The Garden Conservancy's
Open Days

Visit America's Best Private Gardens

2016 Edition

Published and distributed by The Garden Conservancy, Inc.

Distributed by the Garden Conservancy, Cold Spring, New York

Publisher's Cataloging-in-Publication
(provided by Quality Books, Inc.)
The Garden Conservancy's Open Days Directory:
Visit America's Best Private Gardens, 2016 ed., 21st ed.
    p. cm.
    Includes index.
    ISSN: 1087-7738
    ISBN - 13: 978-1-893424-28-9
    ISBN - 10: 1-893424-28-6
1. Gardens—United States—Directories.
2. Botanical gardens—United States—Directories.
3. Arboretums—United States—Directories.
    I. Garden Conservancy
    II. Title: Open Days Directory
    SB466.U65G37 2010   712'.07473
                        QBI00-836

Published by
The Garden Conservancy
P.O. Box 219, Cold Spring, NY 10516

MIX
Paper from
responsible sources
FSC
www.fsc.org
FSC® C103525

The Garden Conservancy's
Open Days 2016
Visit America's Best Private Gardens

Cover photos, from top row, left to right:
1. Ande & Peter Rooney's Garden at Twin Brook Farm, Ulster Park, NY
2. Sleepy Cat Farm, Greenwich, CT
3. Riverhill—Joe & Tamara DiMattio, Saugerties, NY
4. Jeff Pavlat & Ray Clayton Garden, Austin, TX. Photo: Jeff Pavlat.
5. Ande & Peter Rooney's Garden at Twin Brook Farm, Ulster Park, NY
6. Ewig Garden, Upper Grandview, NY
7. Stonegate Farm, Balmville, NY. Photo: Matthew Benson
8. Paxson Hill Farm, New Hope, PA
9. *Growing Beautiful Food: A Gardener's Guide to Cultivating Extraordinary Vegetables and Fruit* by Matthew Benson

Contents

Our Supporters

We gratefully acknowledge the support provided by:

George Ball
W. Atlee Burpee Company
Kayne Foundation
The Leon Levy Foundation
Ruettgers Family Charitable Foundation

Thank you to the garden businesses and public gardens
that support this publication through their advertising and participation.

Partnering Organizations

We are so grateful to the following organizations who partner with us to bring
Open Days to their communities.

Boerner Botanical Gardens
Hales Corners, WI

Chase Garden
Orting, WA

The Cummer Museum of Art & Gardens
Jacksonville, FL

Hardy Plant Society of Oregon
Portland, OR

Hollister House Garden
Washington, CT

Innisfree Gardens
Millbrook, NY

Peckerwood Garden Conservation
Foundation, Hempstead, TX

The Tompkins County Community
Beautification Program, Ithaca, NY

Friends of Villa Terrace Museum & Gardens
Milwaukee, WI

Mary M.B. Wakefield Charitable Trust
Milton, MA

Dedicated to
Henriette Suhr
who loved and supported
our Open Days for twenty years.

Henriette Granville Suhr
(1916 — 2015)

Photo of Henriette by Maria Robledo

Welcome to Open Days

We are proud to be America's only national garden-visiting program.

Since 1995 the Open Days program has been inviting gardeners from around the country to share their gardens and gardening know-how with the public.

Each Open Day is an opportunity to see something new and inspiring. You will find a wide variety of gardens within the *Directory*. They represent the incredible range and definition of what a garden can be: expansive estates and small backyard oases, manicured hedges and wild country gardens, plant collections and outdoor art, edible gardens and gardens that support wildlife.

Open Days also celebrates the people who create gardens, and this year we invite you to spend time with them during our many special programs. We hope you will join us.

Happy Garden Visiting!

Open Days Needs You!

Jacksonville, Florida volunteers make Open Days part of the Cummer Museum of Art & Gardens' annual Garden Month. Photo by Laura Palmer

There are many ways to get involved in Open Days.

By bringing Open Days to your community as a Regional Representative, sharing your own garden as a Garden Host, or welcoming visitors at Open Day gardens as a Greeter, you can be a part of this award-winning nation-wide garden education program.

Regional Representative

Our volunteer Regional Representatives recruit nearly all of the gardens that open each year. They assist us with local publicity, sponsorships, and advertising.

Garden Host

Our Garden Hosts are among America's most passionate gardeners. To nominate your garden—or another garden you know—to be a part of the program, complete our online Garden Nomination Form (visit our website), call or email our office to request a nomination form.

Greeter

Many of our Open Days need volunteers to greet visitors during the day and answer questions in the garden.

Contact Us

The Garden Conservancy's
Open Days Program
P.O. Box 219, Cold Spring, NY 10516
(845) 424-6502 (9 a.m. to 5 p.m. ET)
opendays@gardenconservancy.org

We look forward to hearing from you!

LONGSHADOW®

.COM

What You Need to Know Before You Visit

Open Days are self-guided tours. Simply observe the dates and times the gardens are open and plan your visit.

Where possible, we have scheduled gardens to be within a reasonable driving distance of each other. (Occasionally we find a garden that simply must be included, despite being off the beaten path.) We do our best to make sure published garden directions are accurate. Always check directions before you leave home; bring a map, or GPS system along with garden addresses.

Admission to Gardens

Admission to Open Days gardens begin at $7 per person, children 12 and under are free. You may pay in cash or redeem Open Days admission tickets at the entrance of each garden.

Save on admission by purchasing Open Days admission ticket booklets in advance. Booklets include six tickets for the price of five. That's one free garden visit per booklet. Our members enjoy 50% off! Day passes are also available at some gardens.

Visitors enjoy Jane Garmey's garden.

Open Days Extras

We keep adding extras to our Open Days. You can take advantage of Experts in the Gardens at no cost. Digging Deeper events require advance registration through our website, **opendaysprogram.org,** or by calling our toll-free order line, 1 (888) 842-2442, 9 a.m. to 5 p.m. ET.

ORDER YOUR TICKETS

- Online at **opendaysprogram.org**
- By calling 1 (888) 842-2442
  Monday – Friday, 9 a.m. – 5 p.m. ET

Tickets never expire. Please allow at least 10 business days for USPS delivery.

MEMBERS DISCOUNT: We save the best deals for Garden Conservancy members who may purchase ticket booklets at 50% off. Interested? Learn more about membership at **gardenconservancy.org**

Be the Best Garden Guest

Open Days are special invitations into our Garden Hosts' private gardens. Please reward their generosity by following these simple garden-visiting rules:

 Please sign in at the admissions table. Our volunteer Garden Greeters would love to welcome you.

 Plants and their parts must remain in the garden, no picking, pinching, or removing of plant pieces of any kind.

- Take it with you—do not leave litter in the garden, and please do not smoke!

 Stay on designated paths (and out of the pool!)

- Follow any posted signs or directions.

 Bring a friend, but not your furry friend. Sorry, no animals allowed.

- Children are very welcome at Open Days, and must be supervised at all times.

 Park your car so others can enter and leave the parking area easily.

 Respect the owner's preference for photographs. See garden listing or ask at entry. Tripods are not permitted.

- Restrooms are not available, even if "It's an emergency!" Please go before you arrive, or ask at the admissions table for directions to the nearest public facilities.

- Most gardens featured on Open Days are private and not normally open to the public. Please respect the privacy of these Garden Hosts and only visit their gardens on the dates and times posted.

- Respect the privacy of our Garden Hosts by not contacting them directly outside of the Open Day.

- Many Garden Hosts can be found in the gardens during their Open Day,  identified by their "Garden Host" button. Please say hello! And let them know how much you enjoyed their garden.

SEIBERT & RICE
FINE ITALIAN TERRA COTTA

www.seibert-rice.com
(973) 467.8266

Gardens and Much More!

🏷 Pop-Up Nurseries

How many times have you seen plants at Open Day gardens that you want in your own garden? Now you can buy them on site. We have invited our Garden Hosts' favorite nurseries to set up shop at select Open Days. Instant gratification! Look for the "sale tag" in our garden listings.

Digging Deeper

These programs invite you to take a closer look at the garden world. Sharing their perspectives on the meaning of gardens, specialists of all sorts welcome you into to their garden, farm, studio, or nursery for a tour, demonstration, or tasting on site, or a lecture at a nearby location. The idea is to dig deep and have fun! They require pre-registration, so plan ahead!

Experts in the Garden

Open Days are great places to learn about gardening. Our Garden Hosts and Regional Representatives have asked special guests to join them in their gardens. Whether you want to know more about plants, design, or the practical do-it-yourself stuff, ask the experts! You can get it all at Open Days!

Expanded Online Information

Read more about Open Days gardens, browse photographs, let us know what you think! Visit **opendaysprogram.org.** While you are there, don't forget to sign up for our e-mail reminders. It's the best way to stay up to date on what's happening.

Photos, clockwise from top left: Broken Arrow Nursery / Russian River Flower Schoo / Tovah Martin, Gordon & Mary Hayward, Roger Swain / Landcraft Environments

Join us for Events at White Flower Farm

The Great Tomato Celebration

May 20–22   9:00 a.m.–5:00 p.m.

The Great Tomato Celebration is not to be missed. Go home with treasured heirlooms, modern hybrids, and the top-rated Tomato plants for your garden. Be sure to get here early for the best selections. We'll have over 100 varieties of Tomato seedlings to choose from, plus fertilizers, stakes, ties, containers, and a selection of herbs and vegetables to make this year's garden the best ever. Experts will be on hand each day to answer your questions.

Open House

June 18

Mark your calendars for our Open House day, when we welcome old friends and new for iced tea and Cucumber sandwiches on the lawn by our house. We'll start serving around 2:30. The display gardens should be close to peak and the Begonia House will be hitting its stride. For more information visit whiteflowerfarm.com/events.

3.5 MILES SOUTH OF LITCHFIELD CENTER ON ROUTE 63
STORE OPEN DAILY 9–5:30 • (860) 567-8789

White Flower Farm

PLANTSMEN SINCE 1950

The Garden Conservancy

By participating in Open Days you are supporting a nationwide garden education program and the preservation of gardens all across America. Since Frank Cabot first visited the Ruth Bancroft Garden more than twenty-five years ago and was inspired to start the Garden Conservancy, we have been identifying gardens in need and helping them to become stronger and independent public resources.

Over the years we've partnered with garden owners, community and professional organizations, and local volunteers to help save, preserve, rehabilitate, and rescue more than eighty gardens. At the Garden Conservancy we're passionate about gardens, and determined to help preserve the rich cultural heritage they so often embody. We work to help gardens become viable, sustainable, and valued resources for their communities, a source of inspiration, education, and respite for the public.

Many of our Preservation Partners (both past and present) participate in Open Days. Please make them part of your garden-visiting plans this season and see your support at work.

For more information about our preservation work, visit **gardenconservancy.org/preservation**

Join the Garden Conservancy

Our members are part of a community of garden enthusiasts who share our dedication for saving and sharing outstanding American gardens.

Our members-only events include an annual program at White Flower Farm to be held on June 18 during the Litchfield County Open Day in Connecticut. Members enjoy a behind-the-scenes tour of the nursery and an annual plant sale.

Membership offers you opportunities to explore, learn, and be inspired.

Our members enjoy:
- A free copy of our *Open Days Directory*
- 50% discount on Open Days tickets (advance purchase required)
- Subscription to our print and electronic newsletters
- Discounted admission to Garden Conservancy-sponsored lectures and Digging Deeper programs.
- Participation in our special Member Discount Club
- Subscription to *Better Homes & Gardens*

To Become a Member

Call us at (845) 424-6500, email us at membership@gardenconservancy.org, or visit **gardenconservancy.org/membership**

Nursery & Retail Partners

Our nursery and retail partners bring their choice selections of plants and garden-related merchandise to Open Days. We hope you enjoy browsing their wares and taking a part of Open Days home to your own garden.

Achille Agway, Peterborough, NH
www.achilleagway.com

Adams Fairacre Farms, Poughkeepsie, NY
www.adamsfarms.com

Atlock Farm, Somerset, NJ
www.facebook.com/atlock

Broken Arrow Nursery, Hamden, CT
www.brokenarrownursery.com

Digging Dog Nursery, Albion, CA
www.diggingdog.com

Ellen Hoverkamp Scanner Photography,
West Haven, CT
www.myneighborsgarden.com

Geraniaceae, Richmond, CA
www.geraniaceae.com

Hortulus Farm, Wrightstown, PA
www.hortulusfarm.com

Inspired Gardener, Westmoreland, NH
www.inspiredgardener.com

Merritt Bookstore, Millbrook, NY
www.merrittbookstore.com

Monches Farm, Colegate, WI
www.monchesfarm.com

Opus Plants, Little Compton, RI
www.opusplants.com

Orchard Jewelry, New York, NY
www.orchardjewelry.com

Paxson Hill Farm, New Hope, PA
www.paxsonhillfarm.com

Peckhams Greenhouse,
Little Compton, RI
www.peckhamsgreenhouse.com

Pixie Perennials, WIlton, CT
www.pixieperennials.com

Pondside Nursery, Hudson, NY
www.pondsidenursery.com

Rare Find Nursery, Jackson, NJ
www.rarefindnursery.com

Rocky Dale Gardens, Bristol, VT
www.rockydalegardens.com

Rosedale, Hawthorne, NY
www.rosedalenurseries.com

Telescopes of Vermont, Norwich, VT
www.gardentelescopes.com

White Flower Farm, Morris, CT
www.whiteflowerfarm.com

Woman's Work, Pawling, NY
www.womanswork.com

Gardens by Date

Saturday, April 2

FLORIDA
DUVAL COUNTY

Jacksonville
- Cummer Museum of Art, 10 a.m. to 4 p.m.
- Garden of Mr. & Mrs. David Foerster,
  12 p.m. to 4 p.m.
- Garden of Mr. & Mrs. Preston Haskell,
  12 p.m. to 4 p.m.
- Garden of Ann & David Hicks,
  12 p.m. to 4 p.m.
- Garden of Mr. & Mrs. William H. Morris,
  12 p.m. to 4 p.m.

NEW YORK
TOMPKINS COUNTY

Trumansburg
- Hitch Lyman's Garden, 11 a.m. to 3 p.m.

Saturday, April 9

NEW JERSEY
ESSEX COUNTY

Nutley
- The Mountsier Garden, 10 a.m. to 4 p.m.

Saturday, April 23

CALIFORNIA
ALAMEDA COUNTY

Berkeley
- Our Own Stuff Gallery, 10 a.m. to 4 p.m.

Oakland
- Leianne's Garden, 10 a.m. to 4 p.m.
- Potomac Waterworks, 10 a.m. to 4 p.m.

Orinda
- The Bowyer Japanese Garden,
  10 a.m. to 5 p.m.

Richmond
- Robin Parer's Greenhouse, 1 p.m. to 4 p.m.

Saturday & Sunday, April 23 & 24

NEW YORK
PUTNAM COUNTY

Cold Spring
- Stonecrop, 10 a.m. to 5 p.m.

Sunday, April 24

WESTCHESTER COUNTY

Lewisboro
- The White Garden, 10 a.m. to 3 p.m.

Saturday, April 30

TEXAS
HARRIS COUNTY

Bellaire
- Bellaire Meadow, 10 a.m. to 4 p.m.

Houston
- Alba Garden, 10 a.m. to 4 p.m.
- The Art Compound, 10 a.m. to 4 p.m.
- Baldridge Residence, 10 a.m. to 4 p.m.
- Camberg Garden, 10 a.m. to 4 p.m.
- Habitat Gardens, 10 a.m. to 4 p.m.
- Kyle-Lasseter Garden, 10 a.m. to 4 p.m.

Southside Place
- Southside Glade, 10 a.m. to 4 p.m.

Sunday, May 1

CALIFORNIA
LOS ANGELES COUNTY

Arcadia
- Merrill & Donivee Nash, 10 a.m. to 4 p.m.

Pasadena
- La Casita del Arroyo, 9:30 a.m. to 3:30 p.m.
- Garden of Lisa & Tom Evans, 10 a.m. to 4 p.m.
- Lipsig Garden, 10 a.m. to 4 p.m.
- Lomita Garden, 10 a.m. to 4 p.m.
- Oak Vale, 10 a.m. to 4 p.m.

- Yariv Residence, 10 a.m. to 4 p.m.

C O N N E C T I C U T
FAIRFIELD COUNTY
Greenwich
- Sleepy Cat Farm, 10 a.m. to 4 p.m.

Wilton
- Pixie Perennials, 10 a.m. to 4 p.m.

N E W   Y O R K
DUTCHESS COUNTY
Red Hook
- The Chocolate Factory—Ruth Oja, 10 a.m. to 2 p.m.

Saturday, May 7

C A L I F O R N I A
LOS ANGELES COUNTY
Los Angeles
- The Fletcher Garden, 10 a.m. to 4 p.m.

Santa Monica
- 15th Street Garden, 10 a.m. to 4 p.m.
- Casa Nancina, 10 a.m. to 4 p.m.
- Jaffe Garden, 10 a.m. to 4 p.m.
- Merrihew's Sunset Gardens, 9:30 a.m. to 3:30 p.m.
- The Gardens at Woodacres, 10 a.m. to 4 p.m.

N E W   J E R S E Y
ESSEX COUNTY
East Orange
- The Secret Garden @ 377, 10 a.m. to 4 p.m.

Short Hills
- Garden of Dr. & Mrs. George E. Staehle, 10 a.m. to 2 p.m.
- Greenwood Gardens, 10 a.m. to 4 p.m.

HUNTERDON COUNTY
Glen Gardner
- Woodlove—Lainie & John Beavin's Garden, 12 p.m. to 4 p.m.

MORRIS COUNTY
Convent Station
- The L'Hommedieu Garden, 10 a.m. to 4 p.m.

SOMERSET COUNTY
Far Hills
- The Hay Honey Farm, 10 a.m. to 5 p.m.

N E W   Y O R K
SUFFOLK COUNTY
East Hampton
- Biercuk & Luckey Garden, 10 a.m. to 4 p.m.
- The Garden of Dianne B., 12 p.m. to 4 p.m.
- Edwina Von Gal, 10 a.m. to 4 p.m.
- Garden of Marshall Watson, 10 a.m. to 5 p.m.

WESTCHESTER COUNTY
Chappaqua
- Shobha Vanchiswar & Murali Mani, 10 a.m. to 4 p.m.

Ossining
- The Wildflower Island at Teatown Lake Reservation, 10 a.m., 12 p.m., 2 p.m.

Sunday, May 8

N E W   Y O R K
PUTNAM COUNTY
Cold Spring
- Stonecrop, 10 a.m. to 5 p.m.

Sunday, May 15

N E W   Y O R K
SUFFOLK COUNTY
Mt. Sinai
- Tranquility, 10 a.m. to 4 p.m.

Old Field
- Two Grey Achers, 11 p.m. to 4 p.m.

Stony Brook
- Sue Bottigheimer's Garden, 10 a.m. to 4 p.m.
- Mitsuko En, 2 p.m. to 6 p.m.

Saturday, May 21

C A L I F O R N I A
MARIN COUNTY
Kentfield
- Clipped Perfection, 10 a.m. to 4 p.m.

Ross
- Echoes of the Past, 10 a.m. to 4 p.m.

CONNECTICUT
NEW LONDON COUNTY
Stonington
- Kentford Farm, 10 a.m. to 4 p.m.

NEW JERSEY
BERGEN COUNTY
Allendale
- Monfried Garden, 10 a.m. to 4 p.m.

Wyckoff
- Formerly Tall Trees, 10 a.m. to 4 p.m.

ESSEX COUNTY
East Orange
- The Secret Garden @ 377, 10 a.m. to 4 p.m.

Short Hills
- Greenwood Gardens, 10 a.m. to 4 p.m.

NEW YORK
DUTCHESS COUNTY
Amenia
- Broccoli Hall—Maxine Paetro, 10 a.m. to 4 p.m.
- Mead Farm House Garden, 10 a.m. to 4 p.m.

Dover Plains
- Copperheads, 10 a.m. to 4 p.m.
- Millbrook
- Innisfree Garden, 10 a.m. to 4 p.m.

Wappingers Falls
- Anne Spiegel, 10 a.m. to 4 p.m.

SUFFOLK COUNTY
Cutchogue
- Arnold & Karen Blair, 10 a.m. to 4 p.m.

Flanders
- Garden of Valerie M. Ansalone, 10 a.m. to 4 p.m.

Remsenberg
- The Gardens of Fred Meyer, 10 a.m. to 4 p.m.
- Tuthill Gardens, 10 a.m. to 4 p.m.
- Wintergreen Garden, 10 a.m. to 4 p.m.

Saturday & Sunday, May 21 & 22

RHODE ISLAND
NEWPORT COUNTY
Little Compton
- Sakonnet, 9:30 a.m. to 6 p.m.

Saturday, May 28

MASSACHUSETTS
DUKES COUNTY
Chilmark
- Blueberry Ridge Garden, 10 a.m. to 2 p.m.

Saturday, June 4

CALIFORNIA
MARIN COUNTY
Bolinas
- Garden of Sculpture, 10 a.m. to 4 p.m.
- Visions of Paradise—Sally Robertson Garden & Studio, 10 a.m. to 4 p.m.

Stinson Beach
- Flora & Fauna by the Sea, 10 a.m. to 4 p.m.

CONNECTICUT
NEW HAVEN COUNTY
Stony Creek
- Uptop, 10 a.m. to 4 p.m.

NEW YORK
COLUMBIA COUNTY
Ancram
- Adams-Westlake, 12 p.m. to 4 p.m.

Claverack
- Peter Bevacqua & Stephen King, 10 a.m. to 4 p.m.
- Ketay Garden, 10 a.m. to 4 p.m.

Copake Falls
- Margaret Roach, 10 a.m. to 4 p.m.

Hudson
- Hudson Hood, 11 a.m. to 4 p.m.

West Taghkanic

- Arcadia—Ronald Wagner & Timothy Van Dam, 10 a.m. to 4 p.m.

WASHINGTON
KING COUNTY
Auburn

- Soos Creek Botanical Garden & Heritage Center, 10 a.m. to 3 p.m.

PIERCE COUNTY
Graham

- Old Goat Farm, 10 a.m. to 3 p.m.

Orting

- VanCor Gardens, 10 a.m. to 3 p.m.
- Chase Garden, 10 a.m. to 3 p.m.

Puyallup

- Ernie & Julia Graham, 10 a.m. to 3 p.m.
- Ed Hume's Educational Garden, 10 a.m. to 3 p.m.

Sunday, June 5

CONNECTICUT
FAIRFIELD COUNTY
Ridgefield

- The Barlow Mountain Garden of Helen Dimos & Benjamin Oko, 10 a.m. to 4 p.m.
- Garden of Ken & Margaret Uhle, 10 a.m. to 4 p.m.

Wilton

- Pixie Perennials, 10 a.m. to 4 p.m.

MASSACHUSETTS
NORFOLK COUNTY
Milton

- Garden of Christine Paxhia, 10 a.m. to 4 p.m.
- Shapiro/Bloomberg Garden—the former "Mrs. Holden McGinley Garden" designed by Ellen Biddle Shipman, 10 a.m. to 4 p.m.
- Mary M. B. Wakefield Estate, 10 a.m. to 4 p.m.

SUFFOLK COUNTY
West Roxbury

- Dustman-Ryan Garden, 10 a.m. to 4 p.m.

NEW YORK
PUTNAM COUNTY
Brewster

- Eastward, 10 a.m. to 4 p.m.

WESTCHESTER COUNTY
Bedford

- Leslie & John Needham—River Hills, 10 a.m. to 4 p.m.

Bedford Hills

- Phillis Warden, 10 a.m. to 4 p.m.

North Salem

- Keeler Hill Farm, 10 a.m. to 4 p.m.
- Perrin Garden, 10 a.m. to 4 p.m.

Saturday, June 11

CONNECTICUT
HARTFORD COUNTY
Burlington

- The Salsedo Family Garden, 10 a.m. to 4 p.m.

Plantsville

- The Kaminski Garden, 10 a.m. to 4 p.m.

West Hartford

- The Mayes Garden, 10 a.m. to 4 p.m.

LITCHFIELD COUNTY
Barkhamsted

- Washington Hill, 11 a.m. to 4 p.m.

MASSACHUSETTS
BARNSTABLE COUNTY
North Truro

- Garden of David Kirchner & Scott Warner, Saturday, 10 a.m. to 4 p.m.

Provincetown

- Garden of Bartwbara Cantor, 10 a.m. to 4 p.m.
- Garden of John Derian, 10 a.m. to 4 p.m.
- Garden of Kenn Freed, 10 a.m. to 4 p.m.
- Garden of Alix Ritchie & Marty Davis, 10 a.m. to 4 p.m.

Truro

- Flyte Cottage—The Garden of Kurt D. Gress & Samuel Parkinson, 10 a.m. to 4 p.m.

BRISTOL COUNTY
Rehoboth
- Garden of Marjorie & Don DeAngelis, 10 a.m. to 4 p.m.
- McIlwain Garden, 10 a.m. to 4 p.m.

Seekonk
- Andrew Grossman's Display Gardens, 10 a.m. to 4 p.m.

MISSOURI
LADUE COUNTY
Ladue
- The Jacobs Garden, 10 a.m. to 4 p.m.

St. Louis
- The Jamieson Garden—An Architectural Garden, 10 a.m. to 4 p.m.
- The Shangri-La Garden, 10 a.m. to 4 p.m.
- The David Sherman Woodland Garden, 10 a.m. to 4 p.m.

NEW JERSEY
BERGEN COUNTY
Closter
- Mary's Garden, 10 a.m. to 4 p.m.

Mahwah
- Sisko Gardens, 10 a.m. to 4 p.m.

River Edge
- Anthony "Bud" & Virginia Korteweg, 8:30 a.m. to 4 p.m.

River Vale
- Cupid's Garden—Audrey Linstrom Maihack, 10 a.m. to 5 p.m.

NEW YORK
NASSAU COUNTY
Glen Cove
- Kippen Hill, 10 a.m. to 4 p.m.

Locust Valley
- Nancy Taylor's Garden, 10 a.m. to 4 p.m.

Mill Neck
- John P. Humes Japanese Stroll Garden, 11:30 a.m. to 4 p.m.

Old Westbury
- The Howard Phipps Jr. Estate, 10 a.m. to 4 p.m.

SUFFOLK COUNTY
Bridgehampton
- Entwood Garden, 10 a.m. to 4 p.m.

East Hampton
- The Garden of Dianne B., 12 p.m. to 4 p.m.
- Garden of Arlene Bujese, 10 a.m. to 2 p.m.
- Glade Garden, 10 a.m. to 4 p.m.
- Previti/Gumpel Garden, 10 a.m. to 4 p.m.

PENNSYLVANIA
BUCKS COUNTY
Doylestown
- Fordhook Farm of W. Atlee Burpee Co., 10 a.m. to 4 p.m.

Furlong
- Dark Hollow Farm, 10 a.m. to 4 p.m.

New Hope
- Paxson Hill Farm, 10 a.m. to 4 p.m.

Point Pleasant
- The Gardens at Mill Fleurs, Guided tours only at 10 a.m. & 1:30 p.m.

Wrightstown
- Hortulus Farm, 10 a.m. to 4 p.m.

RHODE ISLAND
PROVIDENCE COUNTY
Providence
- College Hill Urban Oasis, 10 a.m. to 4 p.m.

WASHINGTON
CLARK COUNTY
Battle Ground
- The Bailey Haven, 10 a.m. to 4 p.m.
- Ritchie Garden, 10 a.m. to 4 p.m.

Vancouver
- Dragonfly Hollow, 10 a.m. to 4 p.m.
- The Garden of Roger & Judy McElhaney's Matsu Kaze (Wind in the Pines), 10 a.m. to 4 p.m.
- Seymour-Lueck, 10 a.m. to 4 p.m.

Sunday, June 12

N E W   Y O R K
PUTNAM COUNTY

Cold Spring
- Stonecrop, 10 a.m. to 5 p.m.,
  Tea from 12 p.m. to 4 p.m.

Garrison
- Ross Gardens, 10 a.m. to 4 p.m.

Saturday, June 18

C A L I F O R N I A
MENDOCINO COUNTY

Albion
- The Gardens Surrounding Digging
  Dog Nursery, 10 a.m. to 5 p.m.

Hopland
- Frey Gardens, 10 a.m. to 4 p.m.

Mendocino
- Moss Garden, 10 a.m. to 4 p.m.

Philo
- The Apple Farm, 10 a.m. to 4 p.m.
- Wildwood, 10 a.m. to 4 p.m.

C O N N E C T I C U T
LITCHFIELD COUNTY

Falls Village
- Bunny Williams, 10 a.m. to 4 p.m.

Kent
- Mica Quarry Estate, 10 a.m. to 4 p.m.

Washington
- Highmeadows—Linda Allard, 10 a.m. to 4 p.m.
- Brush Hill Gardens—Charles Raskob Robinson
  & Barbara Paul Robinson, 10 a.m. to 4 p.m.
- Hollister House Garden, 10 a.m. to 4 p.m.

N E W   Y O R K
DUTCHESS COUNTY

Amenia
- Broccoli Hall—Maxine Paetro,
  10 a.m. to 4 p.m.

Thursday, June 23

M A S S A C H U S E T T S
NANTUCKET COUNTY

Nantucket
- Carried Away, 10 a.m. to 3 p.m.
- Joly's Garden, 10 a.m. to 4 p.m.
- Suzy Grote's Garden, 10 a.m. to 4 p.m.
- Patsy's Garden, 10 a.m. to 4 p.m.
- Unicorn's Delight, 10 a.m. to 4 p.m.

Saturday, June 25

C A L I F O R N I A
SAN FRANCISCO COUNTY

San Francisco
- Geary Street Garden, 10 a.m. to 4 p.m.
- Hummingbird Garden, 10 a.m. to 4 p.m.
- Tenderloin National Forest, 10 a.m. to 4 p.m.

N E W   Y O R K
COLUMBIA COUNTY

Craryville
- Rabbit Hill, 10 a.m. to 5 p.m.

Hillsdale
- Texas Hill, 10 a.m. to 4 p.m.

Hudson
- The Happy, 10 a.m. to 4 p.m.

Millerton
- Helen Bodian, 10 a.m. to 4 p.m.

Valatie
- Kevin Lee Jacobs, 10 a.m. to 4 p.m.

DUTCHESS COUNTY

Poughkeepsie
- Dappled Berms—The Garden of
  Scott VanderHamm, 10 a.m. to 4 p.m.

NASSAU COUNTY

Mill Neck
- John P. Humes Japanese Stroll
  Garden, 11:30 a.m. to 4 p.m.

SUFFOLK COUNTY

Amagansett
- Ngaere Macray & David Seeler,
  10 a.m. to 4 p.m.

Bridgehampton
- Stanley & Susan Reifer, 10 a.m. to 3 p.m.

East Hampton
- Carol Mercer, 10 a.m. to 4 p.m.

Montauk
- Richard Kahn & Elaine Peterson, 10 a.m. to 2 p.m.

Sagaponack
- Susan & Louis Meisel, 10 a.m. to 2 p.m.

ULSTER COUNTY

Highland
- Teri Condon—Gardensmith Design, 12 p.m. to 4 p.m.

New Paltz
- Springtown Farmden, 1 p.m. to 4:30 p.m.

Sunday, June 26

ILLINOIS
LAKE COUNTY

Lake Forest
- Pond Ridge, 10 a.m. to 4 p.m.
- Suzanne's Garden, 10 a.m. to 4 p.m.
- Thornewood, 10 a.m. to 4 p.m.

NEW YORK
WESTCHESTER COUNTY

Bedford Hills
- Phillis Warden, 10 a.m. to 4 p.m.

Cortlandt Manor
- Vivian & Ed Merrin, 10 a.m. to 2 p.m.

North Salem
- The Hen & the Hive, 10 a.m. to 4 p.m.

South Salem
- Garden of Bernard Marquez & Tim Fish, 10 a.m. to 6 p.m.

WASHINGTON
KITSAP COUNTY

Bainbridge Island
- Chapman's Garden, 10 a.m. to 4 p.m.
- The Demianew Gardens, 10 a.m. to 5 p.m.
- Peyton Gully Garden, 10 a.m. to 4 p.m.
- Olaf Ribeiro/Nancy Allison, 10 a.m. to 4 p.m.
- The Skyler Garden, 10 a.m. to 5 p.m.

Kingston
- Leaf Works, 10 a.m. to 4 p.m.

Saturday, July 2

NEW YORK
DELAWARE COUNTY

Andes
- Cynthia & Charles Bonnes, 10 a.m. to 4 p.m.
- Mel & Peg's Rustic Cabin Cottage Garden, 10 a.m. to 4 p.m.

East Meredith
- Totem Farm Garden, 10 a.m. to 4 p.m.

Jefferson
- Quaker Hill Farm—Elisabeth Searles & Richard Friedberg, 10 a.m. to 4 p.m.

Roscoe
- Berry Brook Farm—Mermer Blakeslee & Eric Hamerstrom, 10 a.m. to 4 p.m.

Sunday, July 3

NEW YORK
DUTCHESS COUNTY

Pawling
- Hall Christy House Garden, 11 a.m. to 6 p.m.
- Scherer Garden, 11 a.m. to 4 p.m.

Saturday, July 9

CONNECTICUT
LITCHFIELD COUNTY

Washington
- Hollister House Garden, 10 a.m. to 4 p.m.

West Cornwall
- Jane Garmey, 1 p.m. to 5 p.m.
- Michael Trapp, 11 a.m. to 4 p.m.

NEW YORK
DUTCHESS COUNTY

Amenia
- Jade Hill—Paul Arcario & Don Walker, 10 a.m. to 4 p.m.

SUFFOLK COUNTY

Mattituck
- Dennis Schrader & Bill Smith, 10 a.m. to 4 p.m.

Mt. Sinai
• Tranquility, 10 a.m. to 4 p.m.

VERMONT
BENNINGTON COUNTY
East Arlington
• Rogerland, 10 a.m. to 4 p.m.

Manchester
• Garden of Mary & Bob Russell,
  10 a.m. to 4 p.m.
• Turkey Hill Farm, 10 a.m. to 4 p.m.

Manchester Center
• Coventry Cottage—Joan & Lee
  Feglemann's Garden, 12 p.m. to 4 p.m.
• Hildene, The Lincoln Family Home,
  9:30 a.m. to 4:30 p.m.

Sunday, July 10

NEW JERSEY
BERGEN COUNTY
Tenafly
• Linda Singer, 10 a.m. to 4 p.m.

Saturday, July 16

CONNECTICUT
NEW LONDON COUNTY
Stonington
• Kentford Farm, 10 a.m. to 4 p.m.

WISCONSIN
MILWAUKEE COUNTY
Milwaukee
• Renaissance Garden at Villa
  Terrace, 10 a.m. to 4 p.m.

River Hills
• The Chimneys, 10 a.m. to 5 p.m.
• Hill Top House, 10 a.m. to 5 p.m.

OZAUKEE COUNTY
Grafton
• Two Oaks, 10 a.m. to 5 p.m.

Mequon
• Dragonfly Farm, 10 a.m. to 5 p.m.

Sunday, July 17

ILLINOIS
COOK COUNTY
Winnetka
• Nantucket Garden, 10 a.m. to 4 p.m.

LAKE COUNTY
Lake Forest
• Old Mill Farm, 10 a.m. to 2 p.m.

Mettawa
• Mettawa Manor, 10 a.m. to 4 p.m.

NEW YORK
COLUMBIA COUNTY
Canaan
• Rockland Farm, 10 a.m. to 4 p.m.

New Lebanon
• The Tilden Japanese Garden, 10 a.m. to 4 p.m.

Spencertown
• Garden of Linda B. Horn, 10 a.m. to 4 p.m.

PUTNAM COUNTY
Cold Spring
• Stonecrop, 10 a.m. to 5 p.m.

Saturday, July 23

CONNECTICUT
NEW HAVEN COUNTY
Meriden
• Jardin des Brabant, 12 p.m. to 5 p.m.
• George Trecina, 10 a.m. to 4 p.m.

NEW YORK
ULSTER COUNTY
Phoenicia
• Garden of Jim Goss & Joe
  Murray, 10 a.m. to 4 p.m.
• Garden of Roger Griffith, 10 a.m. to 4 p.m.

Saugerties
• Ann Krupp Bryan, 10 a.m. to 5 p.m.
• The Donald Elder & Richard Suma
  Garden, 10 a.m. to 4 p.m.

Willow
• Suzanne Pierot's Garden by the Stream, 10 a.m. to 4 p.m.

WISCONSIN
SHEBOYGAN COUNTY
Sheboygan
• The Christopher Farm & Gardens, 10 a.m. to 4 p.m.

Sunday, July 24

NEW YORK
WESTCHESTER COUNTY
Bedford Hills
• Heffernan Garden, 10 a.m. to 4 p.m.
• Phillis Warden, 10 a.m. to 4 p.m.

Cortlandt Manor
• Vivian & Ed Merrin, 10 a.m. to 2 p.m.

Pound Ridge
• Sara Stein Garden, 10 a.m. to 4 p.m.

South Salem
• Garden of Bernard Marquez & Tim Fish, 10 a.m. to 6 p.m.

Saturday, July 30

CALIFORNIA
ALAMEDA COUNTY
Albany
• Keeyla Meadows, 10 a.m. to 4 p.m.

Berkeley
• Camp Shasta, 10 a.m. to 4 p.m.

Oakland
• Casa de Sueños, 10 a.m. to 4 p.m.

Piedmont
• Mediterranean Delight, 10 a.m. to 4 p.m.

CONTRA COSTA COUNTY
Orinda
• Garden at 520 Miner Road, 10 a.m. to 4 p.m.

CONNECTICUT
LITCHFIELD COUNTY
Lakeville
• Montgomery Glazer Property, 10 a.m. to 4 p.m.

Washington
• Hollister House Garden, 10 a.m. to 4 p.m.

NEW YORK
DUTCHESS COUNTY
Millbrook
• Squirrel Hall, 10 a.m. to 4 p.m.

Millerton
• Hyland/Wente Garden, 10 a.m. to 4 p.m.

Saturday, August 6

MINNESOTA
HENNEPIN COUNTY
Medina
• Wallace Gardens, 10 a.m. to 2 p.m.

NEW JERSEY
MONMOUTH COUNTY
Locust
• Nancy & Dan Crabbe's Garden on the Navesink River, 9 a.m. to 4 p.m.

Red Bank
• Woodland Garden, 9 a.m. to 5 p.m.

Rumson
• Beth Deutch Garden, 10 a.m. to 4 p.m.
• King & Leigh Sorensen, 10 a.m. to 4 p.m.

NEW YORK
DUTCHESS COUNTY
Rhinebeck
• Cedar Heights Farm, 10 a.m. to 4 p.m.
• Cedar Heights Orchard—Arvia Morris, 10 a.m. to 4 p.m.
• Amy Goldman Fowler, 10 a.m. to 2 p.m.

Tivoli
• A Tea Garden in Tivoli, 10 a.m. to 4 p.m.

SCHUYLER COUNTY
Alpine
• Lipari Garden, 10 a.m. to 4 p.m.

TOMPKINS COUNTY
Freeville
• Manzano Garden, 10 a.m. to 4 p.m.

Ithaca
• Orcutt Garden, 10 a.m. to 4 p.m.

Trumansburg
• Filios Garden, 10 a.m. to 4 p.m.
• Heron Ridge, 10 a.m. to 4 p.m.

W I S C O N S I N
MILWAUKEE COUNTY
Hales Corners
• Boerner Botanical Gardens, 8 a.m. to 6 p.m.

River Hills
• Green Fire Woods, 10 a.m. to 4 p.m.
• Kubly Garden, 10 a.m. to 4 p.m.

WASHINGTON COUNTY
Newburg
• Ramhorn Farm, 10 a.m. to 4 p.m.

Sunday, August 7

I L L I N O I S
DU PAGE COUNTY
West Chicago
• The Gardens at Ball, 10 a.m. to 4 p.m.

KANE COUNTY
Elburn
• Hummer Haven, 10 a.m. to 5 p.m.

Saturday, August 13

C O N N E C T I C U T
FAIRFIELD COUNTY
New Canaan
• Dogwood Hill, 10 a.m. to 4 p.m.

Redding
• In Situ, 10 a.m. to 4 p.m.

Weston
• Wells Hill Farm, 10 a.m. to 4 p.m.

M A S S A C H U S E T T S
NORFOLK COUNTY
Needham
• Ellen Lathi's Garden, 10 a.m. to 4 p.m.

Wellesley
• Hunnewell Garden, 10 a.m. to 2 p.m.

P E N N S Y L V A N I A
BUCKS COUNTY
Doylestown
• Fordhook Farm of W. Atlee Burpee Co.,
  10 a.m. to 4 p.m.

New Hope
• Paxson Hill Farm, 10 a.m. to 4 p.m.

W I S C O N S I N
MILWAUKEE COUNTY
Greenfield
• Radler's Rosarium, 10 a.m. to 4 p.m.

Hales Corners
• Boerner Botanical Gardens, 8 a.m. to 6 p.m.

WAUKESHA COUNTY
Dousman
• Lark's Garden, 10 a.m. to 4 p.m.

Waukesha
• The Sievert Garden, 10 a.m. to 4 p.m.

Sunday, August 14

N E W   Y O R K
PUTNAM COUNTY
Cold Spring
• Stonecrop, 10 a.m. to 5 p.m.

Saturday, August 20

N E W   H A M P S H I R E
CHESHIRE COUNTY
Stoddard
• Garden of Jenny Lee Hughes & Edward Yoxen,
  10 a.m. to 4 p.m.

HILLSBOROUGH COUNTY
Francestown
• The Gardens at Juniper Hill Farm,
  9 a.m. to 5 p.m.

Hancock
- Eleanor Briggs' Garden, 10 a.m. to 4 p.m.

Peterborough
- The Gardens of Laura & Jamie Trowbridge, 10 a.m. to 4 p.m.
- Michael & Betsy Gordon, 10 a.m. to 4 p.m.
- Gardens of Maude & John Odgers, 10 a.m. to 4 p.m.

NEW YORK
COLUMBIA COUNTY
Copake Falls
- Margaret Roach, 10 a.m. to 4 p.m.

Hudson
- Versailles on Hudson, 10 a.m. to 2 p.m.

Valatie
- Kevin Lee Jacobs, 10 a.m. to 4 p.m.

Sunday, August 21

NEW HAMPSHIRE
CHESHIRE COUNTY
Walpole
- Distant Hill Gardens—Garden of Michael & Kathy Nerrie, 10 a.m. to 4 p.m.

Westmoreland
- Hudson Garden, 9 a.m. to 5 p.m.

SULLIVAN COUNTY
Acworth
- The Gardens on Grout Hill, 10 a.m. to 4 p.m.

VERMONT
WINDHAM COUNTY
Westminster West
- Gordon & Mary Hayward's Garden, 10 a.m. to 4 p.m.

Saturday, August 27

CONNECTICUT
NEW HAVEN COUNTY
Meriden
- George Trecina, 10 a.m. to 4 p.m.

Sunday, August 28

CONNECTICUT
LITCHFIELD COUNTY
Cornwall
- Something to Crow About Dahlias, 10 a.m. to 4 p.m.

West Cornwall
- Roxana Robinson—Treetop, 10 a.m. to 4 p.m.

Saturday, September 10

NEW JERSEY
ESSEX COUNTY
Montclair
- Claire Ciliotta, 10 a.m. to 4 p.m.

Nutley
- The Mountsier Garden, 10 a.m. to 4 p.m.

Short Hills
- Greenwood Gardens, 10 a.m. to 4 p.m.

Sunday, September 11

CONNECTICUT
LITCHFIELD COUNTY
Bridgewater
- Maywood Gardens, 10 a.m. to 4 p.m.

Roxbury
- Castlebrae Farm, 10 a.m. to 4 p.m.

Washington
- Hollister House Garden, 10 a.m. to 4 p.m.
- Red Mill Farm, 10 a.m. to 4 p.m.

Saturday, September 17

NEW JERSEY
SOMERSET COUNTY
Far Hills
- The Hay Honey Farm, 10 a.m. to 5 p.m.
- Stone House Garden, 10 a.m. to 4 p.m.

NEW YORK
NASSAU COUNTY
Mill Neck
- John P. Humes Japanese Stroll Garden, 11:30 a.m. to 4 p.m.

Sunday, September 18

CONNECTICUT
FAIRFIELD COUNTY
Greenwich
- Sleepy Cat Farm, 10 a.m. to 4 p.m.

Ridgefield
- Ken Eisold's Garden, 10 a.m. to 4 p.m.

Wilton
- Pixie Perennials, 10 a.m. to 4 p.m.

ILLINOIS
LAKE COUNTY
Lake Forest
- The Gardens at 900, 10 a.m. to 4 p.m.

MASSACHUSETTS
MIDDLESEX COUNTY
Carlisle
- The Gardens at Clock Barn—Home of Maureen & Mike Ruettgers, 10 a.m. to 4 p.m.

NEW YORK
PUTNAM COUNTY
Cold Spring
- Stonecrop, 10 a.m. to 5 p.m.

WESTCHESTER COUNTY
Lewisboro
- The White Garden, 10 a.m. to 3 p.m.

North Salem
- Dick Button—Ice Pond Farm, 10 a.m. to 3 p.m.

Saturday, September 24

NEW YORK
DUTCHESS COUNTY
Clinton Corners
- Junto Farm, 10 a.m. to 4 p.m.

Millbrook
- Clove Brook Farm—Christopher Spitzmiller, 10 a.m. to 4 p.m.
- Innisfree Garden, 10 a.m. to 4 p.m.
- Katie Ridder & Peter Pennoyer, 10 a.m. to 4 p.m.

Stanfordville
- Bear Creek Farm, 10 a.m. to 4 p.m.
- Ellen & Eric Petersen, 10 a.m. to 4 p.m.

SUFFOLK COUNTY
Cutchogue
- Arnold & Karen Blair, 11 a.m. to 4 p.m.

Saturday, October 1

NEW YORK
NASSAU COUNTY
Mill Neck
- John P. Humes Japanese Stroll Garden, 11:30 a.m. to 4 p.m.

Sunday, October 2

NEW YORK
PUTNAM COUNTY
Cold Spring
- Stonecrop, 10 a.m. to 5 p.m.

Saturday, October 8

NEW JERSEY
HUNTERDON COUNTY
Stockton
- The Garden at Federal Twist, 10 a.m. to 6 p.m.

PENNSYLVANIA
BUCKS COUNTY
New Hope
- Jericho Mountain Orchards, 10 a.m. to 4 p.m.
- Paxson Hill Farm, 10 a.m. to 4 p.m.

Saturday, October 15

NEW YORK
DUTCHESS COUNTY
Pawling
- The Brine Garden—Duncan & Julia Brine, 12 p.m. to 6 p.m.

Sunday, October 16

DISTRICT OF COLUMBIA
Georgetown
- The Barbara Downs Garden, 10 a.m. to 4 p.m.
- Georgetown Garden: Nancy Gray
  Pyne, 10 a.m. to 4 p.m.
- The Sessum + Biles Garden, 10 a.m. to 4 p.m.

Saturday, October 29

NORTH CAROLINA
ORANGE COUNTY
Durham
- Deer Chase Gardens, 10 a.m. to 3 p.m.

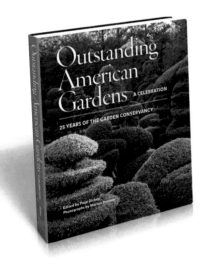

Gardens by Location

California

ALAMEDA COUNTY

Albany
- Keeyla Meadows, Saturday, July 30

Berkeley
- Camp Shasta, Saturday, July 30
- Our Own Stuff Gallery Garden, Saturday, April 23

Oakland
- Casa de Sueños, Saturday, July 30
- Leianne's Garden, Saturday, April 23
- Potomac Waterworks, Saturday, April 23

Piedmont
- Mediterranean Delight, Saturday, July 30

CONTRA COSTA COUNTY

Orinda
- The Garden at 520 Miner Road, Saturday, July 30
- The Bowyer Japanese Garden, Saturday, April 23

Richmond
- Robin Parer's Greenhouse, Saturday, April 23

LOS ANGELES COUNTY

Arcadia
- Merrill & Donivee Nash, Sunday, May 1

Los Angeles
- The Fletcher Garden, Saturday, May 7

Pasadena
- Garden of Lisa & Tom Evans, Sunday, May 1
- Lipsig Garden, Sunday, May 1
- Lomita Garden, Sunday, May 1
- Oak Vale, Sunday, May 1
- Yariv Residence, Sunday, May 1

Santa Monica
- 15th Street Garden, Saturday, May 7
- Casa Nancina, Saturday, May 7
- Jaffe Garden, Saturday, May 7
- The Gardens at Woodacres, Saturday, May 7

MARIN COUNTY

Bolinas
- Garden of Sculpture, Saturday, June 4
- Visions of Paradise—Sally Robertson Garden & Studio, Saturday, June 4

Kentfield
- Clipped Perfection, Saturday, May 21

Ross
- Echoes of the Past, Saturday, May 21

Stinson Beach
- Flora & Fauna by the Sea, Saturday, June 4

MENDOCINO COUNTY

Albion
- The Gardens Surrounding Digging Dog Nursery, Saturday, June 18

Hopland
- Frey Gardens, Saturday, June 18

Mendocino
- Moss Garden, Saturday, June 18

Philo
- The Apple Farm, Saturday, June 18
- Wildwood, Saturday, June 18

SAN FRANCISCO COUNTY

San Francisco
- Geary Street Garden, Saturday, June 25
- Hummingbird Garden, Saturday, June 25
- Tenderloin National Forest, Saturday, June 25

Connecticut

FAIRFIELD COUNTY

Greenwich
- Sleepy Cat Farm, Sunday, May 1, Sunday, September 18

New Canaan
- Dogwood Hill, Saturday, August 13

Redding
- In Situ, Saturday, August 13

Ridgefield
- The Barlow Mountain Garden of Helen Dimos & Benjamin Oko, Sunday, June 5
- Ken Eisold's Garden, Sunday, September 18
- Garden of Ken & Margaret Uhle, Sunday, June 5

Weston
- Wells Hill Farm, Saturday, August 13

Wilton
- Pixie Perennials, Sunday, May 1, Sunday, June 5, Sunday, September 18

HARTFORD COUNTY

Burlington
- The Salsedo Family Garden, Saturday, June 11

Plantsville
- The Kaminski Garden, Saturday, June 11

West Hartford
- The Mayes Garden, Saturday, June 11

LITCHFIELD COUNTY

Barkhamsted
- Washington Hill, Saturday, June 11

Bridgewater
- Maywood Gardens, Sunday, September 11

Cornwall
- Something to Crow About Dahlias, Sunday, August 28

Falls Village
- Bunny Williams, Saturday, June 18

Kent
- Mica Quarry Estate, Saturday, June 18

Lakeville
- The Montgomery Glazer Property, Saturday, July 30

Roxbury
- Castlebrae Farm, Sunday, September 11

Washington
- Highmeadows—Linda Allard, Saturday, June 18
- Hollister House Gardens, Saturday, June 18; Saturday, July 9; Saturday, July 30; Sunday, September 11
- Brush Hill Gardens—Charles Raskob Robinson & Barbara Paul Robinson, Saturday, June 18
- Red Mill Farm, Sunday, September 11

West Cornwall
- Roxana Robinson—Treetop, Sunday, August 28
- Jane Garmey, Saturday, July 9
- Michael Trapp, Saturday, July 9

NEW HAVEN COUNTY

Meriden
- Jardin des Brabant, Saturday, July 23
- George Trecina, Saturday, July 23, Saturday, August 27

Stony Creek
- Uptop - Garden of Fred Bland, Saturday, June 4

NEW LONDON COUNTY

Stonington
- Kentford Farm, Saturday, May 21, Saturday, July 16

District of Columbia

WASHINGTON

Georgetown
- The Barbara Downs Garden, Sunday, October 16
- The Sessums + Biles Garden, Sunday, October 16
- Georgetown Garden: Nancy Gray Pyne, Sunday, October 16

Florida

DUVAL COUNTY

Jacksonville
- Garden of Mr. & Mrs. David Foerster, Saturday, April 2
- Garden of Mr. & Mrs. Preston Haskell, Saturday, April 2
- Garden of Ann & David Hicks, Saturday, April 2
- Garden of Mr. & Mrs. William H. Morris, Saturday, April 2

Illinois

COOK COUNTY

Winnetka
- Nantucket Garden, Sunday, July 17

DU PAGE COUNTY
West Chicago
- The Gardens at Ball, Sunday, August 7

KANE COUNTY
Elburn
- Hummer Haven, Sunday, August 7

LAKE COUNTY
Lake Forest
- The Gardens at 900, Sunday, September 18
- Suzanne's Gardens, Sunday, June 26
- Old Mill Farm, Sunday, July 17
- Pond Ridge, Sunday, June 26
- Thornewood, Sunday, June 26

Mettawa
- Mettawa Manor, Sunday, July 17

Massachusetts

BARNSTABLE COUNTY
North Truro
- Garden of David Kirchner & Scott Warner, Saturday, June 11

Provincetown
- Garden of Barbara Cantor, Saturday, June 11
- Garden of John Derian, Saturday, June 11
- Garden of Kenn Freed, Saturday, June 11
- Garden of Alix Ritchie & Marty Davis, Saturday, June 11

Truro
- Flyte Cottage —The Garden of Kurt D. Gress & Samuel Parkinson, Saturday, June 11

BRISTOL COUNTY
Rehoboth
- Garden of Marjorie & Don DeAngelis, Saturday, June 11
- McIlwain Garden, Saturday, June 11

Seekonk
- Andrew Grossman's Display Gardens, Saturday, June 11

DUKES COUNTY
Chilmark
- Blueberry Ridge Garden, Saturday, May 28

MIDDLESEX COUNTY
Carlisle
- Gardens at Clock Barn—Home of Maureen & Mike Ruettgers, Sunday, September 18

NANTUCKET COUNTY
Nantucket
- Carried Away, Thursday, June 23
- Suzie Grote's Garden, Thursday, June 23
- Joly's Garden, Thursday, June 23
- Patsy's Garden, Thursday, June 23
- Unicorn's Delight, Thursday, June 23

NORFOLK COUNTY
Milton
- Garden of Christine Paxhia, Sunday, June 5
- Shapiro/Bloomberg Garden—the former "Mrs. Holden McGinley Garden" designed by Ellen Biddle Shipman, Sunday, June 5
- Mary W. B. Wakefield Estate, Sunday, June 5

Needham
- Ellen Lathi's Garden, Saturday, August 13

Wellesley
- Hunnewell Garden, Saturday, August 13

SUFFOLK COUNTY
West Roxbury
- Dustman-Ryan Garden, Sunday, June 5

Minnesota

HENNEPIN COUNTY
Medina
- Wallace Gardens, Saturday, August 6

Missouri

ST. LOUIS COUNTY
Ladue
- Jacobs Garden, Saturday, June 11

St. Louis
- The Jamieson Garden: An Architectural Garden, Saturday, June 11
- The Shangri-La Garden, Saturday, June 11
- The David Sherman Woodland Garden, Saturday, June 11

New Hampshire

CHESHIRE COUNTY

Stoddard
- Garden of Jenny Lee Hughes & Edward Yoxen, Saturday, August 20

Walpole
- Distant Hill Gardens—Garden of Michael & Kathy Nerrie, Sunday, August 21

Westmoreland
- Hudson Garden, Sunday, August 21

HILLSBOROUGH COUNTY

Francestown
- The Gardens at Juniper Hill Farm, Saturday, August 20

Hancock
- Eleanor Briggs' Garden, Saturday, August 20

Peterborough
- The Gardens of Laura & Jamie Trowbridge, Saturday, August 20
- Michael & Betsy Gordon, Saturday, August 20
- Gardens of Maude & John Odgers, Saturday, August 20

SULLIVAN COUNTY

Acworth
- The Gardens on Grout Hill, Sunday, August 21

New Jersey

BERGEN COUNTY

Allendale
- Monfried Garden, Saturday, May 21

Closter
- Mary's Garden, Saturday, June 11

Mahwah
- Sisko Gardens, Saturday, June 11

River Edge
- Anthony "Bud" & Virginia Korteweg, Saturday, June 11

River Vale
- Cupid's Garden—Audrey Linstrom Maihack, Saturday, June 11

Tenafly
- Linda Singer, Sunday, July 10

Wyckoff
- Formerly Tall Trees, Saturday, May 21

ESSEX COUNTY

East Orange
- The Secret Garden @ 377, Saturday, May 7, Saturday, May 21

Montclair
- Claire Ciliotta, Saturday, September 10

Nutley
- The Mountsier Garden, Saturday, April 9, Saturday, September 10

Short Hills
- Garden of Dr. & Mrs. George E. Staehle, Saturday, May 7
- Greenwood Gardens, Saturdays, May 7, May 21, September 10

HUNTERDON COUNTY

Glen Gardner
- Woodlove—Lainie & John Beavin's Garden, Saturday, May 7

Stockton
- The Garden at Federal Twist, Saturday, October 8

MONMOUTH COUNTY

Locust
- Nancy & Dan Crabbe's Garden on the Navesink River, Saturday, August 6

Red Bank
- Woodland Garden, Saturday, August 6

Rumson
- Beth Deutch Garden, Saturday, August 6
- King & Leigh Sorensen, Saturday, August 6

MORRIS COUNTY

Convent Station
- The L'Hommedieu Garden, Saturday, May 7

SOMERSET COUNTY

Far Hills
- The Hay Honey Farm, Saturday, May 7, Saturday, September 17
- Stone House Garden, Saturday, September 17

New York

COLUMBIA COUNTY

Ancram
- Adams-Westlake, Saturday, June 4

Canaan
- Rockland Farm, Sunday, July 17

Claverack
- Peter Bevacqua & Stephen King, Saturday, June 4
- Ketay Garden, Saturday, June 4

Copake Falls
- Margaret Roach, Saturday, June 4, Saturday, August 20

Craryville
- Rabbit Hill, Saturday, June 25

Hillsdale
- Texas Hill, Saturday, June 25

Hudson
- Versailles on Hudson, Saturday, August 20
- The Happy, Saturday, June 25
- Hudson Hood, Saturday, June 4

Millerton
- Helen Bodian, Saturday, June 25

New Lebanon
- The Tilden Japanese Garden, Sunday, July 17

Spencertown
- Garden of Linda Horn, Sunday, July 17

Valatie
- Kevin Lee Jacobs, Saturday, June 25, Saturday, August 20

West Taghkanic
- Arcadia—Ronald Wagner & Timothy Van Dam, Saturday, June 4

DELAWARE COUNTY

Andes
- Cynthia & Charles Bonnes, Saturday, July 2
- Mel & Peg's Rustic Cabin Cottage Garden, Saturday, July 2

East Meredith
- Totem Farm Garden, Saturday, July 2

Jefferson
- Quaker Hill Farm—Elisabeth Searles & Richard Friedberg, Saturday, July 2

Roscoe
- Berry Brook Farm—Mermer Blakeslee & Eric Hamerstrom, Saturday, July 2

DUTCHESS COUNTY

Amenia
- Broccoli Hall—Maxine Paetro, Saturday, May 21, Saturday, June 18
- Jade Hill—Paul Arcario & Don Walker, Saturday, July 9
- Mead Farm House Garden, Saturday, May 21

Clinton Corners
- Junto Farm, Saturday, September 24

Dover Plains
- Copperheads, Saturday, May 21

Millbrook
- Clove Brook Farm—Christopher Spitzmiller, Saturday, September 24
- Innisfree Garden, Saturday, May 21, Saturday, July 30, Saturday, September 24
- Katie Ridder and Peter Pennoyer, Saturday, September 24
- Squirrel Hall, Saturday, July 30

Millerton
- Hyland/Wente Garden, Saturday, July 30

Pawling
- The Brine Garden—Duncan & Julia Brine, Saturday, October 15
- Hall Christy House Garden, Sunday, July 3
- Scherer Garden, Sunday, July 3

Poughkeepsie
- Dappled Berms—The Garden of Scott VanderHamm, Saturday, June 25

Red Hook
- The Chocolate Factory—Ruth Oja, Sunday, May 1

Rhinebeck
- Cedar Heights Farm, Saturday, August 6
- Cedar Heights Orchard—Arvia Morris, Saturday, August 6
- Amy Goldman Fowler, Saturday, August 6

Stanfordville
- Bear Creek Farm, Saturday, September 24
- Ellen & Eric Petersen, Saturday, September 24

Tivoli
- A Tea Garden in Tivoli, Saturday, August 6

Wappingers Falls
- Anne Spiegel, Saturday, May 21

NASSAU COUNTY

Glen Cove
- Kippen Hill, Saturday, June 11

Locust Valley
- Nancy Taylor's Garden, Saturday, June 11

Mill Neck
- John P. Humes Japanese Stroll Garden, Saturdays, June 11, June 25, September 17, October 1

Old Westbury
- Howard Phipps Jr. Estate, Saturday, June 11

PUTNAM COUNTY

Brewster
- Eastward, Sunday, June 5

Cold Spring
- Stonecrop Gardens, Saturday & Sunday, April 23 & 24; Sundays, May 8, June 12, July 17, August 14, September 18, October 2

Garrison
- Ross Gardens, Sunday, June 12

SCHUYLER COUNTY

Alpine
- Lipari Garden, Saturday, August 6

SUFFOLK COUNTY

Amagansett
- Ngaere Macray & David Seeler, Saturday, June 25

Bridgehampton
- Entwood Garden, Saturday, June 11
- Stanley & Susan Reifer, Saturday, June 25

Cutchogue
- Arnold & Karen Blair, Saturday, May 21, Saturday, September 24

East Hampton
- The Garden of Dianne B., Saturday, May 7, Saturday, June 11
- Biercuk & Luckey Garden, Saturday, May 7
- Garden of Arlene Bujese, Saturday, June 11
- Glade Garden, Saturday, June 11
- Carol Mercer, Saturday, June 25

- Previti/Gumpel Garden, Saturday, June 11
- Edwina von Gal, Saturday, May 7
- Garden of Marshall Watson, Saturday, May 7

Flanders
- Garden of Valerie M. Ansalone, Saturday, May 21

Mattituck
- Dennis Schrader & Bill Smith, Saturday, July 9

Montauk
- Richard Kahn & Elaine Peterson, Saturday, June 25

Mt. Sinai
- Tranquility, Sunday, May 15, Saturday, July 9

Old Field
- Two Grey Achers, Sunday, May 15

Remsenburg
- Tuthill Gardens, Saturday, May 21
- The Gardens of Fred Meyer, Saturday, May 21
- Wintergreen Garden, Saturday, May 21

Sagaponack
- Susan & Louis Meisel, Saturday, June 25

Stony Brook
- Sue Bottigheimer's Garden, Sunday, May 15
- Mitsuko En, Sunday, May 15

TOMPKINS COUNTY

Freeville
- Manzano Garden, Saturday, August 6

Ithaca
- Orcutt Garden, Saturday, August 6

Trumansburg
- Filios Garden, Saturday, August 6
- Heron Ridge, Saturday, August 6
- Hitch Lyman's Garden, Saturday, March 19, Saturday, April 2

ULSTER COUNTY

Highland
- Teri Condon—Gardensmith Design, Saturday, June 25

New Paltz
- Springtown Farmden, Saturday, June 25

Phoenicia
- Garden of Jim Goss & Joe Murray, Saturday, July 23

- Garden of Roger Griffith, Saturday, July 23

Saugerties
- Ann Krupp Bryan, Saturday, July 23
- The Donald Elder & Richard Suma Garden, Saturday, July 23

Willow
- Suzanne Pierot's Garden by the Stream, Saturday, July 23

WESTCHESTER COUNTY

Bedford
- Leslie & John Needham—River Hills, Sunday, June 5

Bedford Hills
- Heffernan Garden, Sunday, July 24
- Phillis Warden, Sunday, June 5, Sunday, June 26, Sunday, July 24

Chappaqua
- Shobha Vanchiswar & Murali Mani, Saturday, May 7

Cortlandt Manor
- Vivian & Ed Merrin, Sunday, June 26, Sunday, July 24

Lewisboro
- The White Garden, Sunday, April 24, Sunday, September 18

North Salem
- Dick Button—Ice Pond Farm, Sunday, September 18
- The Hen & the Hive, Sunday, June 26
- Keeler Hill Farm, Sunday, June 5
- Perrin Garden, Sunday, June 5

Ossining
- The Wildflower Island at Teatown Lake Reservation, Saturday, May 7

Pound Ridge
- Sara Stein Garden, Sunday, July 24

South Salem
- Garden of Bernard Marquez & Tim Fish, Sunday, June 26, Sunday, July 24

North Carolina

ORANGE COUNTY

Durham
- Deer Chase Gardens, Saturday, October 29

Pennsylvania

BUCKS COUNTY

Doylestown
- Fordhook Farm of W. Atlee Burpee Co., Saturday, June 11, Saturday, August 13

Furlong
- Dark Hollow Farm, Saturday, June 11

New Hope
- Jericho Mountain Orchards, Saturday, October 8
- Paxson Hill Farm, Saturday, June 11, Saturday, August 13, Saturday, October 8

Point Pleasant
- The Gardens at Mill Fleurs, Saturday, June 11

Wrightstown
- Hortulus Farm, Saturday, June 11

Rhode Island

NEWPORT COUNTY

Little Compton
- Sakonnet, Saturday & Sunday, May 21 & 22

PROVIDENCE COUNTY

Providence
- College Hill Urban Oasis, Saturday, June 11

Texas

HARRIS COUNTY

Bellaire
- Bellaire Meadow, Saturday, April 30

Houston
- Alba Garden, Saturday, April 30
- The Art Compound, Saturday, April 30
- Baldridge Residence, Saturday, April 30
- Camberg Garden, Saturday, April 30
- Habitat Gardens, Saturday, April 30
- Kyle-Lasseter Garden, Saturday, April 30

Southside Place
- Southside Glade, Saturday, April 30

Vermont

BENNINGTON COUNTY

East Arlington
- Rogerland, Saturday, July 9

Manchester
- Garden of Mary & Bob Russell, Saturday, July 9
- Turkey Hill Farm, Saturday, July 9

Manchester Center
- Coventry Cottage—Joan & Lee Fegelman's Garden, Saturday, July 9
- Hildene, The Lincoln Family Home, Saturday, july 9

WINDHAM COUNTY

Westminster West
- Gordon & Mary Hayward's Garden, Sunday, August 21

Washington

CLARK COUNTY

Battle Ground
- The Bailey Haven, Saturday, June 11
- Ritchie Garden, Saturday, June 11

Vancouver
- Dragonfly Hollow, Saturday, June 11
- The Garden of Roger & Judy McElhaney's Matsu Kaze (Wind in the Pines), Saturday, June 11
- Seymour-Lueck, Saturday, June 11

KING COUNTY

Auburn
- Soos Creek Botanical Garden & Heritage Center, Saturday, June 4

KITSAP COUNTY

Bainbridge Island
- Chapman's Garden, Sunday, June 26
- The Demianew Gardens, Sunday, June 26
- Peyton Gully Garden, Sunday, June 26
- Olaf Ribeiro/Nancy Allison, Sunday, June 26
- The Skyler Garden, Sunday, June 26

Kingston
- Leaf Works, Sunday, June 26

PIERCE COUNTY

Graham
- Old Goat Farm, Saturday, June 4

Orting
- Chase Garden, Saturday, June 4
- VanCor Gardens, Saturday, June 4

Puyallup
- Ernie & Julia Graham Garden, Saturday, June 4
- Ed Hume's Educational Garden, Saturday, June 4

Wisconsin

MILWAUKEE COUNTY

Greenfield
- Radler's Rosarium, Saturday, August 13

Hales Corners
- Boerner Botanical Gardens, August 6, August 13

Milwaukee
- Renaissance Garden at Villa Terrace, July 16

River Hills
- The Chimneys, Saturday, July 16
- Green Fire Woods, Saturday, August 6
- Hill Top House, Saturday, July 16
- Kubly Garden, Saturday, August 6

OZAUKEE COUNTY

Grafton
- Two Oaks, Saturday, July 16

Mequon
- Dragonfly Farm, Saturday, July 16

Newburg
- Ramhorn Farm, Saturday, August 6

SHEBOYGAN COUNTY

Sheboygan
- The Christopher Farm and Gardens, Saturday, July 23

WAUKESHA COUNTY

Dousman
- Lark's Garden, Saturday, August 13

Waukesha
- The Sievert Garden, Saturday, August 13

Special Programs

Saturday, April 2

FLORIDA
Jacksonville
- Carolyn Marsh Lindsay, Cummer Museum of Art & Gardens

Sunday, April 10

NEW YORK
Millbrook
- Gardening with Nature, Douglas Dockery Thomas, Cary Institute, 2801 Sharon Turnpike

Saturday, April 23

CALIFORNIA
Richmond
- A Passion for Pelargoniums, Robin Parer, Robin Parer's Greenhouse

Saturday, April 23

NEW YORK
Cold Spring
- Rock Garden Plants—Easy to Sublime, Anne Spiegel, Stonecrop Garden (during 10th Annual NARGS sale)

Sunday, May 1

NEW YORK
Millbrook
- Photographing Eden—The Work of Curtice Taylor, Curtice Taylor, Cary Institute, 2801 Sharon Turnpike

Sunday, May 22

NEW YORK
Millbrook
- The Quiet Beauty of Innisfree—A Modern Icon, Kate Kerin, Cary Institute, 2801 Sharon Turnpike

Saturday, May 28

MASSACHUSETTS
Chilmark
- The Dexter Rhododendrons in a Collector's Garden, Peter Norris, Blueberry Ridge Garden

Saturday, June 4

NEW YORK
Copake Falls
- Succulent Love, Kathy Tracey, Margaret Roach's Open Day

Sunday, June 5

MASSACHUSETTS
Milton
- Judith Tankard, Shapiro-Bloomberg Garden

Saturday, June 11

NEW YORK
Mill Neck
- Tea Ceremony, Stephen Morrell, Humes Japanese Stroll Garden

PENNSYLVANIA
Doylestown
- Spring Crops, Plant Hybridizing & Burpee's Top Plant Picks with George Ball, & Henk van der Veldt, Fordhook Farm

Wrightstown
- Listening to the Land at Hortulus Farm, Jack Staub & Renny Reynolds, Hortulus Farm

Saturday, June 25

NEW YORK
Mill Neck
- Tea Ceremony, Stephen Morrell, Humes Japanese Stroll Garden

Sunday, July 17

NEW YORK
Spencertown
- Bringing Back Natural Landscapes with Linda Horn, Barbara, Hughey, and Heather Grimes, Linda Horn's Garden

Saturday, July 30

CONNECTICUT
Lakeville
- *Garden Revolution*—Exploring Natural Landscapes, Larry Weaner, Mongomery Glazer Property
- Jamie Purinton, Mongomery Glazer Property

Salisbury
- Exploring Twin Maples—The Evolution of a Garden, Douglas Dockery Thomas & Deborah Munson, Twin Maples

Saturday, August 6

MINNESOTA
Medina
- Wallace Gardens: A Classical Framework with Jazz Improvisations, Wally Marx, Wallace Gardens

NEW YORK
Rhinebeck
- *Heirloom Harvest: Modern Daguerreotypes of Historic Garden Treasures*, Amy Goldman Fowler, Amy Goldman Fowler's Garden

Tivoli
- *A Tea Garden in Tivoli* with Bettina Mueller, A Tea Garden in Tivoli

WISCONSIN
Newburg
- Preserving Beauty at Ramhorn Farm, Matt Kastell & Scott Sieckman, Ramhorn Farm

Saturday, August 13

PENNSYLVANIA
Doylestown
- Summer Crops, Plant Hybridizing & Burpee's Top Plant Picks, George Ball, & Simon Crawford, Fordhook Farm

MASSACHUSETTS
Needham
- Garden Tips from a Tropical Paradise Near Boston with Kerry Ann Mendez & Ellen Lathi, Ellen Lathi's Garden

WISCONSIN
Waukesha
- Going Green: Communing with Moss in Dale Sievert's Garden, Dale Sievert, The Sievert Garden

Friday, August 19

NEW HAMPSHIRE
Peterborough
- *Outstanding American Gardens*, Page Dickey, Bass Hall

Saturday, August 20

NEW HAMPSHIRE
Francestown
- Garden Q&A, Roger Swain, The Gardens at Juniper Hill Farm

Stoddard
- The Nostril Chronicles: Fragrance in the Garden, Tovah Martin, Garden of Jenny Lee Hughes & Edward Yoxen

NEW YORK
Copake Falls
- *Planting in the Post-Wild World*, Thomas Rainer, Margaret Roach's Open Day

Sunday, August 21

VERMONT
Putney
- Garden Design Master Class with Gordon & Mary Hayward, Gordon & Mary Hayward's garden

Thursday, September 8

NEW YORK

Battery City

- Into the Blue: Pushing the Boundaries on a Rooftop Garden, Fred Rich, Mark K. Morrison & Annie Novak, Fred Rich's Battery Rooftop Garden

Saturday, September 17

NEW YORK

Mill Neck

- Tea Ceremony, Stephen Morrell, Humes Japanese Stroll Garden

Sunday, September 18

MASSACHUSETTS

Carlisle

- Growing Food at Clock Barn Farm—A Program for Families, Annie Novak, Clock Barn Farm

NEW YORK

South Salem

- Making Visual Sense of Your Outdoor Space, Bernard Marquez & Tim Fish, Garden of Bernard Marquez & Tim Fish

Saturday, September 24

NEW YORK

Millbrook

- *A House in the Country*, Katie Ridder, The Garden of Katie Ridder & Peter Pennoyer

Saturday, October 1

NEW YORK

Mill Neck

- Tea Ceremony, Stephen Morrell, Humes Japanese Stroll Garden

Saturday, October 8

PENNSYLVANIA

New Hope

- Seeing the Garden for the Trees— Designing with Trees at Paxson Hill Farm, Bruce Gangawer, Paxson Hill Farm

Sunday, October 16

Georgetown

- Revitalizing the Garden with Compost Tea, Andrea Fillipone & Eric T. Fleisher, Georgetown Garden: Nancy Gray Pyne

Saturday, October 29

NORTH CAROLINA

Durham

- Designing with Nature at Deer Chase Gardens, Justin Waller, Deer Chase Gardens

CALIFORNIA

San Francisco East Bay

Saturday, April 23

🕐 **Hours vary by garden**
(Starting at 10 a.m.)

$7 per garden

 **DIGGING DEEPER:** A Passion for Pelargoniums, Robin Parer's Greenhouse, 10 a.m. & 12 p.m.

ALAMEDA COUNTY

BERKELEY

📍 **OUR OWN STUFF GALLERY GARDEN**
3017 Wheeler Street, Berkeley

🕐 10 a.m. to 4 p.m.

My small urban garden has, over the past thirty-eight years, become mature—that is to say, way over my head—an oasis, and a California world of its, and our own. Unusual subtropical plants still intermingle with sculptures in steel, stone, and ceramic which Mark Bulwinkle, Sara Floor, Ted Fullwood, and I have made. Cevan Forristt helped me do a raccoon-proof koi pond. A collection of bantam chickens have the run of the garden by day and sleep in The Poultry Pagoda (Chicken Kremlin) by night. I have added a "beach," a faux eroded landfill of pebbles and shards. The ex-driveway is now The Big Beauty Garden, where strong colors and bold foliage embrace a ten-foot-tall ceramic, beatific female figure. The "National Collection of Bambusa Ceramica" continues to increase in size and varieties. The garden never holds still.
2013 | ♿ | 📷

Our Own Stuff Gallery, featured in *Outstanding American Gardens: A Celebration—25 Years of the Garden Conservancy*. Photo by Marion Brenner.

⮕ From I-80/I-580 by San Francisco Bay, take the Ashby Avenue/Berkeley Exit. Go 1.5 miles, look for Shattuck Avenue. There are two gas stations at that intersection. Cross Shattuck and turn right onto Wheeler Street. Go to fourth house on left, #3017. Please park on Wheeler or Emerson Street.

OAKLAND

⦿ LEIANNE'S GARDEN
13971 Skyline Boulevard, Oakland
🕐 10 a.m. to 4 p.m.

Enjoy panoramic views of the San Francisco Bay from the many seating areas of this hillside garden. Walls, patios, and paths are built almost completely from recycled materials. Featuring an eclectic and unusual plant collection, garden areas include shade gardens under redwoods and cedars, a cactus and succulent hillside, proteas, orchids and bromeliads, along with beehives, koi, goats and more.

NEW | ♿ | 📷

⮕ In Oakland, take I-580 to the Keller Avenue exit. Go east (uphill) on Keller. When Keller ends at Skyline Boulevard, turn left onto Skyline which has a median strip at this point. Go 0.9 mile and make U-turn at Hansom. Proceed to 13971 Skyline (blue house on bay side of street). Street parking is plentiful.

⦿ POTOMAC WATERWORKS
2451 Potomac Street, Oakland
🕐 10 a.m. to 4 p.m.

In a quiet Oakland neighborhood behind a simple wooden cottage lies an astonishing sight—an unfolding network of water features and private spaces set in the center of a truly secret garden. No less remarkable than the water features are the serenely beautiful garden spaces, sculpture, and stone placements. Grasses, Japanese maples, ginkgos and unusual color/texture plants surround and meet the water in unexpected ways, yet this urban woodland is unlike any found in nature.

Behind the scenes, it is also a demonstration of rainwater collection and reuse technologies serving the water features, drainage and irrigation systems. This lovely garden reminds its visitors that wonders sometime lay hidden in the most unexpected places. The garden has been featured on previous tours (since 1995) and well worth a return visit.

2014 | 📷

⮕ From Highway 13, exit at Joaquin Miller Avenue, and turn left onto the frontage road. At the stop sign, turn right onto Lincoln Avenue and downhill 0.5 mile. Turn left from Lincoln and park on Potomac.

From South Bay, take I-880 north and go east to I-580 at Castro Valley. Follow I-580 to Oakland/San Leandro area and merge onto Warren Freeway/Highway 13 North. Take Exit 13 at Lincoln Avenue/Joaquin Miller and turn left onto Lincoln Avenue. Go downhill 0.5 mile on Lincoln and turn left onto Potomac Street. Please park on street.

ORINDA

⦿ THE BOWYER JAPANESE GARDEN
147 Overhill Road, Orinda
🕐 10 a.m. to 5 p.m.

When we purchased our house more than forty years ago, the surrounding area had no vegetation; cars rounding the curve on the main road appeared to be driving directly into our front door. Our solution was a wooden fence and a small Japanese Zen garden. Later modifications included a waterfall feature and several traditional Japanese garden spaces: a woodland entrance area, an entrance garden, and two courtyard gardens. The main courtyard garden hosts a dry lake and a small island. Our Japanese style house is now surrounded by this tranquil garden.

2014 | 📷

⮕ From Highway 24, take Orinda exit south to Moraga. About 100 yards after stoplight at exit, turn left on Overhill Road. 0.8 mile (just after crest of hill) is a weathered slotted fence on left masking garden. Please park on street.

RICHMOND

 ROBIN PARER'S GREENHOUSE
505 Brookside Drive, Richmond

1 p.m. to 4 p.m.

 DIGGING DEEPER | 10 AM & 12 PM

Robin's Parer's Geraniaceae nursery and greenhouse, open by appointment only, is thought to have the largest selection of rare and unusual pelargoniums in the United States. Visit her 11,000-square-foot commercial greenhouse to see hundreds of pelargonium types in bloom—including scented leaf, Regals (Martha Washingtons), ivy leaf, angel and pansy face. There are also species pelargoniums all from Southern Africa, with flowers in many vivid colors of red, orange, lilac, rose, yellow, pink, and white. Robin is the author of *The Garden Lovers Guide to Hardy Geraniums* (April 2016) and co-organizer of The Hortisexuals, a group made up of horticulture professionals and passionate gardeners. **NEW** | ♿ | 📷

Do not use GPS, MapQuest, Google Maps or Waze. From Highway 580 take the Richmond Parkway exit (if coming from the east it is the second last exit before the Richmond/San Rafael Bridge; if coming from the west it is the first exit after the bridge) and head north on Castro/Richmond Parkway (with the Bay on your left) about 4 miles. At Pittsburg Avenue, turn right (there is a recycling plant on left as you turn); go through one intersection and at the "T" junction turn left onto Fred Jackson Way (formerly Third Street). Go down 1 block to stop sign and turn right onto Brookside Drive. Look along Brookside on left and a few hundred yards down is a sign for Top Hat Orchids and beyond that a Eugenia hedge next to the road. On the other side of the hedge, but before a wooden water tank, turn left down a little road between two rows of greenhouses. I am in the greenhouse half way down on the left. There are pelargoniums outside the door and in the beds in front of the greenhouse. Park on either side of the greenhouse.

 # DIGGING DEEPER

SATURDAY, APRIL 23 | 10 AM & 12 PM | $20
A PASSION FOR PELARGONIUMS
AT: Robin Parer's Greenhouse
      505 Brookside Drive, Richmond

If the thought of "red geraniums" (pelargoniums) recalls that wonderful poem of Theodore Roethke's, 'The Geranium', you might be amazed to discover how fascinating, how varied, and how adaptable "geraniums" really are. Robin's nursery is thought to have the largest selection of rare and unusual pelargoniums in the United States. In this one-hour talk we will look at hundreds of varieties and learn how to identify, propagate and care for these plants successfully. There will also be plenty of time to wander the 11,000 square foot. greenhouse and smell scented leaves or photograph flowers.

Registration is required and space is limited. **Opendaysprogram.org or call 1(888) 842-2442**

Pasadena

Saturday, May 1

🕐 **10 a.m. to 4 p.m.**
$7 per garden

★ Start your day at La Casita del Arroyo, 177 South Arroyo Boulevard, Pasadena, 9:30 a.m. to 3:30 p.m.

Maps and discounted admission tickets will be available there. Admission, free.

LOS ANGELES COUNTY

ARCADIA

📍 **MERRILL & DONIVEE NASH**
1014 Hampton Road, Arcadia

Donivee Nash grew up in Delaware surrounded by the rich culture of nineteenth-century estate gardens like Longwood, Mount Cuba, Winterthur, and Nemours. She brought this garden aesthetic with her to the New England-style saltbox (as this property was in 1938) over thirty-five years ago. Although the house has dramatically grown and enlarged, the parklike ambience of the landscaping remains. Donivee is a collector of specimen plants. Over the years, she added roses and perennials to the existing English-style gardens. She added a poolside pavilion (a miniature version of the one designed by Beatrix Farrand at Dumbarton Oaks), which is a cool oasis during hot summers. In 2009 when Donivee and her husband

Merrill wanted to unify the backyard and reduce water consumption, they called upon well-known garden designer Judy Horton. Out went much of the lawn, in came twenty-plus trees, including a sycamore grove to screen... [Read the full description on-line]

2013 | ♿ | 📷

➲ From the west, go east on I-210. Exit at Rosemead North/Michillinda. Go north on Michillinda, cross Foothill Boulevard, and turn right onto Hampton Road. Continue to the intersection of Hampton and Dexter Roads. The garden is at #1014 Hampton, on the south-west corner of the intersection.

From the east, go west on I-210. Exit at Baldwin Avenue. Turn north onto Baldwin, cross Foothill Boulevard, and turn left onto the second street, Hampton Road. Follow Hampton to the intersection of Dexter and Hampton Roads. Proceed as directed above.

The garden of Merrill & Donivee Nash, featured in *Outstanding American Gardens: A Celebration—25 Years of the Garden Conservancy*. Photo by Marion Brenner.

PASADENA

📍 **GARDEN OF LISA & TOM EVANS**
455 South San Rafael Avenue,
Pasadena

Sited on over two acres of park-like grounds, this gracious gated estate, originally designed by noted architect Louis DuPuget Millar in 1908, was thoughtfully expanded in the 1920s by Roland Coate. It more recently was renovated to fit a more modern lifestyle by the renowned architect David Serrurier. The house is approached on its circular drive, past gardens and tree lined pathways, into an intimate Dimic stone courtyard with a reflecting fountain, rose trellis, camellias, bear lime trees, and Old World olive trees. The rose garden is a formal collection of more than 1,000 specimens representing more than 100 varieties of old garden roses intermingled with newer varieties, grandiflora, hybrid tea, floribunda, and climbing roses. The rear of the yard houses a large, inviting pool framed by a Dimic pool deck, Bacheldered-covered terrace and Bachelder fountain encasing lily pads and aquatic plants. There is a spectacular wisteria terrace, with blooms entwined in a custom...
[Read the full description online]
NEW | ♿ | 📷

➲ From 134 Freeway (1.4 miles), exit at San Rafael Avenue in Pasadena. Travel southeast (right turn from 134 East; left turn from 134 West/210). Turn right onto West Colorado Boulevard, heading west. After several blocks, turn left at first traffic light onto Melrose Avenue (by clock tower). Take a soft left at stop sign onto Avenue 64. Take first left onto Nithsdale Road and go several blocks to San Rafael Avenue. Turn right onto South San Rafael Avenue and find parking.

📍 **LIPSIG GARDEN**
280 California Terrace, Pasadena

Our gardens surround our Thornton Ladd-designed, modernist house completed around 1950. We extensively re-landscaped the grounds around 1990 with the assistance of the late landscape architect Owen Peters of EPT Design. In 2012, we replaced the tennis court that dominated the front of our house with a garden designed by landscape architects Amy Korn and Matt Randolph of Kornrandolph and landscape designer Judy Horton. Our gardens begin with a rustic street frontage of *Pittosporum undulatum* trees shading clumps of dietes, daylilies, society garlic, and other plants. North of our gate, there is an olive tree with a mixed planting below. Going through the gate, one passes beds of roses on either side. The northern bed is bounded by Carolina laurel cherries. Beyond the roses is an arc of lawn backed by white crape myrtles, sweeping around to a broken concrete planter draped with rosemary and featuring...
[Read the full description online]
NEW | ♿ | 📷

➲ Go to Pasadena on the 110, 134, or 210 Freeways. Exit at Orange Grove Boulevard. From the 134 or 210 Freeways, go south on Orange Grove Boulevard about 0.5 mile to Arbor Street and turn right.

From the 110 Freeway, go north on Orange Grove Boulevard about 1.5 miles to Arbor Street and turn left. Drive 2 blocks on Arbor, first to Grand Avenue and then to California Terrace. Turn right onto California Terrace and find a parking spot before California Terrace becomes a private drive three houses in. Do not drive down the private drive. Walk down the private drive to just before it dead-ends at a gated property. The entrance is on right. You will see "280" in large numbers on the wall beside our gate, which will be open.

📍 **LOMITA GARDEN**
1415 Lomita Drive, Pasadena

This is the first time this private estate garden has been included in the Open Days program. The house and garden are designed to take full advantage of the mild, Mediterranean climate where outdoor entertaining can be a year-round activity. The recently updated woodland gardens include heritage oaks, pines, and sweet gum trees that reflect the rustic, architectural character of the house. Pools of white iris and blue agapanthus edge the woodland areas where dogwood and Japanese maples provide seasonal interest under the tree canopy. The secluded, tropical pool and spa garden, replete with five water features, is an alluring view from the floor-to-ceiling windows in the living room and study above. Handcrafted fences and gates grace the boundaries of the gardens, and a herringbone-patterned brick patio under a wisteria-covered arbor welcome the visitor to the family entry garden. Rustic stone, raised-vegetable beds provide the family… [Read the full description online]

NEW | ♿ |

➥ From the 210 freeway, take Exit 26/Lake Street in Pasadena and go south 0.7 mile. Turn right onto Del Mar Boulevard and continue 0.3 mile. Turn left onto South El Molino Drive and continue 1.3 mile, through traffic circle. Turn right onto Woodland Road for 381 feet. Turn left onto Lomita Drive for 364 feet. The garden is on right.

From the 110 Freeway, take the 110 Freeway to the north end and turn right onto Glenarm Street. Turn right onto South Oakland Street, through traffic circle for 0.4 mile. Turn slight left onto Lomita Drive. The garden is on right.

From the 10 Freeway, take Exit 23A-23B/ Atlantic Boulevard north toward Pasadena for 2.5 miles. Continue north as road name changes to Los Robles Avenue 1.0 mile. Turn right onto South Oakland Avenue 479 feet, then a sharp right onto Lomita Drive. The garden is on right.

OAK VALE
375 South San Rafael Avenue, Pasadena

When my husband and I stopped at an estate sale the object of our interest became the garden! As soon as we walked in to the home it became a secondary thought, one look out of the window and the garden became first and foremost. We were captivated by the ducks who were borrowing the turtle pond and yard, secure that no one would bother them. The previous owners had occupied the house for fifty years and were unable to maintain the property in their later years. It needed to be completely restored and upgraded in addition to remodeling the garden. This restoration allowed us to appreciate the siting of this home and create areas that encourage viewing from every room. The 1911 Sumner Hunt-designed house embraces the sloping terraces creating natural divisions in the garden. An arroyo stone-lined runoff "stream" from the mountains runs along the width of the property. Our 100-year-old neighbor remembers deer drinking from it! With winds… [Read the full description online]

NEW | ♿ |

➥ From 134 Freeway (1.4 miles), exit at San Rafael Avenue in Pasadena, go southeast (right turn from 134 East; left turn from 134 West/210). Turn right onto West Colorado Boulevard, and go west. After several blocks, turn left at first traffic light onto Melrose Avenue (by clock tower). Take a soft left at stop sign onto Avenue 64. Take first left onto Nithsdale Road and go several blocks to San Rafael Avenue. Turn right onto South San Rafael Avenue and find parking.

YARIV RESIDENCE
480 Madeline Drive, Pasadena

The Yariv garden is a quintessential example of the Mid-Century Modernism style. The house, designed in 1960 by the notable local architect, Bill Blurock, presents an austere façade to the street that belies the elegance of the interior and rear garden. The front yard was completely updated in the winter of 2015—a water-thirsty front lawn, overgrown trees, and an asphalt driveway were replaced with a contemporary palette reminiscent of Palm Springs. The plantings for the front consist of various different agaves, aeoniums, echeverias, euphorbias, senecios, and *Lippia nodiflora* groundcovers. The elegant branching structure of the seven Jerusalem Thorn trees (*Parkinsonia aculeata*) provide a profusion of yellow flowers in the spring. These trees are native to the Sonoran and Chihuahuan deserts of southwestern United States, northern Mexico as well as the Galapagos Islands. The rear garden was overhauled in 2008. The only remaining element of the back yard is the... [Read the full description online]

NEW | ♿ | 📷

⤵ From the 210 or 134 Freeway, exit onto Orange Grove Boulevard and travel south to Madeline Drive. Turn right. Park on the north side of Madeline only or on Grand Avenue at the bottom of the hill.

From the 110 Freeway exit onto Orange Grove and travel north to second light at Madeline Drive. Turn left. Parking on north side of Madeline Drive only or on Grand Avenue at the bottom of the hill, a very short walk.

LEAD GARDEN
✿ PUBLIC GARDEN

LOS ANGELES COUNTY
PASADENA

◉ **LA CASITA DEL ARROYO GARDEN**
727 South Orange Grove Boulevard, Pasadena
(626) 449-9505, lacasitadelarroyo.org

★ Start your tour here on Sunday, May 1 between 9:30 a.m. and 3:30 p.m. Tickets and maps to all of the Pasadena gardens will be available.

$ Free

See this garden's listing on page 67.

Los Angeles

Saturday, May 7

🕐 **10 a.m. to 4 p.m.**
$7 per garden

★ Start your day at Merrihew's Sunset Gardens, 1526 Ocean Park Boulevard, Santa Monica, 9:30 a.m. to 3:30 p.m.

Maps and discounted admission tickets will be available there. Admission, free.

The Garden at Woodacres, featured in *Outstanding American Gardens: A Celebration—25 Years of the Garden Conservancy*. Photo by Marion Brenner.

LOS ANGELES COUNTY

LOS ANGELES

THE FLETCHER GARDEN
336 Bentel Avenue, Los Angeles

The Fletcher Garden is a study in restraint. While Bob Fletcher's palette of green and white may seem simple at first glance, it is anything but. He was known to show design students a garden devoid of bright colors and flowers and ask them how many colors they saw. When the reply was "green" he would open their eyes to the million shades of green around them—forest, moss, mint, olive, jade, emerald, chartreuse, and so on. Then he would ask them to look at the textures of the leaves and barks—shiny, matte, rounded, pointed, lobed, crinkled, fuzzy, flaky, smooth, ribbed, and on and on. Thinking in this way is how he designed classic, timeless gardens such as this one. Keep your eyes and your mind open as you wander about. Bob's spirit is there guiding you. The garden owner writes this about caring for his work "Bob Fletcher created a timeless garden of beauty and grace. I often describe this garden as my... [Read the full description online]
NEW | ♿ | 📷

⮑ From San Vicente Boulevard in Santa Monica, turn north onto Allenford Avenue/26th Street. Turn right onto Street and then left onto Bentel Avenue.

From Sunset Boulevard, turn south onto Allenford Avenue. Turn left onto South Rockingham and then right onto Hanover and then a quick sharp right onto Bentel.

Please park on the street.

SANTA MONICA

15TH STREET GARDEN
407 15th Street, Santa Monica

Jonathan and Stefanie Greenberg knew that it was time for a change when they realized that they and their three children were not using their garden as anything other than a path from the garage to the kitchen door or for an occasional dip in the pool. They had visited other gardens designed by landscape architect Joseph Marek on previous Open Days and decided to give him a call. Joseph started with the back garden in 2011, developing a plan that included keeping the old pool but eliminating everything else. Gone are the old concrete pool deck and outdated hot tub, a spiral staircase to the studio above the garage and all of the grass. He designed a series of spaces for entertaining at the heart of which is a lively fountain set in a Sweetwater sandstone and Mexican pebble court. The pool was redesigned to include a new Jacuzzi lined in a glittering green glass tile. New long pool steps were added and the pool was re-plastered in a soft sandy green to mimic the color of...
[Read the full description online]

NEW | ♿ | 📷

➥ From San Vicente Boulevard, turn south onto 14th Street. Turn left onto Carlyle Avenue and then right onto 15th Street.

From Montana Avenue, turn north onto 15th Street. Park on the street.

CASA NANCINA
1015 Pier Avenue, Santa Monica

Garden designer, Nancy Goslee Power's own garden, Casa Nancina is discovered behind a barn red gate, where one enters a series of small, colorful courtyards with a tiny house inspired by visits to Brazil and Morocco. The garden unfolds to reveal many places to dine and settle in: a seating group in front of a fireplace, tables and chairs all surrounded by many terracotta pots, with both common and unusual plants and trees. A rare Kashmir cypress weeps over a wall fountain, a path with herringbone pebbles leads to the central courtyard, the heart of the garden. Aubergine cannas and a cushioned bench against saffron stucco walls, tropical looking king palm trees canopying the courtyard, a Majorelle cobalt wall with maiden hair and tree ferns in the back ground, blue morning glories drape over the studio cottage, and a centered long water tank filled with waterlily pads and gold fish make this enchanting petite garden a surprising oasis in suburban Santa Monica.

2005 | 📷

➥ Take I-10 west to Lincoln Boulevard. Turn left, pass Ocean Park Boulevard and continue to Pier Avenue. Turn left and go to end of block. House is on left. Please park on the street.

JAFFE GARDEN
217 16th Street, Santa Monica

Her clients' long love of France was the inspiration for this charming city garden designed by Sally Paul Garden Design. The original garden and pergola was built almost fifteen years ago but a new addition to the house and guest house created an opportunity to link the two together. A large portion of the lawn was removed to create a lovely gravel garden with comfy furniture, boxwoods planted in gravel, citrus in pots and flanked on one side by an aerial hedge of standard 'Saratoga' Bay Laurel trees and on the other, by an olive tree underplanted with a variety of clipped rounded shrubs. The center lawn panel is steel edged with a gravel mow-strip, while rounded boxwoods link the new part of the garden to the original. Old Anduze pots adorn the pergola terrace and entry garden. Lavenders, Little Ollie (and Big Ollie!), boxwoods, Cypress 'Tiny Tim', myrtle, pittosporums, and westringia abound to create a Mediterranean palette that is both pleasing and appropriate.

NEW | ♿ | 📷

➥ The garden is located west of the 405 Freeway and south of Sunset Boulevard. Go west on San Vicente Boulevard to 17th Street and turn south. Turn west onto Georgina and go 1 block. Go south on 16th Street. The house will be on the east side of the street, 1 block south of San Vicente.

THE GARDENS AT WOODACRES
801 Woodacres Road, Santa Monica

Two great modern masters have shaped the experience of Woodacres, Suzanne and Ric Kayne's one-acre garden overlooking the legendary golf course of the Riviera Country Club (it is literally on the sixth hole). In the distance, an expansive view of the Pacific Palisades draws the eye to the horizon. In a bold move, the Kaynes turned to the eminent Belgian firm of Wirtz International to replace a traditional, English-style country garden with something quite different. The task of translating their sensibility to a suburban garden in Southern California fell to local designer Lisa Zeder. Working in tandem, the Wirtzes and Zeder used hedges of Japanese boxwood (*Buxus japonica*) and Carolina cherry (*Prunus caroliniana*) to shape the spaces, transforming the property into a series of serene green terraces, each with a different (but stunning) view. Flowering trees and shrubs enliven the garden spaces, notably the dramatic Chinese flame trees (*Koelreuteria bipinnata*) and... [Read the full description online]

2011 | ♿ | 📷

➥ From 10 Freeway West, exit onto Cloverfield Boulevard and turn right. Turn left onto Santa Monica Boulevard. Turn right onto 14th Street and go north, crossing San Vicente Boulevard onto Woodacres Road. Please park on San Vincente Boulevard.

From 405 Freeway, take the Wilshire exit and go to 14th Street. Proceed as directed above.

Marin County

Saturday, May 21

🕐 **10 a.m. to 4 p.m.**
$7 per garden

MARIN COUNTY

KENTFIELD

📍 **CLIPPED PERFECTION**
11 Meadow Avenue, Kentfield

This organic garden was featured in *Garden Design* magazine and includes an orchard and herb and vegetable gardens. One enters via a formidable gate set in a perfectly-sheared Coast Redwood hedge that hides a secret, rambling garden sanctuary previously designed by Scott Colombo. Fragrant antique roses twist and spill over three archways and along walls of craggy weathered stone. A cobblestone path runs through a series of garden rooms that burst with wild geraniums and lilacs. A unique stone throne is flanked by a pair of blueberry soldiers. The overgrown English garden style at the front of the property contrasts with the more recently redesigned and orderly style of the back pool garden. Globes of teucrium, geranium, boxwood, salvia, and white foxglove—clipped to perfection—create surrounding garden beds. A unique metal trellis planted with honeysuckle, 'Cecil Brunner' roses, and clematis covers a water feature nestled in a redwood hedge. The hornbeam hedge surrounding the nearby soccer field looks magical in all seasons.

NEW | ♿ | 📷

➲ Take 101 North to Sir Francis Drake Boulevard Exit. Exit right onto Laurel Grove. Continue to Meadow Avenue and turn right. The garden is on the left.

ROSS

📍 **ECHOES OF THE PAST**
8 Southwood Avenue, Ross

Walk past the magnificent oak to the right of the driveway and you immediately see

the remnants of an old Japanese garden—a garden previously filled with huge holly trees, enormous camellias, and a bounty of jewel-toned rhodies, and azaleas. The old garden had a number of Japanese elements: a fish pond, a tea house, and one-of-a-kind Japanese maples. The remaining Japanese maple weeps to the left as you enter through the garden gate. The main house nestles into the property in a way that creates a secluded stage for family gatherings. A recently added guest/pool house with an enormous stone fireplace overlooks an edible garden complete with rambling black satin blackberries, five kinds of golden and red raspberries, and espaliered apple and pear trees. The raised beds are replanted seasonally and host a bounty of colorful tulips in spring. This once-overgrown garden area was used as a pasture for horses long ago.

NEW | ♿ | 📷

⮕ Take Highway 101 North to the Sir Frances Drake Boulevard exit to the town of Ross. Turn left onto Lagunitas Road and then right onto Shady Lane. Turn left onto Southward Avenue and go to #8.

Marin County

Saturday, June 4

🕙 **10 a.m. to 4 p.m.**
$7 per garden

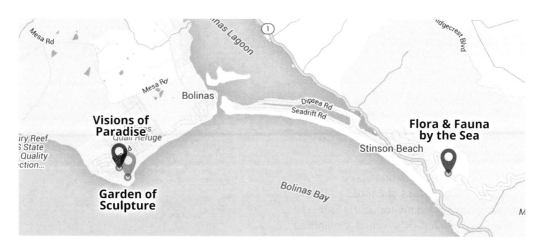

MARIN COUNTY

BOLINAS

📍 **GARDEN OF SCULPTURE**
20 Nymph Road, Bolinas

Landscape architect George Hargreaves is known for designing large urban master plans such as the Stanford's Engineering Quadrangle in Palo Alto, not for work on small, windswept, starkly beautiful sites atop cliffs that gradually step to the ocean as this property does. "The sculpture collection drew me to work on this project," he says. Works by Henry Moore, Richard Long, and Barbara Hepworth are among those in the owner's collection. Hargreaves saw that the sculptures could be arranged in tiers to be viewed individually, as well as seen as a group from a distance. "We created a view corridor that steps down toward the ocean," he says. The flat-stepped terraces along this corridor provide a sculpted vista. Stacked stone fitted together forms retaining walls and the stair treads and paths are covered with crushed granite. At some points the property goes from natural to cultivated landscape. Hedges were used in windy areas where wind blocks were needed. Hedgerows separate the larger landscape from the garden landscape.

NEW | ♿ | 📷

➲ Take Route 101 to the Sir Francis Drake Boulevard Exit and follow Sir Francis Drake to its end in Olema. Turn left onto Route 1 and continue to unmarked right turn to Bolinas, just before the Lagoon. Bear left at the yield sign. Turn left at the first stop sign at the Las Baulines Nursery. Turn right at the next stop sign onto Mesa Road. Turn left onto Overlook Drive. Turn right onto Elm Street. Turn left onto Maple Road. Turn right onto Cherry Drive. Turn left onto Nymph Road. Number 20 is on the left.

📍 **VISIONS OF PARADISE—SALLY ROBERTSON GARDEN & STUDIO**
284 Cherry Road, Bolinas

I like to think of walking through the garden gate as entering an enchanted and magical world. When asked to describe my garden, I like to refer to the title of one of my favorite garden books, "Visions of Paradise." This expression has guided me for nearly four decades. As a painter, I often choose plants as inspiration for a watercolor, but I give much thought to their placement, for the garden itself is a highly orchestrated color palette. As I mature as a gardener, shrubs and trees which give year round structure become more and more important, and well-shaped shrubs mingle well with exuberant roses. Succulents have found their place, along with unusual larger specimens such as the lovely deciduous Dawn

Redwood from China. The pond and water garden offer an idyllic spot to linger and enjoy a reflective moment. The garden is an ever-changing project, evolving year after year, and I hope that even those who have visited in the past will find new inspiration here. Visitors are also invited to visit the studio, where art and garden meet.

2006 | ♿ | 📷

➲ From San Francisco, take Highway 101 across Golden Gate Bridge to first Mill Valley/Stinson Beach/Route 1 exit. Follow Route 1, for 4.4 miles north of Stinson Beach. The Bolinas Lagoon will be on left; as soon as lagoon ends, turn left at unmarked intersection. Bear left at yield sign and continue on towards Bolinas. Turn left at first stop sign at Las Baulines Nursery. Turn right at next stop sign onto Mesa Road, which will take you up onto Bolinas Mesa. Take first real left onto Overlook Drive and continue on to Elm Road and turn right. Go down Elm Road to large green public utilities building on right and turn left onto Maple. Cherry Road is first right and #284 is first house on right.

From East Bay, take Richmond-San Rafael Bridge to Highway 101. You can either take Mill Valley exit and follow directions above or take San Anselmo exit and follow Sir Francis Drake Boulevard until it ends in Olema. Turn right onto Route 1 and proceed to unmarked right turn to Bolinas, just before Bolinas Lagoon, and proceed as directed above. Please park in driveway or along street.

STINSON BEACH

📍 **FLORA & FAUNA BY THE SEA**
6901 Panoramic Highway, Stinson Beach

Huge boulders on a steep hillside provide the framework for this unusual garden perched on the shoulders of Mt. Tamalpais. It was created twenty years ago from a wilderness of brambles, poison oak, and native willows. Now stone walks radiate from a centrally located house to a series of garden rooms defined by their plantings—various fuchsia species, tillandsia and pendulous epiphyllums grow in the shade of ancient bay trees. On the hillside, protea, and dozens of succulent species grow in the sparse soil among the rocks. In the sunny open spaces, azara, pseudocydonia, psoralea, and rare pittosporum shrubs share space with perennials and self-seeding annuals. Water-loving plants such as papyrus and giant gunnera surround the seasonal stream and the koi pond. The garden contains more than 200 species of plants including unusual specimens from the Mediterranean, Australia, New Zealand, Chile, and South Africa. Scattered among the plants are beautiful stone sculptures from Zimbabwe and comfortable weather-worn benches offering diverse views of the garden and the Pacific Ocean below.

2006 | ♿ | 📷

⮫ From Highway 101, exit at Stinson Beach. Follow signs to Route 1 and Stinson Beach (about 12 miles north of exit from Highway 101). Immediately before entering town of Stinson Beach, turn right onto Panoramic Highway and proceed uphill about 0.25 mile. Number 6901 is on right, facing ocean. Please park on overlooks on either side of large bay tree that shelters entrance to property.

The Gardens Surrounding Digging Dog Nursery, featured in *Outstanding American Gardens: A Celebration—25 Years of the Garden Conservancy*. Photo by Marion Brenner.

Mendocino County

Saturday, June 18

🕐 Hours vary by garden
  (Starting at 10 a.m.)
$7 per garden

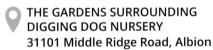

MENDOCINO COUNTY

ALBION

📍 **THE GARDENS SURROUNDING
DIGGING DOG NURSERY**
31101 Middle Ridge Road, Albion

🕐 10 a.m. to 5 p.m.

Nestled among towering redwoods on a rural ridge top, Digging Dog Nursery and its elaborately planted grounds cover approximately two acres. A verdant back-drop of clipped evergreen and deciduous hedges sculpt distinctly separate spaces, thresholds, and views beckoning with anticipation. Inspired by old-style tradition and emphasizing year-round appeal, the garden's dramatic perennial borders, some more than 150-feet-long, are threaded together by pathways and tree-lined trails. This structured layout juxtaposes ebullient plantings, which feature a diverse collection of unusual plants and favored main-stays. The landscape designer and co-owner will be giving two informative, guided tours amidst the nursery's surrounding gardens. Digging Dog Nursery is a mail-order and retail nursery featuring unusual and hard-to-find perennials, ornamental grasses, shrubs, trees, and vines that flourish in a variety of garden settings throughout the country. Plants will be available for sale.

2015 | ♿ | 📷

➲ From the south on Highway 1, turn right onto Albion Ridge Road; from the north on Highway 1, turn left. Go 4 miles east on Albion Ridge Road. Turn right onto Middle Ridge Road (right turn only; this is a three-way intersection). Go 0.3 mile on Middle Ridge Road. You will see a cluster of mailboxes on right and then directly ahead on left, our driveway and a tree with Digging Dog Nursery sign on it. Turn left into driveway, and shortly turn right into parking lot. A green sign on left reads Nursery Parking. Once you pull into the parking lot you will see the farm gates and our welcome sign. Parking lot is small; additional parking along roadside.

HOPLAND

FREY GARDENS
300 Ralph Bettcher Drive, Hopland
🕙 10 a.m. to 4 p.m.

Frey Gardens is a one-acre sustainable, habitat garden. The garden is six years old and is composed of a mix of native plants and others that attract and support a variety of insects and birds, all planted in a naturalistic style. There is also a small vegetable garden. Many rustic structures are found in the garden, such as a hermit's hut, chicken coop, bar, and whimsical gate posts.

2015 | ♿ |

↪ From the South, the garden is 100 miles from San Francisco and Berkeley directly north on Highway 101. It is 1 hour north of Santa Rosa, 30 minutes north of Healdsburg, 15 minutes north of Cloverdale. Go north on Highway 101, from San Francisco through Santa Rosa, Healdsburg, Cloverdale. In Hopland, take the first left at Mountain House Road. Immediately after the bridge behind the gas station on Highway 101, turn right onto MacMilan. Make an immediate left onto Ralph Bettcher Drive. Garden is at #300, the second house on right. Look for signs. Park anywhere along the road or at the closed elementary school across the street. Watch for ditch on left side of road.

From the north, Hopland is approximately 15 to 20 minutes south of Ukiah on Highway 101. Turn right onto Mountain House Road on the south end of Hopland. Immediately AFTER the bridge behind the gas station, turn right onto MacMilan. Make an immediate left onto Ralph Bettcher Drive. Garden is the second

house on the right, #300. Look for signs. Park on the road anywhere, or at the closed school across the street. Watch for the ditch on the left side of the road. Garden is 2 to 3 minutes from Highway 101.

MENDOCINO

MOSS GARDEN
45145 Brest Road, Mendocino
🕙 10 a.m. to 4 p.m.

The surrounding tree-studded state park and coastal headlands of the Pacific Ocean lend an isolated feeling to the Moss Garden. Set back from the strong breezes of the bluff's edge, the house provides a sheltered garden setting, while an ocean view beckons. The charming redwood residence, enhanced with Northern European details, inspired the garden's layout and many of its architectural elements. Aligned with the house, the sunken garden required substantial excavation to lower it beyond harsh winds, thus creating a suitable microclimate for an array of unexpected plants. The leftover soil became the main component in the construction of the rammed earth walls, which retain and partition garden rooms and impart a classic time-worn appeal. Leeward of the house, the protected orchard garden brims with blooms, conveying a blousy exuberance. In contrast, the heather garden features mounding forms in an exposed wind-contoured tapestry of texture color.

2013 | ♿ |

↪ About 1 mile north of the town of Mendocino, turn west off Highway 1 at entry point of Russian Gulch State Park and Point Cabrillo Drive. Continue directly west onto Brest Road. Go about 0.25 miles to a gate that reads "Moss, 45145". Proceed through the gate and park in the noted area.

PHILO

 THE APPLE FARM
18501 Greenwood Road, Philo

🕐 10 a.m. to 4 p.m.

The garden at The Apple Farm is a work in progress. We started in 1984 with a rundown farm labor camp and orchard. The present garden was a barren mess of old car parts, fences, blackberries, and Bermuda grass. Everything you will see has been reclaimed by hand, without sprays or machines. We started with annuals and a kitchen garden close to the old house, which is now our commercial kitchen. We gradually added perennial starts, mostly dug from family gardens in Napa Valley and later added shrubs and a few trees to create the partially shaded microclimate we now enjoy. We created a simple potting shed/greenhouse at the back of the main building in the shell of a building that existed. Luckily it has good sun exposure, unlike the rest of the house. Our children were very young and I spent most of my time outside with them working to make a garden to grow both food and flowers. As the years went by and I started to do bouquets for our local farmers market and my brother's...

[Read the full description online]

2015 | ♿ | 📷

➲ From the Bay area, take 101 North to the last Cloverdale exit, then go West on 128 to Anderson Valley. The sign will say Ft. Bragg and Boonville. It will be about thirty minutes on a winding road, which straightens out at Boonville, from there you have another fifteen minutes to go. Three miles past Philo, at mile marker 20.15, turn left onto Greenwood Road (the sign says Elk and Hendy woods). Go 0.25 mile, The Apple Farm will be on your left at the one lane bridge. If parking lot in front is full, including orchard extra parking, drive by garden on driveway and park in orchard behind the garden.

 WILDWOOD
7990 Highway 128, Philo

🕐 10 a.m. to 4 p.m.

A potager with extensive market gardens surrounded by a mixed shrub border. A good collection of magnolia, acer, and other temperate trees and shrubs, in a park of 150-foot redwood trees.

2012 | ♿ | 📷

➲ From the coast, take Highway 128 South to just before the town of Philo. A sign reading "35 mph ahead" is in the driveway, turn right. Follow gravel road to right of barn and cottages in front of property to house and garden.

From the south, take Highway 128 North, pass the town of Philo about 0.25 mile. On right is a sign reading "45 mph curve ahead", #7990 is on left just after this sign. In middle of curve, mile marker 22.34 is on right. Follow gravel road to right of barn and cottages in front of property to house and garden.

The Gardens of Alcatraz, San Francisco, California

For more than 150 years, a succession of soldiers, families of correction officers, and prison inmates cultivated gardens on rocky, windswept Alcatraz Island in San Francisco Bay. Since 2003, in partnership with the National Park Service and the Golden Gate National Parks Conservancy, the Garden Conservancy has led the effort to restore these long-abandoned gardens, not just for the island's 1.5 million annual visitors to enjoy, but to demonstrate the importance of gardening to the people who lived in this notoriously harsh environment.

...Today, thriving gardens once again surround the somber prison walls, as they did during much of the island's history.

—Excerpted from *Outstanding American Gardens: A Celebration—25 Years of the Garden Conservancy*. Photo by Marion Brenner.

San Francisco

Saturday, June 25

🕐 10 a.m. to 4 p.m.
$7 per garden

SAN FRANCISCO COUNTY

SAN FRANCISCO

📍 **GEARY STREET GARDEN**
735 Geary Street, San Francisco

In the heart of downtown San Francisco lives a secret garden behind twin historic buildings. These structures were erected in the early 1900s in the theater district and are three blocks from Union Square on the dividing line between upper class Nob Hill and the notorious Tenderloin districts. It is extremely urban; however, from the tree-less streets and filthy sidewalks you are just a garden gate away from an amazing urban oasis. Sean Stout and James Pettigrew of Organic Mechanics have designed a lush habitat garden for frogs, fish, bees, butterflies, song birds, humming birds, mourning doves, nesting robins, and more. Even hawks regularly visit, bathing in the mosaic water feature after eating their pigeon in the trees. The garden invites people with its soothing sound of water, many paths, and secret nooks. Recycled materials are used in fresh, creative ways in mosaic paths, unusual planters, and sculpture. Rare and unusual plants are featured in this can't miss urban paradise. Organic Mechanics has won numerous awards including the American Horticulture Society Environment Award and the prestigious Best in Show at the San Francisco Flower and Garden Show. They have appeared on many television programs, newspapers, and magazines. Their design build firm is founded on organic and sustainable principles.

2014| 📸

➲ From Marin, take Route 101 South across

Golden Gate Bridge. Lombard Street becomes Van Ness Avenue/Route 101South take Van Ness Avenue to O'Farrell Street and turn left. Go to Leavenworth Street and turn left onto Leavenworth Street. Turn left onto Geary, #735 is halfway down block on left between Leavenworth Street and Hyde Streets.

From East Bay, take I-80W to Harrison Street at 5th Street. Follow Harrison Street to left onto 6th Street and turn right. Cross Market Street where 6th becomes Taylor Street. Follow Taylor north to Geary Street and turn left. Number 735 is between Leavenworth and Hyde Streets on left.

From South Bay, take I-280 North and exit onto 6th Street. Cross Market Street where 6th Street becomes Taylor Street and go north to Geary Street. Turn left onto Geary. Number 735 is halfway down block between Leavenworth and Hyde on left. There is metered parking or parking garages on two blocks sandwiching the 700 Geary block. This garden is three blocks away from The Hummingbird Garden at the Hotel Mark Twain.

HUMMINGBIRD GARDEN
Hotel Mark Twain, 345 Taylor Street, San Francisco

This garden, designed and built by Organic Mechanics, is nestled between two old high story brick buildings, behind the Mark Twain Hotel. The garden lies smack between the rough edgy urban Tenderloin and the upscale Union Square neighborhoods of San Francisco. This garden is designed for us by hotel guests as well as the bar and restaurant Fish and Farm. The garden, once a slab of concrete, is titled 'The Hummingbird Garden'. The garden contains many habitat plants that tolerate the shade, such as fuchsias and begonias. The hardscape is ninety percent reclaimed materials including memorial waste (beautiful granite, marble, and other stone), rusty weights, manhole covers, saw blades and a huge variety of wood planks to create the boardwalk. The heart of the garden is a large fountain and pond, while a smaller stone water element is for the birds and butterflies. The recycled boardwalk snakes itself through the long space making the garden feel larger. There are three small patios for intimate seating and one large mosaic patio at the end of the boardwalk for larger gatherings. Mark Twain's words still echo in the garden's hardscape, custom etched forever in stone. This garden is a one-of-a-kind hidden gem that is truly a sustainable, artistic habitat.

2014 | ♿ | 📷

⮑ 345 Taylor Street is located between O'Farrell Street and Ellis Street. Street parking may be difficult. There are many public lots in area. Note: This garden is three blocks away from the Geary Street Garden.

TENDERLOIN NATIONAL FOREST
511 Ellis Street, San Francisco

Urban blight is interrupted by bucolic splendor on one of the Tenderloin's grittiest blocks. Once littered with hypodermic needles and garbage, dead-end Cohen Alley has been transformed by a nonprofit artists' collective. A grove of trees is taking root, concrete walls are covered with bright murals, and asphalt has been replaced with mosaic pathways and koi ponds. If you feel so inspired— and really, who wouldn't?—garden tools are available to help maintain San Francisco's scrappiest natural wonder. This forest is a project of the nonprofit Luggage Store gallery in cooperation with the city of San Francisco, which allows the nonprofit to lease the alley for $1 a year. See the Luggage Store's website for upcoming events in the Tenderloin National Forest, including free clothes mending by artist Laureen Moyer on the 15th of each month (weather permitting) and occasional community pizza-making in the garden patio pizza oven.

NEW | ♿ | 📷

⮑ The garden is on Ellis Street between Leavenworth and Hyde Streets.

Getting there with public transportation Bart: Powell. Muni: Powell. Bus: 27, 31, 38

San Francisco East Bay

Saturday, July 30

🕐 **10 a.m. to 4 p.m.**
$7 per garden

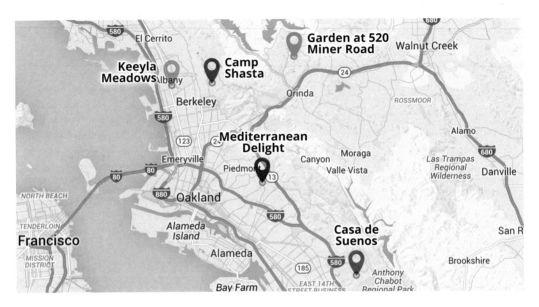

ALAMEDA COUNTY

ALBANY

 KEEYLA MEADOWS
1137 Stannage Avenue, Albany

Keeyla Meadows is a painter, sculptor, and garden designer who makes gardens that are full-scale works of art that you can walk into and be a part of. Her own garden is a living painting of vibrant colors. Keeyla is known as a pioneer in making artistic gardens more accessible to small-scale gardens where color means filling the garden "frame" with attention to detail. Much of the planting color comes in through flowers. The garden is an invitation to local pollinators: 'Hummers', bees, and butterflies. All materials are included in the garden work: painterly pavings, wavy walls, mosaic benches, bronze sculpture, and brilliantly colorful plantings. You will find images of Keeyla's garden in her new book, *Fearless Color Gardens*. Some of Keeyla's handmade pots and garden sculptures will be offered for sale.
2014 | ♿ | 📷

From I-80, take the Gilman Street Exit east about 1 mile to San Pablo Boulevard (large street with a traffic light). Go 2 blocks past San Pablo Boulevard. Turn left onto Stannage Avenue. Go 1 block. Garden is on east side of street.

BERKELEY

 CAMP SHASTA
2645 Shasta Road, Berkeley

We call it "Camp Shasta" because we feel like we are at summer camp living here, in a park-like setting dominated by a house that looks like the National Park Service built it.

The garden is a deep canyon with Codornices Creek running through it year round. It is a mostly woodland setting, partly shaded, with sunnier areas near the house where the potager area, complete with fruit trees and chickens, is located. Because of the size of the property, about three quarters of an acre, I do not strive for a manicured look, but rather a look of tamed and enhanced nature. There are numerous sculptures, the best of which is a two-ton stone face in the creek, carved by Marcia Donahue.

2013 | ♿ | 📷

⮎ From I-80, take the University Avenue exit and go all the way to its end at the campus. Turn left onto Oxford and then turn right in 2 short blocks onto Hearst. Go uphill to the light at Euclid and turn left. Stay on Euclid past Cedar Street 2 short blocks to Hawthorne Terrace and turn right. Go 1 block and turn left onto Leroy. Leroy will turn to the right and come out at the intersection of Rose, Tamalpais, and Shasta Road. Turn right and go uphill on Shasta. Park immediately. Walk up to 2645. Parking is limited to the left side of the street before you reach the garden, or below on Tamalpais, Leroy, etc. There is no parking above the house.

OAKLAND

CASA DE SUEÑOS
11110 Lochard Street, Oakland

In the beginning...a full acre covered with giant eucalyptus, juniper, and ivy has been transformed into a garden paradise. As a landscape designer, my son and our crew have worked continually building stone walls, patios, and pathways, a large koi pond, arbors, a shade house, and a nursery. My travels have inspired me to create lush and interesting plantings... graced with many friends art including Keeyla Meadows, Marcia Donahue, and Vickie Jo Sowell.

2013 | ♿ | 📷

⮎ Take I-580 to Golf Links Road exit. Turn left up hill past Oakland Zoo and go 1.5 miles.

Turn right onto Caloden, then right onto Malcolm, and left onto Lochard Street. Garden is 1.5 blocks on left. Park on street and please do not block neighbor's driveways.

PIEDMONT

MEDITERRANEAN DELIGHT
106 Estates Drive, Piedmont

A very personal creation, this garden displays the owners' sense of whimsical design with a beautiful variety of plant color and texture in a layout that invites exploration. Owners Christina and Stuart have added their own special touches with sculptures, beads, large murals and other surprises that await discovery. Lois and Ernest Rich designed, built and installed a new artistic steel gate with a *Nicotiana* motif and a fence mimicking tall grass in motion. The front and rear laws were removed many years ago. Now, with rustic stone work, gravel paths, large pots and an interesting water feature, the beautiful Mediterranean style house looks at home. Plantings range from a large collection of succulents, kangaroo paws, salvias and woodland plants. With its open spaces and private nooks the garden is truly a creative endeavor. The owners collaborated with Sherry Merciari, a local landscape designer to develop the garden.

2012 | 📷

⮎ From Highway 580 exit toward Park Boulevard, merge onto MacArthur Avenue. Turn left at the traffic light and then slight right at the next light onto Park Boulevard. Turn left onto Estates Drive and go to second house on right.

From Highway 13, exit at Park Boulevard and go west (down the hill) and right onto Estates Drive. Go to second house on right.

CONTRA COSTA COUNTY

ORINDA

THE GARDEN AT 520 MINER ROAD
520 Miner Road, Orinda

The owners built the house and laid out the lower and upper gardens on the one-acre site in 1979 and over time have created a sculpture wonderland with their collection from around the world. A playful abstract metal gate done by local artist, Stan Dann, sets the artistic tone for the guests when they arrive. The lower garden with its boxwood spheres and gently arching pergola was originally designed by Ron Lutsko. In setting a more formal mood, he created rooms of color which sets off the sculpture. These seasonal changes make for something always in bloom. By 2000, garden designer Suzanne Porter updated the plantings throughout and created a continuous garden up to and beyond the house. Subsequently, since 2005, Jane Sylvester has been involved in the next renovation. Through necessary editing, she has replanted various sections entirely as gardens change over time. The rear hillside is much cleaner now as the entire rear garden can once again be seen to the rear arbor. Shade-loving perennials hug the path toward the private terrace near the kitchen.

2013 | &

➲ From San Francisco/Oakland, take the Bay Bridge East. Follow signs to Highway 580 and 24. Take Highway 24 toward Walnut Creek. Go through the Caldecott Tunnel and exit at Orinda. At stop light, turn left. Go back under freeway and BART. At fourth traffic light is Miner Road. Turn right and go to #520. There are mailboxes on left, driveway is directly across the street. Pass the driveway and 2 more houses and turn right onto Valley View for street parking.

From Walnut Creek, take Highway 24 west toward Oakland. Take Orinda exit and follow "village" signs. Turn right onto Camino Pablo. Fourth light is Miner Road. Turn right onto #520. Proceed as directed above.

✤ PUBLIC GARDENS

CONTRA COSTA COUNTY

WALNUT CREEK

THE RUTH BANCROFT GARDEN
1552 Bancroft Road, Walnut Creek
(925) 944-9352,
www.ruthbancroftgarden.org

The three-and-one-half-acre Ruth Bancroft Garden is filled with hundreds of stunning succulents. The Ruth Bancroft Garden, Inc. is a 501(c)(3) nonprofit which owns the Garden and raises funds for its preservation. The Garden is an outstanding example of a water-conserving garden and houses important collections of aloes, agaves, yuccas, and echeverias.

🕐 Tuesday through Sunday, 10 a.m. to 4 p.m. Closed Thanksgiving day, the Friday after Thanksgiving, Christmas day, and New Year's day.

$ $10 general, $8 seniors and students. Free for members, children under 12, Garden Conservancy and AHS Reciprocal Admissions Program members.

➲ From San Francisco or Oakland Drive East on Highway 24, and continue onto I-680 North. Exit Treat Boulevard and turn right. Go about 1 mile, then turn right onto Bancroft Road. Make a U-turn at Stratton Road. The Ruth Bancroft Garden will be on your right.

From Sacramento Drive West on I-80 and exit onto I-680 South. Exit at Treat Boulevard and turn left from the offramp onto North Main Street. Make the next left onto Treat Boulevard. Go about 1 mile, then turn right onto Bancroft Road. Make a U-turn at Stratton Road. The Ruth Bancroft Garden will be on your right.

From San Jose, drive North on I-680. Exit onto Treat Boulevard and turn right. Go about 1 mile, then turn right onto Bancroft Road. Make a U-turn at Stratton Road. The Ruth Bancroft Garden will be on your right.

The Ruth Bancroft Garden, Walnut, Creek, California

When he first saw her garden of succulents in 1988, Frank Cabot knew that Ruth Bancroft had created a stunning work of art. Soon thereafter, the Ruth Bancroft Garden became the first preservation project of the Garden Conservancy, and it is now recognized as one of America's finest public gardens. It is both a typically Californian dry garden, with an emphasis on water-conserving succulents and cacti, and the uniquely personal creation of a designer using plants as sculptural and architectural elements.

...The plan developed by the Garden Conservancy for the preservation of the Ruth Bancroft Garden became the model for other preservation projects to come.

—Excerpted from *Outstanding American Gardens: A Celebration—25 Years of the Garden Conservancy*. Photo by Marion Brenner.

LOS ANGELES COUNTY

PASADENA

LA CASITA DEL ARROYO GARDEN
**727 South Orange Grove Boulevard,
Pasadena, (626) 449-9505,
lacasitadelarroyo.org**

⭐ Start your tour here for the May 1 Pasadena Area Open Day between 9:30 a.m. and 3:30 p.m. Tickets and maps will be available.

La Casita del Arroyo (The Little House on the Arroyo) was built as a community meeting house in 1933, a joint venture by the Pasadena Garden Club and the City of Pasadena. Natural materials from the Arroyo were combined with recycled materials from the velodrome built for the 1932 Olympics as a work project during the Great Depression. In 1988, the Pasadena Garden Club in conjunction with noted land-scape architects Isabel Greene and Yosh Befu designed and installed a water demonstration garden intended as an educational resource for the greater Pasadena community that promoted plants suitable for a Mediterra-nean climate as well as water-saving irrigation systems. In 2010, the Pasadena Garden Club re-designed the Butterfly Garden which leads from the Arroyo up to the main garden and the Casita. As a joint venture with the City, the building may be rented to non-profit groups, weddings and receptions by applying to the City of Pasadena. The gardens, maintained by the Pasadena Garden Club. Visitors may park on the street adjacent to La Casita or come up through the trails in the Arroyo.

🕐 Year round, daylight hours

$ Free

➥ From I-210 in Pasadena, exit south onto Orange Grove Boulevard. Turn right onto Arbor Street to Arroyo Boulevard. Turn right and #177 is on left.

From I-110, continue from end of freeway north on Arroyo Parkway. Turn left onto California Boulevard which dead ends at Arroyo Boulevard. Turn right and continue to #177.

From Highway 101 east, exit at Orange Grove Boulevard, just before the I-210 junction. Turn right onto California Boulevard which dead ends at Arroyo Boulevard. Turn right and continue to #177.

MARIN COUNTY

ROSS

MARIN ART & GARDEN CENTER
**30 Sir Francis Drake Boulevard, Ross
(415) 455-5260, www.magc.org**

Marin Art & Garden Center's eleven acres have a rich history of inspiring artists, gardeners, and conservationists. Founded in 1945 on a former estate property, MAGC is a lively center for learning, cultural programs, and celebrations. It is a hidden jewel in the heart of Marin County. Majestic specimen trees highlight a landscape rich in flowering shrubs and seasonal plantings. Classes, lectures, and workshops are held year-round. Resident groups include the Ross Valley Players, an acclaimed community theater group; Laurel House Antiques, a beloved shopping destina-tion; and the Moya Library—Ross Historical Society, a valuable resource for horticulture and local history.

🕐 Year round, daily, dawn to dusk.

$ Free, guided tours of grounds offered regularly

➥ From 101 North, take the Sir Francis Drake Boulevard exit. Keep right at the fork and continue west for 10 to 15 minutes, depending on traffic. The Marin Art & Garden Center is on right, directly across from the Lagunitas Bridge. Turn into the iron gates and park in the main lot.

From 101 South, take Exit 450B toward San Anselmo, which merges onto Sir Francis Drake Boulevard. Continue west for 10 to 15 minutes, depending on traffic. The Marin Art & Garden Center is on right, directly across from the Lagunitas Bridge. Turn into the iron gates and park in the lot.

Please note: If you enter the above address into Google Maps or another other on-line map service, please be sure to specify that the address is in Ross. Otherwise, you could end up in another town, as there is more than one 30 Sir Francis Drake.

LOS ANGELES COUNTY

FLINTRIDGE

DESCANSO GARDENS
1418 Descanso Drive, Flintridge
(818) 949-4200, www.descansogardens.org
Nestled in the San Rafael Hills just minutes from Los Angeles, Pasadena and the San Fernando Valley, Descanso Gardens is a botanic garden of year-round loveliness with landscapes both rugged and refined. A member-supported garden, Descanso welcomes each year more than 300,000 visitors from around the world who come to explore its Oak Woodland, Camellia Forest, International Rosarium and many other themed gardens. Overarching these gardens are hundreds of beautiful coast live oaks, a naturally occurring woodland in an urban setting. Descanso Gardens is where arts, culture and nature intersect, with family-friendly seasonal festivals and nature-themed programs for all ages. The Sturt Haaga Gallery presents three exhibitions each year featuring works by noted artists. Summer brings extended evening hours with jazz and world music concerts, enjoyed on the Main Lawn while the audience picnics. Descanso Gardens is accredited by the American Association of Museums and is an International Camellia Garden of Excellence.
🕐 Open daily except for Christmas. 9 a.m. to 5 p.m. Last entry is at 4:30 p.m.
$ General $9 / Seniors 65 and over / Students $6. Children (5 to 12 years) $4 / Descanso members and children under 5 free.
➲ Take the 2 North and exit at Verdugo Boulevard. Turn right onto Verdugo Boulevard. Verdugo Hills Hospital is on right. Turn right onto Descanso Drive. Entrance is on right.
From Pasadena and the San Gabriel Valley, take the 210 West and exit at Angeles Crest

Highway. Turn left onto Angeles Crest Highway. Turn right onto Foothill Boulevard. Turn left onto Verdugo Boulevard. Turn left onto Descanso Drive. Entrance is on right.
From the San Fernando Valley, take the 210 East and exit at Angeles Crest Highway. Turn right onto Angeles Crest Highway. Turn right onto Foothill Boulevard. Proceed as directed above.

SAN FRANCISCO COUNTY

SAN FRANCISCO

GARDENS OF ALCATRAZ
Alcatraz Island, San Francisco,
(415) 561-4900, www.alcatrazgardens.org
The gardens were created by inmates, officers, and the families who lived and gardened on Alcatraz Island over its long history as a military fortification and prison, and in its later role as a federal prison. With the help of numerous volunteers, overgrowth has been removed and many of the gardens have been restored to the former beauty of the military and prison eras. More than one million visitors that visit the island every year can now see how the beautiful, well-tended gardens provided the power to transform both a harsh environment and to nourish the human spirit.
🕐 Year round, daily. Closed Thanksgiving, Christmas, and New Year's Day.
🚩 Free docent-led garden tours, Fridays & Sundays, 9:30 a.m. from the Alcatraz dock. Wednesdays a Open Garden viewing called 'Ask the Gardener', 11 a.m. to 2 p.m.
$ There is no fee to visit Alcatraz Island. However there is a charge for the ferry service to and from the island, supplied by a private company under contract with the National Park Service. For schedules, prices, and to purchase tickets in advance (tickets are made available about 90 days in advance) visit www.alcatrazcruises.com or call (415) 981-7625. Alcatraz frequently sells out, as much as a week in advance in summer and near holidays.

Trade Secrets

A two-day event to benefit Women's Support Services

SATURDAY, MAY 14
Rare Plant and Garden Antiques Sale
LionRock Farm, Rte. 41, Sharon, CT
Early buying 8–10am $125
(with breakfast)
Regular admission 10am–3pm $40

SUNDAY, MAY 15
Tour Four Splendid Gardens in
Sharon, Lakeville & Falls Village, CT
10am–4pm $70 *(advance tickets $60)*
Tickets may be purchased at the
gardens

MAY 14 & 15, 2016

TICKETS & FURTHER INFORMATION:

TradeSecretsCT.com
(860) 364-1080

Media Sponsors

*Rain or shine
We regret that we cannot
welcome pets on either day.*

CONNECTICUT

Fairfield County

Sunday, May 1

🕐 **10 a.m. to 4 p.m.**
$7 per garden

🏷️ Pop-up Nursery
Pixie Perennials

FAIRFIELD COUNTY

GREENWICH

📍 **SLEEPY CAT FARM**
146 Clapboard Ridge Road, Greenwich

The thirteen-acre gardens of Sleepy Cat Farm have evolved over the past eighteen years through a close collaboration of the present owner and Virginia-based landscape architect Charles J. Stick. The most recently developed portion of the landscape which borders Lake Avenue includes an extensive greenhouse and potager. The newly constructed "Barn", distinguished by its half-timbered French Normandy vocabulary is surrounded by thyme-covered terraces which provide an elegant stage set for a fine collection of garden ornament, sculpture, and boxwood topiary. The visitor's experience of the garden unfolds as pathways lead from garden room to garden room in a carefully orchestrated series of discoveries. The central portion of the garden is distinguished by two parallel garden spaces, the first is dominated by a long reflecting pool, terminated on the north end by a wisteria-covered arbor and on the south end by a pebble mosaic terrace and fountain basin. One of the great surprises of the tour is the adjacent garden space. Bordered by a...
[Read the full description online]

2014 | 📷

⮑ From I-95 north, take Exit 3 in Connecticut. At bottom of exit ramp, turn left onto Arch

Street (if traveling on I-95 south, turn right). Go under railroad overpass. The next traffic light is Railroad Avenue. Go through light and take next left onto Southview. At top of hill turn right onto Field Point Road. Go through light at West Putnam Avenue, crossing Route 1 between Exxon station and library onto Deerfield. Go through the rotary, taking second exit onto Lake Avenue. Go through another small rotary and pass over a narrow bridge, warned by a sign. Turn left onto Clapboard Ridge Road. It is second driveway; turn before white mailbox marked "146."

WILTON

📍 **PIXIE PERENNIALS**
200 Nod Hill Road, Weston

🏷️ Pixie Perennials

Terraced perennial gardens with a wide variety of unusual plants surround a 1740 homestead set on four acres overlooking a reservoir, home to mature and specimen trees. A small rock garden tucked into the exposed ledge leads to a fish pond. A frog pond is nestled in between rows of flowers. The property features peach trees, an old leaning apple tree, fig trees, kiwi, blueberry bushes, strawberries, raspberries, and a vegetable garden. The kitchen courtyard garden room hosts shade plants: hellebores, brunnera, heuchera, ligularia, shaped boxwoods and other varieties of perennials that live nestled under a giant maple tree. Peonies border one length of the paddock fence leading you to the lilac bushes. A back garden built around the exposed stones showcases tall plants that can be seen from the house. In late summer a stand of perovskia creates a blue backdrop for fall flowering perennials. The garden is a work in progress, ever-changing from year to year. The party barn boasts quarter sawn oak floors, and hosted town dances during Prohibition. Home-grown perennials and shrubs will be for sale on the back patio and adjacent areas. There will be a pop-up boutique in the "party" barn featuring wonderful items for sale by local artisans.

NEW | ♿ | 📷

➥ It is 0.9 mile up on the right from the intersection of Route 33/Ridgefield Road and Nod Hill.

New London County

Saturday, May 21

⏱ **10 a.m. to 4 p.m.**
$7 admission

NEW LONDON COUNTY

STONINGTON

● **KENTFORD FARM**
297 New London Turnpike, Stonington

Kentford Farm is a perennial farm in the making. For eighteen years, Paul Coutu and William Turner have been planting and creating grass pathways and planting beds. The farm dates back to 1727 and the previous owner started planting in 1945. Fifty-foot weeping cherries, a Norway spruce, copper beech, and blue atlas cedar, to name a few, dot this five-acre

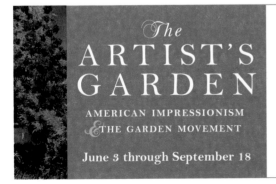

ANNOUNCING HOLLISTER HOUSE
GARDEN STUDY WEEKEND VI

Presented by Hollister House Garden and the Garden Conservancy

September 10 – 11, 2016

Symposium, Great Vendors, & Open Days Garden Tours

Saturday, September 10

Symposium at the Heritage Hotel in Southbury, CT, featuring talks by:

Arne Maynard – celebrated garden designer and author known for his large country gardens; two-time Chelsea Flower Show gold medal winner

David Culp – noted plantsman, garden author and authority, and breeder of hybrid hellebores

Page Dickey – beloved author, passionate gardener, and plant connoisseur

Andy Brand and **Chris Koppel** – plant experts at Broken Arrow Nursery

At the conclusion of the symposium, enjoy cocktails and early buying at the sale of Rare and Unusual Plants at Hollister House Garden.

Sunday, September 11

Garden Conservancy Open Day tour will feature private gardens in Litchfield County.

Sale of Rare and Unusual Plants will be open to the public at Hollister House Garden.

For a full schedule of participating gardens, see the Open Days schedule at gardenconservancy.org.

For more information and to register for the Saturday program, visit www.hollisterhousegarden.org or call (860) 868-2200.

garden. There is a walk-in root cellar built into the hillside and stone walls surround the whole property. For more information, visit www.kentfordfarm.com.

2015 | ♿ | 📷

➲ From New London, take I-95 north to Exit 90/Mystic. Turn left onto Route 27 and go to stop sign in Old Mystic Center. Bear right and go through stop sign, passing Old Mystic Fire Station on left. Bear right at next fork onto North Stonington Road. Pass Clyde's Cider Mill on left. Go to blinking light at intersection of Routes 184 & 201. Turn right onto Route 184 and go east. Kentford Farm is second driveway on left.

From Providence, take I-95 south to Exit 90/Mystic. Turn right onto Route 27. Proceed as directed above. From Norwich, take Route 2 east past Foxwoods Resort Casino. Turn right onto Route 201 South toward Old Mystic. Turn left onto Route 184 East. Kentford Farm is second driveway on left.

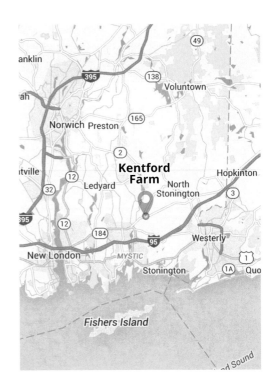

New Haven County

Saturday, June 4

🕐 **10 a.m. to 4 p.m.**
$7 per garden

NEW HAVEN COUNTY

STONY CREEK

📍 **UPTOP—GARDEN OF FRED BLAND**
30-34 Wallace Road, Stony Creek
🕐 10 a.m. to 4 p.m.

This is an intensively cultivated one-acre village weekend garden created by an architect/plant collector. The garden has more than 1,400 species of plants (mostly perennials, shrubs, and small trees) arranged in many gardens: a long double border, three wood-

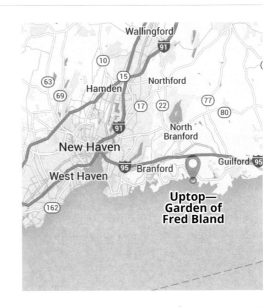

land gardens, a pool garden hidden by a rollicking serpent tapestry hedge, many other hedges and rock walls (all quarried on site), a main cottage and guest cottage with several other outbuildings all purpose-designed to be subservient to the dominant garden. The owner is the Chairman of the Board of the Brooklyn Botanic Garden. The garden was published in Jane Garmey's *The Private Gardens of Connecticut.*

2015 |

➲ Take I-95/Connecticut Turnpike to Exit 56, turning south from the exit onto Leetes Island Road. Go about 1.5 miles to a four-way stop sign. Continue straight through into Stony Creek Village, winding through the village on Thimble Islands Road, past the beautiful harbor and Town Dock on the right. Continue past an open field on the right and left to the next street and turn left on Wallace Road. Wind around to the right until you find 30-34 Wallace on the left.

Fairfield County

Sunday, June 5

🕙 **10 a.m. to 4 p.m.**
$7 per garden

There are also gardens open on this day in nearby Westchester County, NY. See page 197.

 Pop-up Nursery
Pixie Perennials

FAIRFIELD COUNTY

RIDGEFIELD

📍 **THE BARLOW MOUNTAIN GARDEN OF HELEN DIMOS & BENJAMIN OKO**
11 Barlow Mountain Road, Ridgefield

This 1735 saltbox, house of landscape designer Helen Dimos and Dr. Benjamin Oko, is listed on the National Register of Historic Buildings. It is surrounded by perennial gardens that feature peonies, clematis, iris, and roses. Shrub borders contain boxwood, hydrangeas, viburnums, calycanthus and rhododendron. Trees near the house include stewartias, and several native species including dogwoods, a fringe tree, witch hazel, ironwoods, and elms. Further out on the rolling lawn are the many trees planted over the last twenty years by the owner. She believes that, aside from architectural interventions, trees are the strongest elements in shaping spaces and creating

distinct areas in the garden. Among these trees are white and mossycup oaks, a fernleaf beech, a silver linden, and numerous conifers. Near the enclosed vegetable/cutting garden, there are magnolias. Furthest from the house, forming a backdrop at the bottom of the lawn

Garden of Ken & Margaret Uhle, featured in *Outstanding American Gardens: A Celebration—25 Years of the Garden Conservancy*. Photo by Marion Brenner.

are a tupelo, a dawn redwood, and two Alaska cedars. There are also an ornamental grass border, a natural grass border and a wetland edge border of mostly native shrubs. For approximately ten years, the property has been protected by an eight-foot wire deer fence.

2014 | 📷

⮑ From the south and west including North Salem, take Route 684 to Exit 7/Purdys/Sommers. Turn right off the ramp and, at the traffic light, turn left. Then almost immediately take the second right onto Route 116 (see sign). Follow 116 through North Salem where Route 116 is joined briefly by Route 121. Where 116 and 121 divide, turn right (at Vox Restaurant) to stay on 116. From this point, Barlow Mountain Road is 3.1 miles away on left. Turn left (you will see a grass triangle in the middle of the intersection and a boat ramp sign). Number 11 is the fourth driveway on right, across from a red mail box.

From southbound Route 22, take the exit for Routes 6 and 202. At the end of ramp, turn left. In a few miles, turn right onto Route 121. Turn left onto Route 116 by Vox Restaurant. Proceed as directed above.

From westbound I-84, take the exit for Route 7 South. Turn right onto Route 35 toward Ridgefield. Turn right at Copps Hill Road (just before the Copps Hill Shopping Center; Shell station and brick bank building on left). Turn right again at the end of Copps Hill Road onto North Street. Go about 2 miles north. North Street runs into Barlow Mountain Road. Number 11 is on left with mailbox on the right.

There is limited parking. If the parking area at the house is full, or you are concerned about being parked in, please continue past our house and take the first left onto Barlow Mountain Road, and then turn immediately right into the parking area for Pierrepont State Park. It is a very short walk from there to garden, but take great care to walk on right where you are not in the lane of cars approaching over the crest fence of the hill.

📍 GARDEN OF KEN & MARGARET UHLE
54 Silver Spring Road, Ridgefield

This one-acre garden has been designed in a woodland setting among large glacially deposited rocks. A prominent feature of the garden is its man-made winding brook connecting two small lily ponds bordered with yellow and blue flag iris, rushes, and other marginal plants. Woodchip paths meander through the garden characterized by mature oak trees and more than 600 varieties of perennials, shrubs, and understory trees. In another location, a lawn area is surrounded by small groupings of bald cypress, dawn redwood, and a variety of flowering trees. Informal stone steps lead down to a 70' long plank boardwalk through a cypress/tupelo swamp. This garden has been designed, installed, and maintained by the owner, a landscape architect, and is a good example of what can be accomplished on a relatively small property.

2015 | 📷

⮑ From Westchester County, take Route 35 east toward Ridgefield. Turn right onto Peter Parley Drive. (Peter Parley Drive is a very short diagonal street adjacent to a small red school house). It is located approximately 10 miles east of the intersection of 35 with I-684 and the Saw Mill Parkway). When you are on Peter Parley Drive, bear to the left and stop at the stop sign. At the stop sign, do not turn right or left – continue straight across the road (which is not marked) up a small incline and immediately turn right onto Silver Spring Road. Note that after 1.5 miles Silver Spring Road joins with St. John's Road at a "T" intersection. At this point turn right and continue on Silver Spring Road. Number 54 is on the left and fronts on a shared driveway. Please park on Silver Spring Road and walk down the shared driveway. Number 54 is the first house on the right, a one-story light green ranch.

From Northern Fairfield County, take Route 35 west toward New York. Turn left onto West Lane. Make an immediate left onto Silver Spring Road. Note that after 1.5 miles Silver

Spring Road joins with St. John's Road at a "T" intersection. Proceed as directed above.

From Southern Fairfield County take Route 33 east toward Ridgefield. Turn left onto Scarlet Oak Drive. At the end of Scarlet Oak make a right onto Silver Spring Road. Number 54 is on the right and fronts on a shared driveway. Please park on Silver Spring Road and walk down the shared driveway. Number 54 is the first house on the right, a one-story light green ranch.

WILTON

PIXIE PERENNIALS
200 Nod Hill Road, Wilton

Pixie Perennials

Terraced perennial gardens with a wide variety of unusual plants surround a 1740 homestead set on four acres overlooking a reservoir, home to mature and specimen trees. A small rock garden tucked into the exposed ledge leads to a fish pond. A frog pond is nestled in between rows of flowers. The property features peach trees, an old leaning apple tree, fig trees, kiwi, blueberry bushes, strawberries, raspberries, and a vegetable garden. The kitchen courtyard garden room hosts shade plants: hellebores, brunnera, heuchera, ligularia, shaped boxwoods and other varieties of perennials that live nestled under a giant maple tree. Peonies border one length of the paddock fence leading you to the lilac bushes. A back garden built around the exposed stones showcases tall plants that can be seen from the house. In late summer a stand of perovskia creates a blue backdrop for fall flowering perennials. The garden is a work in progress, ever-changing from year to year. The party barn boasts quarter sawn oak

floors, and hosted town dances during Prohibition. Home-grown perennials and shrubs
will be for sale on the back patio and adjacent
areas. There will be a pop-up boutique in the
"party" barn featuring wonderful items for sale
by local artisans.

2015 | 📷

➲ It is 0.9 mile up on the right from the
intersection of Route 33/Ridgefield Road and
Nod Hill.

Hartford & Litchfield County

Saturday, June 11

🕐 **Hours vary by garden**
   (Starting at 10 a.m.)
$7 per garden

HARTFORD COUNTY

BURLINGTON

📍 **THE SALSEDO FAMILY GARDEN**
   15 Half King Drive, Burlington
🕐 10 a.m. to 4 p.m.

Our gardens have been created on a unique
location, a hilltop 1,000 feet above sea level
with a magnificent view of 4,000 acres of wa-
tershed and state forest. Begun in 1977, this
site has undergone various physical transfor-
mations, resulting in stone-walled terraces
that render this acre-plus location usable. The
last big change in 1995 added an expanded

backyard terrace with a pool, post-and-beam
gardener's tool shed, dwarf conifer collection,
vegetable garden, and a collection of hardy
chrysanthemums. The front yard features low-
maintenance lawns punctuated by beds of
native and exotic trees, shrubs, and perennials. The emphasis of this landscape is sustainability with a focus on low maintenance and
minimal water requirements.

2015 | ♿ | 📷

➲ Take I-84 to Exit 39 and go west on Route 4
towards Farmington. Go through Farmington
about 3 miles to Unionville Center to traffic
light; pass Friendlys on left. Bear right onto

J.P. FRANZEN ASSOCIATES ARCHITECTS, P.C.

AWARD-WINNING ARCHITECTURE
LANDSCAPE ARCHITECTURE
PRESERVATION AND PLANNING

PROJECTS FROM MAINE TO HAWAII WITH
OFFICES IN SOUTHPORT AND FAIRFIELD, CONNECTICUT

Photo by Stacy Bass

203.259.0529
www.franzenarchitects.com
• MEMBERS OF THE AMERICAN INSTITUTE OF ARCHITECTS •

Route 4 (Old Masonic Hall on right, church on left). Go 1 mile along Farmington River. At light, turn left onto Route 4 and go up hill towards Burlington. Go about 1 mile and turn left onto Belden Road (fish hatchery sign is on left). Go to stop sign. Turn right onto George Washington Turnpike, and then take next left onto Cornwall. Go up hill and turn right onto Nassahegan, then make second left onto Half King Drive. Go to bottom of cul-de-sac to middle gravel drive with granite mailbox post labeled #15. Please park in cul-de-sac.

PLANTSVILLE

THE KAMINSKI GARDEN
513 Marion Avenue, Plantsville

🕐 10 a.m. to 4 p.m.

"Wow" is usually the first word spoken as visitors pass through the gates and enter the garden. Mature trees anchor the sweeping curves of the oversized garden beds to the earth. Interesting foliage and a succession of bloom keep this garden looking great year round. Shade predominates throughout the space, as does an ever-growing collection of shade-tolerant perennials, shrubs, and Japanese maples. A soothing sense of softness is provided by the use of tumbled bluestone for the patio, the raised garden beds surrounding the deck, and the curved pathways to the free-form pool. Years of organic gardening have resulted in an environment that supports vigorous plant growth and provides a safe haven for the wildlife that live here. We have been working on improving the "curb appeal" of the front yard. We added a granite obelisk and garden courtyard, ripped up the tar that ran up to the house and replaced it with pea stone and granite pavers, added a boulder garden, and installed another shade garden at the front of the house.

2015| ♿ | 📷

⮕ From I-84, take Exit 30/Marion Avenue. From Hartford and I-84 West, turn right at light onto Marion Avenue. From Waterbury and I-84 East, turn left at stop sign at end of exit. At light, turn left onto Marion Avenue. Go about 1 mile, passing Frost Street. Next driveway on right is our house, #513. House is slate blue with detached two-car garage. Please park in driveway.

WEST HARTFORD

THE MAYES GARDEN
90 Richmond Lane, West Hartford

🕐 10 a.m. to 4 p.m.

Shady and serene, this peaceful woodland garden is layered with texture and color for all seasons. Spring wildflowers and bulbs merge into a multitude of hostas and ferns. Peonies and flowering shrubs give way to hydrangeas, roses, and ultimately flowering witch hazel, autumn clematis, and purple gentian. Bird baths and feeders ensure a wide variety of birds while the waterfall's music draws the visitor to the stone patio and fishpond where a dogwood stands on a mossy tree well sheltering a cluster of painted ferns and miniature hostas.

2014 | 📷

⮕ From I-84 East, take Exit 43, left ramp for Park Road toward West Hartford Center. Turn right onto Park Road and then immediately turn left onto Trout Brook Drive. Turn left onto Asylum Avenue. Turn right onto North Main Street/Route 218) Continue through Bishop's Corner intersection. Approximately 1 mile from intersection, turn left onto Sheep Hill Drive. Go to stop sign, bear right #90 is third house on the left.

From I-84 West, take Exit 61, (12 miles) ramp on right for I-291 West towards Windson. At Exit 1 (6 miles), take ramp right for Route 218/Bloomfield. Bear right toward Route 218 .3 miles. Bear left onto Route 218/Cottage Grove Road. Keep straight on Cottage Grove Road through intersection of Route 185. Third right after the section, turn right onto Sheep Hill Drive. Follow to stop sign, #90 is third house on the right.

From I-91 North, take Exit 35B ramp for Route 218 towards Bloomfield. Turn right onto Route 218. Continue straight through intersection of Route 185. Turn right onto Sheep Hill Drive. Follow to stop sign #90 is large brown house-third on right.

From I-90 South, take Exit 32 A/32B, take ramp for I-91 toward Springfield. Keep straight onto Trumbell Street. Turn right onto Route 44. turn right onto Route 218 North. Main Street (continue through Bishop's Corner intersection/about 1 mile turn left onto Sheep Hill Drive. Follow to stop sign; #90 is third house on right.

LITCHFIELD COUNTY

BARKHAMSTED

 WASHINGTON HILL
300 East Hartland Road, Barkhamsted
🕐 11 a.m. to 4 p.m.

This seven-year-old garden shows what two gardeners can do with the challenging one-and-one-half-acre cleared portion of a severely sloped seven-acre wooded lot. Parterres connected by banks and a stairway now provide key features: mitigation of upland run-off, planting spaces along the banks, a thirty-by-fifty-foot, four-square perennial garden punctuated at the inner corners with flowering crabapple trees, a twenty-by-forty-foot potager/cutting garden, lawns, and a 150-foot border created to showcase irises, peonies, Oriental lilies, and annuals. The banks feature nearly 200 deciduous and evergreen shrubs and trees, flowering bulbs, ornamental grasses, alpine outcroppings, perennials, roses, and fruit trees. Large potted tree roses add interest to the ends of the four-square walkways. The entire garden is designed for three full seasons of bloom, from spring bulbs and early peren-nials, to late-flowering aster, salvia, sanguisorba, *Lobelia* cardinalis, sedum, and chrysanthemum. The signature feature of the garden in June is the native mountain laurel that saturates the entire perimeter of the property and the adjacent woodland. The garden is a lovely testament to the ability of plantings to mature

quickly, accomplish design objectives, and create a wonderful year-round outdoor environment.
2015 | ♿ | 📷

➲ From north and east, take I-91 to Exit 40/Bradley Airport. Follow connector road to Route 20 West. Go through East Granby and Granby to Route 219 on left. Take Route 219 to Route 179. Turn right onto Route 179. Go about 800 feet to 300 East Hartland Road on right.

From south and west, take Route 8 to end of divided highway in Winsted. Turn left onto Route 44. Go to Route 318 and turn left. Go through Pleasant Valley, over reservoir dam to Route 219. Turn left and go up hill to Route 179. Go to 300 East Hartland Road. Please park on opposite side of road on shoulder, as far off pavement as possible and use caution when crossing.

Litchfield County

Saturday, June 18

🕐 **10 a.m. to 4 p.m.**
$7 per garden

There are also gardens open on this day in nearby Dutchess County, NY. See page 207.

🏷 Pop-up Nursery
Broken Arrow Nursery / Woman's Work

LITCHFIELD COUNTY

FALLS VILLAGE

📍 **BUNNY WILLIAMS**
1 Point of Rock Road, Falls Village

Interior designer and garden book author Bunny Williams' intensively planted fifteen-acre estate has a sunken garden with twin perennial borders surrounding a fishpond, a parterre garden, a year-round conservatory filled with tender plants, a large vegetable garden with flowers and herbs, a woodland garden with meandering paths, and a pond with a waterfall. There are also a working greenhouse and an aviary with unusual chickens and fantail doves, an apple orchard with mature trees, a rustic Greek Revival-style pool house folly, and a swimming pool with eighteenth-century French coping.

2015 | 📷

➲ From Route 7 North, go to Falls Village. Turn left at blinking traffic light onto Main Street/Route 126. Bear right (still on Route 126). Go to stop sign at Point of Rocks Road. Driveway is directly ahead. Please park in field adjacent to house.

KENT

📍 **MICA QUARRY ESTATE**
44 Kent Hollow Road, Kent

🏷 Broken Arrow Nursery / Woman's Work

Inspired by a strong interest in collecting specimen trees and shrubs, and by studies at the New York Botanical Gardens, the owners have developed this garden over the past thirty years into an expression of their personal development as landscape designer and horticulturist. The massive stone columns at the entrance to the property set the stage for the extensive stonework that gives struc-

The garden of Bunny Williams, featured in *Outstanding American Gardens: A Celebration—25 Years of the Garden Conservancy*. Photo by Marion Brenner.

ture to the landscape. The owner has taken a complete hands-on approach to development of the garden, as all stone work, planting, pruning and sourcing of plants have been done by him. After retiring from his corporate career in New York City, he has also selectively done design, consultation and plant sourcing on request for other projects. The garden contains one of the largest private collections of rare, distinctive and hard to find trees in the Northeast. Crossing a terrace with stunning views of Lake Waramaug and beyond, visitors will come upon a large Koi pond, waterfalls and an entirely unexpected cast bronze fountain. The core purpose of the garden is... [Read the full description online]

2015 | ♿ | 📷

⟳ From Kent, take Route 341 East toward Warren and go about 6 miles. Turn right onto Kent Hollow Road. Go 0.25 mile, house is on right after passing lake on left. Watch for stone walls and two stone columns with lights. Park on road near the pond.

From traffic light in Warren, take Route 341 West toward Kent. Go about 3 miles and turn left onto Kent Hollow Road. Go 0.25 mile, house is on right after passing lake on left. Watch for stone walls and two stone columns with lights. Park on road near the pond.

WASHINGTON

📍 HIGHMEADOWS—LINDA ALLARD
156 Wykeham Road, Washington

High on a hillside, with a beautiful panoramic view of the Litchfield Hills, this garden has Old-World charm. Surrounded by stone walls covered with espaliered fruit trees, climbing roses, and hydrangeas the garden is partly formal and partly potager. A lush rose arbor filled with pale pink and white roses inter-woven with clematis separates the two. Boxwood hedges define the white formal garden enhanced by a variety of green textures. Geometric beds overflowing with fruits, vegetables, herbs, and flowers are a true depiction of potager. This part of the

garden changes yearly; plantings are worked by color and color combination. In this, its first year for bloom, is a newly completed woodland garden. The woodland garden, initially conceived as a woodland trail winding throughout the property, has evolved using a naturalistic approach with native species. The original trees and shrubs have been enriched with additional plantings of azalea, dogwood trees, hellebores, ferns, and spring flowering bulbs. It is inspired by William Robinson's The Wild Garden originally published in 1870 and a more recent expanded edition by Rick Darke. His beautiful photographs and commentary illustrate how well this concept translates to contemporary, sustainable gardening.

2015 | 📷

⟳ From Washington Green at Gunn Memorial Library, turn onto Wykeham Road. Follow for about 1.5 miles until Old Litchfield Road forks left. Stay right on Wykeham for about 0.25 mile. Go up a small hill to a red barn on right. The entrance to garden is opposite barn. Number 156 is on stone wall, proceed through gate to garden.

📍 BRUSH HILL GARDENS—
CHARLES RASKOB ROBINSON &
BARBARA PAUL ROBINSON
Nettleton Hollow Road, Washington

Take a virtual tour of Brush Hill Gardens on www.brushhillgardens.com for a preview of many different areas, including the Moon Garden planted in yellows and purples, the Rose Walk, the Peony and Wheelbarrow Borders, the Serpentine Garden with its garden folly, and up through the Arch into the Woodland Walk with its series of cascading pools and rills. Each area is adorned with structures designed and built by Charles. The garden has been featured in many articles and books, including Rosemary Verey's book, The Secret Garden, and HGTV's "A Gardener's Diary". Barbara's biography, Rosemary Verey: The Life and Lessons of a Legendary Gardener, will be available.

2015 | ♿ |

➥ From I-84, take Exit 15/Southbury. Take Route 6 to Route 47 and turn left. Go 4 miles, passing Woodbury Ski Area on left, and turn right onto Nettleton Hollow Road. Go 4 miles, past intersection of Wykeham and Carmel Hill Roads, and watch for sign to enter parking field on left side of Nettleton Hollow Road. From north at intersection of Route 109 and Nettleton Hollow Road, go south on Nettleton Hollow Road for 0.3 mile, just past Clark Road, look for signs to park in field on right. Brush Hill Gardens is 2 miles north of Hollister House Gardens on Nettleton Hollow Road.

❀ PUBLIC GARDEN

⚲ HOLLISTER HOUSE GARDEN
300 Nettleton Hollow Road, Washington

Situated around an eighteenth-century farmhouse in the Litchfield Hills of northwest Connecticut, this romantic country garden features exuberant plantings set in rambling formal structure and is noted for its subtle and sometimes surprising color combinations. Reminiscent of such classic English gardens as Great Dixter and Sissinghurst, the garden is divided into a series of rooms which open to vistas over the garden and out onto the natural landscape beyond. The garden has been a preservation project of the Garden Conservancy since 2005.

2015 | ♿ |

⏱ Special Open Days June 18, July 9, July 30, and September 11, 10 a.m. to 4 p.m. Otherwise May to September, Friday 2 p.m. to 5 p.m. Saturday 10 a.m. to 4 p.m.

$ $5 requested donation.

➥ From I-84, take Exit 15/Southbury. Take Route 6 North through Southbury and Woodbury. Turn left onto Route 47 North. Go 4 miles, past Woodbury Ski Area on left, and turn right onto Nettleton Hollow Road. Go 1.7 miles. Garden is on right. Please park along the road or follow parking signs through the gate.

Litchfield County

Saturday, July 9

⏱ **Hours vary by garden (Starting at 10 a.m.)**
$7 per garden

There is a garden open on this day in nearby Dutchess County, NY. See page 222.

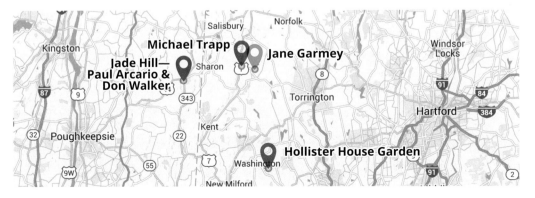

Hollister House Garden, Washington, Connecticut

Set in the picturesque hills of northwestern Connecticut, George Schoellkopf's Hollister House Garden represents an American interpretation of the classic English cottage garden. It reflects its rural New England setting in the unpretentiousness and hardiness of its plantings, while drawing inspiration from Vita Sackville-West's garden at Sissinghurst, where a series of walled or hedged "rooms" enclose horticulturally sophisticated combinations of shrubs, perennials, bulbs, and flowering trees.

—Excerpted from *Outstanding American Gardens: A Celebration—25 Years of the Garden Conservancy*. Photo by Marion Brenner.

WEST CORNWALL

JANE GARMEY
106 Cogswell Road, West Cornwall

🕐 1 p.m. to 5 p.m.

An idiosyncratic garden that began to take shape about twelve years ago and surrounds an 1827 house, shielded from the road by a row of 250-year-old sugar maples. There are two long beds, planted for drama and height with perennials, grasses, and annuals; a small kitchen garden; a boxwood parterre; a formal arrangement of weeping cherry trees; a long water rill; and a bird house village set in a glade of giant petasitis.

2015 | ♿ | 📷

⮑ From Route 7, take Route 128 through West Cornwall. Continue up hill and turn left onto Cream Hill Road. At first crossroads, turn right onto Cogswell Road. House is last one on the left, immediately before the Church.

MICHAEL TRAPP
7 River Road, West Cornwall

🕐 10 a.m. to 4 p.m. .

This Old World-style garden is intimate with cobbled paths, terraced gardens, raised perennial beds, and reflecting pools. Overlooking the Housatonic River, the property has a distinct French/Italian flavor.

2015 | 📷

⮑ From Route 7, take Route 128 East through covered bridge into West Cornwall. Go on Route 128, taking second left onto River Road. House is yellow with gray trim, first on left. Please park in front or in town.

✱ PUBLIC GARDEN

WASHINGTON

HOLLISTER HOUSE GARDEN
300 Nettleton Hollow Road, Washington

🕐 10 a.m. to 4 p.m.

Situated around an eighteenth-century farmhouse in the Litchfield Hills of northwest Connecticut, this romantic country garden features exuberant plantings set in rambling formal structure and is noted for its subtle and sometimes surprising color combinations. Reminiscent of such classic English gardens as Great Dixter and Sissinghurst, the garden is divided into a series of rooms which open to vistas over the garden and out onto the natural landscape beyond. The garden has been a preservation project of the Garden Conservancy since 2005.

2015 | ♿ | 📷

🕐 Special Open Days June 18, July 9, July 30, and September 11, 10 a.m. to 4 p.m. Otherwise May to September, Friday 2 p.m. to 5 p.m. Saturday 10 a.m. to 4 p.m.

$ $5 requested donation. No Open Days admission tickets accepted on September 11 during Garden Study Weekend. Admission on this date is $10 and includes a plant sale.

⮑ From I-84, take Exit 15/Southbury. Take Route 6 North through Southbury and Woodbury. Turn left onto Route 47 North. Go 4 miles, past Woodbury Ski Area on left, and turn right onto Nettleton Hollow Road. Go 1.7 miles. Garden is on right. Please park along the road or follow parking signs through the gate.

New London County

Saturday, July 16

🕐 **10 a.m. to 4 p.m.**
$7 per garden

NEW LONDON COUNTY

STONINGTON

📍 **KENTFORD FARM**
   297 New London Turnpike, Stonington

Kentford Farm is a perennial farm in the making. For eighteen years, Paul Coutu and William Turner have been planting and creating grass pathways and planting beds. The farm dates back to 1727 and the previous owner started planting in 1945. Fifty-foot weeping cherries, a Norway spruce, copper beech, and blue atlas cedar, to name a few, dot this five-acre garden. There is a walk-in root cellar built into the hillside and stone walls surround the whole property. For more information, visit www.kentfordfarm.com.

2015 | ♿ | 📷

⮑ From New London, take I-95 north to Exit 90/Mystic. Turn left onto Route 27 and go to stop sign in Old Mystic Center. Bear right and go through stop sign, passing Old Mystic Fire Station on left. Bear right at next fork onto North Stonington Road. Pass Clyde's Cider Mill on left. Go to blinking light at intersection of Routes 184 & 201. Turn right onto Route 184 and go east. Kentford Farm is second driveway on left.

From Providence, take I-95 south to Exit 90/Mystic. Turn right onto Route 27. Proceed as directed above. From Norwich, take Route 2 east past Foxwoods Resort Casino. Turn right onto Route 201 South toward Old Mystic. Turn left onto Route 184 East. Kentford Farm is second driveway on left.

Fairfield County

Saturday, July 23

🕐 **Hours vary by garden**
(Starting at 10 a.m.)

$7 per garden

FAIRFIELD COUNTY

MERIDEN

📍 **JARDIN DES BRABANT**
131 Corrigan Avenue

🕐 12 p.m. to 5 p.m.

Since 1972, this has been one woman's en-closed garden retreat on three quarters of an acre. The upper lawn features a large beech tree and a perimeter of flowering shrubs, mature conifers, shade perennials, Kousa and Florida dogwoods, and annuals. A nearly 100 foot dawn redwood dominates the lower gardens of shade perennials, roses, annuals, and vines. Grass paths lead toward, and past, a stone-and-stucco storage house with hayr-ack planters. A small potager, an ancient apple tree shading hosta and ferns, and a *Viburnum plicatum* hedge complete the secluded rear garden which dissolves into open lawn.

2015 |

➲ From I-91, take I-691 West to Exit 6/Lewis Avenue. Turn left at end of exit ramp. Turn left at end of Lewis onto Kensington Avenue. Turn left onto Chamberlain Highway. Pass Target store on right and look for Steuben Street immediately after 7-Eleven on left and high-way exit on right. Proceed as directed above. Please park on either side of street. Watch for children in area.

📍 **GEORGE TRECINA**
341 Spring Street, Meriden

🕐 10 a.m. to 4 p.m.

This is a very high-maintenance, one-third-acre suburban garden created over many

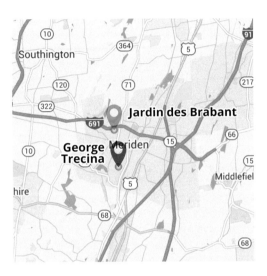

years. With numerous wood, stone, and metal features along with mature conifers and hedges, it has four-season interest. But the real excitement begins as the annuals and tropicals mature over summer. Best seen in July through September, hundreds of con-tainers are filled with succulents, phormiums, and cannas, to name a few. Many specimens have been overwintered for ten or more years. The latest renovations include a formal oval garden with boxwood hedge and central fountain, a rectangular garden of conifers with cedar lattice-work fencing and a shade garden with a quartz stepping stone path and classic Lutyens bench. There are many unique urns of stone, terra-cotta and fiberglass. We will be celebrating our twentieth year of opening the garden.

2015 | ♿ |

➲ From I-91 North, take Exit 18/I-691 West to

Exit 6/Lewis Avenue. Turn right onto Lewis Avenue (which becomes Linsley Avenue) and go to end. Turn right onto Hanover Street to first traffic light. Turn left onto Columbus Avenue to second stop sign. Turn left onto Prospect Avenue and take second right onto Spring Street. Go to fourth house on right, #341. Please park along Spring Street. Persons with walking problems may drive up driveway.

From I-91 South, take Exit 15/Route 68. Turn left onto Route 68 and go about 2.75 miles. Turn right onto Route 150/Main Street. Turn left onto Route 71/Old Colony Road for about 2.25 miles to third traffic light. Turn left onto

Flower Street and go to end. Turn left onto New Hanover Avenue and then first right onto Prospect Avenue. Take first left onto Spring Street.

From I-84, take Exit 27/I-691 East to Exit 5/ Route 71/Chamberlain Highway. Turn right onto Route 71 and go to end. Turn left onto West Main Street and go to first light. Turn right onto Bradley Avenue and go to stop sign. Turn left onto Winthrop Terrace and go to light. Go through intersection up Columbus Avenue to second stop sign. Turn left onto Prospect Avenue and then second right onto Spring Street.

Litchfield County

Saturday, July 30

🕐 **10 a.m. to 4 p.m.**

$7 admission

There are gardens open on this day in nearby Dutchess County, NY. See page 233.

 Book Signing
Larry Weaner, Lakeville

 DIGGING DEEPER: Exploring Twin Maples—The Evolution of a Garden, Douglas Dockery Thomas & Deborah Munson, Salisbury, 4:30 p.m.

 DIGGING DEEPER: Garden Revolution— Exploring Natural Gardens with Larry Weaner; Lakeville, CT; 2 p.m.

 EXPERTS IN THE GARDEN: Jamie Purinton, Montgomery Glazer Property, Lakeville

LITCHFIELD COUNTY

LAKEVILLE

 THE MONTGOMERY GLAZER PROPERTY
120 Millerton Road, Lakeville

 DIGGING DEEPER

 EXPERTS IN THE GARDEN

 Book Signing: 1 to 2 p.m.
Garden Revolution, by Larry Weaner

The main feature of this approximately three-acre lakeside property is a lovely meadow that surrounds both the guest and main house. In the summer of 2009, Bill Montgomery and Lizzie Glazer replaced their uneventful (or dull) lawn with this dynamic and bio-diverse meadow that changes throughout the year and attracts a wonder of birds, dragonflies and butterflies. Their property also includes a formal entry court, kitchen terrace, dining terrace, small cutting and herb gardens, carved old elm tree, and a bio-filtering channel that filters water from the roof before it enters the lake.

NEW |

➲ This garden is at 120 Millerton Road (near intersection of Belgo Road) on the south side or lakeside of the road, 4 miles east of downtown Millerton and one mile west of downtown Lakeville. Limited parking so please park on Belgo Road.

SALISBURY

 TWIN MAPLES
Address will be sent to Digging Deeper ticket holders only

 DIGGING DEEPER ONLY

PUBLIC GARDEN

WASHINGTON

 HOLLISTER HOUSE GARDEN
300 Nettleton Hollow Road, Washington

Situated around an eighteenth-century farmhouse in the Litchfield Hills of northwest Connecticut, this romantic country garden features exuberant plantings set in rambling formal structure and is noted for its subtle and sometimes surprising color combinations. Reminiscent of such classic English gardens as Great Dixter and Sissinghurst, the garden is divided into a series of rooms which open to vistas over the garden and out onto the natural landscape beyond. The garden has been a preservation project of the Garden Conservancy since 2005.

2015 | & |

🕐 Special Open Days June 18, July 9, July 30, and September 11, 10 a.m. to 4 p.m. Otherwise May to September, Friday 2 p.m. to 5 p.m. Saturday 10 a.m. to 4 p.m.

💲 $5 requested donation. No Open Days admission tickets accepted on September 11 during Garden Study Weekend. Admission on this date is $10 and includes a plant sale.

➲ From I-84, take Exit 15/Southbury. Take Route 6 North through Southbury and Woodbury. Turn left onto Route 47 North. Go 4 miles, past Woodbury Ski Area on left, and turn right onto Nettleton Hollow Road. Go 1.7 miles. Garden is on right. Please park along the road or follow parking signs through the gate.

DIGGING DEEPER

SATURDAY, JULY 30 | 2 PM

GARDEN REVOLUTION—EXPLORING NATURAL GARDENS WITH LARRY WEANER

AT: 120 Millerton Road, Lakeville

Principal and Founder of Larry Weaner Associates, Larry's natural landscapes are nationally recognized for their unique blend of environmental science and fine garden design. In

Kim Sokoloff

this sweeping meadow of his design, Larry will discuss the key concepts in creating and maintaining such natural landscapes, and how in addition to being visually engaging, vibrant ecosystems, they are important sources of environmental change.

Registration is required and space is limited. **Opendaysprogram.org or call 1(888) 842-2442**

 # EXPERTS IN THE GARDEN

SATURDAY, JULY 30

JAMIE PURINTON

AT: The Montgomery Glazer Property
120 Millerton Road, Lakeville

Landscape architect Jamie Purinton, who works on the Montgomery Glazer Property, will be available throughout the Open Day to answer questions. Her practice focuses on sustainable design, minimizing our impact on the land, and making distinct and meaningful places.

 # BOOK SIGNING

SATURDAY, JULY 30 | 1 PM – 2 PM

GARDEN REVOLUTION
BY LARRY WEANER

AT: The Montgomery Glazer Property
120 Millerton Road, Lakeville

DIGGING DEEPER

SATURDAY, JULY 30 | 4:30 PM

EXPLORING TWIN MAPLES— THE EVOLUTION OF A GARDEN

A tour with Douglas Dockery Thomas & Deborah Munson

AT: Twin Maples, Salisbury
    Address will be sent to Digging Deeper
    ticket holders only

When the vast meadow is at its peak, award-winning gardener and native plant enthusiast Douglas Thomas and horticulturist Deborah Munson will take guests on a guided tour of Twin Maples, Douglas's spectacular garden in Salisbury, Connecticut. Twin Maples flows smoothly from architecture to nature, from formal garden to field, with extraordinary views of the Litchfield Hills beyond. Douglas and her late husband, Wilmer Thomas, purchased the property in 1996 and built a Georgian-style house and guest cottage designed by David Anthony Easton. They created formal gardens near the house with landscape architect Rodney Robinson and horticulturist Deborah Munson (one in tribute to the work of Russell Page), a woodland garden with Deborah Munson, and a 40-acre wildflower meadow with native plantsman Larry Weaner that figures prominently in his upcoming book, Garden Revolution. Light refreshments will be served.

Registration is required and space is limited. **Opendaysprogram.org or call 1(888) 842-2442**

Fairfield County

Saturday, August 13

🕐 **10 a.m. to 4 p.m.**
$7 per garden

FAIRFIELD COUNTY

NEW CANAAN

📍 **DOGWOOD HILL**
1000 Ponus Ridge Road, New Canaan

Stately urns, roses, dahlias, hydrangeas, zinnias, heliotrope, palm trees, and ornamental grasses abound in Dogwood Hill's splendid August gardenscape. Enjoy a leisurely stroll through this six-acre estate with many garden features designed to please the eye, stimulate the senses, and soothe the soul. Incorporating native plants and classical elements, the property is highlighted by a delightful hillside walking garden. It is a tapestry of rhododendrons and azaleas, hemlock and pines, peonies and roses, lilies and ferns, sweet woodruff and tiarella, clematis and poppies, birch and dogwood, two fountains and classical statuary, a formal sunken garden and a secret garden room. A relaxing pool-side garden combining perennials and tropical plants completes the scene. Dogwood Hill was featured in *Garden Design's* Spring 2015 issue as an "outstanding garden in America" with article by Tovah Martin and photographs by Rob Cardillo. "Making an Entrance," the first chapter in Stacy Bass' book *In the Garden*, is a photo essay depicting Spring at Dogwood Hill. The deer-fenced... [Read the full description online]

2012 | 📷

⮕ From Merritt Parkway, take Exit 36. Turn left onto Route 106. Turn left at traffic light onto Jelliff Mill Road and go about 1 mile to end. Turn right onto Ponus Ridge Road. Go about 2 miles to Wahackme Road on right and gated entrance to property on left. Please park only on west side of Ponus Ridge Road as directed.

REDDING

📍 **IN SITU**
73 Diamond Hill Road, Redding

In Situ is an eight-acre utopia where sculpture, music, fashion and culinary are exhibited in

In Situ, featured in *Outstanding American Gardens: A Celebration—25 Years of the Garden Conservancy*. Photo by Marion Brenner.

the open. Our mission is to provide scholarships to under privileged college students who aspire to attend leading art schools in the United States. We offer our eighteen magnificent and unique garden rooms to companies dedicated to sculpture, music, fashion, or the culinary arts, as a means to stage charity functions, art shows and other corporate events in support of our mission. In Situ is nestled in the rural countryside of Redding, Connecticut. Surrounded by the 312-acre Saugatuck Waterfall Natural Area, the eight-acre property was part of a private estate that was built in 1905. The preserved natural area is a landscape of deciduous woodlands, rocky outcroppings and meadows clearings, permeated by a series of small creeks that empty into the Saugatuck River. In Situ's structures were extensively renovated by architect Robert Orr, who drew upon their heritage as utility buildings by incorporating barn beams as their framework. The house... [Read the full description online]

2015 | 📷

⮑ From the Merritt Parkway/Route 15 North, take Exit 42/Highway 57 toward Westport/ Weston. Go 0.2 mile. At end of ramp at traffic light, turn right onto Highway 57/Weston Road (signs for Weston). Go 3.8 miles. Turn left onto Route 57/Georgetown Road. Go 4.0 miles. Turn right onto Route 107/Redding Road. Go 3.9 miles. Toward the end of the reservoir, cross a small bridge. Turn left to continue on Redding Road/Route 53 North. Pass The Redding Road House and cemetery on right. At flashing light, turn left onto Diamond Hill Road. The Mark Twain Library is on left. Go about 0.25 mile. Garden is on right. Please park on upper road. *Note: The mailbox numbers are not in order.

WESTON

📍 **WELLS HILL FARM**
   3 Wells Hill Road, Weston

Wells Hill Farm strives to model sustainability and the best organic growing practices for small family farms. Companion herbs and flowers are integrated throughout our production gardens. We grow produce intensively on one third of an acre and use our remaining thirteen acres of pastures and woodlands for rotating two mobile chicken coops, one sheep house, and a rabbit hutch—all of which fertilize our pasture, add to our rich compost, control pests and keep weeding around the property to a minimum. Our two livestock guardian dogs keep the animals safe from predation. We do all farming by hand and do not till our soil. Additionally, we grow through four seasons in a 125-foot-high tunnel. Wells Hill Farm sells to restaurants in Fairfield County and New York City, runs a small CSA, and holds farming classes for children and adults. All inputs are carefully considered and almost all of the farm's garden structures and architectural elements are built from downed trees and rocks found on the property.

2014 | ♿ partial | 📷

⮑ From Merritt Parkway South, take Exit 42/ Route 57 toward Westport/Weston.Turn right onto Route 57/Weston Road. Go 0.9 mile and turn right onto Lyons Plains Road. Go 3.6 miles. Lyons Plains Road becomes Kellogg Hill Road 0.7 mile. Cross briefly and jog slightly right onto Old Redding Road 0.04 mile. Turn sharp left onto Kellogg Hill Road and go 0.06 mile. Turn sharp left onto Wells Hill Road. Garden is on the right.

From Merritt Parkway North, take Exit 44 toward Connecticut 58/Fairfield/Redding. Go 394 feet. Turn left onto Congress Street and go 312 feet. Turn right onto Route 58 N/ Black Rock Turnpike and go 3.7 miles Turn left onto Redding Road and go 0.3 mile. Take the 1st right onto Wells Hill Road. Garden is on the right. Please park on the street or in our long driveway toward the right side of the embankment flanking the driveway. Signs directing you to the garden on the right will be posted. Do not enter gates near the house. Please wear good walking shoes as paths and pasture are on an uneven hillside.

New Haven County

Saturday, August 27

🕐 **10 a.m. to 4 p.m.**
$7 admission

NEW HAVEN COUNTY

MERIDEN

📍 **GEORGE TRECINA**
341 Spring Street, Meriden

This is a very high-maintenance, one-third-acre suburban garden created over many years. With numerous wood, stone, and metal features along with mature conifers and hedges, it has four-season interest. But the real excitement begins as the annuals and tropicals mature over summer. Best seen in July through September, hundreds of containers are filled with succulents, phormiums, and cannas, to name a few. Many specimens have been overwintered for ten or more years. The latest renovations include a formal oval garden with boxwood hedge and central fountain, a rectangular garden of conifers with cedar lattice-work fencing and a shade garden with a quartz stepping stone path and classic Lutyens bench. There are many unique urns of stone, terra-cotta and fiberglass. We will be celebrating our twentieth year of opening the garden.

2015 | ♿ | 📷

➲ From I-91 North, take Exit 18/I-691 West to Exit 6/Lewis Avenue. Turn right onto Lewis Avenue (which becomes Linsley Avenue) and go to end. Turn right onto Hanover Street to first traffic light. Turn left onto Columbus Avenue to second stop sign. Turn left onto Prospect Avenue and take second right onto Spring Street. Go to fourth house on right, #341. Please park along Spring Street. Persons with walking problems may drive up driveway.

From I-91 South, take Exit 15/Route 68. Turn left onto Route 68 and go about 2.75 miles. Turn right onto Route 150/Main Street. Turn left onto Route 71/Old Colony Road for about 2.25 miles to third traffic light. Turn left onto Flower Street and go to end. Turn left onto New Hanover Avenue and then first right onto Prospect Avenue. Take first left onto Spring Street.

From I-84, take Exit 27/I-691 East to Exit 5/Route 71/Chamberlain Highway. Turn right onto Route 71 and go to end. Turn left onto West Main Street and go to first light. Turn right onto Bradley Avenue and go to stop sign. Turn left onto Winthrop Terrace and go to light. Go through intersection up Columbus Avenue to second stop sign. Turn left onto Prospect Avenue and then second right onto Spring Street.

Litchfield County

Sunday, August 28

🕐 **10 a.m. to 4 p.m.**

$7 per garden

LITCHFIELD COUNTY

CORNWALL

📍 **SOMETHING TO CROW ABOUT DAHLIAS**
34 Furnace Brook Road, Cornwall

The garden has grown in the past eighteen years to include more than 2,000 plants. It consists of 175 different dahlia varieties producing countless blooms of every shape, color, and size. When in full bloom, the long rows stretch down the gently sloping garden putting on a spectacular and riotous display of color. Tovah Martin recently described the garden as "full spectrum version of Oz, totally outrageous." Every year, new varieties are introduced allowing for a new business selling tubers and fresh-cut stems.

2015 | ♿ |

➲ From Waterbury, take Route 8 north to Exit 44. Turn left onto Route 4 West. Go about 12 miles. The garden is on the right.

From Danbury, take Route 7 north for about 40 miles all the way to Cornwall Bridge. At the intersection of Routes 4 and 7 bear right onto Route 4 and follow for about 3 miles. The garden is on the left side of the road.

WEST CORNWALL

📍 **ROXANA ROBINSON—TREETOP**
218 Town Street, West Cornwall

On the grounds of a family Arts and Crafts house built in 1928, an idiosyncratic hillside garden, incorporating granite ledge, steep ravines, placid greensward, and a wooded hillside sloping down to a lake. The gardens themselves are separated into two areas—the well-mannered Sissinghurst, flat ground, blues, pinks, silvers and purples, stone paths and emerald lawn; and Margaritaville, a wild and rocky ravine, rioting with giant ferns, tithonia, reds and oranges and yellows, salvias and nasturtiums and brilliant hues. Around the gardens are deep woods, with ferns and woodland walks.

NEW |

➲ From West Cornwall: At the covered bridge, (intersection of Routes 7 and 128,) leave the covered bridge behind and go straight up the hill on Route 128 east. Go for 1.19 miles and turn left, at the school, onto Cream Hill Road. Go for 1.4 miles and turn right onto Scoville Road. Go to the end and a "T" intersection (0.7 mile) and turn right onto Town Street. Go 0.36 miles, down into a dip and up the hill again to Treetop.

From Goshen: At the traffic circle, take Route 4 east to the blinking light, about 4 miles. At the light continue straight, up the hill, onto Route 128, about 1 mile. Turn right onto Town Street. Follow Town Street past the white church at North Cornwall to a "Y" intersection, about 1 mile. Bear left (actually stay straight) onto Town Street. Go around a curve to the right. After that big curve we are the second drive on the right. The sign at the driveway says Treetop. The mailbox is on the left and says #218.

WARNING: DO NOT DEPEND ON GPS OR SIRI! THERE IS NO CELL SIGNAL HERE, AND GPS SENDS YOU UP A GOAT TRAIL!

Litchfield County

Sunday, September 11

🕙 **10 a.m. to 4 p.m.**
$7 per garden
$10 Hollister House Garden

★ Start your day at Hollister House Garden in Washington.

🏷 Pop-up Nursery
Rare and Unusual Plant sale at Hollister House Garden as part of Garden Study Weekend VI

LITCHFIELD COUNTY

BRIDGEWATER

 MAYWOOD GARDENS
52 Cooper Road, Bridgewater

This private estate features a sunken perennial garden protected by ten-foot stone walls, a gazebo garden planted with flowers and shrubs to attract butterflies and hummingbirds, a rose garden planted in a French pattern design surrounded by a circle of hemlocks, a woodland path populated by mature beech and cherry trees as well as viburnum and rhododendrons, a ledge garden on an exposed hillside, a heather bed, white garden, herb garden, ornamental kitchen garden, and 4,000-square-foot greenhouse.

2015 | ♿ | 📷

↪ From I-84, take Exit 9 and go north on Route 25 towards Brookfield Village. Turn right onto Route 133 East towards Bridgewater. Cross Lake Lillinonah Bridge and take first right onto Wewaka Brook Road. Go 0.75 mile and turn right onto Beach Hill Road to end. Turn right onto Skyline Ridge. Go 0.5 mile and turn right onto Cooper Road. Please park on right across from greenhouse complex.

Announcing Hollister House
Garden Study Weekend VI

Presented by Hollister House Garden and the Garden Conservancy

September 10 – 11, 2016

Symposium, Great Vendors, & Open Days Garden Tours

Saturday, September 10

Symposium at the Heritage Hotel in Southbury, CT, featuring talks by:

Arne Maynard – celebrated garden designer and author known for his large country gardens; two-time Chelsea Flower Show gold medal winner

David Culp – noted plantsman, garden author and authority, and breeder of hybrid hellebores

Page Dickey – beloved author, passionate gardener, and plant connoisseur

Andy Brand and **Chris Koppel** – plant experts at Broken Arrow Nursery

At the conclusion of the symposium, enjoy cocktails and early buying at the sale of Rare and Unusual Plants at Hollister House Garden.

Sunday, September 11

Garden Conservancy Open Day tour will feature private gardens in Litchfield County.

Sale of Rare and Unusual Plants will be open to the public at Hollister House Garden.

For a full schedule of participating gardens, see the Open Days schedule at gardenconservancy.org.

For more information and to register for the Saturday program, visit www.hollisterhousegarden.org or call (860) 868-2200.

ROXBURY

 CASTLEBRAE FARM
34 Rucum Road, Roxbury

My garden consists of several borders surrounding an eighteenth-century farmhouse. The planting style is "cottagey," with a mixture of shrubs, perennials, and annuals with loosely followed themes, such as a blue border and a rose border. As with many gardeners, I have recognized the need to simplify my gardens with the addition of more shrubs and low-maintenance plants.

2014 | ♿ | 📷

➲ We are about 4 miles outside of the center of Roxbury, on the corner of Bacon and Rucum Road. Take Route 317 towards Woodbury. Bacon Road is a right turn about midway up the second hill (if you see a tiny airport on right you have gone too far). Follow Route 67 from center of town about 4 miles to Rucum Road. Turn left. Our house is the gray house on the corner. Please enter from the driveway up the hill on Rucum from the house.

WASHINGTON

 RED MILL FARM
341 Nettleton Hollow Road, Washington

Informal gardens set off an 1840s farmhouse and historic pre-Revolutionary War sawmill. Intimate spaces on changing levels around the house and conservatory, paved with local granite, feature tropical and half-hardy container plants and vines along with roses and perennials. A white garden with flagstone paving filled with plants is surrounded by trellises with roses and clematis. Sweeping lawns drop to the sawmill area, where native plants, wildflowers, and a wet garden border the millpond and waterways. Amble through a new woodland area with its rocky pool.

2014 | 📷

➲ From I-84, take Exit 15 in Southbury and turn north onto Route 6. Go about 6 miles to traffic light at Route 47, and turn left. Go 4.1 miles, turn right onto Nettleton Hollow Road. Go 1.1 miles and Red Mill Farm is on left; look for a white picket fence.

LEAD GARDEN
❋ PUBLIC GARDEN

WASHINGTON

 HOLLISTER HOUSE GARDEN
300 Nettleton Hollow Road, Washington

★ Start your day here for the September 11 Litchfield County Open Day.

Situated around an eighteenth-century farmhouse in the Litchfield Hills of northwest Connecticut, this romantic country garden features exuberant plantings set in rambling formal structure and is noted for its subtle and sometimes surprising color combinations. Reminiscent of such classic English gardens as Great Dixter and Sissinghurst, the garden is divided into a series of rooms which open to vistas over the garden and out onto the natural landscape beyond. The garden has been a preservation project of the Garden Conservancy since 2005.

2015 | ♿ | 📷

🕐 Special Open Days June 18, July 9, July 30, and September 11, 10 a.m. to 4 p.m. Otherwise May to September, Friday 2 p.m. to 5 p.m. Saturday 10 a.m. to 4 p.m.

$ $5 requested donation. No Open Days admission tickets accepted on September 11 during Garden Study Weekend. Admission on this date is $10 and includes a plant sale.

➲ From I-84, take Exit 15/Southbury. Take Route 6 North through Southbury and Woodbury. Turn left onto Route 47 North. Go 4 miles, past Woodbury Ski Area on left, and turn right onto Nettleton Hollow Road. Go 1.7 miles. Garden is on right. Please park along the road or follow parking signs through the gate.

Fairfield County

Sunday, September 18

🕐 **10 a.m. to 4 p.m.**

$7 per garden

There are gardens also open on this day and a Digging Deeper event in nearby Westchester County, NY. See page 245.

 DIGGING DEEPER: Big Ideas from a Small Garden; Bernard Marquez & Tim Fish; South Salem; NY, 2p.m. & 4:30 p.m. See page 248.

🏷️ Pop-up Nursery
Pixie Perennials

FAIRFIELD COUNTY

GREENWICH

📍 **SLEEPY CAT FARM**
146 Clapboard Ridge Road, Greenwich

The thirteen-acre gardens of Sleepy Cat Farm have evolved over the past eighteen years through a close collaboration of the present owner and Virginia-based landscape architect Charles J. Stick. The most recently developed portion of the landscape which borders Lake Avenue includes an extensive greenhouse and potager. The newly constructed "Barn", distinguished by its half-timbered French Normandy vocabulary is surrounded by thyme-covered terraces which provide an elegant stage set for a fine collection of garden ornament, sculpture, and boxwood topiary. The visitor's experience of the garden unfolds as pathways lead from garden room to garden room in a carefully orchestrated series of discoveries. The central portion of the garden is distinguished by two parallel garden spaces, the first is dominated by a long reflecting pool, terminated on the north end by a wisteria-covered arbor and on the south end by a pebble mosaic terrace and fountain basin. One of the great surprises of the tour is

the adjacent garden space. Bordered by a...
[Read the full description online]

2014 |

⮑ From I-95 north, take Exit 3 in Connecticut. At bottom of exit ramp, turn left onto Arch Street (if traveling on I-95 south, turn right). Go under railroad overpass. The next traffic light is Railroad Avenue. Go through light and take next left onto Southview. At top of hill turn right onto Field Point Road. Go through light at West Putnam Avenue, crossing Route 1 between Exxon station and library onto Deerfield. Go through the rotary, taking second exit onto Lake Avenue. Go through another small rotary and pass over a narrow bridge, warned by a sign. Turn left onto Clapboard Ridge Road. It is second driveway; turn before white mailbox marked "146."

RIDGEFIELD

⬤ KEN EISOLD'S GARDEN
18 Chestnut Hill Road, Ridgefield

This extensive garden on four acres is designed to enhance the features of the landscape: a large open field, a stream, and woodlands. The garden includes a perennial border, a woodland path with two rustic bridges, a shrub border, a grass garden, and a grove of conifers. A gazebo, pergola, several terraces, and a sculpture provide focal points.

2015 | ♿ |

⮑ Five miles from the center of Ridgefield (on the south), 2 miles from I-84 (on the north).

From Ridgefield, go north on Route 116, 3 miles to Ridgebury Road, turn right. Then go 2 miles to Chestnut Hill Road and turn left.

From I-84, take Exit 1/Saw Mill Road. Go 2 miles south to Ridgebury Road (at intersection with George Washington Highway). Go 0.5 mile to Chestnut Hill Road, turn right.

From North Salem, go 2 miles east on Route 116, to Ridgebury Road. Turn left, then go 2 miles to Chestnut Hill Road and turn left. There will be off-road parking in the field.

WILTON

⬤ PIXIE PERENNIALS
200 Nod Hill Road, Wilton

🏷 Pixie Perennials

Terraced perennial gardens with a wide variety of unusual plants surround a 1740 homestead set on four acres overlooking a reservoir, home to mature and specimen trees. A small rock garden tucked into the exposed ledge leads to a fish pond. A frog pond is nestled in between rows of flowers. The property features peach trees, an old leaning apple tree, fig trees, kiwi, blueberry bushes, strawberries, raspberries, and a vegetable garden. The kitchen courtyard garden room hosts shade plants: hellebores, brunnera, heuchera, ligularia, shaped boxwoods and other varieties of perennials that live nestled under a giant maple tree. Peonies border one length of the paddock fence leading you to the lilac bushes. A back garden built around the exposed stones showcases tall plants that can be seen from the house. In late summer a stand of perovskia creates a blue backdrop for fall flowering perennials. The garden is a work in progress, ever-changing from year to year. The party barn boasts quarter sawn oak floors, and hosted town dances during Prohibition. Home-grown perennials and shrubs will be for sale on the back patio and adjacent areas. There will be a pop-up boutique in the "party" barn featuring wonderful items for sale by local artisans.

2015 |

⮑ It is 0.9 mile up on the right from the intersection of Route 33/Ridgefield Road and Nod Hill.

❇ PUBLIC GARDENS

FAIRFIELD COUNTY

NEW CANAAN

IRWIN PARK
848 Weed Street, New Canaan
(203) 966-1591

New Canaan's newest park is best described as a people sanctuary, with benches and chairs scattered among its vast orchard and fields. A one-mile trail winds through the surrounding woods. A highlight takes place in the spring when thousands of daffodils bloom on the great lawn. There is an enchanting Children's Mushroom Maze Garden. The New Canaan Garden Club (a member of The Garden Club of America since 1920) has accepted the stewardship of this property with the help of a family endowment and the town parks department. Dogs must be kept on leads at all times.

🕐 Year round, daily, dawn to dusk.

$ Free

➲ Take Exit 36 off the Merritt Parkway/Route 15 and follow Weed Street to #848 signage and entrance on the left. Also within walking distance of Metro North train station. Limited parking is available for cars and bicycles.

WAVENY WALLED GARDEN AT WAVENY HOUSE IN WAVENY PARK
677 South Avenue & Route 124, New Canaan, (203) 594-3600

The Waveny Walled Garden was originally designed by Frederick Law Olmsted's firm as a formal rose garden. In 1995, the garden was redesigned as a Wedding Garden by a committee of the New Canaan Garden Club horticulture devotees. The design today incorporates roses in a long rose border along one side. The remaining three sides, bordered by brick walks, showcase deep herbaceous borders which include perennials, small trees, flowering shrubs, bulbs, and annuals. Three season of the year this very special space is used weekly for weddings and special events. In this civic endeavor, the New Canaan Garden Club collaborates with the Town Parks and Recreation department. The Garden Club is responsible for the weekly maintenance.

🕐 April through October, daily, dawn to dusk.

$ Free

➲ From the Merritt Parkway/Route 15, take Exit 37 and follow South Avenue into town. Driveway entrance to Waveny Park is on left. The garden is adjacent to Waveny House on the left. Ample parking is available. Dogs must be on leads at all times.

NEW LONDON COUNTY

OLD LYME

FLORENCE GRISWOLD MUSEUM HISTORIC GARDEN
96 Lyme Street, Old Lyme,
(860) 434-5542,
www.florencegriswoldmuseum.org

In addition to the restored Florence Griswold House, where artists of the Lyme Art Colony lived, the Museum features a gallery for changing art exhibitions, education and landscape centers, a restored artist's studio, eleven acres along the Lieutenant River, and extensive gardens. Using Miss Florence Griswold's records, historic photographs, and paintings by members of the famed colony, the garden was restored to its 1910 appearance. Miss Florence's garden features masses of flowers informally arranged in bordered beds. The Rafal Landscape Center offers insight into the history of the region's landscape.

🕐 Year round, Tuesday through Saturday from 10 a.m. to 5 p.m. and Sunday 1 to 5 p.m. Closed Monday.

$ $10 for adults, $9 for seniors, $8 students, $8 groups, and free to children 12 and under

➲ From I-95 take Exit 70 in Old Lyme.

DISTRICT OF COLUMBIA

Washington D.C.

Sunday, October 16

🕙 **10 a.m. to 4 p.m.**
$7 per garden

 EXPERTS IN THE GARDEN: Compost Tea in Nancy Pyne's Garden, with Andrea Filippone & Eric T. Fleisher, Georgetown

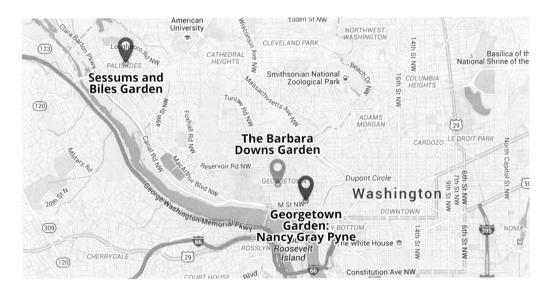

WASHINGTON D.C.

GEORGETOWN

📍 **THE BARBARA DOWNS GARDEN**
3321 P Street NW, Georgetown

Located in Washington, D.C.'s historic Georgetown, this town garden exudes the spirit of Japan, a favorite travel spot of its owner. A dry streambed of randomly placed stones descends from the elevated rear of the garden and meanders to the house, terminating in a circular arrangement of stones that mimick a pool. The centerpiece of the garden, a sculptured millstone-shaped pink granite fountain surrounded by lavender plantain lily (Hosta x 'Honeybells') bubbles with life. Framed by crepe myrtle 'Nantchez' (Lagerstroemia indica 'Natchez'), the terrace of Stoneyhurst flagstone provides a reflective escape in this hidden urban garden.

NEW

⮐ The property is in Georgetown on P Street NW, one block west of Wisconsin Avenue, between 33rd and 34th Streets.

GEORGETOWN GARDEN: NANCY GRAY PYNE
1224 30th Street NW, Georgetown

🎓 EXPERTS IN THE GARDEN

A journey through this secret garden in the heart of Georgetown takes the visitor up a series of formal terraced gardens and past a number of outbuildings that include a library, two greenhouses, and a freestanding theater. It culminates in a decorative walled vegetable garden designed and planted by Washington Post garden writer, Adrian Higgins. The garden had been assembled over the course of a century or more, but it was given its character in the 1930s as one of the major Washington projects of a pioneering landscape architect named Rose Greely. The main terrace is a walled garden perched above the house. Its most animated feature, a geometric fountain, is aligned with both the rear entrance of the house and, at right angles to it, a rectangular lawn framed by a path and boxwood plantings. The upper garden functions as its own formal garden of shrubs and small trees, as well as an entrance for the theater, known as the playhouse, and the larger greenhouse (and potting shed). The upper garden is also a place of paths. One leads to a parking lot at the end of an alley. Another passes a long boxwood walk that leads past a fenced swimming pool, which was once an ornamental garden and, later, a tennis court. The vegetable garden is bounded by more brick walls and by the back of the garage and a cedar fence. The space, sixty feet by thirty feet, also contains the second greenhouse built by Nancy Gray's husband, Gordon Gray, who was a passionate orchid grower.

NEW | 📷

➲ The garden is located between M and N Streets in the historic neighborhood of Georgetown.

 SESSUMS + BILES GARDEN
5081 Lowell Street, N.W.

The Sessums + Biles Garden is a horticultural treasure where sustainability and design embrace. The client, a passionate gardener bored with traditional "green on green" landscapes, commissioned a garden with careful consideration to all seasons and where plant form, texture, and color are of equal importance. The result is a dynamic, ever-changing tapestry of predominantly native trees, shrubs, perennials, and groundcovers. Sweeping paths, walls, terraces, and a water feature form the backbone of this unique garden. No herbicides or fertilizers are used, and pesticide use is strictly limited to the aging stand of hemlocks. The site is not irrigated, site water is reclaimed, and all garden material is composed on site. The garden is also a Certified Wildlife Habitat through the National Wildlife Federation and the client is physically involved in all aspects of the garden's maintenance.

2010 | 📷

➲ The garden is located less than 1 mile from American University in upper northwest Washington D.C. Street parking is available; no parking on site.

EXPERTS IN THE GARDEN

SUNDAY, OCTOBER 16

COMPOST TEA IN NANCY PYNE'S GARDEN

with Andrea Filippone & Eric T. Fleisher

AT: Georgetown Garden: Nancy Gray Pyne
     1224 30th Street NW, Georgetown

In 2011, Nancy Gray Pyne hired the New York-based firm, F2 Environmental Design. Andrea Filippone is a boxwood expert who is on a crusade to get people to move beyond the sickly standard English and American box varieties to embrace lesser-known hybrids that are elegant and agreeably pungent, but better garden plants. Eric T. Fleisher is the organic guru in the firm, who believes that the basis of all successful gardening is an understanding and nurturing of the soil biosphere. Healthy soil is rich in beneficial bacteria and fungi, some of which work directly with plant roots to nourish and protect their symbionts. Some of these microbes are eaten by tiny creatures that release nitrogen as they feed, Fleisher explained. It is a system that relies on good soil structure, lots of choice compost incorporated into the earth and the absence of chemical fertilizers and pesticides.

❁ PUBLIC GARDEN

WASHINGTON

**DUMBARTON OAKS GARDENS &
DUMBARTON OAKS PARK**
1703 32nd Street, N. W.
(202) 339-6401, www.doaks.org

The Dumbarton Oaks Gardens and Dumbarton Oaks Park were designed as one project by noted architect Beatrix Farrand in cooperation with her clients, Mr. & Mrs. Robert Woods Bliss, who purchased the property in 1920. The design, mostly completed in the 1920s and 1930s, progressed from formal terraced gardens near the house to an informal, naturalistic landscape in the stream valley below, with designed views between them. In 1940, the Blisses gave the house and related formal gardens to Harvard University as a research center and conveyed the twenty-seven-acre, naturalistic landscape to the National Park Service. Dumbarton Oaks Park is managed by the National Park Service, Rock Creek Park.

🕐 Gardens open March 15 through October 31, Tuesday through Sunday, 2 p.m. to 6 p.m. Park open year round, daily, dawn to dusk

💲 $10 adults, $8 senior citizens 60 and older, $5 for students and children (12 and under)

➲ The gardens' entrance is at R and 31st Streets, N.W., 1.5 blocks east of Wisconsin Avenue. Park along street. Park's entrance is north on Lovers Lane from R Street, east of 31st Street; Lovers Lane runs between Dumbarton Oaks Gardens' east wall and west edge of Montrose Park. Entrance is on left at bottom of hill.

FLORIDA

OUR PARTNER IN FLORIDA

This Open Day is part of the Cummer Museum of Art & Gardens annual Garden Month. Every March, the Cummer Museum of Art & Gardens celebrates Garden Month through a variety of garden-related activities and exhibitions. This year's Garden Month will include tours, lectures, concerts, and art workshops for visitors of all ages.

Azaleas bloom in the English Garden at the Cummer Museum.

Jacksonville

Saturday, April 2

🕐 **12 p.m. to 4 p.m.**

$30 Day Pass, includes admission to Cummer Museum

★ Start your day and purchase day passes at Cummer Museum, 829 Riverside Avenue.

 EXPERTS IN THE GARDEN: CAROLYN MARSH LINDSAY at the Cummer Museum

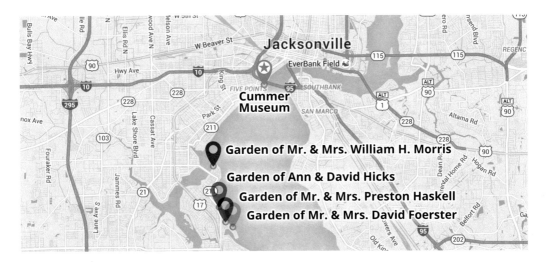

DUVAL COUNTY

JACKSONVILLE

 GARDEN OF MR. & MRS. DAVID FOERSTER
5023 Yacht Club Road, Jacksonville

A majestic magnolia tree forms the centerpiece of a grass-covered lawn and bricked riverfront garden overlooking downtown Jacksonville in the distance. On either side are trimmed vine-covered brick walls. Low-level boxwood hedges border the bulk headed river, forming a background for two seasonal areas for annuals, which are separated by a brick walkway leading from a large elevated terrace to the river. A classical columned arbor covered by wisteria, provides a shady area overlooking the pool. Clipped boxwood hedges border the terrace and the river room

of the house. The entire garden area, featured in *Seasons* magazine, was designed by landscape architect Robert L. Hartwig and planted by award-winning landscape architect P.D. Shoemaker.
NEW

➲ Driving south on Route 17/Roosevelt Boulevard, turn left onto Verona. Then turn right onto Ortega Boulevard. Continue to left on Morven Road. Continue to left on Yacht Club Road.

📍 **GARDEN OF MR. & MRS. PRESTON HASKELL**
4971 Morven Road, Jacksonville

The Haskell Gardens comprise three acres of lush plantings, a contemporary house, and fourteen large abstract outdoor sculptures that are integrated into the landscape.

ESCAPE

REFRESH YOUR PERSPECTIVE
AT THE CUMMER GARDENS

The historic Cummer Gardens are an ideal destination for a morning of quiet contemplation, a midday stroll by the St. Johns River, and an evening of reflection beneath the Cummer Oak. Visit today to experience the Cummer family's living legacy.

CUMMER MUSEUM
ART | GARDENS | EDUCATION

cummermuseum.org

The initial design for the riverfront property was created by landscape architect Wayne O. Manning, Jr., circa 1978. The landscape scheme for the property includes medium-density woods of live oaks and magnolias, with screening shrubbery including viburnum, holly, ligustrum, anise, and oleaster. The road to the west is screened by a multi-layered tall hedge with azaleas, sago palms, and holly ferns planted in the foreground. Curving hedges of varying heights define spaces within the property and set off the outdoor sculpture. A lawn opens to St. Johns River on the east side of the estate. Other plantings include aspidistra, pittosporum, podocarpus, ilex, and jasmine, which covers an arbor and the fences around the tennis court. Ground covers include liriope, juniper, and mondo grass. Flowering annuals are added for color.

NEW

➲ Driving south on Route 17/Roosevelt Boulevard, turn left onto Verona. Then turn right onto Ortega Boulevard. Continue and turn left onto Morven Road.

GARDEN OF ANN & DAVID HICKS
4705 Ortega Boulevard, Jacksonville

In 1991, two riverfront properties and houses were joined, creating one family house and garden. Mary Palmer Dargan of Dargan Landscape Architects (Atlanta, Georgia) was engaged to integrate the grounds. In keeping with the formal Colonial Revival style of the "new" house, Dargan created terraces and private garden rooms on the front, shaded side of the property. A walk through an arched pergola along the side of the property opens to a sunny expansive view of the St. Johns River. A classical arbor with limestone columns overlooks an oval lawn and a lovely terraced parterre rose garden, reached by a set of English steps. Judy Drake and Gerry Crouch of Sunscapes Landscape Design, installed the garden in 1995 and have maintained and augmented the garden for twenty years.

2014

➲ Driving south on Route 17/Roosevelt Boulevard, turn left onto Verona and then right onto Ortega Boulevard.

GARDEN OF MR. & MRS. WILLIAM H. MORRIS
3700 Oak Point Avenue, Jacksonville

This property was purchased as a vacant lot in 1996. Over the next few years, plans for the gardens and house were developed with construction complete in 2003. Formal gardens surround the English Baroque-style house with more natural gardens away from the house. It is one of the few riverfront properties without a bulk head, which allows for a natural transition to the river. A number of water features complement the riverside setting of the gardens which were designed and laid out by the owners. The gardens provide a setting for a collection of outdoor sculptures which the owners have collected over the years. The gardens continue to evolve as the owners visit other gardens in their travels.

NEW

➲ Driving south on Route 17/Roosevelt Boulevard, turn left onto Verona. Then turn left onto Ortega Boulevard. The garden is on the right on Oak Point Avenue.

LEAD GARDEN
❋ PUBLIC GARDEN

DUVAL COUNTY
JACKSONVILLE

✪ THE CUMMER MUSEUM OF ART & GARDENS
829 Riverside Avenue, Jacksonville, (904) 356-6857
www.cummer.org/visit

★ Start your day here on April 2 for the Jacksonville Open Day. Tickets and maps will be available here.

EXPERTS IN THE GARDEN

🕐 Special Garden Conservancy Open Day, Saturday, April 2, 12 p.m. to 4 p.m. Otherwise, Tuesday 10 a.m. to 9 p.m.; Wednesday through Saturday 10 a.m. to 4 p.m.; Sunday, 12 p.m. to 4 p.m. Closed Mondays and July 4th, Thanksgiving, Christmas Eve, Christmas Day, New Years Eve, and New Years Day.

$ Free for Open Days visitors on April 2 Open Day when purchasing a day pass. Free on Tuesday from 4 p.m. to 9 p.m. and first Saturday of every month. Otherwise $10 adults, $6 seniors (62+), military, and students (with ID). Children 5 and under free. College students with ID free Tuesday–Friday, 4 p.m. to 9 p.m.

The Cummer Gardens, acknowledged by the National Register of Historic Places, have a fascinating history and bear the imprint of some of the foremost names in landscape design and horticulture, including Ossian Cole Simonds, Ellen Biddle Shipman, Thomas Meehan & Sons, and the fabled Olmsted firm. The Museum's two-and-one-half acres of historic gardens are unique examples of early twentieth-century garden design, featuring reflecting pools, fountains, arbors, antique ornaments, and sculptures. The majestic Cummer Oak has a canopy of more than 150 feet and is one of the oldest trees in Jacksonville.

➲ Traveling north on I-95 South, take Exit 352A. Take ramp right for Forest Street toward Riverside Avenue. Turn left onto Forest Street. Turn right onto Route 211S/Riverside Avenue. Bear right onto Route 211/Riverside Avenue. Museum is on left.

Traveling south on I-95 North, take Exit 351A. Take ramp right and follow signs for Park Street. Turn left onto Park Street. Turn right onto Riverside Avenue. Museum is on left.

Museum parking on Riverside Avenue (directly across from Museum), additional lot on corner of Riverside Avenue and Post Street.

🎓 EXPERTS IN THE GARDEN

SATURDAY, APRIL 2 | 12 – 4 PM
CAROLYN MARSH LINDSAY
AT: Cummer Museum of Art & Gardens
    828 Riverside Avenue, Jacksonville

Carolyn Marsh Lindsay will be at the Cummer Museum of Art & Gardens to talk about her work on the massive restoration effort of the Museum's Italian Garden which she initiated after locating original plans designed by Ellen Biddle Shipman in the landscape architect's archives at Cornell University. Carolyn is committed to beautification and served as the first female president of the American Horticultural Society. She is also a landscape designer and the owner of a nursery.

ILLINOIS

Chicago's North Shore

Sunday, June 26

🕐 **10 a.m. to 4 p.m.**

$7 per garden

LAKE COUNTY

LAKE FOREST

📍 **POND RIDGE**
808 South Ridge Road, Lake Forest

This Howard Van Doren Shaw gardeners' cottage was originally part of a large estate (Robert P. Lamont House c. 1924), with a pond separating the cottages from the owners' house. When we bought the property in 1998 the cottage had undergone several renovations and the garden consisted mostly of concrete and junipers. We asked our landscape architect, Douglas Hoerr, to design a low-maintenance garden using primarily boxwood and groundcover. Boxwood hedges and large mounds, together with gravel paths, emphasize the horizontal axis of the cottage. The concept is closer to a French jardin rather than an English cottage garden—no beds of flowering perennials or annuals. Recent updates have been designed and planted by Kemora Landscapes.

2015 | 📷

➲ From Highway 41, if exiting west onto Old Elm Road, turn north (right) onto South Ridge Road and go 0.5 mile. From Highway 41, if exiting west onto Westleigh Road, turn south (left) onto Ridge Road and go 0.5 mile. Please park on South Ridge Road, no driveway parking.

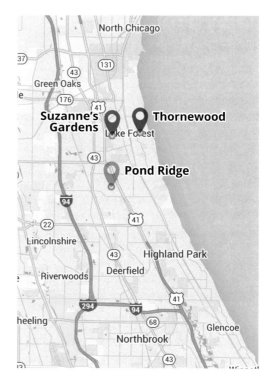

📍 **THORNEWOOD**
1070 Meadow Lane, Lake Forest

Originally the head gardener's cottage and part of the estate to the north, the house has a long history of professional gardeners in residence, including the current owner. Today a visitor meanders through a series of garden rooms, each with its own unique theme. There is the rain garden and a woodland garden featuring native plants, a shade garden featuring ornamental plantings, and a formal lily pond flanked by two mini-bogs with pitcher plants in the central lawn. The working garden is where the garden shed and potted dwarf tree collection reside. There is also a vegetable garden, rose garden, and more than sixty varieties of woody plants alone and... well, you'll see...

2015 | ♿ partial | 📷

⮌ From downtown Lake Forest take Deerpath Road east to the stop sign at Sheridan Road (4 blocks). Turn left (north) and continue past the stop sign at Westminster (1 block) and turn right at the next street, which is Woodland Road (2 blocks). The first cross street is Meadow Lane (1 block), take a right (south) and it is the first house on the right. Park on the west side of the street only; do not park in driveway.

📍 SUZANNE'S GARDENS
283 West Laurel Avenue, Lake Forest

Situated adjacent to the Lake Forest Open Lands' Haffner Meadow, Suzanne's Gardens transition seamlessly from native vegetation to more formal perennial beds. Here, you'll find indigenous plants that spill over from the neighboring prairie and woodlands to mingle with non-natives that are typical of more traditional European gardens. Every effort has been made to ensure that non-natives remain in aesthetic and ecological harmony with the conservation lands. Indeed, healthy land stewardship has been a priority throughout. The sustainable approach to gardening has been influenced by Dennis Nyren's longtime services on the Boards of Directors associated with LFOLA and Conserve Lake County. In spring 2012 the gardens received the Conservation at Home Award from Conserve Lake County for implementing sustainable practices such as prioritizing native plants and conserving, storing and cleaning water on-site. Native plants require less water and chemicals in order to prosper, they, retain rainwater and they purify runoff. They also complement the natural ecology of the area, providing habitat and nourishment to native animals. Non- native plants—many from as far away as China—do not provide these same benefits since they have been cultivated locally for fewer than 100 years, preventing native animals from developing a symbiotic relationship with them. In 1999 when the Nyrens purchased the house, five ancient Elms shaded the yard—now there is only one graceful shady lady left. But this loss created an opportunity: borders were expanded, allowing sun-loving plants to thrive where there were once only shade plants. Meander the yard but also, enjoy a moment of quiet reflection sitting under a cathedral of towering pines along a path that leads to an Open Lands Prairie Preserve. Below, a carpet of spring trillium and other ephemerals followed by blooms and grasses which create a subtle melding of colors and textures.

2014 | ♿ | 📷

⮌ From the intersection of Green Bay Road and Deerpath Road, go north on Green Bay Road to Laurel Avenue about 0.25 mile. Turn left and go west on Laurel Avenue. Please park on Laurel near the "T" with Private Lane. Go south on Private Lane to #283.

Chicago's North Shore

Sunday, July 17

🕐 Hours vary by garden
(Starting at 10 a.m.)

$7 per garden

COOK COUNTY

WINNETKA

📍 **NANTUCKET GARDEN**
777 Bryant Avenue, Winnetka

🕐 10 a.m. to 4 p.m.

The cedar-shingled Nantucket-style house, built in 1916 by Edwin Clark, with its flower-filled window boxes, provides a beautiful background for this enchanting country garden created over the last thirty years. As you enter the rear gardens you pass a shrub border extending the length of the south property with boxwood, variegated dogwood, and other shrubs. A terraced perennial garden of various shades of pink, blue, and white flowers cascades down the hillside. The garden includes many old flower favorites, stone walls, and roses climbing on trellises near a rose garden. A ravine garden, best seen from the bridge, features giant and variegated butterburs, hostas, Joe Pye weed, grasses, and iris. On your way to the bridge one passes a boxwood knot garden surrounded by a yew hedge and backed by an arrowwood viburnum hedge as well as a woodland area with different varieties of ferns, hostas, and ground covers.

2008 | ♿ | 📷🏠

➲ From Edens Expressway/I-94 north, take Willow Road exit. Go to Hibbard Road and turn left. Go straight to dead-end at Tower Road and turn right. Go east to Sheridan Road and turn right. Go 2 blocks to Humboldt Avenue and turn right. Go 1 block to Bryant Avenue. Our house is on right.

From Edens Expressway/I-94 south, take

Tower Road exit and proceed as directed above.

LAKE COUNTY

LAKE FOREST

📍 **OLD MILL FARM**
499 West Old Mill Road, Lake Forest

🕐 10 a.m. to 2 p.m.

Once a working dairy farm siring championship bulls, this property consisted of a

1929 English Tudor-style house and several out-buildings eventually demolished by the original owner when selling a large portion of the property. Jens Jensen designed the original master plan for the entire property. The current owners purchased the property from the original owner's estate for their family residence, dreaming of restoring the property and house. Collaborating with John Mariani and Jim Osborne of Mariani Landscape, they've created a truly magical garden. Old Mill Farm focuses on the potager garden of boxwood partitions filled spring to fall with bulbs and annuals for flower arranging and herbs and vegetables for cooking. Next to this garden is a berry patch and, unusual for this northern climate, a bed of Italian figs. Two perennial borders are adjacent to the potager garden. One border focuses on perennials with annuals added for seasonal color. The other border is a butterfly garden surrounded by yew hedges. Other garden features include an orchard, a woodland garden, and a prairie restoration.

2014 | ♿ | 📷

⮌ From Route 41 North, take Route 22 West/Half Day Road. Turn right onto Route 43/Waukegan Road and go about 0.5 mile to first street on right, Old Mill Road. Turn right and go east to end of street. House is last drive on right. Please park along north side street.

METTAWA

📍 **METTAWA MANOR**
25779 St. Mary's Road, Mettawa
🕐 10 a.m. to 4 p.m.

The house and grounds were built in 1927 as a family compound. Donna LaPietra and Bill Kurtis are only the second owners in the manor's rich history and have been working for the past twenty-three years to refurbish some garden areas and create new ones. The centerpiece is a walled English-style garden with forty-foot perennial borders on either side of a sunken lawn that leads to a spring

walk and rose room centered on an old fountain. Outside the east gate is a golden garden and an orchard/meadow bordered by a fenced potager, cutting garden, and circular herb garden. The sixty-five-acre property has two ponds, a fifteen-acre prairie, a parkland of specimen trees and is surrounded by a newly reclaimed oak-hickory forest. The most recent additions include a silver garden, a bronze garden, an ornamental lily pool, aqua-theatre, a three-tiered mound, a grass labyrinth with central fire pit, with a tree house overlook, and a shrubbery with island beds. This year's Open Day will be celebrated with activities and festivities throughout the grounds.

2015 | 📷

⮌ Take I-94/Edens Expressway to Route 41. Exit at Route 60 West, go 3 miles to St. Mary's Road, and turn left just past horse stables to Open Days signs on left of St. Mary's Road marking driveway entrance.

Elburn & West Chicago

Sunday, August 7

🕐 **Hours vary by garden**
   (Starting at 10 a.m.)
$7 per garden

🚩 Guided Tour
   The Gardens at Ball

DU PAGE COUNTY

WEST CHICAGO

📍 **THE GARDENS AT BALL**
   622 Town Road, West Chicago

🕐 10 a.m. to 4 p.m.

🚩 Guided tours available throughout the day

Guests will enjoy the opportunity to visit The Gardens at Ball, usually reserved for the wholesale customers of the 111-year-old Ball Horticultural Company, a world leader in the breeding, production, distribution and marketing of horticultural products. There will be more than ten acres of gardens to view including redesigned perennial beds and new rose displays. Thousands of annual, perennial and vegetable varieties will be showcased in beds, containers and baskets along with flowers and vegetables in the All-America Selections evaluation trials. Guides will be available throughout the day to give garden tours and answer questions. Allow two hours or more to visit these exceptional gardens. Port-o-potties will be available for guests.

2015 | ♿ | 📷

➲ Turn north onto Town Road off Roosevelt Road/ Route 38 in West Chicago. Watch for signs to turn left into the parking and main garden entrance just north of the main building complex. West Chicago

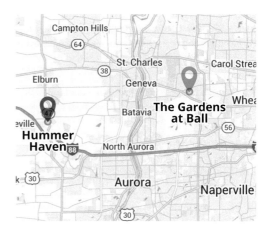

KANE COUNTY

ELBURN

📍 **HUMMER HAVEN**
   43W712 Willow Creek Drive, Elburn

🕐 10 a.m. to 5 p.m.

This entire property is a riot of color that begins in early spring with tens of thousands of blooming bulbs and continues through November with several hundred species of perennials, lilies, bulbs, and shrubs. We grow many unusual plants that are normally found in warmer climates. We have three landscaped ponds with waterfalls, the largest has a stream that leads to a quarry type pond. One hundred and twenty tons of quarry rock were used in building the ponds. Our gardens are host to butterflies, birds, dragonflies, and amphibians, a colony of bats and other wildlife. The back gardens are interlaced with winding stone paths, where we are continually adding new planting areas populated with unusual and new plants. For those who enjoy bird watching, we have an assortment of birds that frequent the gardens; you are guaranteed to see many Ruby-throated Hummingbirds. We have been a Certified National Wildlife Habitat since 1991, a certified Monarch Waystation and a Xerces Society Pollinator Habitat.

2015 | ♿ | 📷

➥ Take Route 47 South through Elburn for about 6 miles. Go straight through stop sign at Main Street to first street on right, Willow Creek Drive. Garden is at second house on right.

From east, take Fabyan Parkway at Randall Road west about 3.5 miles to end at Main Street. Turn right and go 3.5 miles to Route 47. Turn left at stop sign and go to first street on right. Garden is at second house on right.

From south and I-88, take exit for Route 56 and follow to Route 47. Turn right onto Route 47. Go about 4 miles and cross I-88. Continue another mile to second Willow Creek Drive entrance. Turn left and go to second house on right. Please park on street.

Chicago's North Shore

Sunday, September 18

🕓 **10 a.m. to 4 p.m.**

$7 per garden

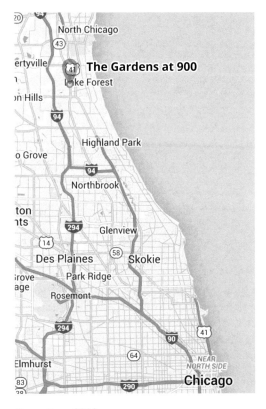

LAKE COUNTY

LAKE FOREST

📍 **THE GARDENS AT 900**
1065 Acorn Trail, Lake Forest

The Gardens at 900 are a sensitive renovation and interpretation of the original entry building complex and gardens of Elawa Farm. Originally designed by architect David Adler in 1917 for A. Watson and Elsa Armour, the buildings had been abandoned for nearly a decade before being acquired by Craig Bergmann and Paul Klug. Both private residence and the design offices for Craig Bergmann and Paul Klug, the use of buildings and garden areas at 900 respectively regard the history of the site, while also fostering creativity within its existing framework. Formal borders, a shade garden, an orchard, a new swimming pool garden, and a motor court constitute the garden today. A relatively young garden (2010), The Gardens at 900 are an excellent example of how quickly a landscape can be transformed with the strategic placement of plant material and a focused, collaborative vision.

2015 |

The garden is 2.7 miles north of Route 60 and 1.4 miles north of Deerpath Road. One block south of Middlefork Drive/Westmoreland Road traffic light. Please use the Acorn Trail entrance. Turn west from Waukegan Road/ Route 43 onto Middlefork Drive and take the first left on to Acorn Trail. Please park on the street and walk down the designated path at #1065.

✿ PUBLIC GARDENS

COOK COUNTY

GLENCOE

CHICAGO BOTANIC GARDEN
1000 Lake Cook Road, Glencoe
(847) 835-5440, www.chicagobotanic.org

The Chicago Botanic Garden, one of the treasures of the Forest Preserve District of Cook County, is a 385-acre living plant museum featuring twenty-four distinct display gardens surrounded by lakes, as well as four natural areas. The Garden's programs educate visitors of all ages about plants and the natural world, from day campers to high school students, to certificate, Masters and PhD students to lifelong learners. The Visitor Center houses the Plant Information Service, Garden Café and Garden Shop. The Regenstein Center houses exhibition halls, the Lenhardt Library and Greenhouses. The Plant Conservation Science Center houses the Green Roof Garden and Visitor Gallery with interactive interpretation of the plant research being done behind the scenes.

🕐 Year round, daily, 8 a.m. to dusk, with extended summer and winter holiday season hours.

💲 Free. Parking fees apply.

➲ Located 0.5 mile east of Edens Expressway/ Route 41 on Lake Cook Road.

DU PAGE COUNTY

WHEATON

CANTIGNY
1 South 151 Winfield Road, Wheaton
(630) 668-5161, www.cantigny.org

The Formal Gardens, opened in 1977, are a prime example of a relaxed Midwest display landscape, created to be calm and free flowing. The formal gardens encompass about 30 acres of ornamental landscapes. Two of the many highlights include the Rose Garden and the one-acre Idea Garden, designed to educate and inspire home gardeners. A variety of programs are offered throughout the year, including floral workshops, gardening lectures, free tours and monthly bird walks. Spanning nearly thrity acres, this lush horticultural masterpiece is one of the largest display gardens in the Midwest, showcasing perennials, ground covers, flowering bulbs, shrubs and trees. In addition, the gardens include more than 160,000 annuals, all grown in Cantigny's renowned greenhouses. Visitors are encouraged to stroll the gardens throughout the four seasons to witness their ever-changing beauty. Please visit cantigny.org for more information including hours, parking fees, directions and a calendar of upcoming events or call 630.668.5161

🕐 November through April, Monday through Sunday, 9 a.m. dusk. May through October, Monday through Sunday, 7 a.m. to dusk. *Cantigny Gardens & Grounds are closed all of January and Monday through Thursday in February.

💲 $5 per car; bus rates available. Weekday, off peak rates $2 per car.

➲ Take I-88 west to Winfield Road exit. Go north about 2 miles. Entrance is on right before Roosevelt Road/Route 38.

MASSACHUSETTS

Martha's Vineyard

Saturday, May 28

🕐 **10a.m. to 2 p.m.**
$7 admission

 DIGGING DEEPER: The Dexter Rhododendrons in a Collector's Garden at Blueberry Ridge Farm, Chilmark 3 p.m.

DUKES COUNTY

CHILMARK

📍 **BLUEBERRY RIDGE GARDEN**
19 Blueberry Ridge Lane, Chilmark

 DIGGING DEEPER

The garden is located on approximately four acres and was started in 2002, so many of the plantings are still young, with the largest, most mature rhodies at close to fourteen years old. It is located in a low area between two sets of hills to the north and south, crisscrossed by old stone walls. Native species to this area are highbush blueberry (*Vaccinium corymbosum*), cinnamon and royal fern (*Osmunda cinnamo-*

mea and *regalis*), summersweet (*Clethra alnifolia*), swamp azalea (*Rhododendron viscosum*), holly and inkberry (*Ilex opaca* and *I. glabra*), sheep laurel (*Kalmia angustifolia*) under a canopy of tall pitch pines (*Pinus rigida*), red and white oak, beetlebung or tupelo (*Nyssa sylvatica*) and swamp maples (*Acer rubrum*). There are also spring ephemerals which may have gone past including anemone, *Trientalis borealis*, and star flower. The main plant collections include more than 1,200 rhododendrons, Japanese maples and hydrangeas with smaller groupings of mountain laurel, epimedium, and tree peonies. In the fenced in yard behind the house are two large herbaceous perennial,... [Read full description online]

2015 | ♿ |

➲ Three miles west (sign to Menemsha) of intersection of North Road and State Road. Go 0.25 mile past Tea Lane to Blueberry Ridge Lane on left. Garden entrance is 0.25 mile on right. Cars must park near deer gate, which will lower as car passes over it. Limited 10 cars at one time.

 DIGGING DEEPER

SATURDAY, MAY 28 | 3 PM

THE DEXTER RHODODENDRONS
IN A COLLECTOR'S GARDEN

with Peter Norris

AT: Blueberry Ridge Garden
     19 Blueberry Ridge Lane, Chilmark

In the early twentieth century, the hybridizing and propagation efforts of Charles Owen Dexter were responsible for over 80% of all rhododendrons in the US. Today, his influential role is virtually unknown to any but rhododendron enthusiasts. Late in life, Dexter moved to Sandwich, MA, where he created at least 145 varieties of rhododendrons. These Dexter hybrids are noted for their dense foliage, robust stature, and flowers—often exquisitely scented—of superior size and color. Dexter rarely kept written records of his crosses and he never named them. As a result, only a limited record of his important accomplishments remained. Shortly after Dexter's death, horticulturists began working to locate, catalogue, propagate and preserve as many of the Dexter hybrids as possible. Today's host, Peter Norris, was part of this massive effort as a member of the informal Sandwich Club. At their peak bloom and fragrance, Peter will introduce participants to many of Dexter's spectacular hybrids, and tell the fascinating story of this individual and the efforts to preserve his creations.

Registration is required and space is limited. **Opendaysprogram.org or call 1(888) 842-2442**

Greater Boston Area

Sunday, June 5

🕐 **10 a.m. to 4 p.m.**

$7 per garden

★ Start your day at the Mary M. B. Wakefield Estate in Milton. Maps will be available.

 EXPERTS IN THE GARDEN: Judith Tankard, Shapiro/Bloomberg Garden, Milton, 10 a.m. to 4 p.m.

OUR PARTNER IN THE BOSTON AREA

MARY M.B. WAKEFIELD ESTATE

 Each June, the Wakefield Estate welcomes visitors to celebrate the annual blooming of hundreds of Polly Wakefield's kousa dogwood trees during "Dogwood Days". As host garden, the Wakefield Estate has helped us line up three remarkable gardens, some with historical pedigrees and others representing remarkable accomplishments of local gardeners and landscape designers. Begin your day at the Wakefield Estate, pick up a map and head out to see some or all of these great and inspiring gardens. A guided tour of the Wakefield Estate will be offered at 1:00 p.m., rain or shine.

NORFOLK COUNTY

MILTON

 GARDEN OF CHRISTINE PAXHIA
1027 Brush Hill Road, Milton

Christine Paxhia created her garden of sensory splendor from nothing. She says, "when we first moved in, there was not one desirable plant." After clearing out the overgrown invasives beneath the white pines and Norway spruce that surround the property, Paxhia began to assess her options. She designed her garden based on what would grow well in the different pockets and zones of her garden with an emphasis on an abundance of color, texture, and aromatic plants and flowers. Today, her garden offers months of delight with a wide array of unusual perennials, viburnums, lilacs, and peonies. A blend of sun and shady areas of the garden offered an oppor-

tunity for Paxhia to play with groupings and fragrant compositions such as with her pairing of an unusual carpet dianthus (with a smell of cinnamon) and a white lilac 'hyacinthiflora' making for a heady mix for the passersby. Her collection of peonies includes not only the standard single and double varieties but also tree and intersectional plants chosen for their fragrance or unusual attributes. Her "shade wonderland" incorporates a broad spectrum of native and woodland plants with an emphasis on textures and colors. Paxhia considers her garden a "teaching garden" enabling her to play the role of *Brush Hill Garden Guru* that became the name of her business, but she is quick to add that it is not a cookie cutter garden nor is it perfectly manicured, preferring a more natural look. While she's committed to including as many native plants as she can (especially to support her beehive), she confesses she can't do without select ornamentals like the peonies, striving rather for a "happy mix."

NEW

➲ From Route I-95/128, take Exit 2B in Canton for Route 138 North. Bear right on Canton Avenue, then take an immediate left in order to effectively turn onto Brush Hill Road. Go approximately 1 mile, #1027 is on the left.

From the Wakefield Estate, turn left onto Brush Hill Road and go 1 mile, #1027 is on left.

 SHAPIRO/BLOOMBERG GARDEN— THE FORMER "MRS. HOLDEN MCGINLEY GARDEN" DESIGNED BY ELLEN BIDDLE SHIPMAN
582 Blue Hill Avenue, Milton

 EXPERTS IN THE GARDEN

The extraordinary Shapiro/Bloomberg Garden is a carefully preserved historic garden designed for Mrs. Holden McGinley by Ellen Biddle Shipman in 1925, at the peak of Shipman's illustrious career as one of America's premiere landscape architects. A stunning example of Shipman's garden design philosophy of closely integrating house and garden, the garden has an axis luring the visitor out from the house's garden room across the lawn into the walled garden. There, another axis transitions through a series of three long, narrow descending garden rooms, each on a successively lower level and each with its own distinctive character. Most of the original detail is intact including an original bluestone rill which traverses the uppermost panel. This garden shows how Shipman often skillfully combined formal and wild gardens in a compressed suburban setting. Shipman was known for her walled gardens stating, "planting, however beautiful, is not a garden. A garden must be enclosed... or otherwise it would merely be a cultivated area." Using this prototypical layout here, the garden is enclosed and surrounded by high whitewashed brick walls which match the mansion. Recently acquired by Ellen Shapiro and her husband Michael Bloomberg, this important garden now receives the protection and care it so richly deserves. Open Day visitors are fortunate to have this rare opportunity to glimpse an intact masterwork by the "Dean of American Women Landscape Architects."

NEW

➲ From Route I-93, take Exit 2B in Canton for Route 138 North. Travel 3.2 miles, continuing on Route 138/Blue Hill Avenue. #582 is on the right.

From the Wakefield Estate, turn right onto Brush Hill Road, then turn left onto Route 138/Blue Hill Avenue. Travel approximately 2 miles north to #582 on the right.

SUFFOLK COUNTY

WEST ROXBURY

 DUSTMAN-RYAN GARDEN
353 Park Street, West Roxbury

This garden reflects the creative efforts of a mighty team: Christie Dustman, professional Garden Designer and Patti Ryan, a professional furniture maker. In their own personal garden, these two artists have let nothing hinder their zeal for plants, stone and whimsy.

The garden is in its tenth season and its transformation was done in phases, keeping only a privet hedge and one Andromeda. The garden uses plants and objects as sculptures in an array of vignettes and intentional views. By showcasing some plants and objects against the background of plants and elements, this garden has many levels of complexity and interest. As members of the Conifer Society, you will find more than fifty different conifers, as well as rare and unusual plants. It is the reclaimed and cast off items used as art and decoration like basketball hoops and organ pipes that often command the most "ooohs and ahhhs".

2014 | ♿ | 📷

➲ From Route 128/I-95 North, take Route 1/ Providence Highway north from Exit 15A or 15B. At Washington Street, bear slightly right and proceed north about 2 miles. Turn left onto Lagrange Street about 0.2 mile past Maplewood Street. Go 0.3 mile and turn right onto Robin Street, just past Searle Road. Take the third left onto Park Street. The garden is at #353. Please park along street.

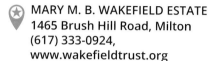

LEAD GARDEN
✳ PUBLIC GARDEN

NORFOLK COUNTY
MILTON

📍 **MARY M. B. WAKEFIELD ESTATE**
1465 Brush Hill Road, Milton
(617) 333-0924,
www.wakefieldtrust.org

★ Start your day here on the June 5 Greater Boston Open Day.

🕐 Special Garden Conservancy Open Day Saturday, June 5, 10 a.m. to 4 p.m.

💲 $5 during Open Day

This Open Day coincides with the Wakefield Estate's own Dogwood Days, timed to give the public a rare opportunity to enjoy our collection of hundreds of Chinese Dogwoods at their spectacular peak bloom.

See this garden's listing on page 120.

🎓 EXPERTS IN THE GARDEN

SUNDAY JUNE 5 | 10 AM TO 4 PM
JUDITH TANKARD
AT: Shapiro-Bloomberg Garden, Milton, MA

Judith B Tankard will be at the Shapiro-Bloomberg Garden to talk about the importance of this historic garden and its famous designer, Ellen Shipman. Designed in the 1920s as a series of stunning outdoor rooms, it was embellished with Shipman's signature water features, garden ornament, and flower borders. The Massachusetts Horticultural Society commended it for its "great charm and restraint." Judith is a landscape historian and author of books on Shipman and other landscape architects. She is a Garden Conservancy Fellow and an Open Days host on Martha's Vineyard.

Eric Roth

Outer Cape

Saturday, June 11

🕐 **10 a.m. to 4 p.m.**
$7 per garden

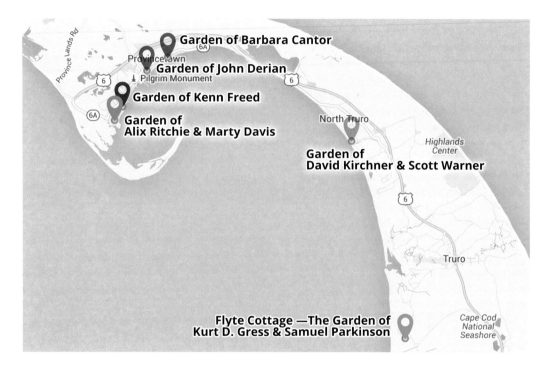

Parking in Provincetown:

The MacMillan Pier Lot, in Provincetown Center (at Lopes Square, near the intersection of Commercial and Standish Streets) is convenient to the Garden of John Derian and Garden of Barbara Cantor.

The West End Parking Lot (located on Commercial Street, roughly across from 50 Commercial Street) is convenient to the Garden of Alix Ritchie & Marty Davis and the Garden of Kenn Freed. There is also limited metered parking on Commercial Street itself further down from the parking lot.

Visit the Town of Provincetown's website, (www.provincetown-ma.gov) for more parking information.

BARNSTABLE COUNTY

NORTH TRURO

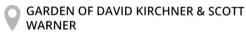

📍 **GARDEN OF DAVID KIRCHNER & SCOTT WARNER**
6 & 8 Twine Field Road, North Truro

Our garden surrounds two vine-covered, late-nineteenth-century cottages atop a challenging windswept site overlooking Cape Cod Bay. Slightly less than an acre in size, the garden is dominated by romantic cottage-style plantings of perennials, flowering shrubs, and self-seeding annuals and biennials in a cool color palette. The garden also includes a "hot" border that comes to life in summer in shades of orange, red, and violet; a large collection of succulents displayed on decks and along walkways; a "Mediterranean" planting in front of a south-facing dry-stack wall sheltering plants generally not hardy in this Zone 7A location; and a wooded glade filled with newly planted native shrubs and other shade lovers. A highlight of our garden is a collection of more than eighty different kinds of roses—climbers, ramblers, and shrubs—most of which are heirloom and old garden varieties. We have designed the garden so that planted areas merge seamlessly with the native grasses, beach plums, bayberries, wild roses, and red cedars that occur naturally on the site.

NEW | 📷

➲ From Boston/Mid-Cape: From Route 6 East, take the North Truro/Shore Road exit (to the left), which puts you on Route 6A (Shore Road). Continue on 6A for approximately 1.2 miles (passing Truro Vineyards on right) until you reach a blinking traffic light/four-corner intersection. (The Salty Market is a landmark at this intersection.) Here, turn left onto Pond Road, which dead ends into the Cold Storage Beach parking lot. Park in the beach parking area (See parking instructions.)

From Provincetown: From Route 6 West, take the Highland Road/North Truro exit (approximately 6 miles from Provincetown). Turn right following sign marked North Truro/Pond Village. At the blinking traffic light/four-corner intersection, (The Salty Market is on your right), cross Route 6A and continue straight onto Pond Road. Pond Road dead ends into the Cold Storage Beach parking lot. Park in the beach parking area (See parking instructions.)

Please park in the Cold Storage Beach lot at the end of Pond Road, above Cape Cod Bay. As you enter the beach parking lot, to far right you will see a tall cedar fence with an open gate that leads into the garden. Enter here.

PROVINCETOWN

📍 **GARDEN OF BARBARA CANTOR**
546 Commercial Street, Provincetown

A striking feature of this town garden is its long brick walkway flanked with beds of billowing catmint punctuated by bearded iris, larkspur, and California poppies. The garden also features perfectly framed views out to Provincetown Harbor and charming borders filled with climbing roses, peonies, lupine, geraniums, thalictrum, crambe, and other cottage garden plants. Elements of structure are provided by classic white picket fencing and neatly trimmed privet hedges. Along Commercial Street, a spreading zelkova tree shelters a mixed planting of lady's mantle, foxglove, columbine, and other plants that flourish in the dappled shade beneath.

NEW | 📷

➲ We do not recommend driving from garden to garden in Provincetown. Instead, follow the suggested parking instructions provided for the gardens and walk to the gardens from the suggested public parking areas for each.

📍 **GARDEN OF JOHN DERIAN**
396 Commercial Street, Provincetown

The small town garden of designer John Derian surrounds an historic and unique eighteenth-century house as well as the Provincetown outpost of John Derian Company's New York City-based shop. A remarkable feature of the garden is a ten-foot-high hornbeam enclosure that shelters a large raised bed—filled with a constantly changing seasonal "menu" of vegetables, herbs, and cut flowers—surrounded by a thick straw mulch that brings a bit of the country to this garden in the center of town. The house's elegant front façade is complemented by a loose planting of native bayberry rising above a well-manicured privet hedge. A mixed herbaceous and shrub border provides color and screening for an area reserved for outdoor entertaining.

NEW | 📷

➲ We do not recommend driving from garden to garden in Provincetown. Instead, follow the suggested parking instructions provided for the gardens and walk to the gardens from the suggested public parking areas for each. Visitors will enter the garden from Law Street.

GARDEN OF KENN FREED
70A Commercial Street, Provincetown

Visitors to this small town garden surrounding an historic nineteenth-century house are greeted by cloud-pruned boxwood in the front garden and a gravel area filled with a riot of self-seeding lupines, corn poppies, larkspur, ox-eye daisies, foxgloves, and California poppies. Other features include a spectacular display of coleus of all shapes and colors in an array of pots; a mixed planting of hardy and tender perennials (including thalictrum, euphorbia, veronicastrum, salvias in variety); and a rock wall with a hot and dry western exposure covered with a mosaic of sedums accented by sempervivums massed in a well-curated collection of unique containers.

NEW |

↻ We do not recommend driving from garden to garden in Provincetown. Instead, follow the suggested parking instructions provided for the gardens and walk to the gardens from the suggested public parking areas for each. Enter the garden from West Vine Street.

GARDEN OF ALIX RITCHIE & MARTY DAVIS
8 Commercial Street, Provincetown

This large garden, completely hidden from the road, is full of surprises. It features a wide variety of creative plantings that take advantage of the many microclimates found on the site. The garden includes cottage-style borders with color schemes that evolve through the seasons, changing from sparkling silvers and whites in June (spires of white foxgloves, drifts of ox-eye daisies, and statuesque Scotch thistles) to rich and vibrant hot colors later in summer and into fall, when crocosmias, salvias, and agapanthus provide bold interest. Visitors will encounter a succession of garden vignettes—a potager, box hedging, charming groupings of pots, azaleas, clematis in variety,

historic outbuildings, and a tranquil shade garden with ferns, epimediums, hostas, rodgersias, and spring ephemerals—culminating in a hillside covered by a grove of native tupelos.

NEW |

↻ We do not recommend driving from garden to garden in Provincetown. Instead, follow the suggested parking instructions provided for the gardens and walk to the gardens from the suggested public parking areas for each.

TRURO

FLYTE COTTAGE —THE GARDEN OF KURT D. GRESS & SAMUEL PARKINSON
9 Ryder Beach Road, Truro

This Cape Cod garden has been in the making for about twelve years and is an ever-changing and expanding place set on a tranquil hill with distant views of Cape Cod Bay. It has the advantage of temperate Truro seasons brought about by the ocean's proximity, and being set back from the shore, it is partly protected from punishing winter winds. The garden is made up of several different areas that are tightly planted with a mixture of shrubs, trees, roses, herbs, and perennials set within stone paths, walls, picket fences, and garden structures. The garden's color palette is primarily blue, white, and yellow except within the Pink Garden (which is, as you guessed, mostly shades of pink). The garden also includes a number of collected garden pieces and ornaments made of stone and metal to add companionship to the plants. While neither formal nor wild, the garden is overall rather exuberant in fullness as it sits peacefully within the Cape Cod landscape.

NEW |

↻ From Boston/Mid-Cape, take Route 6 East to Pamet Road/Truro Center exit and bear right toward South Pamet Road/Truro. You will very shortly reach a "T" intersection; there, turn right and follow the sign toward Truro Center. At the next "T" intersection, turn left onto Truro Center Road, and then take an immediate right onto Depot Road. After 0.5 mile, bear left at the fork onto Old County Road. Continue on Old County Road for approximately 1.7 miles, then turn right onto Ryder Beach Road. The property is approximately 0.1 miles on the right. (Follow parking instructions for 9 Ryder Beach Road).

From Provincetown, take Route 6 West and turn right onto Truro Center Road (about 9 miles from Provincetown). Continue on Truro Center Road for 0.8 mile, then take slight right onto Depot Road. In 0.5 mile, bear left at the fork onto Old County Road. At 1.7 miles, turn right onto Ryder Beach Road. The property is about 0.1 mile on right. (Follow parking instructions for 9 Ryder Beach Road). Visitors are asked to park along Ryder Beach Road on the side of the street opposite from the driveway. Very limited parking is available near the house for those who are physically challenged.

Bristol County

Saturday, June 11

🕐 **10 a.m. to 4 p.m.**
$7 per garden

🏷 Pop-up Nursery
Tranquil Lake Nursery

There are gardens open on this day in nearby Providence, RI. See page 276.

BRISTOL COUNTY

REHOBOTH

📍 **GARDEN OF MARJORIE & DON DEANGELIS**
134 Hillside Avenue, Rehoboth

The garden is a fenced in garden surrounding a pool and patio with broad views of nearby fields. The garden and plantings in the front of the house were recently redesigned and replanted. A new fence and stone wall were installed as main features of the garden. Consequently, it is a young garden that features annuals and grasses for color and textures.

NEW | ♿ partial | 📷

➲ Take I-95 to 195 East and cross the George

Washington Bridge. Keep right to exit onto Route 44. Bear right at the fork in exit ramp onto Taunton Avenue. Follow Route 44 through East Providence, and Seekonk, to Rehoboth. Taunton Avenue turns slightly right and becomes Waterman Avenue in 0.2 mile. Turn left onto Hall Street and go 0.1 mile. Turn right onto Route 44/Taunton Avenue and go 4.8 miles. Turn left onto River Street and go 0.5 miles. Turn left onto Hillside Avenue.

MCILWAIN GARDEN
37 Medalist Drive, Rehoboth

This young garden abuts a golf course, providing expansive views in the English landscape tradition. Optimal plantings have been chosen for the range of challenging ecosystems from rocky/dry soil to windy sites with wet soil. A cluster of trees with filtered sunlight hosts rhododendrons, azalea, pieris, enkiantus, hellebores, and more. Most of the garden enjoys full sun. This is a garden for all seasons with the blossoms of the Okame cherries, saucer and star magnolias ushering in early spring followed soon thereafter by daffodils, grape hyacinth, Spanish bluebells, ground phlox, and PJM azalea. Early May sees the arrival of tulips, azaleas, the sweetly fragrant *Viburnum carlessi*, and lilies of the valley. By mid-May, the bearded iris have opened, along with the chives, allium, bleeding heart, and rhododendrons. By June, this is followed in swift succession by dogwoods, Virginia magnolia with lemon-scented blossoms, peonies, Dutch iris and gumpo azalea, coral bells, catmint, campanula, clematis and *Geranium bikova*. By late June, summer has arrived with hydrangea, roses, foxgloves, garden phlox, daisies, veronica, lavender, astilbe, blue salvia, anise hyssop, and Russian sage. Fall comes with assorted mums and asters and flaming fall foliage of a variety of Japanese maples along with red berries on the viburnum, holly trees, and winterberry. The red-twig dogwood shrubs maintain winter interest along with the topiary boxwood and mottled bark of the Stewartii tree. An herb garden with armillary sphere under planted with alpine strawberries is flanked by a blueberry/raspberry patch, pergola, and roses with lavender.

NEW

➲ From I-195 take Exit 1 in Massachusetts for Route 114A. (Do NOT take Exit 7 in Rhode Island to Barrington via Route 114.). Proceed north on Route 114A through several lights to Route 44/Taunton Avenue. Turn right and go east through Seekonk and into Rehoboth where you will see a flashing yellow light. Proceed east about 0.9 mile to Mills Plaza on left. Drive another 0.3 mile to Bairos Construction followed by the cluster of stores of Winthrop Commons on left. Immediately after Winthrop Commons, turn left onto River Street (it is hard to see). On River Street, cross the 4-way stop, continue about 0.4 mile (passing Tranquil Lake Nursery on right) and turn left onto Hillside Avenue. Drive 0.8 mile, passing the Hillside Country Club on right, and turn right at the next road marked by a sign for Hillside Estates. This is Medalist Drive; proceed to the first house on the right which is #37 (red brick with white columns).

SEEKONK

ANDREW GROSSMAN'S
DISPLAY GARDENS
393 Fall River Avenue, Seekonk

My gardens, which border the Martin Wildlife Refuge and the Runnins River, showcase a wide variety of perennials, shrubs, and grasses. The property includes a blue-and-white garden, a hot colored garden with a checkerboard thyme patio, a cottage garden planted with roses and other old-fashioned favorites, and a rustic pond surrounded by bog plantings. There is also a cutting garden currently planted with tea roses and dinner plate dahlias. The property is featured in Design New England's 2016 March/April issue and is currently a finalist in HGTV's Gorgeous Gardens competition.

2011 | ♿ partial |

⮑ From Providence, take I-95 east to Exit 1/
Seekonk/Barrington/Route 114A. You are now
about five minutes from the house. At exit
traffic light, bear left for Seekonk. Go through
two more lights. At flashing light, bear left and
stay on Route 114A/Fall River Avenue (do not
go straight). Gristmill Restaurant and parking
lot are on right, then a large yellow house
on left. Take gravel driveway, marked by two
white wooden columns, immediately past
the yellow house on left, opposite parking lot
for Vinny's Antiques. The gardens are at end
of driveway. Please park in driveway or in lot
across street.

From I-95 West, proceed as directed above,
but turn right off the exit and only go through
one light before flashing light.

✳ PUBLIC GARDEN

BRISTOL COUNTY
REHOBOTH

📍 **TRANQUIL LAKE NURSERY**
45 River Street, Rehoboth
(508) 252-4002, tranquil-lake.com

🕐 9 a.m. to 5 p.m.

🏷 Tranquil Lake Nursery

🚩 Guided Tour: **10 a.m.**

$ Free

See this garden's listing on page 137.

Nantucket Open Day

Thursday, June 23

🕐 **Hours vary by garden
(Starting at 10 a.m.)**
$7 per garden

NANTUCKET COUNTY
NANTUCKET

📍 **CARRIED AWAY**
6 Salt Marsh Road, Nantucket

🕐 10 a.m. to 3 p.m.

At Carried Away, you'll see a variety of
unique garden spaces with different themes.
From the boxwood parterre courtyard that
is adorned with planters and roses, to the
cutting garden mixed with unique varieties of
specialty plants, to the expansive perennial
borders that deliver you to the waters edge to
view Nantucket harbor and a perfect view of
town. Trellises of blooming roses abound the

estate creating a dreamy feel as you wander this garden peninsula in Monomoy.

NEW

⮑ From the rotary take Milestone Road. Bear left at Monomoy Road. Salt Marsh Road is the first road on left. Please park on Monomoy Road and walk down Salt Marsh to the Last house straight ahead.

📍 JOLY'S GARDEN
42 Shimmo Pond Road, Nantucket
🕐 10 a.m. to 4 p.m.

A family house for three generations, Low Shimmo, was originally the Shimmo Yacht Club when it was built in the late 1920s. A naturalist's garden Low Shimmo was designed for avid birders, attracting all types of feathered friends. The garden sits nestled into the dune at the bottom of Shimmo Pond Road and features sweeping views of the harbor accented by classic Nantucket Hydrangeas on the waterside. On the entry side of the house are two garden rooms. One is the entry garden highlighting a traditional perennial border. The other is an enclosed terrace garden featuring a steep grade planted with naturalizing perennials, annuals and grasses. The *Stewartia* in this area is noteworthy and thriving. This is the quintessential seaside house and garden.

NEW | ♿ partial | 📷

⮑ From the rotary take Milestone Road bear left onto Polpis Road. Turn left onto Shimmo Pond Road before Moors End Farm, follow the dirt road staying to the left at every opportunity. You will reach 42 on the left; drive by the driveway and park in the Shimmo Association parking lot between 42 and 46 Shimmo Pond Road.

Parking for this garden and Patsy's Garden is at the Shimmo Association parking lot.

📍 SUZIE GROTE'S GARDEN
16 Cathcart Road, Nantucket
🕐 10 a.m. to 4 p.m.

Traveling down the dirt road to this property one finds a house tucked among all native Nantucket woodland plants and beautiful specimen trees. Rounding the corner to the back is an unexpected treat—a riot of color framing an exquisite view of the harbor! Lush perennials, overflowing pots, stone walls, a blue stone terrace, an outdoor room, and a split-rail fence in the distance all add to the enjoyment of this garden. It's amazing that this garden is only one year old.

NEW

⮑ Head toward Milestone Road on Monomoy Road. Bear left onto Boston Ave which turns into Brewster Avenue then bear left onto Cathcart Road. Number 16 is on left.

📍 PATSY'S GARDEN
42 Shimmo Pond Road, Nantucket
🕐 10 a.m. to 4 p.m.

This garden was created as an exuberant country garden, mixed with wildflowers, favorite hollyhocks, wild sweet peas, cabbages, roses, hydrangea, Cape Cod rambling roses, and a 'grounding' of boxwood—a collector's garden from a world traveler and gardener wanting to enjoy her summer season on Nantucket. A year later we removed ninety percent of the new garden in order to install an enormous new septic system so a small exercise pool could be added. As all available space was taken, Mrs. Walsh inspired me to simply fill in the only other place we could— the slope of the hill. A large retaining wall was built, filled, faced with native stone, the exercise pool installed, and the garden recreated while moving several of the large cherry trees outside the hedgerow to the slope. The garden was reinstalled and we continue to do what gardeners do—experiment, tweak, transplant, try new introductions, inherit heirloom plants, fight off clever bunnies and crafty deer.

NEW

➲ From the rotary take Milestone Road bear left onto Polpis Road. Turn left onto Shimmo Pond Road before Moors End Farm, follow the dirt road staying to the left at every opportunity. You will reach 42 on the left; drive by the driveway and park in the Shimmo Association parking lot between 42 and 46 Shimmo Pond Road.

Parking for this garden and Joly's Garden is at the Shimmo Association parking lot. Handicapped/disabled drop-off is available in the upper driveway.

📍 **UNICORN'S DELIGHT**
60 Monomoy Road, Nantucket
🕐 10 a.m. to 4 p.m.

Step through the privet archway into a jewel-box garden reminiscent of Monet's paintings of Giverny. Designed for summer enjoyment, this garden combines the sensibilities of self-sufficient plantings with playful expressions of calming colors, textures, and movement.

NEW! | 📷

➲ Continue on Monomoy Road, following the road as it makes a right turn. Number 60 Monomoy is on the left. Please park along the road. Parking on garden's side of the street only. Do not block neighbor's mailboxes. Parking on garden's side of the street only. Do not block neighbor's mailboxes.

Greater Boston

Saturday, August 13

🕐 **Hours vary by garden
(Starting at 10 a.m.)**

$7 per garden

 DIGGING DEEPER: Garden Design Tips from a Tropical Paradise Near Boston, with Ellen Lathi & Kerry Ann Mendez, Needham, 2 p.m.

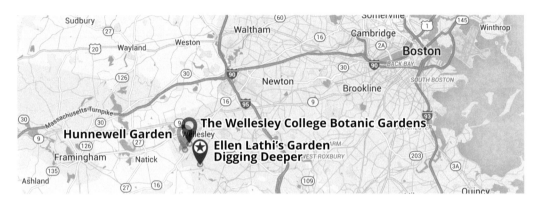

NORFOLK COUNTY

NEEDHAM

 **ELLEN LATHI'S GARDEN
119 Locust Lane, Needham**

🕐 10 a.m. to 4 p.m.

The woodland surrounding our house inspired the gardens that now wind through the forest, around the bog, and through a sunny mixed border toward the house. Here, an abundance of spring-flowering bulbs, shrubs and trees, summer annuals and perennials, fall-blooming ornamental grasses, and winter evergreens all celebrate the individuality of our New England seasons. Highlighted are collections of Japanese maples, beech, deciduous conifers, bamboos and grasses of every type, and large-leafed plants, which love wet and boggy conditions. Using very few flowers in the garden, we attempt to achieve a bold, colorful effect through the seasons using gold and burgundy foliage, leaf variegation, and texture. The garden, now nine years old, is spread over the two-acre property, connected by a series of stepping-stone and mulched paths with transitions punctuated by lichen-covered natural stone and rustic garden ornaments. Destinations we particularly enjoy include a stone gathering area in the woods, a natural bog and creek, a folly at the end of a Nyssa-lined allée, a covered bridge with a special view, and most recently, an oval front entrance garden. The garden is the glue that binds us, a magical place that allows us to dream and play as the years go by. Within this plot of land that we love, where change is the only constant, native woodland and designed landscape are celebrated together.

2008 | ♿ | 📷

➲ Take Route 128 to Exit 21/Newton-Wellesley/Route 16. Turn right off ramp and follow Route 16 west towards Wellesley just over 3 miles to where 5 streets meet in Wellesley Square. Take most extreme left turn onto Grove Street and go 1.8 miles to end. Turn right onto Charles River Street. Go 0.2 mile to first street on right, Locust Lane. Turn right (white rocks at mouth of street) and go 0.2 mile to second house from end, #119. Please park on street.

 HUNNEWELL GARDEN
845 Washington Street, Wellesley

🕐 10 a.m. to 2 p.m.

Four generations of the Hunnewell family have had a hand in this estate garden, which includes a formal azalea garden and pinetum. Greenhouses produce delicate camellias, exotic orchids, flowers, and fruit. The highlight of your visit is bound to be the whimsical yet monumental clipped evergreens, which adorn the sloping shores of Lake Waban.
2004

➲ From Massachusetts Turnpike/I-90 west, take Exit 16. Follow signs to Route 16 west/Washington Street. Follow about 5 miles,

passing through Wellesley Hills, to center of Wellesley. Follow Route 16/South Natick/Holliston. Next traffic light marks entrance to Wellesley College. Proceed 0.6 mile to #845. Follow parking instructions.

 # PUBLIC GARDEN

WELLESLEY

 THE WELLESLEY COLLEGE BOTANIC GARDENS
727 Washington St, Wellesley
www.wellesley.edu/wcbg

🕐 Outdoor spaces open daily, dawn to dusk.
$ Free

See this garden's listing on page 140.

 **DIGGING DEEPER**

SATURDAY, AUGUST 13 | 2 PM
GARDEN DESIGN TIPS FROM A TROPICAL PARADISE NEAR BOSTON
AT: Ellen Lathi's Garden, 119 Locust Lane, Needham

Ellen Lathi's breathtaking gardens—featuring ten-foot banana trees and lush compositions of perennials, flowering shrubs, conifers and ornamental trees—have been showcased in numerous gardening magazines. Join Kerry Ann Mendez, award-winning speaker, author and designer, as she and Ellen lead an informal master class in this inspirational garden, sharing practical insights on how to create or enhance your own piece of paradise.

Registration is required and space is limited. **Opendaysprogram.org or call 1(888) 842-2442**

Carlisle Open Day

Sunday, September 18

 10 a.m. to 4 p.m.
$7 admission

 DIGGING DEEPER: Growing Food at Clock Barn Farm—A Program for Families, Carlisle

MIDDLESEX COUNTY

CARLISLE

 GARDENS AT CLOCK BARN—HOME OF MAUREEN & MIKE RUETTGERS
453 Bedford Road, Carlisle

 DIGGING DEEPER

The Gardens at Clock Barn have been created by the Ruettgers over the last thirty years. The house and drying barn date back to 1790. As you enter the gardens through an arched gate, you walk by the old barn which has trays filled with herbs and flowers from the cutting garden beyond. These trays were built in the late 1930s as a Works Progress Administration project for the drying of digitalis leaves for medicinal use. A grape arbor leads into a walled garden with four quadrants anchored by antique roses and mixed borders with sweeps of foxgloves, *Salvia viridis*, and nepeta intertwined with salad greens and edible herbs. A second tier is flanked by two reflecting pools fringed by *Allium senescens montanum* and an herbal tapestry design mirrored on each side. A greenhouse and potting area houses a collection of more than forty varieties of scented geraniums on one side and pots of kaffir limes, Meyer lemons, figs, bay, and rosemary on the other. Exiting the glass house, a canopy of 100-year-old oaks provides shade for paths that wind through a series of woodland gardens and past a small pond and water feature bordered by hakonechloa. Hosta divisions from the garden of Francis Williams anchor the first shade garden. Favorite plantings in these gardens include anemones, epimedi-

ums, *Kirengeshoma palmata*, *Jeffersonia dubia*, and shade-loving peonies. The path widens as you exit the gardens through a hornbeam arch to finish the tour below the face of The Clock Barn.

2009 | ♿ | 📷

➲ From Boston, take Route 24 south to Exit 14A and merge onto I-495 South. Take Exit 7A for Route 24 North toward Boston. Merge onto Route 24 North and go about 18 miles. Take Exit 21B to merge onto I-93 South toward I-95. Continue on I-95 North for 21 miles. Take Exit 31B for Route 4 North/Route 225 West. Merge onto Bedford Street/Route 225/Route 4 and continue to follow Route 225/Route 4 for 2.8 miles. Turn left at Carlisle Road/Route 225. Turn right to stay on Carlisle Road/Route 225 and follow to destination on right.

Gardens at Clock Barn—Home of Maureen & Mike Ruettgers, featured in *Outstanding American Gardens: A Celebration—25 Years of the Garden Conservancy*. Photo by Marion Brenner.

 DIGGING DEEPER

SUNDAY, SEPTEMBER 18

GROWING FOOD AT GARDENS AT CLOCK BARN—A PROGRAM FOR FAMILIES

AT: Gardens at Clock Barn—Home of Maureen & Mike Ruettgers, 453 Bedford Road, Carlisle

Renowned urban farmer, author, and Manager of the Edible Academy at New York Botanical Garden, Annie Novak, will team up with passionate gardener Maureen Ruettgers, and staff from the Clark Farm organic CSA to offer a family program at the breathtaking Gardens at Clock Barn. Learn about growing and preparing vegetables and herbs. Participants of all ages will get inspired to get their hands dirty and enjoy the fresh fruits of their labor.

Registration is required and space is limited. **Opendaysprogram.org or call 1(888) 842-2442**

❇ PUBLIC GARDENS

BRISTOL COUNTY

REHOBOTH

TRANQUIL LAKE NURSERY
45 River Street, Rehoboth
(508) 252-4002, www.tranquil-lake.com

Tranquil Lake Nursery features two acres of display gardens and ten acres of day lily and iris fields. The Siberian Irises and early season day lilies should be blooming in the fields. You will also see more that ten acres of fields of Siberian Iris and Japanese Iris and day lilies. Tranquil Lake Nursery is the largest grower of these plants in the northeast, with more than 3,000 cultivars of day lilies and more than 300 varieties each of Siberian and Japanese Iris. The Siberian Irises and early season day lilies should be blooming in the fields. You will also have the opportunity to wander among two acres of display gardens at Tranquil Lake Nursery, where you will see a diverse variety of perennials, grasses, shrubs and vines. The gardens include a number of perennial borders, mixed perennial and shrub gardens, an Entry Garden, an ornamental vegetable garden, a thyme bench, container herb garden, a new entry garden, an ornamental grass garden, a pond-side water garden, a purple garden designed to attract hummingbirds, a bog garden, a dry-scree garden, spectacular container plantings brimming with annuals and perennials, a pool with a water rill and a rain garden, bog water garden, and a new children's garden. Many of the plants in the garden are also available for sale.

🕐 Wednesday through Sunday from 9 a.m. to 5 p.m., April 22 through July 31; Wednesday through Saturday from 9 a.m. to 5 p.m., August 1 through September 30. Guided tour (free) at 10 a.m. on June 11th for Open Days visitors.

$ Free

➲ From the West, take Route 195 East out of Providence. Stay on Route 195 to Exit 1 in Massachusetts not in Rhode Island. A large "Raymour and Flanagan" furniture store on right. Turn left off ramp onto Route 114A northbound. Continue to Route 44 and turn right (approximately 3.7 miles) to Winthrop Commons on left and Rehoboth Recreation Center on right. Take an immediate left onto River Street. At stop sign go straight continuing on River Street. The nursery is about 0.3 mile further on right. During bloom season the fields of flowers light the way.

BERKSHIRE COUNTY

STOCKBRIDGE

BERKSHIRE BOTANICAL GARDEN
Routes 102 & 183, Stockbridge
(413) 298-3926, berkshirebotanical.org

Established in 1934 and revered as one of the older public display gardens in the United States, Berkshire Botanical Garden encompasses fifteen acres of land in the heart of the Berkshires. Visitors to the Garden enjoy over 3,000 species and varieties of herbaceous and woody plants that thrive in Zone 5A. Nineteen display gardens blend intimate landscapes with seasonal palettes and tapestries of fragrant and colorful perennials and over 2,000 annuals. Two mixed border gardens, perennial borders for sun and shade, a children's garden, rock garden, and native plant gardens are among the many favorite display areas. Former guest gardeners Martha Stewart (Heirloom Flower Garden), Page Dickey (Terraced Herb Garden), Jack Staub (Vegetable and Fruit Gardens), and Anthony Archer-Wills (Pond Garden) were joined in 2011 by Michael Marriott with the installation of a new rose garden planted with David Austin Roses. The 2015 theme, "Celebrate Water in the Garden" presents both informative and whimsical displays revolving around the essential element of water, from both a design perspective and a fundamental resource. Educational programs and special events offered year round.

🕐 May 1 through Columbus Day, daily

PLANTS
and Answers

THE BE-A-BETTER-GARDENER (BBG) PLANT SALE

MOTHER'S DAY WEEKEND
FRIDAY & SATURDAY, MAY 6 & 7

Annuals • Perennials • Vegetables
Expert Gardening Advice • Rare Trees & Shrubs
Woodland Plants • Containers • Tools
Answers to your Garden Questions
Garden Flea Market & Silent Auction

Plus... a variety of craft, food, and garden vendors!

EARLY BUYING FOR BBG MEMBERS: FRIDAY 9:00 -11:00 AM.

Hours for the general public: Friday 11:00 am – 5:00 pm, Saturday 9:00 am – 5:00 pm.

at the intersection of Rt. 183 & 102, Stockbridge, MA **berkshirebotanical.org**

9 a.m. to 5 p.m. Group tours available by appointment.

$ $15 adults, $14 seniors, $12 students; members and children 12 and under, free.

⮌ From the east, take I-90/Massachusetts Turnpike to Exit 2. Follow Route 102 west through Stockbridge. Entrance on left 0.1 mile past intersection with Route 183. From the west, take the New York State Thruway to Exit B3. Follow Route 22 south 0.8 miles to Route 102, then 5.9 miles east through west Stockbridge to entrance on right.

DUKES COUNTY

TISBURY

THE POLLY HILL ARBORETUM
795 State Road, Tisbury, (508) 693-9426,
www.pollyhillarboretum.org

The Polly Hill Arboretum is a unique Vineyard landscape. Crisscrossed by old stonewalls surrounding open meadows this national register-listed property is home to a collection of more than 1,600 woody plants that Polly Hill began planting from seed in 1958. At any season the Arboretum offers beauty, tranquility and abounds with horticultural and botanical rarities!

🕐 Grounds are open every day, sunrise to sunset. Visitor Center is open from Memorial Day to Columbus Day from 9:30 a.m. to 4 p.m., with daily tours at 10 a.m. in July and August. Otherwise tours are by appointment.

$ $5, members & children under 12 are free

⮌ The Arboretum is located on the island of Martha's Vineyard, in the town of West Tisbury. For directions see our website.

MIDDLESSEX COUNTY

FRAMINGHAM

NEW ENGLAND WILD FLOWER SOCIETY'S
GARDEN IN THE WOODS
180 Hemenway Road, Framingham
(508) 877-7630, www.newenglandwild.org

Only twenty-one miles from Boston, Garden in the Woods is a magical spot unlike any other botanic garden. Its sharp, glacier-made ridges spill into narrow valleys. Two miles of meandering paths lead through a towering canopy of trees to a pond, a wooded bog, numerous springs, and an ever-flowing brook. Set among forty-five acres, this living museum showcases a wide variety of rare and common native plants in naturalistic settings. For families looking to teach their children about the natural world, for adults who can't decide between a stroll in the garden and a walk in the woods, and for anyone curious about the diversity of New England's wildflowers and woody plants, Garden in the Woods offers a unique experience in a tranquil and beautiful place. Many native plants are available for purchase at the Garden Shop, which also offers snacks and a selection of gifts for gardeners.

🕐 Mid-April through October, Tuesday through Sunday and holiday Mondays 9 a.m. to 5 p.m. Last admission at 4:30 p.m. Guided walking tours Tuesday through Friday and holiday Mondays at 10 a.m. and on weekends at 2 p.m. No reservations are necessary for guided walking tours. There is no additional charge for these tours.

$ $12 Adults (18-64), $9 Seniors (65+), $6 Youths (3-17), Children under 3 admitted free. Active servicemen and women and their spouses admitted free with valid military ID. Veterans receive 50 percent discount with proof of service. Members at the Individual with Garden Access level and higher levels admitted free.

⮌ Take Route 128 to Route 20 West. Follow Route 20 8 miles and turn left onto Raymond Road for 1.3 miles to Hemenway Road, then bear right up the hill to the Garden entrance.

From the Massachusetts Turnpike to Exit 12/Route 9 East. Stay on Route 9 for 2.4 miles to the Edgell Road exit. Turn left at the lights at the top of the exit ramp onto the Route 9 overpass and Edgell Road. Follow Edgell Road 2.1 miles to the traffic lights. Turn right onto Water Street, then left onto Hemenway Road.

Continue 1.0 miles. (The road name changes to Eisenhower Road.) Turn left onto Catherine Road and take the first left off Catherine Road to the entrance.

From Route 9 Westbound, follow Route 9 into Framingham and take the exit marked Route 30 West (Same exit for Framingham State College). At top of ramp turn right onto Edgell Road and follow directions above. There are green Garden in the Woods signs which point the way from Route 9.

NORFOLK COUNTY

MILTON

MARY M. B. WAKEFIELD ESTATE
1465 Brush Hill Road, Milton
(617) 333-0924, www.wakefieldtrust.org

Open Days coincides with the Wakefield Estate's own *Dogwood Days*, timed to give the public a rare opportunity to enjoy our collection of hundreds of Chinese Dogwoods (*Cornus kousa*) at their spectacular peak bloom. Polly Wakefield grew most of these trees from seed or cuttings collected from the Arnold Arboretum. The dogwoods are planted throughout Polly's Formal Garden and Terrace Rooms along with other rare trees and shrubs, as well as lining either side of the Fountain Path Allée, that spans the entire length of the garden. It is truly a magnificent sight to behold. Gardens and nurseries surround a farmhouse circa 1730 and a 1794 Georgian mansion. The Wakefield-Davenport Estate takes its name and purpose from Mary "Polly" Wakefield, who lived most of her life at the estate. The estate is managed by the Mary M. B. Wakefield Charitable Trust which is committed to promoting life-long participatory learning using the land and resources of the Wakefield estate. Through collaborative partnerships with schools and community organizations, the Wakefield Trust carries out this mission through providing educational opportunities, tours, presentations, workshops, hands-on training, internships and other programs

covering a variety of subjects, including local history, ecology, horticulture, agriculture, archival work and historic preservation.

🕐 Special Garden Conservancy Open Day Saturday, June 5 from 10 a.m. to 4 p.m.; otherwise, estate is open Monday through Friday. A guided tour of the Wakefield Estate will be offered at 1 p.m., rain or shine.

$ $5 during Open Day

⮑ From Route I-95/128, take Exit 2B in Canton for Route 138 North. Bear right on Canton Avenue, then take an immediate left onto Brush Hill Road. Wakefield Estate entrance is the first opening in the stonewall on your left, 200 feet from the intersection and across from Fuller Village.

WELLESLEY

THE WELLESLEY COLLEGE BOTANIC GARDENS
727 Washington St, Wellesley
(781) 283-3094, www.wellesley.edu/wcbg

On a campus renowned for its beauty, these public gardens offer respite and superb learning resources. The Alexandra Botanic Garden has specimen trees and shrubs from around the world in a picturesque landscape. A tiny brook winds through the garden from a waterfall to Paramecium Pond. The H. H. Hunnewell Arboretum has several different habitats, including a maple swamp, meadow, and fragments of different forest types, with mostly native species. Other specialized gardens include a bog garden, a dwarf conifer garden, a butterfly garden, and our Edible Ecosystem Teaching Garden. Visit the Margaret C. Ferguson Greenhouses to experience plant life from the deserts of Mexico and Africa to the rainforests of Malaysia and Brazil. Seasonal displays combine with permanent collections to present an ever-changing immersion in the world of plants.

🕐 Outdoor spaces open daily, dawn to dusk. The Margaret Ferguson Greenhouses are open 8 a.m. to 4 p.m. every day of the week during the academic year.

$ Free

⮁ The Wellesley College Botanic Gardens' Visitor Center is adjacent to the Science Center and greenhouses. All visitors to the Wellesley College Botanic Gardens should park in Wellesley College's Gray Lot. For visitors with a handicap plate or placard: one handicap space is available right in front of the Visitor Center.

Participants in classes and programs held at the Wellesley College Botanic Gardens' Visitor Center should note: during the academic year when the College is in session, parking on campus is restricted. Use of the College's Davis Parking Facility or carpooling from off-campus is strongly encouraged.

MINNESOTA

Twin Cities

Saturday, August 6

🕐 **10 a.m. to 2 p.m.**
$7 per garden

HENNEPIN COUNTY

MEDINA

 WALLACE GARDENS
2700 Parkview Drive, Medina

🕐 10 a.m. to 2 p.m.

 DIGGING DEEPER

"Wallace Gardens is the finest private formal garden in America created from scratch during this century!" Of the sixty American gardens featured in international best seller, *1001 Gardens You Must See Before You Die*, Wallace Gardens is the only private garden. All others are public and supported by municipalities or foundations. See more than a dozen garden rooms: Monet Color Garden, Black & White Garden, Ornamental Grasses Garden, Roman Sculpture Garden, Mondrian Garden, Knot Garden, Tuscan Temple, Lattice Pavilion, Pentagon Arbor.

➲ Follow I-394 West and Route 12 West to Wayzata Boulevard in Wayzata. Take the exit toward Long Lake/Orono/County Road 112 from Route 12 W. Continue on Wayzata Boulevard. Take Willow Drive North to 2700 Parkview Drive.

 DIGGING DEEPER

SATURDAY, AUGUST 6 | 10 AM TO 12 PM
WALLACE GARDENS—A CLASSICAL FRAMEWORK WITH JAZZ IMPROVISATIONS
AT: Wallace Gardens
2700 Parkview Drive, Medina

During the Digging Deeper event, Wally Marx, the creator and owner of Wallace Gardens will lead a two-hour tour through the two dozen garden rooms and areas. Because of the groups' small size, each person will have the opportunity to get into detail with Wally about the design philosophy, plantings, building materials, maintenance, etc. While internationally acclaimed by garden professionals, keep in mind that Wallace Gardens has been created totally from scratch during this century by a self-taught gardener. Never open to the public, this guided tour will give insights that are unavailable to others. It will show the possibilities open to all.

Registration is required and space is limited. **Opendaysprogram.org or call 1(888) 842-2442**

MISSOURI

St. Louis

Saturday, June 11

🕐 **10 a.m. to 4 p.m.**
$7 per garden

ST. LOUIS COUNTY

LADUE

📍 **THE JACOBS GARDEN**
2 Daryl Lane, St. Louis

When visitors approach this garden, they see a classic red brick house with beautiful windows and welcoming pots of blooming flowers. However, when we enter by the side gate, the real garden begins. We see perennials and shrubs framed by a fence. As we walk through dappled shade by a wisteria-covered fence on our way into the garden, we see hellebore, heuchera, hosta, ligularia, ferns, hydrangea, dogwood, and boxwood—in addition to pots of annuals that provide color and interest. The pool includes a dock and one of the several seating/dining areas. The shape of the pool was governed by the owners' love of the dock and the feeling of being a part of the pool that the dock provides. Rock paths with stepping stones meander next to stately pine trees and hammocks, also enjoyed by the owners dog. This garden, designed by Horticulturalist Robert Dingwall, is easily maintained and truly lived in by the owners...and the dog.

NEW | ♿ | 📷

➔ Exit I-64 on Lindbergh, heading north. Turn right onto Conway Road, then left onto Daryl Lane. The garden is at the first house on the right on Daryl Lane.

ST. LOUIS

📍 **THE JAMIESON GARDEN:**
AN ARCHITECTURAL GARDEN
45 Portland Place, St. Louis

Located in St. Louis' Central West End, this mid-century house is half the size of its stately neighbors and the only modernist residence to have been built on an historic street of Beaux Arts and Georgian style mansions. Designed by Frederick Dunn in 1948, construction of the house was initially met with contention and controversy. When the owner acquired it in the late 1990s, the residence was in its original red brick with tan louver siding. After extensive research and consultation with Terence Riley, formerly curator of Architecture at MoMA, the owner elected to change the exterior to a painted white finish, consistent with modernist structures of the early twentieth century. This decision served both to unify the building materials and to enhance the scale of the house in relation to its neighbors. Following renovations to the main residence, guest house and garage/pool house, the owner contacted Moynihan & Associates to create a new landscape plan for the property, compatible with the modernist vision. The exterior hardscape... [Read the full description online]

NEW | ♿ | 📷

➲ From I-64, take the Skinker Boulevard or McCausland Avenue exit and head north to Lindell Boulevard. Take a right on Lindell, a left on Lake Avenue and a left on Portland Place. Lake Avenue is between Union Boulevard and Kingshighway Boulevard.

THE SHANGRI-LA GARDEN
9440 Old Bonhomme Road, St. Louis

This magnificent garden was transformed by the owners from a tennis court into an imaginative and creative paradise. The garden was designed and conceived according to Feng Shui principles, so there are no straight lines— only curves. There are many reveals, the first of which occurs when the visitor rounds the corner from the side of the house and sees the overall garden. The garden integrates 275 tons of boulders and diverse plantings of trees and shrubs that surround a free-form pool with its own waterfalls. To the back of the garden is a berm with boulders and multicolored foliage. Those who venture to the top

of the berm will find a springhead feeding a small stream which cascades down to a waterfall, splashing into a koi pond, which surrounds the guest house.

2013 | 📷

➲ From I-170, take the Ladue Road exit and proceed west to Dielman Road (0.5 miles). Turn north on Dielman (0.8 mile) to a four-way intersection with Old Bonhomme Road. Proceed west on Old Bonhomme to the 3rd driveway on left. Parking is off Old Bonhomme Road on White Rose Lane. No Parking on the property.

THE DAVID SHERMAN WOODLAND GARDEN
919 Tirrill Farm Road, St. Louis

The David Sherman Woodland Garden is a hidden treasure. The multifaceted garden isn't visible from the street, but, proceeding up the gravel driveway, visitors are greeted by beautiful vintage containers that are always decorated with seasonal flair to create the intimacy of an elegant country estate. The garden was conceived by David and Susan Sherman. When their puppy, Sasha, outgrew her large chain link playpen, they saw an opportunity to create a woodland garden full of interesting plant combinations and garden features, such as a fountain for attracting birds and butterflies. To bring their vision to life, they called on landscape designer, Rand Rosenthal. He took on the challenge and has guided the transformation since the early 90s. Over the years, he made a series of progressive changes to expand and enhance the original concept. Susan and David wanted their Midwest home to feature the same bright colors as their home in Naples, Florida. The perfect solution: surrounding the terrace with vintage containers filled with brightly colored... [Read the full description online]

NEW | ♿ | 📷

➲ Take the Lindbergh exit off Highway 64. Take Lindbergh to Conway; right turn onto Conway. Daryl Lane is the first street on left.

NEW HAMPSHIRE

Peterborough

Friday, August 19

 DIGGING DEEPER

FRIDAY, AUGUST 19 | 7 PM

OUTSTANDING AMERICAN GARDENS,

AT: Bass Hall, 19 Grove Street, Peterborough

In this talk, Page shows and describes a variety of private gardens in the U.S. and in Europe that especially appeal to her because of their strong sense of design, atmosphere, or spirit of originality. She will feature gardens that she has visited through Open Days (a program she co-founded in 1995) and that she has written about in numerous books, most recently *Outstanding American Gardens* which she edited to celebrate the Garden Conservancy's 25th Anniversary. She ends with some pictures of her own garden which is a favorite simply because it is hers.

Tickets will be available at local retailers, at the door, online at opendaysprogram.org or by calling 1 (888) 842-2442.

Monadnock Area

August 20, Saturday

 Hours vary by garden
(Starting at 9 a.m.)

$7 per garden

Pop-up Nurseries:
Achille Agway / Broken Arrow Nursery
/ Opus Plants / Telescopes of Vermont/
Rocky Dale Gardens

 EXPERTS IN THE GARDEN:
Tovah Martin, at Garden of Jenny Lee
Hughes & Edward Yoxen, Stoddard

EXPERTS IN THE GARDEN:
Roger Swain, at the Gardens at
Juniper Hill Farm, Francestown

CHESHIRE COUNTY

STODDARD

GARDEN OF JENNY LEE HUGHES &
EDWARD YOXEN
471 Center Pond Road, Stoddard

10 a.m. to 4 p.m.

EXPERTS IN THE GARDEN

After clearing old hillsides in 2006 for views
and sheep, stone terraces were added next
to the old farmhouse—in part to create a
platform for growing ornamental plants that
volunteer to grow in gravel and to have a
salad garden close at hand. The mixed garden,
consisting of meadows, hills, and a lake view
surrounds a working edible garden and an
ornamental mixed border. Each spills into the
frames of other in a manner that brings the
two together but still retains the individuality
of both. Sheep get moved around to keep the
open spaces. Their wool is not sold or used
for spinning but rather is used at the bottom
of the composted garden beds to help retain
moisture on soil which is mostly freely drain-
ing. Designed by owner Jenny Lee Hughes,
whose clients' gardens have been featured
in local and national publications, the garden

features trees, understory plantings, ground covers, hedges, specimens, re-seeding annuals, perennials, herbs, fruits, and vegetables The aim is a garden that feels natural in its surroundings, yet brings something unforgettable to it.

NEW | ♿ partial | 📷

➲ From Peterborough, take Route 202 to Hancock/Route 123. Take Route 123 through the town of Hancock to Route 9 in Stoddard. Turn right and go 2 miles and then turn left onto Route 123/Stoddard. Go 3 miles, turning left just before the church. Take School Street for one-eigth of a mile to Center Pond Road on the left. Drive .75 mile to #471 Hadley Farm on left. Drive in and park in the pasture to right. Total driving time from Peterborough is 30 minutes.

Please park along the driveway in the pasture at #471 Center Pond Road on the left.

If using GPS, set your destination to School Street, 03464. Take first left off of School Street. Which is Center Pond Rd.

HILLSBOROUGH COUNTY

FRANCESTOWN

📍 **THE GARDENS AT JUNIPER HILL FARM**
151 Reid Road, Francestown

🕐 9 a.m. to 5 p.m.

 Broken Arrow Nursery

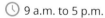 EXPERTS IN THE GARDEN

The Gardens at Juniper Hill Farm surround an eighteenth-century saltbox house and farmstead that remain much as they were 200 years ago. The approximately two acres of gardens surrounding the farm might best be described as "country formal." There is a courtyard garden, a formal lilac garden leading to a frog pool, a whimsical stumpery, a tranquil Mediterranean-inspired "clipped green" garden, a formal potager, and a pool house modeled after the garden pavilion at Hidcote. Scattered throughout the garden are many planted containers and more than

150 boxwoods representing eleven different varieties. Because winter interest was an important consideration in the original layout of the garden, strong architectural lines have become an important design element. The house and garden have been featured several times in both regional and national magazines. For photos and more info on Juniper Hill go to www.juniperhillfarmnh.com or Notes From Juniper Hill on Facebook.

2014 | 📷

➲ From Peterborough, take Route 123 north/ Route 202 east toward Greenfield. Just past Belletete's Hardware on left, turn right toward Greenfield on Route 136 east. Go about 5.4 miles, then turn left onto Francestown Road/ Route 136 east. Go east about 2.9 miles, then look for Reid Road on right. After right onto Reid Road, Juniper Hill Farm is second drive on left.

From the center of Francestown, at Meeting House, follow Route 136 west toward Greenfield. Go about 1.4 miles and look for Reid Road on left. After left onto Reid Road, Juniper Hill Farm is second drive on left.

HANCOCK

📍 **ELEANOR BRIGGS' GARDEN**
86 King's Highway, Hancock

🕐 10 a.m. to 4 p.m.

 Telescopes of Vermont

The garden has grown up around Hancock's first house, a dark 1776 clapboard farmhouse nestled on the slope of Skatutakee Mountain. Goldfish swim among lotus in a forty-eight-foot reflecting pool running along a 1970 kitchen addition. Beyond the pool, parallel borders, designed and maintained by Diane McGuire, stretch away from the house. In the woodland border, witch hazel, azaleas, and snakeroot blend into the forest. Opposite, red, pink, and blue annuals and perennials stand against an old stone wall. You will find an informal herb garden next to the kitchen on the other side of the wall and a terraced vegetable and cutting garden next to the weathered barn below. The borders are arranged in an "S" configuration so that one can wander endlessly in a rather small area. Old roses flank the front door and appear in other beds as well.

2010 | ♿ | 📷

➲ From I-91 North, take Exit 3 for Route 9 East into Brattleboro. Go to Route 123 towards Hancock (about 40 miles). Take the second right onto Hunt's Pond Road (about 5 miles). Go 0.5 mile and left onto King's Highway, a dirt road. Go 0.5 mile and park on the road next to the short driveway on the right up to a large barn.

PETERBOROUGH

📍 THE GARDENS OF LAURA AND JAMIE TROWBRIDGE
29 Cornish Road, Peterborough

🕐 10 a.m. to 4 p.m.

🌿 Rocky Dale Gardens

We purchased this property seventeen years ago after falling in love with the 1763 cape surrounded by big maples, wandering myrtle, and lichen-covered stone walls. We set about creating a long, curving perennial border along the stone wall facing west with a view of the rolling hills beyond as a backdrop. Over the years, the character of the border has evolved from traditional perennials to a mixture of perennials, shrubs, bulbs, annuals, and specialty trees. Tried-and-true heirloom plantings with newer and more unusual plants have been used to create an eclectic, yet harmonized, landscape. We've added numerous shade gardens and a kitchen patio that serves as an ideal location for containers of large tropical plants and succulents. The property also includes several terraced vegetable gardens.

2014 | ♿ | 📷

➲ From the intersection of Route 101 and Route 202 in Peterborough, go west on Route 101 up the hill. Take the third left onto Old Dublin Road. Then take the third left onto Four Winds Farm Road. Take the first left onto Cornish Road. The house is second on right— an old shingled cape.

📍 MICHAEL & BETSY GORDON
14 High Street, Peterborough

🕐 10 a.m. to 4 p.m.

🌿 Opus Plants

This small garden in the village was designed by a plantsman to be an extension of the house. The house and garden are situated on a hill and the garden is terraced on three levels. The upper level was designed to be enjoyed from the street. The middle level is laid out formally using yew hedges and a century-old granite wall foundation. The lowest level is an informal woodland garden and is a work in progress. The garden was planted with a mixture of unusual trees, shrubs, perennials, grasses, annuals and bulbs. Plants were selected primarily for interesting foliage and textures.

2014 | ♿ partial | 📷

➲ From the lights at the intersection of Route 101 and Route 202 in Peterborough, take Route 101 west up the hill to Elm Street. Turn right onto Elm Street. At the stop sign, cross the intersection and take gentle left hand turn up the hill onto High Street. The garden is the third house on the left: a white clapboard house with a picket fence across the street from the Elementary School.

📍 GARDENS OF MAUDE & JOHN ODGERS
130 Four Winds Farm Road, Peterborough

🕐 10 a.m. to 4 p.m.

🌿 Achille Agway

More than thirty years ago, John and Maude cleared their land and began building their home. The gardens quickly emerged, drawing inspiration from English border gardens and Maude's work as an artist who is intrigued with texture, color, and design. A soft palette and flowing shapes are used to create tranquility. Stonewalls and granite pieces complement the New England countryside. John built the house, a small post- and-beam barn (that now serves as a garden shed), the curved wooden arbors, an artistic wooden fence with moon gate, a unique bluestone patio, and a small pond. Woodland and vegetable gardens have been recently added. There are many places for quiet reflection: chairs placed around the gardens, the curved patio that emulates the garden shapes, attached garden room, a retreat in the woods, or by the pond, complete with frog song.

2014 | ♿ partial |

➥ From the intersection of Route 101 and Route 202/Grove Street in Peterborough, take Route 101W towards Keene. In less than 0.5 mile turn left onto Elm Street. Turn right onto Old Dublin Road. In about 0.75 mile turn left onto Four Winds Farm Road (dead-end road). Garden is 0.6 mile on left (fifth driveway after Cornish Road fork.) Red wooden sign on tree at bottom of driveway reads: "130." Please park on right side of road.

From Route 101 West in Keene, head to Peterborough through Marlborough and Dublin. Shortly after the Good Shepherd Lutheran Church bear right onto Old Dublin Road. In less than 0.25 mile, turn right onto Four Winds Farm Road. Proceed as directed above.

From Route 202 North in Hancock, take Route 202 to Peterborough. At Peterborough Library on corner of Route 202 and Main Street, turn right and cross bridge. Continue straight up hill, turning left onto Elm Street. At stop sign, cross Route 101 staying on Elm Street. Proceed as directed above.

🎓 EXPERTS IN THE GARDEN

AUGUST 20, SATURDAY | 10 AM TO 11:30 AM

GARDEN Q&A

with Roger Swain

**AT: The Gardens at Juniper Hill Farm
151 Reid Road, Francestown**

Come meet Roger Swain. Bring your enthusiasm and your gardening questions. He'll be glad to provide both encouragement and advice. Known as 'the man with the red suspenders' and recognized by millions, Roger Swain was host of the popular PBS TV series, *The Victory Garden* for fifteen years. He is the author of five books, was writer and Science Editor at *Horticulture Magazine* for thirty years, and is the recipient of the American Horticultural Society Award for Writing. In 1996, Roger was awarded the Massachusetts Horticultural Society Gold Medal for his 'power to inspire others.'

EXPERTS IN THE GARDEN

AUGUST 20, SATURDAY | 3 PM
NOSTRIL CHRONICLES
—A NOSE'S TOUR OF THE GARDEN
with Tovah Martin

AT: Garden of Jenny Lee Hughes & Edward Yoxen,
     471 Center Pond Road, Stoddard

Tovah Martin talks about fragrance, plus we'll sample the aromatic wares and learn a lot about plant scents in the process. Bring your nose: a smellathon will be included.

Kindra Clineff

Monadnock Area

August 21, Sunday

🕐 **Hours vary by garden
(Starting at 9 a.m.)**

$7 per garden

There is a garden open on this day in nearby Windham County, VT. See page 286.

🏷 Pop-up Nurseries:
The Inspired Gardener / Rocky Dale Gardens / Telescopes of Vermont

DIGGING DEEPER: Walking Design Workshop; at Gordon & Mary Hayward's Garden; Westminster West, VT; 4 p.m. See page 287.

CHESHIRE COUNTY

WALPOLE

DISTANT HILL GARDENS— GARDEN OF MICHAEL & KATHY NERRIE 507 March Hill Road, Walpole

10 a.m. to 4 p.m.

Telescopes of Vermont

At Distant Hill Gardens we consider the entire fifty-eight-acre property to be a garden, from the cultivated ornamentals and vegetables, to the native plants of our forest, fields, and wetlands. We use the term 'Garden' broadly to include the growing of any plants, and believe in the importance of plants, their cultivation and their use in the landscape to help foster an ecological balance between humans and the land. Some of the highlights of Distant Hill Gardens included cultivated gardens with more than 400 varieties of labeled plants, a large biodiverse variety of native plants and trees, and numerous vernal pools, swamps and wetlands. A boardwalk travels over a floating cranberry bog, and a large stone circle was built with stones from the property. The three-acre 'Milkweed Meadow' is for monarch butterflies and dozens of creative sculptures can be enjoyed throughout the gardens. Don't miss the new half-mile accessible nature trail. For more information visit: www.distanthill.org.

2012 | ♿ | 📷

➲ From the post office in downtown Walpole, go south on Main Street a few hundred feet from the post office. Turn left onto Prospect Hill Road (look for a 'Distant Hill Gardens' lawn sign at every major intersection from here on). Go 0.75 mile up a steep hill. Just past the Hooper Golf Course turn left onto Maple Grove Road. Go 0.75 mile. Stay left of Toles Automotive then bear right onto March Hill Road. Go 2.25 miles. The driveway is on left with a 'Distant Hill Gardens' lawn sign directly across from our mailbox, 507 March Hill Road (just past a large run-down arched roof barn on the right).

From the bandstand on Central Square in Keene take Court Street north out of Central Square 2.5 miles to your second traffic circle. (Note: Go straight through the first traffic circle at the Hospital.) Take the first exit out of the second traffic circle, a right turn, just past the entrance to a 7/11 convenience store on the right (it's more like straight ahead). Look for a sign a bit down the road for Surry/ Alstead. This is Route 12A North, but there is no sign. Go 8 miles on Route 12A. Turn left onto Walpole Valley Road (look for a 'Distant Hill Gardens' lawn sign just before the turn on the left). Go 2 miles up a steep hill. Turn left onto March Hill Road (another 'Distant Hill Gardens' lawn sign). Go 0.25 mile. The driveway is on right with a 'Distant Hill Gardens' lawn sign directly across from our mailbox, 507 March Hill Road.

From the intersection of Route 10 and Main Street in Gilsum, go south on Route 10 for 0.6 miles. Turn right onto Surry Road (at the beautiful and historic Stone Arch Bridge) Go 2.5 miles to the end of the road. Turn a right onto Route 12A North. Go 1.2 miles. Turn left onto Walpole Valley Road (look for a 'Distant Hill Gardens' lawn sign). Go 2 miles. Turn left onto March Hill Road (another 'Distant Hill Gardens' lawn sign). Go 0.25 mile. Driveway is on right with 'Distant Hill Gardens' lawn sign directly across from our mailbox, 507 March Hill Road.

WESTMORELAND

HUDSON GARDEN 73 Wentworth Road, Westmoreland

9 a.m. to 5 p.m.

The Inspired Gardener

Begun in the mid-nineties, this eclectic one-and-one-half-acre Westmoreland garden melds elements of formal and informal design. Stone walls, terraces, water features, and free-form beds filled with uncommon woody and herbaceous plants complement the sloping property. Visitors will find much to delight in as they stroll along grassy paths from one garden space to the other.

2011 | ♿ partial | 📷

⮑ From I-91, take Exit 3/Brattleboro, through traffic circle onto Route 9 East. Go 5.4 miles and turn left onto Route 63 North. Go 8.3 miles to Route 12 and turn left. Go 0.02 mile and turn right onto Wentworth Road. Gardens are 0.03 mile on left.

Route 12 North from Keene. Go north on Route 12 from traffic light at the intersection of Routes 12 & 9. Go 12 miles and turn right onto Wentworth Road. Gardens are 0.03 mile on left. Please park on left on grass beside road.

From Walpole, go south on Route 12 to Walpole/Westmoreland town line. Wentworth Road is second left after sign for "Steve's Equipment." (About 0.04 mile past sign) Turn left. Gardens are 0.03 mile on left.

SULLIVAN COUNTY

ACWORTH

📍 **THE GARDENS ON GROUT HILL**
Grout Hill Road, Acworth

🕐 10 a.m. to 4 p.m.

🔖 Rocky Dale Gardens

The gardens on Grout Hill were developed by owners G. Kristian Fenderson and Alston Barrett over a period of nearly five decades from an abandoned farm and house dating from the 1790s. The gardens and other planted areas are several acres in extent. They serve as a laboratory for Kristian's landscape design business and also showcase the owners' personal favorites. The garden features many mature examples of rare and unusual woody and herbaceous plants in a variety of environments. Seasonal annuals and containers also form a large part of the summer display. Azaleas, rhododendrons, viburnums, conifers, magnolias, beech trees, and old roses are just a few of the areas of emphasis.

2003 | 📷

⮑ From the south and east (Keene/Marlow), take Route 10 north to Route 123A west/south, a left turn. continue about 2 miles. Bear left following Route 123A along the river for less than 0.5 mile. At first cross road, turn right onto Grout Hill Road. Cross wooden bridge, go up hill passing Russell Road on right and Ball Road on left. Please park in the field on the right just after the small red Grout Hill Schoolhouse.

From Alstead, at Kimec's station (east end of Alstead village) bear left and follow Route 123A east/north along Cold River to South Acworth Village. Continue east on Route 123A for 2.25 miles. About 0.75 mile after passing Echo Valley Road on left, turn left onto Grout Hill Road and proceed as directed above.

✻ PUBLIC GARDENS

MERRIMACK COUNTY

NEWBURY

THE FELLS
456 Route 103A, Newbury
(603) 763-4789, www.thefells.org

The historic gardens at The Fells—created and nurtured by three generations of Hay family until 1969—surround the twenty-two-room Colonial Revival-style summer home first established by statesman John Milton Hay (1838-1905) in 1891. By then, Hay had served as President Lincoln's private secretary; he later served two other U.S. Presidents as Secretary of State. Over the years, the property changed hands and the gardens fell into disrepair. In 1995 volunteers began to manage the property. In 1997, they formed a nonprofit known today as The Fells. In 2008, The Fells became the owners of eighty-four acres of the original 1,000-acre site. Aided by the Garden Conservancy in 1995, The Fells began the meticulous process of renovating the beautiful gardens. Visitors may now see five formal garden areas, wide sweeping terraced lawns, and lichen-covered stone walls that result in a varied landscape that includes both natural and cultivated elements. Lake and mountain views prevail. The Pebble Court entrance is home to boxwood, lilacs, a yew hedge, a magnificent Enkianthus, and the beautiful "Hebe." A hundred-foot-long stone wallprovides structure for a dazzling perennial border, and high walls and a cascading fountain frame a rose garden of hybrid tea roses. A large rock garden, bordered by an impressive heather bed, was created with onsite granite and contains 650 alpine and rock garden plants. The Old Garden, the first to be created on the property, consists of Rhododendron-lined "secret" paths, fountain and stone tea table, and was restored in 2011.

🕐 Grounds open year round, daily, dawn to dusk. Main House open seasonally, Memorial Day through Columbus Day. Check website for days and hours.

💲 $10 adults; $8 seniors and students; $4 ages 6-17; 5 and under, free.

➲ From I-89 south take Exit 12/Route 11. Turn right and take an immediate left. Continue 5.6 miles. The Fells is on right. Park in lot and walk the quarter-mile driveway to the house and gardens.

NEW JERSEY

Essex County

Saturday, April 9

🕙 **10 a.m. to 4 p.m.**
$7 admission

ESSEX COUNTY

NUTLEY

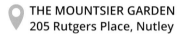 **THE MOUNTSIER GARDEN**
205 Rutgers Place, Nutley

For the last twenty-three years Richard Hartlage has worked with Silas Mountsier and Graeme Hardie on their garden in Nutley, New Jersey. "Our collaboration and friendship grew through a chance meeting with Graeme in Raleigh, North Carolina. The outcome is the most favorite in my portfolio. The original property has expanded from one-half acre to over two acres during the last two decades, as Silas and Graeme purchased adjacent parcels. The garden evolved through collaboration, with not an ill-considered decision; sometimes with disagreement, sometimes embraced immediately, but always with consensus. The garden has deep personal meaning for the three of us and represents the history of a friendship built in physical space. For visitors, the emotional content is palpable with every detail and vista. Though a strolling garden at its heart, the garden offers many places to sit and rest the eye and contemplate the crucible of a visitor's life and the vast collection of figurative and modern art. The garden is bold in its layout and unfolds through a progression... [Read full description online]

2014 | ♿ partial | 📷

➲ From the Lincoln Tunnel or Exit 16, from I-95/New Jersey Turnpike, go west on Route 3. From Garden State Parkway, go east on Route 3. From both directions, go to Main Avenue/Nutley/Passaic exit. At end of exit ramp, turn left and go through two traffic lights (three lights if coming from west). After this light, go straight ahead. Rutgers Place is fourth street on left. Come up Rutgers Place to top of hill; when road flattens, #205 is on right.

Northern New Jersey

Saturday, May 7

🕐 **Hours vary by garden
(Starting at 10 a.m.)**

$7 per garden

ESSEX COUNTY

EAST ORANGE

📍 **THE SECRET GARDEN @ 377
Harrison Park Towers, 377 South
Harrison Street, East Orange**

🕐 10 a.m. to 4 p.m.

This one-acre, formal Italianate garden designed by William T. Gotelli, celebrates its sixtieth birthday in 2016! This unique garden sits atop our parking garage at Harrison Park Towers and is entered through our lobby. We have a number of dwarf conifers and other shrubs which came from Gotelli's personal gardens in South Orange prior to his donation of plants and trees to The National Arboretum (Google: Gotelli Dwarf Conifer Collection for a walking tour of their collection.) At the end of his life, he moved into this building so that he could enjoy this lifetime design achievement. The garden has just completed a number of major restoration steps to recover from

a large construction project in 2009 involving the drainage system and garage. This garden has extensive collections of Azalea, Hydrangea, Lilac, Hosta, Peony, Tree Peony and a variety of spring blooming trees. The Secret Garden@377 is a very special feature of this almost 300-unit cooperative apartment community. An excellent history of The Secret Garden from Matters Magazine can be found at: http://digital.turn-page.com/i/123615-spring-2013. Other than our Open Days dates, The Secret Garden @ 377 is available for tours by appointment only, call Ron Carter at (973) 202-4728 or email: rcarter31@aol.com.

2015 | 📷

➲ From I-280 East take exit for Harrison Street/Clinton Street/East Orange. Turn right onto Harrison Street and cross Central Avenue. Proceed along Harrison past a large open lot on right. Pass East Highland Avenue and turn right into 377 South Harrison. Note a large sign: 377 and turn immediately prior to it. Park in The Visitors Parking Lot and walk to the front entrance under the overhang nearest South Harrison Street. Alternate parking is available along Elmwood Avenue which is a left turn off Harrison immediately in front of the building. Ignore the signs about permits and be careful crossing South Harrison at the cross walk.

From I-280 West take Exit 12A toward Clinton Street/East Orange. Follow along onto Freeway Drive westbound. Turn left onto South Harrison Street. Cross Central Avenue. Proceed as directed above

SHORT HILLS

GARDEN OF DR. & MRS. GEORGE E. STAEHLE
83 Old Hollow Road, Short Hills
🕐 10 a.m. to 2 p.m.

Our garden is in an old quarry. Over the years we have cleared and planted it ourselves after a local landscaper told us it was impossible and to let it stay wild. We started about forty years ago with azaleas, rhododendrons, and wildflowers, then went on to hostas, hellebores, daylilies, geraniums, primulas, and other perennials. We continue to collect and plant experimentally.

2015 | 📷

➲ From Route 24 West, take Hobart Gap Road exit. Turn right at traffic light onto Hobart Gap Road. At blinking light, road name changes to White Oak Ridge Road. At next light (1 mile), turn right onto Parsonage Hill Road. Continue to "T". Turn left onto Old Short Hills Road and go about 0.5 mile to second street on right, Old Hollow Road. Garden is at #83, fifth house on right. Please park along street.

HUNTERDON COUNTY

GLEN GARDNER

WOODLOVE—
LAINIE & JOHN BEAVIN'S GARDEN
103 Green Oaks Road, Glen Gardner
🕐 12 p.m. to 4 p.m.

Our garden, predominantly shade with native and naturalized wildflowers and bulbs, consists of a series of garden rooms and woodland paths over six acres enclosed in a double deer fence. It was created from a woodland over a thirty-five-year period while building our stone house. Like all gardens, it is still in progress. There are perennial gardens, ferns, hosta, clethra, and daylily collections, inviting benches, a hypertufa "room," a pergola, an attached greenhouse, a tiny frog pond, and garden steps between levels. In 2004, "Ivan the Terrible" flooded through the property. To remedy this, there is now a 150-foot stream with a waterfall to carry the run-off terminating in a frog pond. Please stop for light refreshment on the breezeway. We look forward to welcoming you.

2015 | ♿ |

➲ From I-78, take Exit 17. Go north on Route 31 for 5.6 miles to fourth traffic light at Glen Manor Drive. Turn right onto School Street and then turn right onto Main Street (about 0.1 mile). Take first left onto Hill Road. After 1.1 miles, turn left onto Spruce Run Road, which ends in a "T" 0.8 mile later. Turn right onto Red Mill Road; go 0.4 mile and bear right. Go 0.5 mile more and turn right onto Green Oaks Road. The driveway is first left; gate will be open. The driveway is a circle; bear to right around circle and park behind last car on right.

MORRIS COUNTY

CONVENT STATION

THE L'HOMMEDIEU GARDEN
12 Concord Lane, Convent Station
🕐 10 a.m. to 4 p.m.

The rear terrace of this small suburban oasis is an extension of the living space of the owners residence, and has a fish pond with a waterfall which can be heard both throughout the garden and within the house. This garden has a wide range of growing conditions—from full sun to deep shade—and is comprised of a series of garden rooms that lead from this

terrace. These "rooms" consist of a rose garden, a bench garden (which is a black-and-white flowering bulb garden in the Spring), a shady woodland aisle, and a swing garden, which is planted to emulate a native Adirondack-inspired woodland. Further along, one is lead to a knot garden, a sunny deck with planters of herbs off the kitchen, and a cutting garden. This garden, by landscape designer and horticulturist John Sulpy, Jr. of Eldridge Design, still focuses on Spring bulbs, however in the last decade, it has developed horticulturally into a garden of four-season interest, with particular focus on texture and subtle color in Summer's changing light conditions and an increase in the use of vegetables to make it more sustainable.
2015 | ♿ | 📷

➲ From I-287 south, take Exit 35. At top of ramp, bear right onto Madison Avenue. Get in left lane for the next light. Turn left onto South Street. Stay on South Street, passing over I-287, through next light, after which you turn left onto Woodland Avenue. Pass Municipal Complex and make left onto Bennington Road, the immediate right onto Concord Lane; #12 is on the right.

From I-287 North, take Exit 35. At light at head of ramp, make right onto South Street then immediate left onto Woodland Avenue. Pass Municipal Complex, the left onto Bennington Road. Take an immediate right onto Concord Lane; #12 is on the right.

From the north or south, the garden is about 1 mile from I-287. Please park on Concord Lane.

SOMERSET COUNTY
FAR HILLS

 THE HAY HONEY FARM
130 Stevens Lane, Far Hills
🕐 10 a.m. to 5 p.m.

The extensive gardens of the Hay, Honey Farm lie nestled between rolling hills along the North Branch of the Raritan River. The transition from cattle farm to garden began in 1989, and while Black Angus cattle still graze the nearby hayfields, honeybees have become the only 'livestock' allowed within the gates. Over the years, a wide variety of plant material, including hundreds of trees and shrubs, has been carefully added to the landscape in a naturalistic manner, with a respect for the history and topography of the site, and consistent with the broader surrounding atmosphere of Pleasant Valley. The plant collections reflect the diverse interests of the owners and the resident horticulturists, and show the results of a long term vision and dedicated horticultural attention to plant care. Garden areas created near the homes include a dwarf conifer/spring bulb garden, a large walled perennial border, hosta gardens, a native meadow, and a large kitchen garden. Year-round springs feed a small stream which

originates in the wild garden, and flows...
[Read full description online]

2015 |

⮑ From I-95/New Jersey Turnpike, take I-78 West. Then take I-287 North to Exit 22B (or Exit 22 if coming from north). Stay on Route 206 North. At fourth traffic light, turn right onto Holland Avenue. At end, turn left onto Peapack. Turn right onto Willow Avenue. Go 1 mile and turn left onto Branch Road. At 0.7 mile, cross the green steel bridge onto a private gravel road. Follow signs to park at The Hay Honey Farm. Park here for the Stone House Garden also and volunteers will direct you.

❋ PUBLIC GARDEN

ESSEX COUNTY

SHORT HILLS

📍 **GREENWOOD GARDENS**
274 Old Short Hills Road, Short Hills

🕐 10 a.m. to 4 p.m.

Special Garden Conservancy Open Day.
See this garden's listing on page page 172.

Bergen & Essex County

Saturday, May 21

🕐 **10 a.m. to 4 p.m.**

$7 per garden

BERGEN COUNTY

ALLENDALE

📍 **MONFRIED GARDEN**
15 Stone Fence Road, Allendale

Our garden is an ongoing labor of love. We have retained the old yews, rhododendrons, and mature trees on our half acre, but everything else has been the result of nineteen years of addition and subtraction. In keeping with this philosophy, I have recently added many species of Alliums to the front garden borders in an effort to discourage deer. I have also introduced more small shrubs for year-round interest and to reduce maintenance. The backyard garden in years past has been partly shaded, but this year our neighbors' huge Norway maple was cut down, leaving the west border in almost full sun. It is too early to know how this will effect the existing plantings, but I am looking forward to being able to incorporate more sun loving perennials—

time will tell! The arch festooned with Rosa 'Zepherine Drouhin' and Clematis 'Jackmanii' leads into shady raised-bed garden room filled with hostas, ferns, astilbe, and potted tender tropicals. The path continues through a woodland garden planted with spring ephemerals, epimediums, ferns, hellebore, actaea,… [Read full description online]

2015 |

⮐ From the south, take Route 17 North through Paramus. After the Hollywood Avenue Exit stay right. Take the second Sheridan Avenue exit to Waldwick (westbound). Go under Route 17, then immediately bear right up ramp. Turn left onto Prospect Avenue. At first traffic light, turn left onto Franklin Turnpike. At next light, turn right onto Wyckoff Avenue. Go through two lights, then at third light, turn right onto Crescent Avenue (there is a 7-11 and a Walgreens at this intersection). In about 0.5 mile, will see "Welcome to Allendale" sign. In a short distance the road will go downhill. At bottom of hill, turn left onto Beresford Road. Go one block and turn right onto Schuyler Road. Go one block, and turn right onto Stone Fence Road. Our garden is at the third house on right.

From the north and New York State Thruway, take Exit 15 to Route 17 and Route 287 South. At end of exit ramp, stay left onto Route 17 South. Go about 4.5 miles and exit onto Lake Street Ramsey. At top of ramp bear left to traffic light. Go straight through light onto Crescent Avenue. Go straight through three more lights (Franklin Turnpike, Hillsdale Avenue, Brookside Avenue) After Brookside, the road curves and goes downhill. At bottom of the hill, turn right onto Beresford Road and proceed as directed above.

From Manhattan, take George Washington Bridge to Route 4 West/North. After Spring Valley Road, get in right lane. Exit onto Route 17 North. Go through Paramus and follow directions above from the south.

From the west, take Route 287 to Route 208 and Route 4. Go to Route 17 North. Follow directions above from the south.

WYCKOFF

FORMERLY TALL TREES
16 Colonial Drive, Wyckoff

After being cultivated for more than twenty years as a shade garden on a standard suburban lot, storm damage necessitated the removal of the majestic trees and transformed it to a sunnier property. It is still a garden for all seasons with spring bulbs, mahonia, and rhododendrons in abundance. Then more color arrives in the summer with coleus, plectranthus, and salvias sharing space with other annuals, hydrangeas, and hibiscus 'Diana'. In the fall, golden arums, and cyclamen and winter interest comes from varieties of hellebores. By rearranging beds, this avid collector still pampers 150 varieties of hosta, rare ferns, and unusual arisaemas which led to an article in the New York Times where she quoted: "When I like a plant, I usually love the leaves first." Along the side of the property is an ever-expanding collection of handmade troughs opposite a pair of embossed cellar doors she crafted. This long-time Open Days garden has been imaginatively reinvented and warrants another visit.

2014 |

⮐ From George Washington Bridge, take Route 4 West to Route 208 North/Oakland about 7.5 miles to Ewing Avenue. Go down exit ramp and turn right onto Ewing. Go to traffic light and turn right onto Franklin Avenue. Go through two lights to first street on right, Godwin Drive, and turn right. First left is Colonial Drive. Garden is at #16 on right.

From I-287, take Route 208 south. Exit onto Ewing Avenue. Turn left at stop sign and go to light. Turn right onto Franklin Avenue. Proceed as directed above.

EAST ORANGE

 THE SECRET GARDEN @ 377
Harrison Park Towers, 377 South
Harrison Street, East Orange

This one-acre, formal Italianate garden designed by William T. Gotelli, celebrates its sixtieth birthday in 2016! This unique garden sits atop our parking garage at Harrison Park Towers and is entered through our lobby. We have a number of dwarf conifers and other shrubs which came from Gotelli's personal gardens in South Orange prior to his donation of plants and trees to the National Arboretum (Google: Gotelli Dwarf Conifer Collection for a walking tour of their collection.) At the end of his life, he moved into this building so that he could enjoy this lifetime design achievement. The garden has just completed a number of major restoration steps to recover from a large construction project in 2009 involving the drainage system and garage. This garden has extensive collections of Azalea, Hydrangea, Lilac, Hosta, Peony, Tree Peony and a variety of spring blooming trees. The Secret Garden @377 is a very special feature of this almost 300-unit cooperative apartment community. An excellent history of the Secret Garden from *Matters Magazine* can be found at: http://digital.turn-page.com/i/123615-spring-2013. Other than our Open Days dates, The Secret Garden@377 is available for tours by appointment only by calling Ron Carter at 973.202.4728 or email: rcarter31@aol.com.

2015 |

 From I-280 East take exit for Harrison Street/Clinton Street/East Orange. Turn right onto Harrison Street and cross Central Avenue. Proceed along Harrison past a large open lot on right. Pass East Highland Avenue and turn right into 377 South Harrison. Note a large sign: 377 and turn immediately prior to it. Park in The Visitors Parking Lot and walk to the front entrance under the overhang nearest South Harrison Street. Alternate parking is available along Elmwood Avenue which is a left turn off Harrison immediately in front of the building. Ignore the signs about permits and be careful crossing South Harrison at the cross walk.

From I-280 West take Exit 12A toward Clinton Street/East Orange. Follow along onto Freeway Drive westbound. Turn left onto South Harrison Street. Cross Central Avenue. Proceed as directed above.

❊ PUBLIC GARDEN

ESSEX COUNTY

SHORT HILLS

GREENWOOD GARDENS
274 Old Short Hills Road, Short Hills

Special Garden Conservancy Open Day.
See this garden's listing on page page 172.

Bergen County

Saturday, June 11

🕐 **Hours vary by garden
(Starting at 8:30 a.m.)**

$7 per garden

BERGEN COUNTY

CLOSTER

📍 **MARY'S GARDEN
188 Cedar Lane, Closter**

🕐 10 a.m. to 4 p.m.

Charm abounds throughout this residential property. Start with the colorful front beds of perennials within boxwood borders, then continue to the back where this formality morphs into a welcoming and serene private yard. Clematis playfully climb walls and peek through rhododendrons, while hostas keep company with artistic blends of summer annuals. Follow stone paths outlined by mazus to the arbor covered with ivy and roses that leads to a secluded seating area. As you exit, turn and take in the whole view to see once more how each element of color, texture, and plant combinations contribute to the overall tranquility of this cottage garden.

2014 | 📷

⮑ From the south, take the Palisades Parkway North to Exit 2. At end of ramp, turn left onto Route 9W South. Go to next traffic light at Closter Dock Road and turn right. At top of the hill, go through a1 flashing light and two traffic lights. At the second traffic light, there is an Exxon gas station on right and a "Welcome to Closter" sign across the road. Go through light on Closter Dock Road. After a short distance, the road takes a sharp right turn. Go through flashing light to traffic light. Closter Dock Road turns left. Go through center of Closter. At the end of town, there is a fork in road. Go left onto Harrington Avenue. Go two blocks

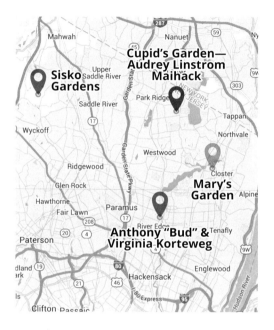

to Cedar Lane and turn left. Garden is three quarters of the way up Cedar Lane.

MAHWAH

📍 **SISKO GARDENS
113 Fardale Avenue, Mahwah**

🕐 10 a.m. to 4 p.m.

Paul has been working on this three-and-one-half acre property for twenty eight years. The property was all woods beyond the house. Major tree removal has opened the property to sunlight and sunset views. The terraces, pool gardens, and lower lawn area have all been developed by the homeowner. Note the koi pond and pool area surrounded by terraced gardens which include iris, grasses, roses, coreopsis, echinacea, phlox, hydrangea, colorful annuals, and vegetables. A former industrial arts teacher, Paul is a self-taught artist working primarily with metal and wood with work internationally . Please note his many metal sculptures throughout the property. Last year, Paul and his wife Janet were featured artists in 201 magazine.

NEW |

➲ From Route 208 take the Russell Avenue Exit toward Wyckoff business district (left). Follow Wyckoff Avenue through 4 stoplights and turn left onto Fardale Avenue.

From Route 17, exit at Lake Street to Ramsey business district (Main Street). Go through Main Street which becomes Wyckoff Avenue. Turn right onto Fardale Avenue. If you come to a stoplight, you've gone 2 blocks past Fardale Avenue. Follow signs to parking.

Please note there is a good amount of walking required as the property sits off of Fardale Avenue. Please park on the right side of driveway only as this is a shared driveway (slightly on lawn is OK). Cars will be able to turn around at the end of the driveway next to the studio. This is a turnaround area only.

RIVER EDGE

📍 ANTHONY "BUD" & VIRGINIA KORTEWEG

800 Summit Avenue, River Edge

🕐 8:30 a.m. to 4 p.m.

Edgecroft is a unique terraced property laid out in 1910 by Italian artisans. One hundred Carrara marble steps lead to a swimming pool surrounded by a stone-columned pergola draped in roses, wisteria, and honeysuckle. A gated brick courtyard entrance with a slowly maturing allée of hydrangeas to greet guests. Hydrangeas provide a warm welcome with hues of pinks and lavender interspersed with a variety of mixed perennials. There are also rare *Cryptomeria* 'Lobbii', rhododendrons, azaleas, a *Magnolia* virginiana, a tiered bronze angel fountain, a Victorian-style perennial garden with David Austin antique roses and

favorite perennials, a formal garden with crepe myrtles, azaleas, and a fountain with a copy of Verrocchio's fifteenth- century bronze "Cupid with Dolphin." A series of three koi ponds interspersed with nine waterfalls cascade down terraces edged with aged pines, golden larches, flowering cherry trees, dogwoods, *Styrax* japonicus, hydrangeas, wild strawberries, and creeping roses. Bronze water statuary, stone benches, and stone... [Read full description online]

2015 | ♿ | 📷

➲ From George Washington Bridge, take Route 4 West to Route 17 North. Take Midland Avenue/River Edge exit. Go east about 2 miles to "T" and turn right onto Kinderkamack Road. Go south to first traffic light. Turn right onto Lincoln Avenue up a cobblestone hill. Walled property on right is Edgecroft. Turn right onto Summit Avenue. Number 800 is immediately on right. Please park along street and enter through open gates. From I-80/Garden State Parkway, take Route 17 North and proceed as directed above.

RIVER VALE

📍 CUPID'S GARDEN— AUDREY LINSTROM MAIHACK

690 Edward Street, River Vale

🕐 10 a.m. to 5 p.m.

Due to a severe storm in 2011, the center of my garden changed from a patio shaded by tall trees to a sun garden full of color. A surrounding border of conifers, pines, and shrubs form a private semi- shaded garden. Short paths lead from decks to ponds, patio, and greenhouse. Varied gardens are adorned with rocks, shells, ground covers, rose trellises, early perennials, potted tropicals, and bonsai plants. Spring has many azaleas, bulbs, wisteria, dogwoods, weeping cherry, and Scotch broom. Later, iris, peonies, dianthus, and roses make way for foxgloves and assorted perennials, as well as water plants, daylilies, hostas, ferns, and herbs. Fall color starts the retreat to the potting shed and cedar greenhouse, my winter garden. Outside, under the watchful eye of Cupid, hawks and doves, as well as many other birds, frogs, rabbits, chipmunks, "Woody" the woodchuck, raccoons, and Mr. Skunk all visit the fish in the ponds.

2015 | ♿ | 📷

⮕ From the Garden State Parkway North, take Exit 172, last exit in New Jersey. Turn right onto Grand Avenue east. Pass Kinderkamack Road (railroad tracks) and go over hill to "T" (about 3 miles). Turn right onto South Middletown Road, which becomes River Vale Road, for 0.5 mile to right on Thurnau Drive

(first right after Forcellati Nursery). First right is Edward Street. Ours is first house on right. Please park on street.

From Palisades Parkway, take Exit 6W. Travel west on Orangeburg Road to fourth traffic light and turn left onto Blue Hill Road at end of reservoir. Go 1.4 miles to a stop sign. Turn left onto River Vale Road and proceed as directed above.

Bergen County

Sunday, July 10

🕐 **10 a.m. to 4 p.m.**
$7 per garden

BERGEN COUNTY

TENAFLY

📍 **LINDA SINGER**
170 Tekening Drive, Tenafly
🕐 10 a.m. to 4 p.m.

I designed this romantic garden to include bluestone walks and patios, fieldstone sitting walls, rose-and-vine-covered arbors and trellises, stone ornaments, a swimming pool, and a small vegetable garden enclosed by a white picket fence. There are perennial and mixed borders. A cottage garden is of special interest for a wide variety of flowering shrubs. The greatest challenge is thwarting the legions of deer, moles, voles, field mice, and rabbits that love the garden as much as I do. I have lots of volunteer plants to give away if you do the bending.

2015 | ♿ partial | 📷

⮕ From Palisades Parkway, take Exit 1/ Englewood/Palisades Avenue. Turn right at

first traffic light onto Sylvan Avenue/Route 9W, drive north about 3 miles. Turn left at light onto East Clinton Avenue. Go 0.5 mile and turn right onto Ridge Road. Go one block and turn right onto Berkeley Drive. Go one block and turn left onto Highwood Road. Go 2 blocks and turn right onto Tekening Drive. House is third on right. A sign with #170 is high on a tree. Please park on street.

Monmouth County

Saturday, August 6

🕐 **Hours vary by garden**
  (Starting at 9 a.m.)
$7 per garden

MONMOUTH COUNTY
LOCUST

📍 **NANCY & DAN CRABBE'S
GARDEN ON THE NAVESINK RIVER
904 Navesink River Road, Locust**

🕐 9 a.m. to 4 p.m.

The property, 150 feet high on a hill overlooking the Navesink River, was originally developed to showcase a Japanese bonsai collection created by the owner's aunt. The bonsai have moved on to a county park and the garden has been extended and currently reflects its original bones coupled with a love of naturalistic English garden flowers and shrubs. It is a peaceful and rustic space.

NEW | 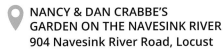

➲ Take Exit 109 on the Garden State Parkway. Continue straight onto Half Mile Road. Continue to dead end. Turn right onto West Front Street and continue to the first light. Turn left onto Hubbard Road and continue to the first light. Turn right onto Navesink River Road. Continue 4.5 miles to 904 Navesink River Road (Black mailbox with a red crab) on the right.

RED BANK

WOODLAND GARDEN
215 McClees Road, Red Bank

🕐 9 a.m. to 5 p.m.

Varied semi-sunny garden featuring shrubs and perennials in a carefree manner, scattered around driveway walls. Shade-loving perennials fill the woods around the house. Indigenous rock walls were created from the site and built by the owner.

NEW |

⮑ Take Navesink River Road to McClees Road, #215 is on the west side, with a white gravel drive.

RUMSON

BETH DEUTCH GARDEN
8 North Ward Avenue, Rumson

🕐 10 a.m. to 4 p.m.

The garden is centered around a 400-foot pier that goes to a dock over a tidal river. The garden features many interesting plants with a wide variety of colors and textures. The garden was planted so that certain plants will be in bloom at almost all times during the summer. The garden also features a robotic sculpture Heliotropis by the well known kinetic sculptor Anthony Castronovo. Heliotropis is a custom solar robotic sculpture made of bronze, kiln-formed glass, and custom electronics. This techno-biotic sculpture changes its form and behavior and responds to its environment via sensors that track temperature, light, and seismic activity. Heliotropis creates a visual link between its physical form and the conditions of its immediate environment. This relationship explores the interactions between machine and nature, as well as the interactions between man and nature. As computers and artificial intelligence proliferate and become woven into all aspects of our human existence, the desire to protect the environment and promote healthy ecologies must also grow.

2015 |

⮑ Take the Garden State Parkway to Exit 109 East. Take Route 520 East, but turn left onto Ward Avenue by Holy Cross Church directly before crossing the Sea Bright Bridge. At the north end of Ward Avenue turn right onto divided road which is North Ward Avenue. Continue on North Ward Avenue to # 8 located on left near dead end. Street parking available.

KING & LEIGH SORENSEN
7 North Ward Avenue, Rumson

🕐 10 a.m. to 4 p.m.

The house, a former windmill and barn, looks at five miles of salt marsh, a river, and the distant Manhattan skyline. The design of the landscape reflects this view to the north—islands of perennials, shrubs, and trees that are salt-water tolerant and grouped naturalistically. Numerous publications have featured the gardens starting with the January 1983 issue of House Beautiful. Leigh, who is a landscape designer, has a collection of bonsai and a flock of chickens. King raises honeybees and five varieties of lettuce. The property floods in storm tides.

2015 | ♿ | 📷

⮑ From Garden State Parkway, take Exit 109. Turn east onto Newman Springs Road and after 1.5 miles turn left onto Broad Street. After 0.75 mile turn right onto Harding Place and go east 5 miles (road name changes to Ridge, then Hartshorne). At end, turn left onto North Ward Avenue. Our driveway is a continuation of North Ward Avenue.

Essex County

Saturday, September 10

🕐 **10 a.m. to 4 p.m.**
$7 per garden

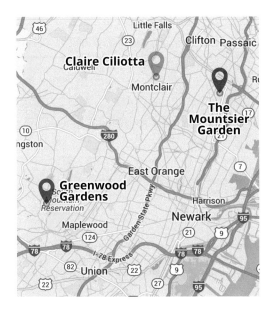

ESSEX COUNTY

MONTCLAIR

 CLAIRE CILIOTTA
279 Park Street, Montclair

Welcome to my garden! There are lots of lovely new changes that I've made in the last two years! The front garden now has a lovely curving path and new broad steps to the house. You will get to see what I've done with the plantings! Then, follow the brick path around the side of the house and look for the climbing roses, baptisias, smoke bushes and a lovely Japanese maple. Open the new gate to a meditation garden—watch the birds at the feeder, notice the Mayan rock wall with its spirit windows surrounding a moon-shaped pond. Enjoy the mounds of hakonechloa and the clump bamboo but don't miss the tree

bench with the tree's newly made clay animal totems surrounded by hydrangeas, roses, and hellebores. Follow the path to the Balinese platform floating in a sea of ferns and day lilies. Take a moment to enjoy the privacy, then walk back to the new deck with its wonderful steel-wire railing. Come up and see the garden from this vantage point! Welcome to my garden! Iced tea will be served!

2012 | ♿ partial |

➲ From the Garden State Parkway, take Exit 151/Watchung Avenue. Turn right if you are coming from the north, left if from the south. Continue five traffic lights or so on Watchung Avenue. The last traffic light will be North Fullerton. Go through traffic light and make the next right (Valero gas station on corner) onto Park Street. Number 279 Park is about ten houses on right.

From Route 3, take Grove Street Exit, turn left onto Grove Street. Continue past the cemetery. Turn right (only way possible) at the traffic light at end of cemetery. Go half-way up hill, turn left onto Park Street, continue about 1.5 miles to #279 (right past Gordonhurst intersection). The garden is on the left.

NUTLEY

 THE MOUNTSIER GARDEN
205 Rutgers Place, Nutley

For the last twenty-three years Richard Hartlage has worked with Silas Mountsier and Graeme Hardie on their garden in Nutley, New Jersey. "Our collaboration and friendship grew through a chance meeting with Graeme in Raleigh, North Carolina. The outcome is the most favorite in my portfolio. The original property has expanded from one-half acre to over two acres during the last two decades, as Silas and Graeme purchased adjacent parcels. The garden evolved through collaboration, with not an ill-considered decision; sometimes with disagreement, sometimes embraced immediately, but always with consensus. The garden has deep personal meaning for the three of us and represents the history of a friendship built in physical space. For visitors, the emotional content is palpable with every detail and vista. Though a strolling garden at its heart, the garden offers many places to sit and rest the eye and contemplate the crucible of a visitor's life and the vast collection of figurative and modern art. The garden is bold in its layout and unfolds through a progression... [Read full description online]

2014 | ♿ partial | 📷🖿

➲ From the Lincoln Tunnel or Exit 16, from I-95/New Jersey Turnpike, go west on Route 3. From Garden State Parkway, go east on Route 3. From both directions, go to Main Avenue/Nutley/Passaic exit. At end of exit ramp, turn left and go through two traffic lights (three lights if coming from west). After this light, go straight ahead. Rutgers Place is fourth street on left. Come up Rutgers Place to top of hill; when road flattens, #205 is on right.

✻ PUBLIC GARDEN

ESSEX COUNTY

SHORT HILLS

⚲ **GREENWOOD GARDENS**
274 Old Short Hills Road, Short Hills

Special Garden Conservancy Open Day.
See this garden's listing on page page 172.

Somerset County

Saturday, September 17

🕐 **Hours vary by garden (Starting at 10 a.m.)**
$7 per garden

🏷 Pop-up Nursery
Broken Arrow Nursery

SOMERSET COUNTY

FAR HILLS

 THE HAY HONEY FARM
130 Stevens Lane, Far Hills

10 a.m. to 5 p.m.

 Broken Arrow Nursery

The extensive gardens of the Hay, Honey Farm lie nestled between rolling hills along the North Branch of the Raritan River. The transition from cattle farm to garden began in 1989, and while Black Angus cattle still graze the nearby hayfields, honeybees have become the only 'livestock' allowed within the gates. Over the years, a wide variety of plant material, including hundreds of trees and shrubs, has been carefully added to the landscape in a naturalistic manner, with a respect for the history and topography of the site, and consistent with the broader sur-rounding atmosphere of Pleasant Valley. The plant collections reflect the diverse interests of the owners and the resident horticulturists, and show the results of a long term vision and dedicated horticultural attention to plant care. Garden areas created near the homes include a dwarf conifer/spring bulb garden, a large walled perennial border, hosta gardens, a native meadow, and a large kitchen garden. Year-round springs feed a small stream which originates in the wild garden, and flows... [Read full description online]

2015 |

⮑ From I-95/New Jersey Turnpike, take I-78 West. Then take I-287 North to Exit 22B (or Exit 22 if coming from north). Stay on Route 206 North. At fourth traffic light, turn right onto Holland Avenue. At end, turn left onto Peapack. Turn right onto Willow Avenue. Go 1 mile and turn left onto Branch Road. At 0.7 mile, cross the green steel bridge onto a private gravel road. Follow signs to park at The Hay Honey Farm. Park here for the Stone House Garden also and volunteers will direct you.

 STONE HOUSE GARDEN
121 Stevens Lane, Far Hills

10 a.m. to 4 p.m.

All the buildings and walls are of old Penn-sylvania stone, the paths and terrace are of Vermont schist. One goes through the beech hedge into the courtyard, planted with low-growing Rhus aromatica and Spanish bluebells. The path, which encircles the house, leads through the medallion garden to the crescent border, planted for spring bloom and fall color, past the kitchen garden, terrace, and Mimi's garden, down stone steps to the bog, which, in the spring, hosts an explosion of primula candelabra, fern, and skunk cabbage.

2015 | ♿ |

⮑ From I-95/New Jersey Turnpike, take I-78 West. Then take I-287 North to Exit 22B (or Exit 22 if coming from north). Stay on Route 206 North. At fourth traffic light, turn right onto Holland Avenue. At end, turn left onto Peapack Road. Turn right onto Willow Avenue. Go 1 mile and turn left onto Branch Road. At 0.7 mile, cross the green steel bridge onto a private gravel road. Follow signs to park at The Hay Honey Farm, and walk next door to the Stone House Garden; volunteers will be on hand to direct you.

Hunterdon County

Saturday, October 8

🕐 **10 a.m. to 6 p.m.**
$7 per garden

🏷️ Pop-up Nursery
Broken Arrow Nursery / Atlock Farm

There are also gardens open on this day in nearby Bucks County, PA. See page 272.

 DIGGING DEEPER: Seeing the Garden for the Trees—Designing with Trees, with Bruce Gangawer, Paxson Hill Farm, New Hope, PA. See page 273.

HUNTERDON COUNTY

STOCKTON

📍 **THE GARDEN AT FEDERAL TWIST**
208 Federal Twist Road, Stockton

🕐 10 a.m. to 6 p.m.

🏷️ Broken Arrow Nursery / Atlock Farm

When we moved into a mid-century house overlooking the woods, I immediately knew only a naturalistic, informal garden would be appropriate to the place. The garden is hidden. You enter through the house, where you first glimpse the landscape, a sunny glade, through a wall of windows. Huge perennials and grasses evoke an "Alice in Wonderland" feeling (many plants are taller than you). The garden is in the New Perennial tradition: plants are massed in interwoven communities, and emphasize structure, shape, and form—which are long lasting—rather than flower. Begun as an experiment to explore garden making in the challenging conditions of unimproved, heavy, wet clay, the garden is ecologically similar to a wet prairie, and is maintained by cutting and burning. Much of the garden peaks in mid-July, when plants reach mature height and flower, then a second peak occurs in October when low sunlight makes the grasses glow in yellows, russets, and golds. Two small ponds attract hundreds of frogs, insects, and wildlife. Many gravel paths open...
[Read full description online]

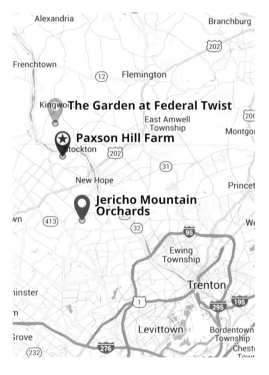

2015 | ♿ | 📷

➲ From the New York City area, take I-78. Take Exit 29 for I-287 toward Route 206/Route 202/Morristown/Somerville. Keep left at the fork and continue onto I-287 South for about 4 miles. Take Exit 17 onto Route 202 and continue to Flemington (about 19 miles). At the traffic circle, continue to the opposite side, and continue on Route 202 (about 10.8 miles) to the last exit in New Jersey, to Lambertville and Route29. At the foot of the exit, turn left, then at the bottom of the exit, turn right onto Route 29/River Road/Daniel Bray Highway. Continue north, passing through the village of Stockton, for a total of 5.1 miles from Lambertville. On the right is a large sign for Hidden Valley Nursery. Federal Twist Road is immediately past the sign. Turn right and drive up Federal Twist Road 2.9 miles to #208. Park on the right side of the road (the house side), taking care to leave the left lane open.

From western Philadelphia suburbs, take the I-276 East/Pennsylvania Turnpike east to Exit 343. Exit on Route 611 North toward Doylestown. In about 10 miles, exit onto Route 202N/New Hope. In about 10 miles, continue on Route 202 past New Hope, and cross toll bridge over Delaware River, exiting immediately on the New Jersey side toward Lambertville. At the foot of the exit, turn left onto Route 29 N/River Road/Daniel Bray Highway. Proceed as directed above.

From northern New Jersey or the Hudson River Valley, take I-287 south, take Exit 17 onto Route 202 and continue to Flemington (about 19 miles), at the traffic circle continue to the opposite side, and continue on Route 202 (about 10.8 miles) to the last exit in New Jersey, to Lambertville and Route 29. At the foot of the exit, turn left, then at the bottom of the exit, turn right onto Route 29/River Road/Daniel Bray Highway. Proceed as directed above.

✳ PUBLIC GARDENS

ESSEX COUNTY
MONTCLAIR
VAN VLECK HOUSE & GARDENS
21 Van Vleck Street, Montclair
(973) 744-4752, www.vanvleck.org

Begun at the turn of the century, these gardens have been developed by several generations of committed horticulturists. The plan is largely formal, responding to the Mediterranean style of the house. The extensive collection of rhododendrons and azaleas, including several named for family members, is renowned. Also of note are the many mature plant specimens.

🕐 Year round, daily, dawn until dusk.

$ Free

➲ From Garden State Parkway north, take Exit 148/Bloomfield Avenue. Stay in left lane of exit ramp through first traffic light and take jug-handle under the GSP back to Bloomfield Avenue; turn right (west) at light. Proceed for 2.5 miles through Bloomfield, Glen Ridge, and Montclair town centers. Turn right onto North Mountain Avenue (Montclair Art Museum is on left). Proceed through 1 light (Claremont Avenue) and take next left onto Van Vleck Street; Van Vleck House & Gardens is on left.

From GSP south, take Exit 148/Bloomfield Avenue. Follow service road (paralleling the GSP) through 1 stop sign and 2 lights. Turn right (west) at the third light onto Bloomfield Avenue. Proceed as directed above.

From New York City, take Lincoln Tunnel to Route 3 west. Exit at Grove Street, Montclair. Turn left at top of exit ramp onto Grove, proceed 3.9 miles to Claremont Avenue, turn right. Proceed 0.9 mile to fifth light. Turn right onto North Mountain Avenue and proceed as directed above.

From I-280, take Exit 8B/Prospect Avenue. Proceed north 2 miles to Bloomfield Avenue, turn right, and proceed 0.5 mile to third light.

Turn left onto North Mountain Avenue. Proceed through 1 light (Claremont Avenue) and take next left onto Van Vleck Street. Van Vleck House and Gardens is on left.

SHORT HILLS

GREENWOOD GARDENS
**274 Old Short Hills Road, Short Hills
(973) 258-4026,
www.greenwoodgardens.org**

Since the early twentieth century, Greenwood Gardens was a private retreat with formal Italianate gardens graced by colorful tiles, rustic stone tea houses, mossy-pebbled walks, and vistas stretching for miles into the surrounding wooded hillsides. Careful preservation work and imaginative horticulture have returned much of the garden to its original Arts and Crafts design. Greenwood Gardens is endorsed by the Garden Conservancy as a Preservation Project Garden.

🕐 Special Garden Conservancy Open Days 2016: May 7, May 21, and September 10, 10 a.m. to 4 p.m., otherwise April through October, Sunday, Monday, and Tuesday from 10 a.m. to 4 p.m.

$ $7

➲ From Garden State Parkway, take Exit 142. Take I-78 west to Millburn and take Exit 50B. At top of exit ramp, turn right onto Vauxhall Road and proceed to its end, about 0.8 mile. At end of Vauxhall, turn left onto Millburn Avenue. In about 1 mile, road jogs slightly to right and changes to Essex). At third traffic light turn right onto Old Short Hills Road and go up hill about 0.5 mile to stone gateposts marking entrance of Greenwood Gardens, 274, on right. Turn here and follow signs to parking lot.

From New Jersey Turnpike/I-95 south, take Exit 14/Newark Airport. Stay right through tollbooth, and take I-78 local west to Millburn, and get off at Exit 50B. Proceed as directed above.

From Route 24 west, take Hobart Gap Road exit. Turn right at light onto Hobart Gap Road. At blinking light, road name changes to White Oak Ridge Road. At next light (1 mile), turn right onto Parsonage Hill Road. Continue to "T" junction. Turn left onto Old Short Hills Road and go about 0.6 mile where road widens at stone gate marked with signs for Greenwood Gardens.

SOMERSET COUNTY

FAR HILLS

LEONARD J. BUCK GARDEN
**11 Layton Road, Far Hills
(908) 234-2677,
www.somersetcountyparks.org**

The Leonard J. Buck Garden is a nationally known rock garden, developed by its namesake in the 1930s. It lies in a woodland stream valley where natural rock outcroppings have been uncovered. There are extensive collections of pink and white dogwoods, azaleas, rhododendrons, wildflowers, ferns, alpines, and rock-loving plants.

🕐 April through November, weekdays, 10 a.m. to 4 p.m.; Saturday, 10 a.m. to 5 p.m.; Sunday, 12 p.m. to 5 p.m. December through March, weekdays, 10 a.m. to 4 p.m. Closed major holidays. Group tours available.

$ $3 suggested donation; $1 seniors and children.

➲ From I-287 north, take Exit 22B; from I-287 south, take Exit 22. At end of exit ramp, take Route 202/206 north, staying right to continue north on 202. Follow signs to Far Hills and Morristown. At Far Hills train station, turn right before tracks onto Liberty Corner/Far Hills Road. Travel 0.9 mile to Layton Road and turn right. Garden is on left.

NEW YORK

Tompkins County

Saturday, April 2

🕐 **11 a.m. to 3 p.m.**
$7 per garden

🏷 Pop-up Nursery
Temple Nursery

In case of rain, Hitch Lyman's garden will welcome visitors on April 3rd.

This date is also subject to change due to the appearance of the snowdrop collection!

TOMPKINS COUNTY

TRUMANSBURG

📍 **HITCH LYMAN'S GARDEN**
3441 Krums Corners Road,
Trumansburg

🏷 Temple Nursery

This garden features a collection of more than 400 snowdrop varieties (galanthus) planted in a woodland setting as well as other early spring flowers. The 1848 Greek Revival-style farmhouse was moved to this site in 1990. Please note: due to rough terrain this garden is not handicapped accessible nor appropriate for small children. In case of rain, the garden will welcome visitors April 3rd. Plants will be offered for sale from the Temple Nursery.

2015 | 📷

➲ From Ithaca, go north on Route 96 about 6 miles. Turn right onto Krums Corners Road. Go to sixth driveway on left. Please park on road.

Dutchess County

Sunday, April 10

 DIGGING DEEPER

SUNDAY, APRIL 10 | 3 PM

GARDENING WITH NATURE

Douglas Dockery Thomas talks about Twin Maples

AT: Cary Institute Auditorium
    2801 Sharon Turnpike, Millbrook, NY

Passionate gardener and native plant enthusiast Douglas Thomas will introduce guests to the changing seasons at Twin Maples, her spectacular garden in Salisbury, Connecticut, and describe the process of planting sustainable wildflower meadows that flourish and become more beautiful each year. Twin Maples flows smoothly from architecture to nature, from formal garden to field, with extraordinary views of the Litchfield Hills beyond. Douglas and her late husband, Wilmer Thomas, purchased the property in 1996 and built a Georgian-style house and guest cottage designed by David Anthony Easton. They created formal gardens near the house with landscape architect Rodney Robinson and horticulturist Deborah Munson (one in tribute to the work of Russell Page), a woodland garden with Deborah Munson, and a 40-acre wildflower meadow with native plantsman Larry Weaner that figures prominently in his upcoming book, *Garden Revolution: How Our Landscapes Can Be a Source of Environmental Change* (Timber Press, May 2016). Douglas Thomas and Deborah Munson will lead a tour of this extraordinary garden at a Digging Deeper event for the Garden Conservancy's Open Days program on Saturday, July 30.

Twin Maples has been featured in numerous publications and was documented by the Millbrook Garden Club for the Smithsonian's Archives of American Gardens. In 2011, **Douglas Thomas** received the Place Maker Award from the Foundation for Landscape Studies for "creating a landscape of extraordinary environmental sensitivity and beauty." They went on to note that "In its entirety, Twin Maples exemplifies place making as an art form of great importance." Douglas is a member of the Horticulture Committee at New York Botanical Garden, as well as the Advisory Council for their School of Professional Horticulture; the Advisory Council of the Ladybird Johnson Wildflower Center; a Managing Director of the Metropolitan Opera; and a Board Member and Meadows Committee Co-Chair for the Dumbarton Oaks Park Conservancy.

Deborah Munson is a sought-after horticulturist in the region and has worked on Twin Maples since the gardens began. She has been a driving force behind Trade Secrets since its inception.

Registration is required and space is limited.   **opendaysprogram.org**   **1(888) 842-2442**

Putnam County

Saturday & Sunday, April 23 & 24

SATURDAY, APRIL 23

 Stonecrop Gardens
10th Annual NARGS Plant Sale
9 a.m. to 3 p.m.

 DIGGING DEEPER: Rock Garden Plants
—Easy to Sublime, with Anne Spiegel,
Stonecrop Gardens, Cold Spring, 11 a.m.

(Anne Spiegel's garden will be open for
the May 21 Dutchess County Open Day.
See page 187.)

✳ SPECIAL PUBLIC

COLD SPRING

⭐ **STONECROP GARDENS**
81 Stonecrop Lane, Cold Spring
(845) 265-2000, www.stonecrop.org

 10th Annual NARGS Plant Sale, April 23

DIGGING DEEPER, April 23

Special Garden Conservancy 2016 Open Day
on April 24, 10 a.m. to 5 p.m. featuring Tea in
the Garden. Visitors may purchase tea and
cake from 12 p.m. to 4 p.m.

Other upcoming 2016 Open Days: May 8,
June 12, July 17, August 14, September 18, and
October 2

Stonecrop Gardens, originally the home
of Frank and Anne Cabot, became a public
garden in 1992 under the direction of Caroline
Burgess. Frank Cabot is also the founder of
the Garden Conservancy. At its windswept
elevation of 1,100 feet in the Hudson Highlands, Stonecrop enjoys a Zone 5 climate. The
display gardens cover an area of about twelve
acres and incorporate a diverse collection of
gardens and plants including woodland and
water gardens, a grass garden, raised alpine

SUNDAY, APRIL 24

Stonecrop Gardens Special Open Day
🕐 **10 a.m. to 5 p.m.**
$5 admission

 Tea in the Garden at Stonecrop Gardens
12 p.m. to 4 p.m.

stone beds, a cliff rock garden, perennial beds,
and an enclosed English-style flower garden.
Additional features include a conservatory,
display alpine house, a pit house with an
extensive collection of choice dwarf bulbs, and
systematic order beds representing over fifty
plant families.

➲ From Taconic State Parkway, take Route
301/Cold Spring exit. Travel 3.5 miles to
Stonecrop's entrance on right. A sign reading
"Stonecrop Gardens" marks the driveway.

From Route 9, take Route 301 east 2.7 miles
and turn left at the entrance.

Photo: M. Doren

STONECROP GARDENS

81 Stonecrop Lane, Cold Spring, New York
845.265.2000 www.stonecrop.org

Stonecrop Gardens consists of 15 acres of gardens at a windswept elevation of 1,100 feet in the Hudson Highlands in Cold Spring, New York.

Come see our diverse collection of gardens and plants
• Conservatory • Enclosed Flower Garden • Woodland Garden
• Mediterranean Garden • Alpine Rock Ledge • Systemic Order Beds

❋ Plants for sale / Membership available ❋
....

Our mission is to uphold and demonstrate the highest standards of horticultural practice and to promote the use of such standards among amateur and professional gardeners through aesthetic displays and educational programs.
....

Stonecrop is open Monday – Saturday
April – October, 10 a.m. – 5 p.m.
Admission $5

Guided group tours (10 or more people) available by appointment

---

❋ 2016 Garden Conservancy Open Days ❋
April 24, May 8, June 12, July 17, August 14, September 18, October 2
Join us for Tea in the Garden (noon – 4 p.m.)

DIGGING DEEPER

SATURDAY, APRIL 23 | 11 AM

ROCK GARDEN PLANTS
—EASY TO SUBLIME

A Lecture by Anne Spiegel

AT: Stonecrop Gardens, 81 Stonecrop Lane, Cold Spring

To help celebrate Stonecrop's 10th annual NARGS plant sale, noted gardener Anne Spiegel will showcase an array of choice rock garden plants for fellow gardeners at every level, along with practical tips for growing them successfully. Anne will draw on her many years of experience as a dirt gardener (she won the prestigious Linc & Timmy foster Millstream Garden Award "for an outstanding contribution to the North American Rock Garden Society for creating a superior garden" for her garden in nearby Dutchess County), her friendships with great rock gardeners around the world, as well as her insights (and photographs) gleaned from a lifetime of hiking in mountains and high deserts looking at plants in the wild.

For more information on the Stonecrop NARGS sale, please visit www.stonecrop.org

You can visit Anne Spiegel's garden during the Saturday, May 21 Dutchess County Open Day. See page 187.

Registration is required and space is limited. **Opendaysprogram.org or call 1(888) 842-2442**

Westchester County

Sunday, April 24

🕐 **10 a.m. to 3 p.m.**
$7 admission

WESTCHESTER COUNTY

LEWISBORO

📍 **THE WHITE GARDEN**
199 Elmwood Road, Lewisboro

The native oak-hickory forest provides a "sacred grove" setting for the modern Greek Revival-style house. The gardens were designed by Patrick Chassé, ASLA, and completed in 1999. Nearest the house the gardens are clas-

The White Garden, featured in *Outstanding American Gardens: A Celebration—25 Years of the Garden Conservancy*. Photo by Marion Brenner.

sically inspired, including a nymphaeum, pergola garden, labyrinth, and theater court, and additional hidden gardens include a perennial ellipse and "annual" garden, a conservatory "jungle" garden, and an Asian-inspired moss garden. Several water features accent the landscape, and native plantings dominate in areas outside the central gardens. Many sculptures enrich this landscape and one can visit a Temple of Apollo on an island in the main pond. In spring, over 300,000 daffodils bloom in the woodland. Woodland walking paths weave over a meandering brook and through a shady dell. Several glasshouses can be seen, including a new state-of-the-art greenhouse that supports the gardens. Head gardener

Eric Schmidt, who ably orchestrates the rich garden plantings throughout the property, is on hand for questions.

2015 |

➲ From Route 15/Merritt Parkway, take Exit 38 and follow Route 123 North through New Canaan into New York state. Town of Lewisboro and village of Vista are first signs encountered. Go past Vista Fire Department about 0.25 mile. Just after shingled Episcopal church on right, Route 123 bears left and Elmwood Road bears right. Go about another 0.25 mile just over a hill. At beginning of a gray stockade fence on right is driveway at #199.

Dutchess County

Sunday, May 1

🕐 **10 a.m. to 2 p.m.**
$7 admission

🌷 DIGGING DEEPER: Photographing Eden—The Work of Curtice Taylor, with Curtice Taylor, Millbrook, 3 p.m.

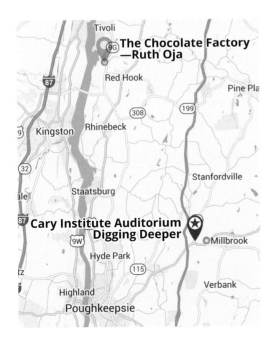

DUTCHESS COUNTY

RED HOOK

📍 **THE CHOCOLATE FACTORY—RUTH OJA**
21 Cedar Hill Road, Red Hook

Built on the ruined foundation of a 1895 Livingston grist mill, this garden combines English style naturalism with the Hudson Valley ideal of the picturesque. The site slopes steeply down to a dramatic waterfall on the Sawkill Creek, which powered the mill and then the chocolate factory which briefly replaced it. The garden was designed to take advantage of the factory ruins, the layered rocky terrain, and the surrounding woods. A path of pine needles winds its way through a woodland garden of native shade plants and shrubs where thousands of spring bulbs bloom before trees leaf out. In the limited sunny areas, there are perennial gardens of roses, phlox, campanula, and bee balm. Shady terraces and woods border a brick walk which curves downhill to old brick courtyards and gardens enclosed by restored stone factory walls. One last turn reveals the waterfall and its associated shade garden of daffodils, astilbe, foxglove, and broad- leafed evergreens. This is an organic garden living in harmony with its natural and historic surroundings.

2015 |

➲ Follow directions to Bard College gardens, Blithewood Arboretum etc. Turn west at

Route 9G and Annandale Road/River Road/ Route 109. Go around the Annandale Triangle, directly across is Shafer House and Cedar Hill Road sign. Chocolate Factory is second house on this unpaved dirt driveway/road.

🌀 DIGGING DEEPER

SUNDAY, MAY 1 | 3 PM

PHOTOGRAPHING EDEN: THE WORK OF CURTICE TAYLOR

AT: Cary Institute Auditorium
    2801 Sharon Turnpike, Millbrook, NY

The work of award-winning garden photographer, Curtice Taylor, has been published in every major shelter magazine in the US and UK, as well as in numerous books. He has been teaching photography at the School of Visual Arts in New York City since 1981. A true Renaissance man, Curtice has written for *Interview*, *Rolling Stone*, *Village Voice*, *Modern Photography* and *House and Garden*, and his photos and other artwork have graced the covers of many books, albums and CDs. Last year, Curtice released a book with author Carolyn Seebohm, *Rescuing Eden: Preserving America's Historic Gardens* (Monacelli) that has received rave reviews internationally. In this lecture, Curtice will talk about his creative process, using images as well as outtakes from *Rescuing Eden*. His book will be available at a book signing following the lecture.

Registration is required and space is limited. **Opendaysprogram.org or call 1(888) 842-2442.**

The Hamptons:South Fork

Saturday, May 7

🕐 **Hours vary by garden
(Starting at 10 a.m.)**

$7 per garden

SUFFOLK COUNTY

EAST HAMPTON

📍 **BIERCUK & LUCKEY GARDEN
18 Sayres Path, East Hampton**

🕐 10 a.m. to 4 p.m.

Our four-season woodland garden under a high oak canopy shelters a collection of rhodo-dendrons, azaleas, kalmia, pieris, understory trees, perennials, bulbs, and tropicals in season. A mostly sunny, rear corner contains a pool designed as a pond with a waterfall and is surrounded with plantings which peak mid-July through October. Winding paths and stone walls enhance a sense of depth and elevation change on a mostly flat acre. There is something in bloom every season.

2015 |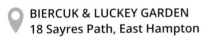

➥ From Montauk Highway/Route 27 turn right onto Sayre's Path. House is first driveway on right. Please park along road.

📍 **THE GARDEN OF DIANNE B.
86 Davids Lane, East Hampton**

🕐 12 p.m. to 4 p.m.

Dianne believes that if she religiously plants at least 1,000 new bulbs each autumn that the Real Spring Garden she aspires to—blankets of flowing color in old English gardens—will come true. This garden is in its eleventh year and the pictures that have so inspired her are beginning to be a reality. She loves *Fritillaria* and you will find them—at least a dozen kinds—under twisting branches, popping out of stone sculptures and nodding among the cultivated moss under a huge seventy-five-year-old pink *Magnolia grandiflora*. Favoring the unusual, she hopes you will see the real vivacity of variegation in the new growth of trillium, ligularia and hepatica while savoring the gloriously poignant leafing out of many Japanese maples, elegant small specimen treasures and rare variegated conifers. Her collection of Jack in the Pulpits grows as she can source new ones (difficult to do), but *Arisaema ringens* 'Black Mambo' should be at its most seductive. Look under trees and around corners, you never know what you might find. This is an ever-evolving, layer-upon-layer... [Read the full description online]

2015 | ♿ | 📷

⮑ On Route 27/ Main Street going east, pass East Hampton Town Pond and Guild Hall then turn right onto Davids Lane (just after the big white columned church). The garden is three-quarters of the way down the street on left—just before the East Hampton Duck Pond. Enter through the garden gate. Please park in the direction of traffic.

 EDWINA VON GAL
962-964 Springs Fireplace Road
🕐 10 a.m. to 4 p.m.

I am a landscape designer and environmentalist, my goal is to create beautiful gardens without synthetic chemicals. My garden is my laboratory as well as an ecological refuge of sorts. It is on a protected salt marsh so much of it is not available for me to intercede, which makes the fabulous view stress free. The rest of the four-plus acres contain a variety of natural restoration and garden areas, in various stages of progress: a meadow, woodland, and moss garden, all full of voracious deer. I explore different ways to create interest with plants they don't eat, and selectively plant and protect those they do. My one deer-proof area—a fenced garden that contains vegetables, shrubs and flowers—is where I get to do most of my gardening. It is surrounded by beds with attempts at reliably deer-proof flowering plants for the bees and butterflies. I do not remove any biomass from the property so I explore various uses of the materials generated, such as log walls from invasive trees, and hay stacks of the meadow cuttings.

NEW | ♿ | 📷

⮑ Follow North Main Street out of East Hampton and bear right onto Springs Fireplace Road. Property is 4.5 miles on the left. Please park on the street.

 GARDEN OF MARSHALL WATSON
253 Kings Point Road, East Hampton
🕐 10 a.m. to 5 p.m.

Set on a bluff overlooking Gardiner's Bay, this home maintains two gardens. One that is a thoroughfare for a large herd of hungry deer that faces punishing ocean winds and salt, and one that is partially fenced and partially walled. The entire property is transitioning to fully organic. The Charlestonian gates welcome you to the interior designer's garden. A gravel forecourt bordered by a holly stilt hedge, rhododendron bed, and gated potager features a wisteria-draped carriage house/potting shed and a neoclassic gazebo which overlooks the walled garden. Note the log-rounds walkway built from cherry and oak trees felled by Hurricane Sandy. A gentle fountain greets you as you circle around the organic vegetable garden and ascend the Italian inspired-circular stairs. The gazebo is surrounded by cascading maples and a unique euonymus groundcover where variegated irises and allium pop through. As you proceed along the formal gravel entrance, flanked by boxwood and agapanthus, the first of many pear and apple espaliers appears... [Read the full description online]

2015 | ♿ | 📷

⮑ Drive east on Route 27/Montauk Highway through East Hampton. Before the windmill and right after Newtown Lane, bear left onto North Main Street. Go under the train trestle. Continue on North Main, through the traffic light, until the road forks. Bear left at the fork onto Three-Mile Harbor Road. Travel several miles past East Hampton Point, past the Bay Kitchen Bar, until you come to a very sharp right turn, or dogleg, at the bottom of the hill. After this dogleg, turn left onto Kings Point Road. Follow this to #253, on the right. The house is on the water. Please park alongside the road next to the garden and gates.

Westchester County

Saturday, May 7

🕐 **10 a.m. to 4 p.m.**
$7 admission

The Wildflower Island at Teatown Lake Reservation in Ossining will also be open on this day.

WESTCHESTER COUNTY

CHAPPAQUA

📍 **SHOBHA VANCHISWAR & MURALI MANI**
76 Castle Road, Chappaqua

🕐 10 a.m. to 4 p.m.

This modest-sized organically maintained garden won the 2007 Golden Trowel award from Garden Design magazine. It features a cottage garden of bulbs and perennials, a Belgian espalier of fruit trees, a grape arbor, an herb garden, a checkerboard garden, and a "meadow" with naturalized bulbs and a greenhouse. There are many European touches like rose arbors, window boxes, a fountain, and Anduze pots. There is also a terrace with a canopied dining area. A vertical garden of mostly ferns and inspired by Patrick Blanc was installed two springs ago. It has been a steep learning curve and we look forward to when it is mature. Presently, we are enjoying sharing it in its infancy. Modest in size, our garden is rich in detail and has a great deal of visual appeal. This garden was featured in the 2010 "Best of" issue of *Westchester Home* magazine.

2015 | ♿ | 📷

➲ From lower Westchester County and New York City, take Saw Mill Parkway North to Exit 32. Follow signs for Route 120 South through hamlet of Chappaqua. Cross parkway. Turn left at "Y," and then left onto South Greeley, then right onto King Street. Halfway up King Street, turn left onto Castle Road. Look for Samalin Investment Counsel at crossing. House is #76 with post-and-rope railing. Please park

on street, staying clear of front of garden, driveway, and walkways.

From upper Westchester County, take Saw Mill Parkway south to Exit 32. Make two right turns and proceed as directed above from Route 120 South.

✳ PUBLIC GARDEN

OSSINING

📍 **THE WILDFLOWER ISLAND AT TEATOWN LAKE RESERVATION**
1600 Spring Valley Road, Ossining

🚩 Guided Tours: 10 a.m. / 12 p.m. / 2 p.m.
Reservations are required. (914) 762-2912, ext.110 by May 5. $5 per person.

See this garden's listing on page 261.

The Area's Widest Selection of Fine Garden Plants

rosedale
NURSERIES, INC.

51 Saw Mill River Road, Hawthorne, NY 10532
(914) 769-1300 • Fax: (914) 769-8770
Open daily 9–5:30 • *www.rosedalenurseries.com*

Putnam County

Stonecrop Gardens Special Open Day featuring Tea in the Garden

SUNDAY, MAY 8

Garden is open 10 a.m. to 5 p.m.
$5 admission

☕ Visitors may purchase tea and cake from 12 p.m. to 4 p.m.

Other upcoming 2016 Open Days: June 12, July 17, August 14, September 18, and October 2. See Stonecrop Gardens' full listing on page 259.

Long Island's North Shore

Sunday, May 15

🕐 **Hours vary by garden**
   (Starting at 10 a.m.)

$7 per garden

SUFFOLK COUNTY

MT. SINAI

TRANQUILITY
42 Jesse Way, Mt. Sinai
🕐 10 a.m. to 4 p.m.

The Becker garden can be described as an explosion of color, fragrance, sound, and texture. Hundreds of perennials, shrubs, trees, and annuals are combined with water features, lawn art, and recently relocated garden trails that allow the visitor to enter the owner's vision of a impressionistic garden painting. Garden footpaths wind through the extensive garden allowing the visitor to immerse themselves in the sights and sounds of nature and escaping the general stress of modern lifestyles. Unique shrubs and flowers create interest and winding paths permit the visitor to stroll and enjoy the sights, sounds, and fragrance of nature.

2015 | ♿ | 📷

➲ Take the Long Island Expressway to Exit 63/Route 83. Go north to Canal Road. Turn left and then take the first right onto Autumn Road. Go to end. Turn right onto Wheat Path and then take the first left onto Jesse Way. Number 42 is on left.

OLD FIELD

TWO GREY ACHERS
88 Old Field Road, Old Field
🕐 11 a.m. to 4 p.m.

Designed, executed and largely maintained by its owners to provide seasonal interest everyday of the year, this garden, adjacent to Conscience Bay on Long Island's North Shore, uses conifers large and small, rhododendrons, azaleas, Japanese maples, and companions to create a tapestry of color, texture, and form. Its favorable maritime microclimate is reflected in the broad range of taxa thriving in this extensively planted landscape. Those visitors returning to the garden since it was last included on the Conservancy's Open Days Program will see a somewhat expanded and much matured landscape.

2013 | ♿ | 📷

➲ Take Route 495/Long Island Expressway to Exit 62. Take Route 97/Nicolls Road North to end at Route 25A. Turn right onto Route 25A and then left at the first traffic light. Go through four stop signs to end at the stone bridge. Turn left over stone bridge onto Old Field Road. Go about 2 miles to #88 on the left. There is no name on the mailbox, but the number 88 shows clearly. There is no roadside parking in the Village of Old Field. Cars should pull off the roadside onto the front lawn.

STONY BROOK

SUE BOTTIGHEIMER'S GARDEN
61 Cedar Street, Stony Brook
🕐 10 a.m. to 4 p.m.

My neighbors' trees create a sense of space. It enlarges the sense of my own garden's size. Within one half acre, raised beds, shrubs, and small evergreens divide the garden into distinct spaces—the front, lower garden; a back lawn with surrounding beds; a shade garden; a north side, and a south side—with different kinds of plantings. In the sunny areas, grassy paths lead from area to another—while wood chip paths go through shady ones. In May, the beds are filled with exuberantly blooming azaleas and companion plants, the shady paths bordered by rare plants and columbines. Recent changes: the February 2013 ice storm gutted a witch hazel, star magnolia, and crape myrtle, but they are now on the mend; a large berm surrounds a newly landscaped work area in the back of the garden; a new and well-designed tool house has brought order to the 1001 things every gardener needs to lay hands on; and an area tucked above the driveway is slowly emerging as a densely planted bed jointly created and tended together with my wonderful neighbor.

2015 | ♿ | 📷

➲ From I-495/Long Island Expressway, go

north on Nicoll Road until it ends at Route 25A. Turn left and proceed to second traffic light at Cedar Street. Turn right and go 0.4 mile to #61. Please park on the street.

📍 **MITSUKO EN**
68 Aspen Lane, Stony Brook
🕐 2 p.m. to 6 p.m.

In a quarter-acre landscape behind a 1967 neo-colonial house, a stream emerges beside a miniature village called Tokuno Mura, cascades beneath a stone slab, through a cluster of boulders, and under an arched wooden bridge to reach a twenty-by-forty-foot lily pond at the base of a hill. A tea house beside a pebble beach, bronze cranes, concrete lanterns, a roofed cedar and bamboo fence with a high covered gate, and a wisteria arbor help to complete the theme. Flowering and evergreen trees and shrubs, whether Japanese or not, are arranged and shaped to give the impression that this is a bit of Japan.

2015 | ♿ | 📷

➲ From Route 347, turn north onto Stony Brook Road (by Hess gas station). Go 2 miles, passing a fire station blinker and two traffic lights. Winding down hill, slow down and signal for a right turn onto Mills Road. Follow to Aspen Lane and continue to #68 where Aspen meets Acorn Lane.

From Route 25A, go south on Stony Brook about 0.5 mile, passing Dogwood Lane and Dairy Farm Road before you reach Mills Road. Proceed as directed above. Please park on street.

Dutchess County

Saturday, May 21

🕐 **10 a.m. to 4 p.m.**
$7 per garden

Pop-up Nursery
Copperheads

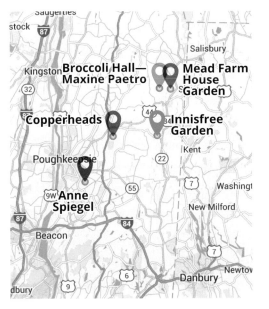

DUTCHESS COUNTY

AMENIA

📍 **BROCCOLI HALL—MAXINE PAETRO**
23 Flint Hill Road, Amenia

Visitors to Broccoli Hall describe this English-style cottage garden as "incredible," "inspirational," "magical"—and they come back again and again. Starting in 1986 with an acre and a half of bare earth, Maxine Paetro collaborated with horticulturist Tim Steinhoff to create a series of enchanting garden rooms. Broccoli Hall offers an apple tunnel, a brick courtyard, a lavish display of spring bulbs blooming with crabapples in May, an extensive border of iris, peonies, and old shrub roses flowering in June, a tree house with long views, and a secret woodland garden with a teddy bears' picnic. We have some new rustic carvings this year by woodsman/artisan Hoppy Quick; new bears, new stairs, new chairs, and some exceptionally charming bird feeders. See photos of Broccoli Hall at www.broccolihall.com.

2015 |

⮕ From Route 22 North, go towards Amenia. Go west on Route 44 to Route 83 North/Smithfield Road. Go 2.5 miles to dirt road on right, Flint Hill Road. Turn right. Garden is first on left. Please park on Flint Hill Road. Be careful of ditches.

📍 MEAD FARM HOUSE GARDEN
224 Perry's Corners Road, Amenia

On the site of a 250-year-old farmyard, this mature garden winds around a fair approximation of a nineteenth-century horse barn and utilizes rocky outcroppings and the stone foundations of long-gone farm buildings as the visual anchors of the perennial beds. Our objective was to suggest that the gardens occurred naturally in the environment rather than being impressed upon it. The base of an old silo has become a deck from which one can gaze over a small pond at the distant landscape. Features include a bog garden and some interesting trees.

2015 | 📷

⮕ From Routes 22, 44 & 343 at only traffic light in Amenia, take Route 22/44 north about 1 mile. Turn left at Maplebrook School onto Perry's Corners Road. Go about 1 mile to clapboard farmhouse on right. Please park on street.

DOVER PLAINS

📍 COPPERHEADS
1249 Route 343, Dover Plains

🏷️ Unusual plants for sale, home-grown from seed!

For the first time ever Copperheads will open its gardens to visitors. The Greek Revival-style house, with expansive views of the Berkshire Mountain foothills, was built in the nineteenth century on the slopes of Plymouth Hill. For more than a hundred years, Copperheads

was a dairy farm comprising more than 1,000 acres. During the Civil War, the Dutch family that owned the property migrated West, the house fell into disrepair and the land became secondary growth forest. The present owners have spent decades repairing, rebuilding, and designing the garden. The current property is approximately forty acres of which five acres are house and gardens. Developing a garden on a significantly sloping site was a challenge. Taking advantage of the terrain, and influenced by English garden design, the owners created a number of garden areas or garden rooms. A perennial garden is enclosed by tall hedges. The upper half of this garden is guarded by bronze mastiffs while the lower garden has a frog pond. A boxwood parterre adjacent to the house functions as both a... [Read the full description online]

NEW |

⮕ From the Taconic State Parkway take Route 44 exit east toward Millbrook, 1.8 miles. Continue straight on Route 82 1.9 miles. At the traffic light continue straight on Route 343 6.3 miles to Bretti Lane parking. If Bretti Lane is not on your map/GPS, it is the north side of Route 343 0.4 mile east of Route 24. Take Route 22 to Route 343 west toward Millbrook 1.6 miles to Bretti Lane parking. If Bretti Lane is not on your map/GPS, it is 1.6 miles west of Route 22. Parking entrance and entrance to property on Bretti Lane immediately off of Route 343. Please do not park on Route 343.

WAPPINGERS FALLS

📍 ANNE SPIEGEL
299 Maloney Road, Wappingers Falls

The dramatic natural setting of this rock garden is the first thing visitors notice. The massive and beautiful outcrop has been enhanced by a series of stone-walled raised beds constructed on stepped ledges and cliffs and planted with choice specimens. Included in the extensive screes and sand beds will be found alpines on many a rock gardener's wish list: *Astragalus*, *Oxytropis,* and *Penstemon* are exceptionally well represented, but the list could go on. The north end of the garden had to be rebuilt after the tornado of 2000; the south end has been extended and developed into a series of tufa and crevice beds which have reached the top of the cliff and the natural crevices on the back of the cliff are now being planted. The sunny and windy garden is never watered due to an inadequate well and there is continuing experimentation with xerophytic and drought tolerant plants. There is also a separate fenced stream garden, home to plants that like wet feet, and a new area beyond the north end of the cliff is being developed for hellebores and other shade lovers. This garden is a testament to both Nature and Nurture: the site is spectacular, but the dedicated hand of the gardener is everywhere adeptly and discreetly in evidence. The garden received the prestigious Linc and Timmy Foster Millstream Garden Award in 2011 from the National Rock Garden Society. **2014** | ♿ | 📷

➲ From Taconic State Parkway North, take Noxon/Lagrangeville exit. Turn left off ramp and proceed 0.4 mile to stop sign and turn right onto Noxon Road. Go about 2.2 miles to Maloney Road on left, then 1.5 miles to garden on left. From Taconic State Parkway South, take Arthursburg Road exit. Go 3.2 miles to Maloney Road on left and proceed as directed above. Please follow parking and exit signs carefully.

❋ PUBLIC GARDEN

MILLBROOK

 INNISFREE GARDEN
362 Tyrell Road, Millbrook
(845) 677-5268,
www.innisfreegarden.org
See this garden's listing page 257.

The Hamptons

Saturday, May 21

🕐 **10 a.m. to 4 p.m.**
$7 per garden

SUFFOLK COUNTY
CUTCHOGUE

 ARNOLD & KAREN BLAIR
4560 Vanston Road, Cutchogue

Our three-acre Peconic Bayfront property overlooks a seventeen-acre beach and wetland protected preserve deeded to The Nature Conservancy—a haven for migratory and nesting sea birds. The gardens flow from an eighty-foot elevation down to sea level via numerous winding paths with various landings and overlooks. A park-like one-and-one-half acre woodland garden features numerous spring flowering shrubs and trees under towering oaks. A wandering rustic path leads to a massive log gazebo fronting a wetland we lovingly rescued from invasive vines and replanted with indigenous bayberry, high tide bush, and native grasses which put on a late Fall delightful burst of color. Extensive stone walls surround a pool tucked into the hillside. Rolling lawns, numerous specimen evergreens, antique and salvaged garden ornaments, and 180-degree bay views with magnificent sunsets enhance a magical spot on the North Fork. Our garden is self-designed and features plenty of natives. It has evolved over twenty seven years of experimenting, transplanting, learning, and re-transplanting. Our garden is a living, breathing, perpetual work that will never finish.

2015 |

⮕ Take Route 25 East from Riverhead. At the second traffic light in Cutchogue, turn right onto Eugenes Road. Turn right onto Skunk Lane. Bear right and continue all the way to the Bay where road curves right over causeway. At end of causeway road forks. Take right fork which is Vanston Road. House is 0.9 mile on right on Vanston Road.

FLANDERS

 GARDEN OF VALERIE M. ANSALONE
86 Risa Court, Flanders

Welcome to my garden. It has been evolving over the past twenty- eight years. My original goal has not changed: create a park-like setting that will welcome me home. The one-acre property was originally filled with oaks, pitch pines, and berryless blueberry bushes. Today there is a native oak canopy as you stroll through winding garden paths to find rhododendrons, azaleas, conifers, magnolias, perennials, hydrangeas, landscape trees, and bulbs. The woodland walk, with sitting areas to enjoy the environment, leads to my 4,000-gallon koi pond where you will meet Chester, Parker, and Bella—a few of my Japanese koi. My garden was featured on the East End, on News 12, and in the Home and Garden supplement to the News Review and other North Fork local newspapers. My garden is designed to provide color and foliage every season.

2015

⮕ From Route 27/Sunrise Highway, take Exit 64N/Route 104. Take first right onto Pleasure Drive, then first left onto Risa Court. Number 86 has white gate. Garden is about two minutes from Route 27 exit.

REMSENBURG

 THE GARDENS OF FRED MEYER
7 Tuthill Lane, Remsenburg

In 1976 when this municipal planner and his English wife were looking for a second home to escape to for peace and solitude they revisited Remsenburg that was familiar to him from childhood days. They found a farm building (chicken coop, since expanded) nestled away among a cedar forest; it then became a series of garden rooms accented with a collection of architectural and whimsical elements. After walking up a long bluestone driveway, the first indication of something special is the use of espaliered Hollywood junipers on the façade of this home. Passing through the gates to the deer-fenced garden, the visitor is greeted by a glorious perennial border of iris, peonies, hollyhock, roses, and other perennials anchored with clematis on tripods. The homeowner says the border is designed to delight with color. Leaving the well-groomed blue spruce, 'Fat Albert', a visitor is presented with a choice of two paths carved out of the cedar forest. As Yogi Berra said, "When you come to a fork in the road, take it," because either way opens your visit... [Read the full description online]

2013 | ♿ | 📷

➲ From the west, take Sunrise Highway to Exit 62. Turn right at the stop sign to Montauk Highway. Turn left and go through Eastport Hamlet. After the railroad underpass and just past Speonk sign, bear right onto South Country Road. Go past the post office, two streets to Tuthill Lane. Garden is at third driveway on right.

From the east, take Sunrise Highway to Exit 63/Westhampton Beach. Go south on Montauk Highway and turn right at the traffic light. Go west 2.8 miles to Nidgyn Avenue to end. Turn right and then left onto driveway.

📍 TUTHILL GARDENS
16 Tuthill Road, Remsenburg

The Schwartz garden is an estate of thirteen-plus acres. From the rear raised patio there is a parterre of two very long beds on either side of a wide grass path. The gardens comprise mature tree peonies, azaleas, and dogwoods all edged with a yew hedge. There is also formal garden of Knock Out roses and two rows of mature Alberta spruce trees. Some of the acreage is wetland and a large pond.

NEW | 📷

➲ From the west, take Sunrise Highway to Exit 62. Turn right at the stop sign to Montauk Highway. Turn left and go through Eastport Hamlet. After the railroad underpass and just past Speonk sign, bear right onto South Country Road. Go past the post office, two streets to Tuthill Lane.

From the east, take Sunrise Highway to Exit 63/Westhampton Beach. Go south on Montauk Highway and turn right at the traffic light. Go west 2.8 miles to Nidgyn Avenue to end. Turn right and then left onto Tuthill Lane. Please park on the street.

📍 WINTERGREEN GARDEN
34 Nidzyn Avenue, Remsenburg

Welcome to Wintergreen Garden. Storied features abound—patterned brick patios, paths, seating, statuary, pool, fish pond, children's playhouse, folly and 'great lawn'—all on a mini estate scaled 0.6 acre. What began as a low maintenance alternative to a lawn, the garden has been our amateur exercise in adapting to forty years of nature's challenges and changes. Lovingly laid recycled brick paths form a Celtic cross diagonally traversing the backyard. A smaller brick circle path knots the garden together, punctuated by an armillary sphere. The paths inspire a meditative four-season garden of hope and healing. Varying sun and shade pockets have been planted to extend color from late winter's flowering hellebore colonies, to November's re-blooming irises. May's forget-me-nots blanket soil amid the early season mixed borders. Our garden is a sanctuary to multiple bird and wildlife species, as well as a sensory delight to humans. The hummingbirds return with their antics in May. Bees buzz, bunnies bounce. May your spirit soar.

NEW | 📷

➲ From Long Island Expressway take Exit 70 South. Continue on County 111 for 1.1 mile. Turn right (west) onto Gordon Street for 289 feet. Turn left (south) onto Eastport-Manor Road for 2.1 miles. Turn left (east) onto Route 80 East for 2.1 miles. Turn right (south) onto Nidzyn Avenue. The garden is on left in 0.4 mile.

From Sunrise Highway take Exit 61 South and go south on Eastport-Manor Road for 0.7 miles. Turn left (east) onto Route 80 for 2.1 miles. Turn right (east) onto Nidzyn Avenue. The garden is on left in 0.4 mile.

Dutchess County

Sunday, May 22

 DIGGING DEEPER

SUNDAY, MAY 22 | 3 PM

THE QUIET BEAUTY OF INNISFREE—
A MODERN ICON

AT: Cary Institute Auditorium
  2801 Sharon Turnpike, Millbrook, NY

Recognized as one of the world's ten best gardens, Innisfree is a powerful icon of mid-twentieth century design. Join Innisfree Landscape Curator (and Garden Conservancy Open Days Director of Recruitment) Kate Kerin as she tells the story of this unique landscape, which has been compared to the Great American novel—love, wealth, loss, perseverance, innovation, and quiet triumph. Innisfree merges Modernist ideas with traditional Chinese and Japanese garden design principles resulting in a distinctly American stroll garden—a sublime composition of rock, water, wood and sky achieved with remarkable ecomony and grace.

Registration is required and space is limited. **Opendaysprogram.org or call 1(888) 842-2442**

Columbia County

Saturday, June 4

🕐 **Hours vary by garden**
  (Starting at 10 a.m.)

$7 per garden

🏷 Pop-up Nursery
  Pondside Nursery / Broken Arrow Nursery

 DIGGING DEEPER: Succulent Love,
  Katherine Tracey, Copake Falls

COLUMBIA COUNTY

ANCRAM

📍 **ADAMS-WESTLAKE**
  681 County Route 7, Ancram

🕐 12 p.m. to 4 p.m.

Two writers, Abby Adams, who writes about gardens and interiors, and her late husband, crime novelist Donald Westlake, authored the various plantings on this former farm in a pastoral Columbia County valley. The gardens have evolved over twenty-five years reflecting the owners' deepening involvement with the larger landscape. Flower beds, a walled swimming pool enclosure, an ornamental frog pond, and a courtyard herb garden frame the 1835 farmhouse. A small orchard and a cutting garden/vegetable plot continue the farm-

ing tradition. Behind the house, strategically placed paths and sitting areas guide the visitor through the landscape to a deep natural ravine where a spring-fed pond faces a field of wildflowers. A winding creek has recently been liberated from its tangle of thorny multiflora roses to be replaced by wild and native plant species. Above the ravine, high meadows offer sweeping views.

2014 | 📷🚩

⮎ From Taconic State Parkway, exit at Jackson Corners (mile 71); turn right onto Route 2. Continue (Route 2 becomes Route 7), following signs for Ancram. At "Y," turn right, staying on Route 7. Our house is just past Gallatin Town Hall (about 7 minutes from the Taconic) on left; look for #681 on a red mailbox. (GPS address is 681 Route 7, Gallatin).

CLAVERACK

📍 **PETER BEVACQUA & STEPHEN KING**
Willmon Road & Route 23B, Claverack

🕐 10 a.m. to 4 p.m.

🏷️ Pondside Nursery

Step through the gate of this garden and you'll find yourself in a magical, private world. This two-acre garden, located in the hamlet of Claverack, feels much larger because of its division into many garden spaces—spaces designed with a careful eye to color, form, and especially texture. One area unfolds upon the next with its own sense of individuality. Among the features are the sun garden (surrounded by architectural yew hedges), the evening garden, the greenhouse borders, and many unusual trees and shrubs. The garden continues to evolve. What was once a small orchard is becoming a conifer garden. A boxwood cloud hedge, inspired by the work of Jacques Wirtz, replaces an old rose border. Also, the owners are developing a border consisting of primarily shrubs and small trees. The garden has been featured in the *New York Times*, *New York Spaces* magazine, *Berkshire Living* magazine, *Gardens of the Hudson Valley* (Monacelli Press), and the recently published *Private Gardens of the Hudson Valley* (also by Monacelli Press).

2015 | ♿ | 📷

⮑ From Taconic State Parkway, take Exit 82 and go northwest towards Hudson and Rip Van Winkle Bridge. At first traffic light, turn right onto Route 9H/Route 23. At next light, (Claverack Market and post office will be on right), turn left onto Route 23B. After about 0.8 mile turn right onto Willmon Road. Please park on left.

📍 **KETAY GARDEN**
6121 Route 9H & Route 23, Claverack

🕐 10 a.m. to 4 p.m.

An allée of large maples and ash forms the entrance to the garden. Our ten-acre property can be viewed as three large sections—even though these sections contain divisions within

them. There is a very large garden in front of the house and a smaller intimately planted one behind, which leads to the third section—an expansive meadow in the distance framed by views of the Catskill Mountains. The front garden is bordered by a semi circle of forsythia that shields the garden from the road and encloses the house and front gardens which consist of rooms created with shrubs, perennials and trees. An iron, circular bench surrounds an oak tree and is a great place to sit in spring when the irises and redbud are in bloom. The garden behind the house has a large pergola off the house which is covered with yellow trumpet vine and looks over the garden and meadow beyond. From this garden, a curving mown path leads down the hill, through the meadow and then along the side of the property bordered by our "homage to Tuscany"—a line of tall narrow Irish juniper, which can, when you squint, look like a row of cypress. In the distance are the barn and the Catskill Mountains. A smaller rustic pergola covered with kiwi (which is yet to fruit) and roses is set away from the house with a stone terrace to the side. Two Adirondack chairs sit there for anyone who wishes to watch the sunset or just enjoy the breeze on the meadow.

2015 | ♿ | 📷

⮑ From Hudson, take Route 23B toward Great Barrington. Turn right onto Route 9H/Route 23. The garden is about an eighth of a mile on the right. The driveway is bordered by a black rail fence. It is right before you get to the big Victorian house also on the right.

COPAKE FALLS

📍 **MARGARET ROACH**
99 Valley View Road, Copake Falls

🕐 10 a.m. to 4 p.m.

🏷️ Broken Arrow Nursery

The garden, about twenty-five years of age, reflects my obsession with plants, particularly those with good foliage or of interest to

Margaret Roach's garden, featured in *Outstanding American Gardens: A Celebration—25 Years of the Garden Conservancy*. Photo by Marion Brenner.

wildlife, and also my belief that even in Zone 5B, the view out the window can be compelling and satisfying all 365 days. Sixty kinds of birds have been my longtime companions, along with every native frog and toad species, and we are all happy together. Informal mixed borders, shrubberies, frog-filled water gardens and container groupings cover the steep two-and-one-third-acre hillside, a former orchard with a simple Victorian-era farmhouse and little outbuildings set in Taconic State Park lands on a rural farm road.

2015 | |

➲ From Route 22 (5 miles south of Hillsdale, 13 miles north of Millerton) take Route 344 towards Taconic State Park signs. Bear right onto Valley View Road after park entrance and brown store, over metal bridge and past camp. After High Valley Road on left, stay right another 100 feet to green barn and house on left. Parking on High Valley or opposite house.

⊛ CHURCH OF ST. JOHN IN THE WILDERNESS
261 State Route 344, Copake Falls

 DIGGING DEEPER VENUE

HUDSON

◉ HUDSON HOOD
72 North Third Street, Hudson
🕐 11 a.m. to 4 p.m.

This urban shotgun-style garden is in the middle of the city, centered on a century-old tulip tree and composed of a wide range of topiaries of holly, boxwood, spruce, privet, and heather. The garden transforms into a tall "exotic jungle" in summer with grasses, rare plants and native specimens. The garden also contains a Modernist-inspired sunken walled garden with square koi pond and collection of contemporary sculptures. The adjoining garden, centered on grid form, contains raised vegetable garden and gravel walks.

2015 | ♿ | 📷

⮑ From Route 9 in Hudson, turn west onto Columbia Street. Go 0.6 mile and turn right onto North Third Street to the end. Plenty of on street parking as well as free parking behind the High School building directly across the street.

WEST TAGHKANIC

ARCADIA—RONALD WAGNER & TIMOTHY VAN DAM
733 Taghkanic Road, West Taghkanic

🕐 10 a.m. to 4 p.m.

Our early Greek Revival-style farmhouse is set in a pastoral landscape. An avenue of sweet gum trees lining the formal drive, is planted in forced perspective to visually extend the approach to the house. The gently rolling hillside is punctuated by a magnificent grove of black locust trees, a developing grove of deciduous conifer trees including bald cypress, metasequoia, and larch, and a wild-flower meadow rises to the north. The informal plantings include the lilac walk and rhododen-dron and hydrangea beds. A large pond is the focus of surrounding naturalistic plantings giving to views of the wetland beyond. Symmetrical twin terraces at the house feature an arbor-covered stone dining table on the south and perennial border on the north.

2015 | ♿ | 📷

⮑ From center of village of Livingston/Route 9, go east on Church/Livingston Road, passing red brick Dutch Reformed Church, and go east about 2 miles, to Taghkanic Road. Turn right and go to third house on right, #733. From the Taconic State Parkway, take Hudson/Ancram, Route 82 exit. Drive northwest on Route 82, past Taconic Diner with neon Indian. About 1 mile from Taconic Parkway, turn left onto Livingston Road. Go 0.5 mile up a winding hill to Taghkanic Road on left. Turn left and go to third house on right, #733.

🌱 DIGGING DEEPER

SATURDAY, JUNE 4

SUCCULENT LOVE

AT: **Church of St. John in the Wilderness**
    261 State Route 344, Copake Falls

Katherine Tracey of Avant Gardens Nursery explores our love affair with succulents. With twenty-five years of nursery experience—selling both retail and mail-order—and a particular passion for foliage and especially succulents, Katherine will share her tips for growing and designing with succulents.

Registration is required and space is limited. **Opendaysprogram.org or call 1(888) 842-2442**

Putnam & Westchester County

Sunday, June 5

🕐 **10 a.m. to 4 p.m.**
$7 per garden

There are also gardens open on this day in nearby Fairfield County, CT. See page 74.

🚩 Guided Tour: Eastward

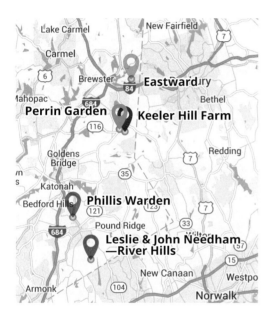

PUTNAM COUNTY

BREWSTER

📍 **EASTWARD**
28 Reynwood Drive, Brewster

🚩 Guided tours available:
11:30 a.m. / 1:30 p.m.

Eastward boarding and training stable has been established for fifteen years, and its gardens have evolved. We now have some lovely, maturing specimen trees, Our dominant feature is five large mixed borders each dedicated to a color theme with abundant bloom throughout the season. In addition we have a 200- foot-long garden in the shade of our indoor arena featuring shade-loving plants, including many native woodland

species. It is matched by a semi-formal sunny bed with an eclectic mixture of shrubs, perennials, and annual bedding plants. As a botanist, I have incorporated as wide a variety of different species as possible, in the various environments I can provide. A good number of specimen trees acquired over the past fifteen years are scattered throughout all the gardens, which include more than fifteen separate garden areas. A newer feature is a large enclosed decorative (and practical) vegetable and herb garden mainly planted in raised beds and containers which we are intensively cultivating for local markets. There are guided tours through the entire garden at 11:30 a.m. and again at 1:30 p.m. for anyone interested in detailed information about the plants and their culture.

2015 | ♿ | 📷

➲ From east, take I-84 to Exit 1/Saw Mill Road and turn right at end of ramp. Turn left at light onto Route 6 West. Go 1.5 miles and turn right onto Joe's Hill Road. Go 1 mile and turn right onto Reynwood Drive. From west, take I-84 to Exit 20N/Route 22 North to first light. Turn right at Milltown Road, then 1.5 miles to a right fork onto Federal Hill Road (after small bridge). Go 0.25 mile and turn right onto Joe's Hill Road, then go 0.75 mile and turn left onto Reynwood Drive.

From south, take I-684 North to Brewster, go on Route 22 North, and proceed as directed above from west. From north, take Route 22 South and turn left onto Milltown Road, then proceed as directed above.

WESTCHESTER COUNTY

BEDFORD

 LESLIE & JOHN NEEDHAM —RIVER HILLS
14 Mianus River Road, Bedford

A lovingly-restored 1790s Dutch Colonial-style house sits high on the property overlooking the Mianus River Gorge. All of the terraces and gardens have been designed to complement this full panoramic view. The property meanders on many levels with dining terraces, various gardens, and seating areas for savoring select views. Stone walls and steps lead from the higher perch through casual plantings, a fruit orchard, and a woodland walk. The gardens are intentionally designed in a loose style to blend the antique with the new and tie it all in with the larger pastoral setting.

2015 | ♿ |

⮕ From the Bedford Village Green, take Route 172 East/Pound Ridge Road east towards Pound Ridge. Turn right at Village Mobil Station onto Long Ridge Road. Go 0.7 mile and take next possible right onto Millers Mill Road. Go down the hill and across small bridge. Then take immediate left onto Mianus Road. Number 14 Mianus River Road is 2.1 miles from Millers Mill Road, the last house on the left before East Middle Patent Road. "River Hills" is on the mailbox, across from the driveway. Please park along the road.

BEDFORD HILLS

 PHILLIS WARDEN
531 Bedford Center Road,
Bedford Hills

This garden of many facets includes perennial borders, three water gardens, a formal vegetable garden, wildflower garden, a fern garden, a marsh garden, a tree platform overlooking the marshlands, a woodland walk, a hidden garden, and a formal croquet court. The garden extends over seven acres, the back four acres of which are a study in what deer do not eat.

2015 |

⮕ From Bedford Village, take Route 22 towards Katonah to intersection at Bedford Cross. Garden is on left. Please park at Rippowam School and walk to #531.

NORTH SALEM

 KEELER HILL FARM
64 Keeler Lane, North Salem

The approach to Keeler Hill Farm is up a driveway of maple trees with horse paddocks on each side. A courtyard reveals the house, a converted dairy barn. Gardens surround the many farm buildings which are home to horses, geese, ducks, guinea fowl, dogs, and cats. The gardens closest to the house are broken into rooms providing privacy and visual surprises. There is a friendship garden filled with friends' castoffs. The lilac walk has been expanded and is now a lilac lair with nice views of the farm fields. A path from the more formal gardens leads to the vegetable gardens and the orchard.

2015 |

⮕ From I-684 North, take Exit 7/Purdys. Turn right off exit ramp onto Route 116 East and go about 5 miles. Cross over Old Route 124/ June Road. Route 116 will join up with Route 121 about 1 mile after June Road intersection. Bear left at that intersection. About 1 mile up road, turn right onto Keeler Lane. Go 0.5 mile. On left, you will see seven yellow barns. Turn in gate with sign on left pillar that reads "Keeler Hill Farm" and "Keeler Homestead" on right pillar. Go up driveway to parking.

 PERRIN GARDEN
676 Titicus Road, North Salem

A curved driveway partially lined with bottle-brush buckeye and fragrant sumac leads to a rise revealing an English-style country house bordered by an apple orchard to one side, a woodland garden on another side and a grass meadow in the front. Visitors pass through a series of beech-and yew-lined courtyards to get to the front door. In the rear, formal gardens surrounded by stone walls contain mature perennials and provide lovely views of preserved land in the distance. A small brick and flagstone area surrounded by perennials offers an intimate spot for dining under a sweet gum tree. Below the formal gardens, a transition garden combines native grasses with blueberry bushes and gives way to a wildflower meadow. The property continues to evolve in its incorporation of more and more native plants to provide a habitat for wildlife and a more sustainable landscape for the future.

2014 |

➲ From I-684 North, take Exit 7/Purdys. Follow Route 116 east to North Salem. At intersection of Routes 116 and 121, turn left and go 0.25 mile and turn left into driveway. Go up driveway to designated parking area.

Nassau County

Saturday, June 11

🕙 **10 a.m. to 4 p.m.**
$7 per garden

🌱 DIGGING DEEPER: Tea Ceremony at the John P. Humes Japanese Stroll Garden, with Stephen Morrell, Mill Neck, 10 a.m.

NASSAU COUNTY

GLEN COVE

📍 **KIPPEN HILL**
89 Walnut Road, Glen Cove

Kippen Hill is a seven-year-old garden that encompasses five smaller gardens situated on one-and-one-half acres. There is the variegated garden with 'Dragon's Eye' pine

and Japanese forest grass, variegated hosta and acuba. A formal garden of English-style borders with a central axis bubbler fountain is the anchor to the site. An Asian garden, with an aviary pagoda, is home for our Asian-native egg-laying hens. Coltsfoot from the Humes Japanese Stroll Garden and black bamboo are featured here along with a majestic 100-year-old boulevard cedar that was planted when the house was first built in 1910. A small vegetable garden with heirloom tomatoes, hosts a collection of antique nineteenth-century American garden equipment. The front roomy lawn is our croquet gaming garden with English-style borders making a perfect back drop for this quintessential British pastime. A Lord and Burnham greenhouse dating to 1925 was rescued and restored from a famed Gold Coast estate over three years ago by Dean and Jonathan. This outbuilding doubles as a site...
[Read the full description online]

2015 | ♿ | 📷

➲ Take Exit 39 North on Glen Cove Road from the Long Island Expressway/I-495. Follow Glen Cove Road several miles to the town of

Glen Cove. Turn right at the light onto Bridge Street in front of the Glen Cove Police Station. Proceed to Highland Road and turn right on Highland Road. Drive up the hill to the first stop light. Cross Walnut Road and park on the lawn marked with parking signs on left. Walk to our garden by following the signs to #89 Walnut Road around the corner.

LOCUST VALLEY

NANCY TAYLOR'S GARDEN
227 Piping Rock Road, Locust Valley

Entering from Piping Rock Road are two white posts, the drive leads to an entrance court enclosed by a natural stone wall. From there, one walks through a gate on the left to a bluestone walk around the house, planted with shade-loving shrubs and perennials to a small terrace. The walk leads to a main terrace with plant beds, a fountain, and an arbor. The terrace overlooks a lawn surrounded by azaleas and rhododendrons, a bird bath, and an allée leading down to a rustic arbor. On the left is natural stone walk through the woods that comes out onto the allée. Walking from the terrace to the right through a gate into a small oval garden with a gravel path, there is a shed on the left, planted with hydrangeas, hostas astilbe and behind a boxwood hedge. Following the gravel walk to the right through a gate into the back drive is a garden on the left, next to a small "necessary" inspired from Charleston gardens. Follow the drive back to the entrance court.

NEW | ♿ | 📷

⟳ Coming from the south, from Route 25A turn north onto Wolver Hollow Road at the Old Brookville Police Booth. Turn left onto Piping Rock Road at the stop sign. Go through the traffic light at Chicken Valley Road going north. My house is at #227 Piping Rock Road, the drive just past Pink Woods Lane on the left. Coming from the north, it is the third driveway south of Frost Pond Road on the west side of Piping Rock Road. PLEASE NOTE: THE NUMBERS ON PIPING ROCK ROAD ARE NOT IN SEQUENCE!!

OLD WESTBURY

HOWARD PHIPPS JR. ESTATE
75 Post Road, Old Westbury

Built in 1935, the house was designed by Adams and Prentice with a landscape by Umberto Innocenti. Rhododendrons have been bred and raised here since the beginning and their hybridization continues today. Entering through a formal flower garden, one crosses a grass terrace which overlooks the swimming pool and meadow, set between two diagonal avenues of American beech. To the east, a wide grass path climbs a hill planted with hybrid rhododendrons and uncommon shrubs. An easy walk of about three-quarters of a mile takes a visitor through a Japanese garden, down the meadow to the trial grounds of new rhododendron seedlings, and returns to the house through mature plantings of flowering shrubs, trees, and a hydrangea garden.

2014 | ♿

⟳ Take the Long Island Expressway to Exit 39. Proceed straight along service road for 2 miles. Turn right at traffic light intersection of Post Road, bear right at far end of pond. Take first driveway on the left, 75 Post Road, "Erchless." Go up winding driveway to house.

From the Grand Central Parkway/Northern State Parkway, take Exit 32 to Post Road in Westbury. Turn left at end of ramp. Cross traffic light intersection of Jericho Turnpike. Continue past Westbury High School on right. Take second driveway on the right after the high school, 75 Post Road, "Erchless." Continue up drive to the house.

✳ PUBLIC GARDEN

MILL NECK

 JOHN P. HUMES JAPANESE STROLL GARDEN
Oyster Bay Road & Dogwood Lane, Mill Neck, (516) 676-4486

 DIGGING DEEPER | 10 a.m.

A seven-acre gem of landscape design, the garden provides a retreat for passive recreation and contemplation. The views, textures, and balance of elements in the garden follow Japanese aesthetic principles, encouraging a contemplative experience. The garden suggests a mountain setting beside a sea, where gravel paths represent streams forming pools and cascades, eventually flowing into the ocean, represented by a pond.

🕐 April 30 through October, Saturdays and Sundays, 11:30 a.m. to 4 p.m. Private tours and tea ceremony demonstrations by appointment. Call for reservations.

💲 $10 adults

➲ The garden is located on the North Shore of Long Island about 26 miles from Manhattan and one mile from Planting Fields Arboretum, and the Long Island Railroad's Oyster Bay Line. Taxis are available.

By car from west, take I-495/Long Island Expressway to Exit 39/Glen Cove Road. Follow Glen Cove Road north to Route 25A/Northern Boulevard. Turn right and continue past LIU Post on the right, past Route 107 to the next traffic light at Wolver Hollow Road. The Old Brookville Police station is on the left. Turn left, and follow Wolver Hollow Road to the "T". Turn right onto Chicken Valley Road. Pass Planting Fields Arboretum on right and continue straight through yellow blinking light and continue one half mile to Dogwood Lane. Turn right. Parking is immediately on right.

From the east: Take I-495/Long Island Expressway to Exit 41N to Route 106N to Route 25A/Northern Boulevard. Turn left onto Route 25A and follow to the second traffic light. Turn right onto Wolver Hollow Road. Old Brookville Police State is on the right. Proceed as directed above.

DIGGING DEEPER

SATURDAY, JUNE 11 | 10 AM | $15

TEA CEREMONY

AT: John P. Humes Japanese Stroll Garden
 Oyster Bay Road and Dogwood Lane, Mill Neck, NY

Tour of the very special John P. Humes Japanese Stroll Garden with its curator Stephen Morrell. Stephen will explain the design aspects of Japanese gardens and the art of the tea ceremony. A landscape architect specializing in Japanese-style gardens, Stephen has studied in Japan and is a practitioner of Zen Buddhism and the tea ceremony. He will explain the history of tea ceremony and present formal tea to one lucky guest recipient.

See this garden's listing on page 258.

This program will be held again on June 25, September 17, and October 1.

Registration is required and space is limited. **Opendaysprogram.org or call 1(888) 842-2442**

John P. Humes Japanese Stroll Garden, Mill Neck, New York

A rare example of traditional Japanese garden design in the American Northeast, this garden was inspired by a trip to Japan that John and Jean Humes took in 1960. Both were fascinated by Buddhist aesthetics and enchanted by their visits to the ancient gardens of Kyoto. When they returned from their travels, they transformed a corner of their wooded Long Island property into a Japanese-style garden and imported a traditional teahouse as its centerpiece.

—Excerpted from *Outstanding American Gardens: A Celebration—25 Years of the Garden Conservancy*.
   Photo by Marion Brenner.

The Hamptons: South Fork

Saturday, June 11

🕐 **Hours vary by garden**
   (Starting at 10 a.m.)
$7 per garden

SUFFOLK COUNTY

BRIDGEHAMPTON

 ENTWOOD GARDEN
100 Chase Court, Bridgehampton
🕐 10 a.m. to 4 p.m.

This is an informal but structured seven acre, contoured landscape seeking to combine intimate gardens, intriguing plant, tree and rock specimens, welcoming habitats, expansive views, and recreational spaces. Originally a flat potato field, it centers around two large naturalistic koi ponds nurtured by wetland filter systems, surrounded by open lawn and arboretum areas which in turn give way to border plantings of mature evergreen and deciduous trees, hidden paths, and shade gardens.

Entering through the front gate, you are greeted by a colorful cottage garden partially shaded by a mature crabapple, a Japanese pagoda-tree and yellow deodar cedar. Continuing west under a weeping atlas-cedar archway, you pass a small Asian-style pond and garden on the left and a kitchen, lily, and rose garden on the right. A partially hidden path under a stand of cedars of Lebanon leads to a hidden koi pond overhung by Himalayan pines. Crossing north through the pond on stones set in the water, the path opens onto a lawn bordered on the left by Alaskan cedar, ... [Read the full description online]

➲ Take Route 27 to Bridgehampton. Go north onto Sag Main Turnpike then take immediate left fork onto Lumber Lane. Go north 1 mile. Turn left onto Chase Court. Number 100 is last house on right.

If coming from Sag Harbor, go south onto Sag Main Turnpike. Turn right onto Scuttle Hole Road. Then turn left onto Lumber Lane. Take the first right onto Chase Court to #100 (last house on right). Please park on the street. **NEW | ♿ | 📷**

➲ Take Route 27 to Bridgehampton. Go north onto Sag Main Turnpike then take immediate left fork onto Lumber Lane. Go north 1 mile. Turn left onto Chase Court. Number 100 is last house on right. If coming from Sag Harbor, go south onto Sag Main Turnpike. Turn right onto Scuttle Hole Road. Then turn left onto Lumber Lane. Take the first right onto Chase Court to

#100 (last house on right). Please park on the street.

EAST HAMPTON

GLADE GARDEN
44 Glade Road, East Hampton
🕐 10 a.m. to 4 p.m.

Tranquility and serenity are the main reactions to a half-acre niche carved from the native woodland. The overall impression is one of green textures, but hiding in plain sight is a collection of rare and unusual flowering trees, shrubs, and groundcovers. Hellebores, camellias, and minor bulbs hold sway through April and are succeeded by daphnes, epimedium, fragrant early rhododendrons, and other woodland plants in May. During the summer, color comes from a progression of hydrangeas and other flowering shrubs and trees, including crape myrtles and a collection of Asiatic and American clethra.

2015 | 📷

⮌ From Route 27/Montauk Highway, turn left at traffic light in East Hampton. Pass town pond, go through village, and turn left at windmill. Pass under railroad bridge and turn right at fork to Springs Fireplace Road. In about 3 miles, turn left onto Woodbine and take an immediate right onto Glade Road. Please park along road, not on grass.

GARDEN OF ARLENE BUJESE
40 Whooping Hollow Road, East Hampton
🕐 10 a.m. to 2 p.m.

Situated on a sloping half-acre, the landscape comprises four rooms. A flower garden bordered by evergreens surrounds a goldfish pond in the rear of the house. Brick walkways weave throughout. The front property is terraced into three levels, each with evergreen backdrops to create a "green" environment in winter. Twenty or so sculptures are strategically placed around the property, including large works by William King, Han van de Bovenkamp, Alfonso Ossorio, Dennis Leri, Arline Wingate, and Calvin Albert. Favored trees are flowering fruit specimens, conifers, and deciduous trees and shrubs including a variety of hydrangeas. The garden has been personally created and maintained by the curator/art dealer over a period of twenty-five years, with the aim of offering a meditative "walk-around—sit here and there" environment for all seasons.

2015 | 📷

⮌ Take Route 114 from Sag Harbor or East Hampton, about 4 miles. Turn right onto Whooping Hollow Road. Please park along street.

THE GARDEN OF DIANNE B.
86 Davids Lane, East Hampton
🕐 12 p.m. to 4 p.m.

This is a small garden with big ideas that echoes Dianne's former career in fashion. The weaving of texture, color, layers, shapes and accessories comes naturally to this bulb and tuber fanatic with a specialty in *Arisaema* and Arums. *Allium* in all their guises—the stranger the better—and lilies of the unexpected kind —especially eucomis, callas and species types are everywhere. The brilliant Orientals come later. Peonies, tree and otherwise, and iris of all kinds (she especially likes the late Japanese ensatas) embrace her cool color palette, as do a frenzy of clematis hanging on the new leaves of specimen maples and dwarf dogwoods. Just making their fabulous moody display are many of her most exotic late blooming Jack in the Pulpits. Look under trees, delve among the many varieties of ferns and peek around corners —there are treasures tucked everywhere. And pay attention to the tips of the many conifers—much of the new growth should be at its explosive best. This is an ever-evolving garden that doesn't depend on flowers for its drama. Her garden sets the stage for her well-read blog Dirtier, which is the progeny of her cult gardening book, *Dirt*.

2015 | ♿ | 📷

⮑ On Route 27/ Main Street going east, pass East Hampton Town Pond and Guild Hall then turn right onto Davids Lane (just after the big white columned church). The garden is three-quarters of the way down the street on left—just before the East Hampton Duck Pond. Enter through the garden gate. Please park in the direction of traffic.

PREVITI/GUMPEL GARDEN
230 Old Stone Highway, East Hampton
🕐 10 a.m. to 4 p.m.

This outdoor environment was developed over the last twenty-five years as a series of exterior rooms. Outdoor sculptures created by the owners are scattered through-out the property. Paths featuring petasites, hydrangea, andromeda, and rhododendrons wind through a cedar grove along the east side of the house. Casual lawn and plantings with a tree house featuring dragon and hawk heads make up the east lawn. There is a sun garden with stone terraces and fountain. The shade garden is a cool, quiet, and restful glade featuring hostas and ferns. Woodland paths along the west edge of the property bring you past several sculptures into the fire pit area. A few steps further to the tranquil Pop's Garden with red dragons guarding the area. For the more daring visitor, there is a walking path off Pop's Garden through one acre of wetland woods. This is an ongoing project and we are just beginning to develop its potential (close-toed shoes preferred for this walk). Then, on past the tented "dining room" to the arbor sitting area at the base of the artist's studio. The studio, accessed by a spiral stair tower, will be open for visitors. Move past the formal, on-axis games lawn to the pool patio. You may end your tour with a brief rest in the fabric-shaded pergola which creates a shady haven at the west end of the patio (note the carved fox and cardinal heads on the ends of the beams).

2015 | 📷

⮑ From center of East Hampton, take Montauk Highway/Route 27 to first traffic light past windmill. Turn left onto Accabonac Highway. Drive 4 miles to stop sign at forked intersection. Cross main road and turn right onto north-most fork, Old Stone Highway. Drive 0.25 mile to #230 (mailbox on tree). Please park on main road and walk up drive to first house on right.

Putnam County

Sunday, June 12

🕐 **Hours vary by garden
(Starting at 10 a.m.)**
$7 ($5 at Stonecrop Gardens)

☕ Tea in the Garden at
Stonecrop Gardens

GARRISON

 ROSS GARDENS
43 Snake Hill Road (Travis Corners),
Garrison

🕙 10 a.m. to 4 p.m.

This garden is a series of vignettes that flow into each other on five acres overlooking the Hudson River. The gardens are designed and maintained by the owner, Arthur Ross, and include a water garden, a moon (white) garden, meditation garden, rock garden, interesting daylilies, a fern garden, shrub garden (azaleas, rhododendrons, mountain laurels), cutting gardens, and garden sculptures, along with a waterfall and a new koi pond. Garden paths give easy access to many unusual flowers.

2007 | 📷

➲ Take Route 9 to Garrison Golf Course. Turn west onto Snake Hill Road. Garden is 0.25 mile on left. Parking is available for 30 cars at any one time.

 # SPECIAL PUBLIC

PUTNAM COUNTY

COLD SPRING

 STONECROP GARDENS
81 Stonecrop Lane, COLD SPRING
(845) 265-2000, www.stonecrop.org

🕙 10 a.m. to 5 p.m.

Special Garden Conservancy 2016 Open Day on June 12, 10 a.m. to 5 p.m. featuring Tea in the Garden. Visitors may purchase tea and cake from 12 p.m. to 4 p.m.

See this garden's listing on page 259.

Stonecrop Gardens Special Open Day featuring Tea in the Garden

SUNDAY, JUNE 12

Garden is open 10 a.m. to 5 p.m.
$5 admission

☕ Visitors may purchase tea and cake from 12 p.m. to 4 p.m.

Other upcoming 2016 Open Days: July 17, August 14, September 18, and October 2. See Stonecrop Gardens' full listing on page 259.

Dutchess County

Saturday, June 18

🕐 **10 a.m. to 4 p.m.**
$7 per garden

There are also gardens open on this day in nearby Litchfield County, CT. See page 82.

DUTCHESS COUNTY

AMENIA

📍 **BROCCOLI HALL—MAXINE PAETRO**
23 Flint Hill Road, Amenia

🕐 10 a.m. to 4 p.m.

Visitors to Broccoli Hall describe this English-style cottage garden as "incredible," "inspirational," "magical"—and they come back again and again. Starting in 1986 with an acre and a half of bare earth, Maxine Paetro collaborated with horticulturist Tim Steinhoff to create a series of enchanting garden rooms. Broccoli Hall offers an apple tunnel, a brick courtyard, a lavish display of spring bulbs blooming with crabapples in May, an extensive border of iris, peonies, and old shrub roses flowering in June, a tree house with long views, and a secret woodland garden with a teddy bears' picnic. We have some new rustic carvings this year by woodsman/artisan Hoppy Quick; new bears, new stairs, new chairs, and some exceptionally charming bird feeders. Photos of Broccoli Hall can be seen at www.broccolihall.com.

2015 |

➲ From Route 22 North, go towards Amenia. Go west on Route 44 to Route 83 North/Smithfield Road. Go 2.5 miles to dirt road on right, Flint Hill Road. Turn right. Garden is first on left. Please park on Flint Hill Road. Be careful of ditches.

Columbia County

Saturday, June 25

🕐 **Hours vary by garden (Starting at 10 a.m.)**

$7 per garden

COLUMBIA COUNTY

CRARYVILLE

📍 **RABBIT HILL**
158 Maiers Road, Craryville

🕐 10 a.m. to 5 p.m.

Forty years ago, my husband Richard and I bought a tiny "get-away". A nineteenth-century farmhouse set in fifty-seven acres of a second-growth woodland. Today, the tiny house, wrapped in additions, is unrecognizable. The gardens, then non-existent became our joy and creating a landscape was Richard's passion for years. Unfortunately he passed away this May and all of the plants and trees miss him. I am continuing to work on the garden without him. We cleared a woodland for a large lawn and opened land to reveal a view of the Berkshires. Richard raised the canopy of a large wooded area and planted many species and varieties of decorative understory trees, shrubs, shade perennials, and ground-covers that are now seen by strolling on a network of stone paths that interlace the woodland grove. A moss garden is contained within the grove and it is bordered by an allée planted with specimen trees and shrubs and, to the east, by "Moby Dick", a rock outcropping, several hundred feet long, uncovered by hand digging over several years. Whale-shaped and...
[Read the full description online]

2015 | ♿ |

➲ From the Taconic State Parkway, exit east at Manor Rock Road. Go 1 mile to fork and turn right onto Maiers Road. Ten feet on left are five mailboxes and our driveway with a

sign, "158 Maiers Road." Park on the road and walk into the property. If you are handicapped have a friend drive you in.

From intersection of Route 22 and 23 at Hillsdale, go west on Route 23 exactly 4 miles to County Route 11/Beauty Award Highway. Go south 2.2 miles to Craryville Road. Turn right and go 0.8 miles to fork in road. Bear right onto Manor Rock Road and go 1.5 miles to Maiers Road fork. Keep left about ten feet. Our driveway is just past five mailboxes. Please park on Maiers Road and walk in.

HILLSDALE

 TEXAS HILL
411 Texas Hill Road, Hillsdale

🕐 10 a.m. to 5 p.m.

Our garden atop Texas Hill in Hillsdale began ten years ago after we completed the restoration of our newly purchased house, leaving behind our Germantown house and garden after twenty five years. We acquired this 1967 "modern ranch" from the family of the original owners. There was no garden to speak of—just a few peonies, lots of vinca and epimedium, rhododendron, and a few sad tulips. But the rocky ridge-line property had much to offer: excellent big views, interesting variety of terrains, old and newer stone walls and patios, established trails through the woods, and a beautifully sighted spring fed pond. Accentuating and highlighting these assets has been our over-riding goal from the outset. However, the elevation (Zone 4), brutal exposure, deer herds, and the rocky terrible soil presented unusually difficult challenges. Initially we created two protected courtyards using existing structures and new fencing, planting beds with perennials and small scrubs and dwarf trees. Beyond these early beds and courtyards, we planted large groups of evergreen... [Read the full description online]

NEW

⮑ From the Taconic State Parkway, exit onto Route 23 East. Go 0.2 mile and turn left onto County Road 11. Go another 0.2 mile and turn right onto Carlson Road. Road becomes Texas Hill Road after intersections of Lockwood Road. Number 411 is on the right, about 3 miles from the Taconic.

HUDSON

 THE HAPPY
331 Mt. Merino Road, Hudson

🕐 10 a.m. to 4 p.m.

The garden is about a decade old and accompanies a 1973 brick ranch. The existing elements were a couple of white pines, a half dozen apple trees, a magnolia, and a pool. First I installed a fence to keep the deer out of the immediate back yard so that I could plant what I wanted and not have to worry about what would be their dinner. The gardens now include four species of magnolia, a collection of more than twenty different chamecyparis, collections of hostas, viburnums, sedums, optunia, peonies, junipers, and azaleas—with lots a variegated leaves, chartreuse leaves, humongous leaves, diminutive leaves, and everything in between. Structure is provided by typical border plants like boxwood and taxus, but also by hydrangeas, hibiscus, hachenochloa, and fothergillas. Garden beds are laid out with modernist elements and are much deeper than typical gardens. There is the striped garden with rows of perennials and shrubs. There are areas that are enclosed on all sides to make you feel held and secure as well as open areas with far ranging views, that are freeing and expansive. Form and function are dominate. The rooms have been created for specific purposes: entry, entertaining, growing food, strolling, and lounging as well as providing for nature and wildlife through food sources and habitat.

NEW | ♿ | 📷

⮑ One mile north of the Rip Van Winkle Bridge and 3 miles south of Hudson's Warren Street. Parking is available on the front lawn of the house.

MILLERTON

 HELEN BODIAN
359 Carson Road, Millerton

🕐 10 a.m. to 4 p.m.

Our garden began twenty years ago with the construction of a naturalistic rock garden. Over time, as our collection of rare and unusual plants grew and demanded more appropriate settings, the garden evolved into a series of different environments, linked together by paths that pass by a pond and through rolling fields and connect to many woodland trails.

Today, in addition to the rock garden, there is a traditional square border planted with large perennials and shrubs, a walled garden displaying potted greenhouse plants around a small pool, and an ornamental vegetable garden. This year, to replenish the soil in the vegetable garden, half will be planted with a mixed cover crop (green manure).

2015 | ♿ | 📷

➲ From Millerton, take Route 22 to intersection of Routes 44 and 22 and go north on Route 22 for 4 miles. On right, you will see a sign for Columbia County and on left, Carson Road. Turn onto Carson Road and go up hill for 1 mile. On left are a tennis court and a metal barn, on right, a white farmhouse with a modern addition. Please park in field next to barn. From Hillsdale, take Route 22 South about 14 miles from traffic light in Hillsdale. Look for a sign on left for Dutchess County and Carson Road on right.

VALATIE

📍 **KEVIN LEE JACOBS**
3007 Main Street, Valatie

🕐 10 a.m. to 4 p.m.

Kevin Lee Jacobs wears three hats: cookbook author, serious gardener, and creator of the well-known website "A Garden for the House" (www.agardenforthehouse.com). His house is on the National Register of Historic Places. He has designed numerous gardens on his urban property: a Woodland Garden, a winding Serpentine Garden, two Kitchen Gardens, and a formal Boxwood Garden.

2014 | 📷

➲ From Claverack and points south, take Route 9H north. Take the Valatie exit. Turn left onto Route 9 North. Continue 0.6 mile to Main Street. Turn left onto Lake Street (the first left) and then an immediate left into the driveway. The house is a big white Victorian with green shutters.

Dutchess County

Saturday, June 25

🕐 **10 a.m. to 4 p.m.**
$7 admission

There are also gardens open in nearby Ulster County on this day. See page 214.

🏷 Pop-up Nursery
Adams Fairacre Farms

DUTCHESS COUNTY

POUGHKEEPSIE

📍 **DAPPLED BERMS—THE GARDEN OF SCOTT VANDERHAMM**
74 Colburn Drive, Poughkeepsie

🏷 Adams Fairacre Farms

The garden is situated on a one-acre property within a 1950s (IBM- era) suburban com-

munity. As a result of the mature growth trees which dominate the grounds, a shade perennial garden was created and cultivated over eighteen seasons of weekend gardening. The assembled collection of plants, spread throughout numerous beds and man-made berms, relies heavily on the juxtapositions of color, texture, and form to bring interest and natural beauty to the garden. One of the highlights of the garden is the collection of more than 105 different hosta cultivars numbering more than 214 specimens, all labeled for ease of identification.

2015 |

➲ From Route 9, take Spackenkill Road/Route 113 East 2 miles to Colburn Drive. (Please Note: Colburn Drive is a U-Shaped street with two entrances onto Spackenkill Road. Number 74 Colburn is closest to the more western entrance.) Turn right off of Spackenkill Road onto Colburn Drive to #74 on the left; please park on the street.

From the Taconic State Parkway heading south, exit at Route 44 West. Take Route 44 west approximately 12 miles to Main Street, Poughkeepsie. Continue on Main Street to Raymond Avenue/Route 376. Turn left on Raymond Avenue. Travel south on Raymond Avenue (past Vassar College) to Hooker Avenue. Turn left and continue on Route 376 to Zack's Way. Turn right at Zack's Way (which becomes Boardman Road) and follow to Spackenkill Road/Route 113. Turn right on Spackenkill Road and then left onto Colburn Drive. Please park on the street.

From the Taconic State Parkway heading north: exit at Route 55 West. Take Route 55 West approximately 14 miles to Raymond Avenue and proceed as directed above.

Nassau County

Saturday, June 25

🫖 DIGGING DEEPER

SATURDAY, JUNE 25 | 10 AM | $15

TEA CEREMONY

AT: John P. Humes Japanese Stroll Garden
     Mill Neck, NY

Tour of the very special John P. Humes Japanese Stroll Garden with its curator Stephen Morrell. Stephen will explain the design aspects of Japanese gardens and the art of the tea ceremony. A landscape architect specializing in Japanese-style gardens, Stephen has studied in Japan and is a practitioner of Zen Buddhism and the tea ceremony. He will explain the history of tea ceremony and present formal tea to one lucky guest recipient.

See this garden's listing on page 258.

This program will be held again on September 17 and October 1.

Registration is required and space is limited. **Opendaysprogram.org or call 1(888) 842-2442**

The Hamptons: South Fork

Saturday, June 25

🕐 **Hours vary by garden
(Starting at 10 a.m.)**

🔖 Pop-up Nursery
The Bayberry

$7 per garden

SUFFOLK COUNTY

AMAGANSETT

📍 **NGAERE MACRAY & DAVID SEELER
50 Montauk Highway, Amagansett**

🕐 10 a.m. to 4 p.m.

🔖 The Bayberry

David is the owner of the Bayberry Nursery and the garden reflects his personal taste—or at least his enthusiasms. Originally a wildflower meadow, the patios, courtyard garden, and cutting gardens evolved over thirty years. His most recent enthusiasm, a three-quarter-acre pond built in 2006, required the construction of a new wing on the house, designed to feel like a boathouse. David's wife Ngaere maintains the grounds (with gardener Teresa Pascual), but has NO say in the design. She puts up with this because, in this area at least, she thinks he knows what he is doing.

2009 | ♿ | 📷

➲ Go to the Bayberry Nursery at 50 Montauk Highway, 2 miles east of East Hampton and 0.25 mile west of the Village of Amagansett.

Follow signs at the Bayberry to the parking area for Garden Conservancy visitors.

BRIDGEHAMPTON

📍 **STANLEY & SUSAN REIFER
5 Paumanok Road, Bridgehampton**

🕐 10 a.m. to 3 p.m.

The Reifer Garden was designed by Jian Guo Xu, a noted Chinese artist. Using his considerable artistic skills, he has created a complex of graceful gardens on five acres that incorporate Taoism, Confucianism, and Buddhism. Employing Chinese craftsmen, he has constructed numerous pavilions, bridges, and water features interconnected by winding paths and illuminating viewing points. With the horticultural collaboration of Whitney's Landscaping, he has painted the garden in a vivid tapestry of colors and textures which echo the strains of Chinese classical music.

2014 | 📷

➲Take Montauk Highway/Route 27 to Snake Hollow Road in Bridgehampton (Bridgehampton National Bank is on the corner.) Go north.

Turn left at stop sign onto Mitchells Lane. At traffic circle go right onto Scuttlehole Road. Make immediate left onto Millstone Road. Go approximately 1 mile and turn right onto Old Sag Harbor Road. Take first left onto Paumanok Road. Park in the cul-de-sac and follow sign to garden entrance.

CAROL MERCER
33 Ocean Avenue, Bridgehampton
🕐 10 a.m. to 4 p.m.

An undeniable partnering of pattern, movement, and color makes this garden glow and come alive. Mercer and her partner, Lisa Verderosa, have a thriving garden design business called The Secret Garden, Ltd.; they received accolades for the design of the roof garden at the 2003 Kips Bay Designer Showhouse in New York City. Previous years' recognition includes the Gate House Gardens at the 2003 Villa Maria Designer Showhouse, Water Mill, New York and gold medal awards at several of the New York City flower shows. The garden was a cover story in Garden Design magazine, and appeared in *House Beautiful*, *Garden Style*, *Victoria*, *Martha Stewart Living*, *Design Times*, and *Oprah's O at Home* magazines, as well as in *Seaside Gardening*, *The Garden Design Book*, *Sanctuary: Gardening for the Soul*, *The Natural Shade Garden*, *Landscape with Roses*, *Garden Stone*, *Hot Plants for Cool Climates*, and most recently, in *Cottage Gardens*. It was also featured in *Newsday* in 1999 and appeared in the Time/Life book series, *Beds & Borders*, *Gardening Weekends*, and *Shade Gardening*.
2014 | ♿ | 📷

➲ From Route 27/Montauk Highway, proceed east through Water Mill, Bridgehampton, and Wainscott to East Hampton. At traffic light at head of pond, turn right onto Ocean Avenue. House, #33, is fourth on left. White stone driveway is marked by a small gray sign. Please park as directed.

MONTAUK

RICHARD KAHN & ELAINE PETERSON
224 West Lake Drive, Montauk
🕐 10 a.m. to 2 p.m.

Since 1977, we have explored the horticultural world through the transformation of a garden first planted in 1931 around a Tudor-style house. Situated on the Montauk peninsula which is surrounded by an endless expanse of water and sky, the property is protected by large, original, non-native plantings of oak, silver maple, and privet which buffer the gardens on all sides except the east which faces Lake Montauk. This protective enclosure within an often inhospitable, very exposed geography gives the place its alluring lushness and its delight to those who first (or repeatedly) enter here from outside. It offers the illusion of peaceful retreat, romance and mystery, whereas, in fact, it has witnessed innumerable hurricanes and northeasters. Throughout the gardens which surround the house we have tried to create space for quiet observation and contemplation. We have encouraged the local bird and insect populations by growing what they like and not using poisons, and they have rewarded us with great variety, filling the air with their sounds and movements. We have... [Read the full description online]
2015 | ♿ | 📷

➲ From Montauk Highway/Route 27, go past village of Montauk 0.8 mile. Turn left onto West Lake Drive (signs for Montauk Harbor/Route 77/Montauk Downs). Garden, #224, is 1.2 miles on right. Please park along road, not on grass.

SAGAPONACK

SUSAN & LOUIS MEISEL
81 Wilkes Lane, Sagaponack
🕐 10 a.m. to 2 p.m.

Our property encompasses more than 100 specimen trees, with a focus on special beeches. Susan uses the flower color of several hun-

dred perennials as if it were paint on canvas to create the visual effects I enjoy seeing.
2011 | ♿ | 📷

⮕ From Route 27/Montauk Highway, go to Sagg Main Street. Turn south. Go past red

schoolhouse on right and general store. Turn left onto Hedges Lane. Go 0.5 mile and take next left onto Wilkes Lane. Garden is at second house on right. Please park along road.

Ulster County

Saturday, June 25

🕐 **Hours vary by garden (Starting at 12 p.m.)**

$7 per garden

There are also gardens open in nearby Dutchess County on this day. See page 210.

ULSTER COUNTY

HIGHLAND

📍 **TERI CONDON— GARDENSMITH DESIGN**
50 Hillside Avenue, Highland

🕐 12 p.m. to 4 p.m.

Nestled in an old apple orchard with a view of the Shawangunk Ridge, this intricate garden is comprised of intimate spaces and surprises in unexpected places. Garden designer, Teri Condon and sculptor Richard Gottlieb have combined their talents creating a feast for your eyes. An akebia-draped pergola, recessed patio, and stone fire circle are woven together with serpentine stepping stone paths that seduce you from one delicacy to the next. Striking foliage combinations paired with architectural forms create a serene yet whimsical garden experience.

2014 | 📷

⮕ From the New York State Thruway, take Exit 18. Turn right at first light after toll onto Route 299. Go 0.2 mile to next light and turn left onto North Ohioville. Turn right onto Old Route 299 (there is an antique store on corner). Go about 0.7 mile to Plutarch Road and turn left. Go another 0.5 mile to Hillside Avenue and turn left. Bear left where drive splits. Garden is on top of hill.

NEW PALTZ

📍 **SPRINGTOWN FARMDEN**
387 Springtown Road, New Paltz

🕐 1 p.m. to 4:30 p.m.

A writer once proclaimed my garden to be very much a "man's garden"; perhaps it is. The emphasis is on fruits and vegetables, but the whole works is woven into planting of flowers and ornamental shrubs. I try to grow a year-round supply of pretty much every kind of vegetable except rhubarb and Jerusalem artichoke. Fruits include many varieties of dwarf apples and pears, grapes, and numerous uncommon fruits such as pawpaws, persimmons, gooseberries (twenty or so varieties), currants, and medlars. Out in the adjoining hayfield is a 100-foot trellis of hardy kiwis and a swale bordered by chestnut and hazelnut trees.

2014 | ♿ | 📷

➲ From I-87/New York State Thruway, take New Paltz/Route 299 West exit through New Paltz. Cross bridge and take first right onto Springtown Road. Bear right at fork; house is #387, about 3 miles on left.

From Kingston, take Route 32 South. Go about 2 miles, after passing Rosendale, to Tillson Road. (Postage Inn is on left). Turn right. Turn left at stop sign onto Springtown Road. House is #387 and is about 1.5 miles on right. Please park along street or driveway.

Westchester County

Sunday, June 26

🕐 **Hours vary by garden (Starting at 10 a.m.)**

$7 per garden

WESTCHESTER COUNTY

BEDFORD HILLS

📍 **PHILLIS WARDEN**
531 Bedford Center Road, Bedford Hills

🕐 10 a.m. to 4 p.m.

This garden of many facets includes perennial borders, three water gardens, a formal vegetable garden, wildflower garden, a fern garden, a marsh garden, a tree platform overlooking the marshlands, a woodland walk, a hidden garden, and a formal croquet court. The garden extends over seven acres, the back four acres of which are a study in what deer do not eat.

2015 | 📷

➲ From Bedford Village, take Route 22 towards Katonah to intersection at Bedford Cross. Garden is on left. Please park at Rippowam School and walk to #531.

Vivian & Ed Merrin's garden, featured in *Outstanding American Gardens: A Celebration—25 Years of the Garden Conservancy*. Photo by Marion Brenner.

CORTLANDT MANOR

 VIVIAN & ED MERRIN
2547 Maple Avenue, Cortlandt Manor
🕐 10 a.m. to 2 p.m.

The "STUMPERIE" garden is now complete and is open (what a wonder out of the hurricane Sandy). The Merrin garden has been featured in several books and magazines. The most spectacular of which is *The New Garden Paradise: Great Private Gardens of the World.* On a pond with a "pond house" is a paradise of lotus, 500 of them. More than 300 moun-

tain laurels surround the garden, in a planting that makes them part of the total landscape. Mixed borders flow in and out of the six- or seven-acre garden, containing indigenous plants as well as species and rare cultivars. The Merrins have four greenhouse structures in which are kept the rare tropical plants, all of which are on display during the summer months. There is a lotus pond which will be in bloom. It is a sight to behold. A dramatic lookout of glass and wood takes the viewer to oversee the property and lake that is part of the property. The garden has been done with the expertise of Patrick Chassé. We also have an expanded new vegetable garden for you to see. In June, visitors will see seventy-two peonies, 200 herbaceous peonies, a cactus garden, hundreds of hellebores, arisamae of... [Read the full description online]

2015 |

➲ From the Taconic State Parkway, take Route 202 exit. Turn left towards Peekskill. Go 2.5 miles, then turn left at traffic light onto Croton Avenue, just past Cortland Farm Market. Go 1.2 miles to blinking light/stop sign and turn right onto Furnace Dock Road. Go 0.8 mile to blinking light/stop sign and turn left onto Maple Avenue. Go 0.9 mile to private road on right. Go 0.2 mile to #2547 on left.

NORTH SALEM

THE HEN & THE HIVE
9 June Road, North Salem

🕐 10 a.m. to 4 p.m.

Starting from scratch, our eleven-year-old gardens have evolved to both ward off and take advantage of the ever-present white tailed deer. All gardens are organically culti-vated featuring open flowerscapes, wildflower meadow paths, and woodlands. Only the vegetable and berry gardens are deer fenced and while we try to take advantage of deer-re-sistant plantings, they are interspersed with flowers that although favored by most herds, make it safely through the summer months. Incorporating seating areas, stone, and even a bit of water, one never knows what they will find on our productive four acres.

2015 | 📷

➲ From I-684 take Exit 7. Take Route 116 toward Salem Center approximately 5 miles. Turn right onto June Road. We are between 116 and 121. House is 0.2 mile south of the North Salem Post Office.

SOUTH SALEM

GARDEN OF
BERNARD MARQUEZ & TIM FISH
74 Hemlock Road, South Salem

🕐 10 a.m. to 6 p.m.

The Garden is a hybrid of design discipline and fun! It consists of several garden rooms on different levels. Plantings consist of a variety of boxwoods, some uncommon in the northeast. There are also a variety of conifer cultivars and other broadleaf evergreens. Water elements, stone work and a view of the Pound Ridge Reservation are highlights. Annuals, perennials, artifacts and containers complete the experience.

2015 | ♿ | 📷

➲ From the west take I-684 to Exit 6/Route 35. Go east to Route 123, south to Mill River Road to Lake Kitchawan Road to Hemlock Road. All are one directional turns.

Delaware County

Saturday, July 2

🕐 **10 a.m. to 4 p.m.**
$7 per garden

DELAWARE COUNTY

ANDES

📍 **CYNTHIA & CHARLES BONNES**
265 Bussey Hollow Road, Andes

Our garden is on a hillside facing the western Catskills with four ponds descending toward the mountain view. Around the house and large barn, part of a former dairy farm, are several formal garden spaces defined by native stone walls. They include a perennial border, a fountain terrace and a vegetable garden. An allée of Japanese lilacs ascends the hillside and informal plantings edge two of the ponds and a connecting stream.

2013 | ♿ | 📷

➲ From the village of Andes, take Route 1/ Tremperskill Road for 5.3 miles to Bussey Hollow Road. Turn right and go for 2.6 miles to driveway on right, Post Box 265. From the south, take Route 30 along the Pepacton Reservoir in the direction of Andes. Cross the bridge and turn left towards Andes. Go 2.7 miles to Bussey Hollow Road. Turn left and go for 2.6 miles to driveway on right, Post Box 265. Please park along side of road.

📍 **MEL & PEG'S RUSTIC CABIN COTTAGE GARDEN**
733 Crescent Hill Road, Andes

Perched on the side of a hill deep in the Catskills, our garden takes full advantage of a beautiful borrowed view that is seamlessly integrated throughout the garden setting. Wind your way up a long sinewy driveway and you are greeted by the boisterous 'garden proper' which was carved out of the steep slope and is held up by a massive boulder retaining wall. Multiple entrances beckon you to enter. Slip in through a cedar arbor covered in grapes, or take the stone path through the conifer garden and meander along gravel and mulch paths through a lush array of small trees, shrubs, perennials, and grasses that create a whimsical, enchanted garden experience. Step down the rustic stone staircases, or exit through a mass of hydrangeas, to explore the smaller garden rooms including: a large mixed garden in the shape of a footprint with wide mulch paths, a couple of small shade gardens, a labyrinth (recently over-hauled) and a small country vegetable garden. This is a garden that you find yourself immersed in and one you will experience with all of your senses—... [Read the full description online]

NEW | & | 📷

⮕ From Route 28 in Kingston drive the 50 miles to Margaretville and continue 6.5 miles further toward the village of Andes. You will pass County Route 6 on the right and continue through the very curvy narrow valley until the next right which is Crescent Hill Road. From Andes take Route 28 about 4.5 miles from the Andes General Store until you reach Crescent Hill Road on your left. Turn onto Crescent Hill Road and continue for 0.7 mile until you come to 733 which is our driveway on the left.

EAST MEREDITH

TOTEM FARM GARDEN
581 Rathbun Hill Road, East Meredith

On four acres of sloping land, the garden at Totem Farm has expanded outward from the old farm house and ice house, towards the fields of wildflowers that surround the place on three sides. A big leaf room, a moon garden, a lilac walk, a very old apple orchard, a recently planted plum orchard, a pond walk, and some living willow tunnels for the chickens, are defined by fences, stone walls, and hedges and connected by paths and stone stairs.

2013 | 📷

⮕ From Oneonta, take Route 23, turn right onto Pindar's Corners/Prosser Hollow Road. Bear left onto Rathbun Hill Road (4 miles). Continue past mail box 581 and park above house. From Delhi, take Route 10, turn left onto Mer-

edith Street/Route 28 and go 7.4 miles. Turn right onto Meridale-Davenport Center Road/Route 10 by Dutch Deli and 2.9 miles. Pass Jersey Road on right and big Dairy Barn. Take next left onto Rathbun Hill Road. Parking will be on the left. Please park in open field above house. There will be signs for parking.

JEFFERSON

QUAKER HILL FARM—ELISABETH SEARLES & RICHARD FRIEDBERG
2121 Quaker Hill Road, Jefferson

We bought this hilltop farm in the Western Catskills many years ago but did not really start to develop the garden until we moved up from New York City about twenty years ago. Since then we have shaped a landscape of broad lawns, trees, perennial borders, stonewalls, and three ponds in an effort to highlight the lovely mountain view but also to create a sense of comfort and enclosure. The area that was the old farm rock "dump" is now a rock garden; an existing pond was enlarged for livestock and for better views from the house; a living willow gazebo provides shelter and a lovely vista of the pond and distant mountains; and a swimming pond feeds a series of naturally landscaped smaller ponds across the road from the house. Richard's large sculptures are displayed on the property.

2013 | & | 📷

⮕ From Route 23 take Teedlebrook Road, Jefferson, New York for 2.1 miles. Turn left at crossroads onto Quaker Hill Road and continue 0.6 miles. Garden is on left at 2121 Quaker Hill Road.

ROSCOE

BERRY BROOK FARM—MERMER BLAKESLEE & ERIC HAMERSTROM
310 Henderson Hollow Road, Roscoe

Our garden began in 1990 on this old, defunct farm. It took its form from the dry stream bed that runs between the house and the horse barn, and reaches toward a large rock in the woods surrounded by ferns. The beds are dense and deep, the plants encouraged to retain some of their wildness. The stone work is both old and ongoing: the hand-hewn flagstones of the terrace, the walls circling the house and running along the pastures where the horses graze, the stone bridge leading to a milk house, the large stone path snaking through a swampy meadow. Antique trucks and farm equipment are settled about. The house, barns, and front porch are open to everyone as they are considered part of the garden.

2013 | ♿ | 📷

⮕ From Route 17 northwest, take Exit 94. Turn left off ramp onto Route 206 west. Go 3 miles. Turn right onto Beaverkill Valley Road.

Go 6.9 miles (this turns into Berry Brook Road) and turn right onto Henderson Hollow Road, a small, dirt road.

From Route 17 southeast, take exit 94. Turn left onto Stewart Avenue in Roscoe and left again at the traffic light onto Route 206 west. Continue for 2.8 miles and turn right onto Beaverkill Valley Road. Follow the directions above.

From the north, follow Route 30 southwest from Margaretville. After crossing the Pepacton Reservoir, continue 7 miles, then turn left onto Holiday Brook Road. Go 4 miles (this turns into Berry Brook Road) and take a sharp left onto Henderson Hollow Road, a small, dirt road. Go all the way to the end. There will be signs for parking.

Dutchess County

Sunday, July 3

🕐 **Hours vary by garden (Starting at 11 a.m.)**

$7 per garden

PAWLING

📍 **HALL CHRISTY HOUSE GARDEN**
5 Meeting House Road, Pawling

🕐 11 a.m. to 6 p.m.

The gardens were designed by the owners to complement their eighteenth-century house and setting with many levels and rooms echoing the layout of the house. The main garden is a courtyard garden with brick paths, three lily pools, perennial garden, shade gardens, and white garden edged by the house, garage, gazebo and hidden natural-form pool. On the perimeter of these gardens, you will find a small orchard and herb garden with faux well which is actually a buried 1,000-gallon cement tank to collect roof water for watering the potager. Most of the property is left as

fields which become buttercup meadows in June. The last garden is truly a secret pond and woodland garden with natural woodland plants mingling with specimen trees and shrubs. Here, the bulbs, trilliums, may apples, and epimedium reign in spring under magnolias and weeping cercis with the Japanese maples dazzling in fall. All is maintained solely by the owners themselves.

2015 | 📷

➲ From Brewster at junction of I-684 and I-84 go north on Route 22 for about 9 miles. Route 311 to Patterson and a Mobil station are on the left. Take a slight right up South Quaker Hill Road. At about 3 miles, turn left onto Mizzentop Road (a 4-way intersection; if you reach Laurel Mountain Road, you have gone 0.5 mile too far.) Follow Mizzentop Road North which becomes Quaker Hill Road for about 3.2 miles. Turn right onto Meeting House Road (if you reach Oblong Lane you have gone 0.3 mile too far) The Hall Christy House is the driveway on left just after the old Oblong Meeting House which may be open for a tour if you are interested. (Do not go down the long straight driveway that appears as an extension of Meeting House Road, it is a private driveway.) There is parking in the circular driveway, but those who are mobile, please park on the road and walk down the driveway or on the path to left after the gate through the meadow to the pond and woods garden before coming to the gardens.

📍 **SCHERER GARDEN**
10 Birch Hill Road, Pawling
🕐 11 a.m. to 4 p.m.

Over thirty years ago we moved a 200-year-old house and barn to our scrubby, rocky site on Quaker Hill. In collaboration with Robin Zitter, we have created the garden we dreamed of, a naturalistic, traditional cottage garden. Woodland paths are filled with rhododendrons, ferns and spring blooming bulbs. In the garden close to the house the beds are now deeper and filled with shrubs, sedges, grasses

and interplanted with perennials. The pool area is a hidden, rocky gem filled with color. A knot garden/herb garden in the back is a focal point and enhances the western views. Our garden is featured in Jane Garmey and John M. Hall's book, *Private Gardens of the Hudson Valley*.

2014 | 📷

➲ Take I-684 to Route 22/Pawling exit. Go about 9 miles to Route 311 and turn right onto South Quaker Hill Road. At stop sign (about 3 miles), turn right onto Birch Hill Road. We are #10 on right. Please park on road.

From Connecticut, take Route 37 through Sherman, and turn onto Wakeman Road. Akin Hall Library is on right, Hill Farm on left. Turn left and continue south; this becomes Birch Hill Road. Please park on road.

Dutchess County

Saturday, July 9

🕐 **10 a.m. to 4 p.m.**

$7 admission

There are also gardens open on this day in nearby Litchfield County, CT. See page 85.

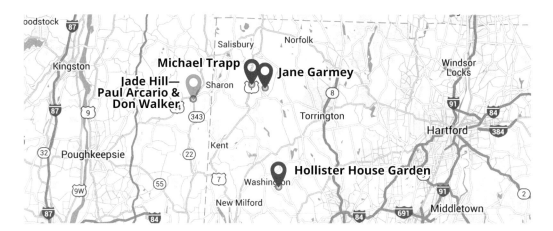

DUTCHESS COUNTY

AMENIA

 JADE HILL—
PAUL ARCARIO & DON WALKER
13 Lake Amenia Road, Amenia

Starting as a rocky hillside that was mostly lawn, Jade Hill has grown into a stroll garden designed to be a tapestry of texture and color. Favorite plants went in first: Japanese maples, conifers, and a bamboo grove. Innumerable wheelbarrows of compost and mulch (wheeled uphill!) helped create beds of shrubs and perennials; hand- dug pools were put in for goldfish and lotus. The main bed along the driveway is anchored by golden barberries and purple smoke trees (coppiced each year)—with roses, peonies, Siberian iris, phlox and other perennials filling in—and backed by a 'Purple Fountain' weeping beech. Jade Hill borders the wetlands that were once Lake Amenia, and our property is on the site of what was intended to become a lakeside community consisting of dozens of small lots. Over the years we were able to acquire some of the adjacent parcels, which quickly became new garden rooms. One addition was the rose garden, another was a gold-themed garden, viewed from a cantilevered "Oriental" pavilion meant to show off carved wooden window panels purchased at a flea market years ago. The garden was featured in the September 2006 issue of *Better Homes & Gardens* and the July 2007 issue of *Hudson Valley* magazine.

2015 | 📷

➲ From the traffic light in Amenia at Routes 22, 44, and 343, take Route 44 West. Make first left after 55 mph sign onto Lake Amenia Road. A gated driveway is after fifth house on right. Please park on road.

The Hamptons: North Fork

Saturday, July 9

🕐 **10 a.m. to 4 p.m.**
$7 per garden

🏷 Pop-up Nursery
Broken Arrow Nursery /
Landcraft Environments

SUFFOLK COUNTY

MATTITUCK

📍 **DENNIS SCHRADER & BILL SMITH**
1200 East Mill Road, Mattituck
🏷 Broken Arrow Nursery /
Landcraft Environments

Set in the heart of the North Fork's wine region, this three-plus-acre garden surrounds a restored 1840s farmhouse. In 2008, the house went through a major renovation and the gardens and terraces surrounding it have since been redesigned. The deck, porches, and stone terraces are filled with hundreds of container plantings. There are many perennial and mixed shrub borders throughout the garden that can be accessed by numerous winding paths. Garden rooms hedged in by hornbeam and boxwood, feature various themed gardens within. Additionally, there is a vegetable/herb garden, a formal knot garden, several bog plantings, meadow gardens and a woodland shade area. The garden also features rustic arbors, trellises, stone walls, and a Tiki hut that contains a collection of exotic plants. The newest meadow garden surrounds the "Ruin"—a subterranean stone grotto partially covered with a sedum green roof. The three roundels located in the eastern part of the garden are made from locust wood harvested from the property. The roundels...
[Read the full description online]
2015 | ♿ | 📷

➲ From I-495/Long Island Expressway, take Exit 73/Route 58 and follow to Route 25. Go through town of Mattituck, past Love Lane to Wickham Avenue. Turn left and go past railroad tracks and traffic light. Stay straight on Wickham and it will turn into Grand Avenue. Take Grand about one mile to East Mill Road. Turn left and look for #1200. Please park along street.

MT. SINAI

📍 **TRANQUILITY**
42 Jesse Way, Mt. Sinai

The Becker garden can be described as an explosion of color, fragrance, sound, and texture. Hundreds of perennials, shrubs, trees, and annuals are combined with water features, lawn art, and recently relocated garden trails that allow the visitor to enter the owner's vision of a impressionistic garden painting. Garden footpaths wind through the extensive garden allowing the visitor to immerse themselves in the sights and sounds of nature and escaping the general stress of modern lifestyles. Unique shrubs and flowers create interest and winding paths permit the

Dennis Schrader & Bill Smith's garden, featured in *Outstanding American Gardens: A Celebration—25 Years of the Garden Conservancy*. Photo by Marion Brenner.

visitor to stroll and enjoy the sights, sounds, and fragrance of nature.

2015 | ♿ | 📷

➲ Take the Long Island Expressway to Exit 63/Route 83. Go north to Canal Road. Turn left and then take the first right onto Autumn Road. Go to end. Turn right onto Wheat Path and then take the first left onto Jesse Way. Number 42 is on left.

Columbia County

Sunday, July 17

🕙 **10 a.m. to 4 p.m.**
$7 per garden

We are proud to partner with the Berkshire Botanic Garden to bring you this Open Day. See their listing in the Massachusetts chapter on page 137.

 DIGGING DEEPER: The Art & Science of Meadow Restoration; with Linda Horn, Heather Grimes & Barbara Hughey; Spencertown, 2:30 p.m.

COLUMBIA COUNTY

CANAAN

📍 **ROCKLAND FARM**
180 Stony Kill Road, Canaan

The garden comprises a variety of areas that flow one from another over about ten acres of our property. A 450-foot-long rock ledge runs parallel to the front drive and is topped by a dry garden. A raised terrace on the west side of the house features exotic and tropical plants, many in containers. Behind the house is a sequence of garden rooms: a lavender garden contained within a raised hornbeam hedge, a pool garden surrounded by perennial beds, a water garden, a sundial garden, a rock garden and a fenced vegetable and cutting garden. A hydrangea allée leads from here to either a lawn with a seating area nestling within sweeps of perennials, or to steps up to a small, wooded knoll, with paths offering intermittent views of the garden and the hills beyond and connecting a folly, a water feature and a stumpery. A massive pine bench in a pine grove overlooks a three-acre lake in the middle-distance. Our garden has been featured in magazines and in the books *Great Gardens of The Berkshires*, *Private Edens*, and *Private Gardens of The Hudson Valley*.

2015 | ♿ | 📷

➡ From west, take Route 295 (last exit before toll going north on Taconic State Parkway) through East Chatham to flashing traffic light

at intersection of Route 5 in Canaan. Immediately after intersection, turn left onto Upper Queechy Road and then left again at end. Look for a parking sign.

From east, take Route 295 from Route 41 in Massachusetts or from Route 22 in New York past Queechy Lake on right, and Stony Kill Road is the first dirt road on right. Go about 0.5 miles and look for a parking sign.

NEW LEBANON

📍 **THE TILDEN JAPANESE GARDEN**
576 Route 20, New Lebanon

Nestled at the gateway to New Lebanon, this garden celebrates its heritage from the Shakers, Governor Samuel Tilden, and Shuji's Restaurant. The brilliance of red bridges acts as a foil for 'Nikko' iris, weeping jades, 'Casablanca' lilies, ginkgos, and many specimen plants. Waterfalls provide sustenance to grasses and pebbled shores with koi lurking beneath water lilies. Ancient lanterns stand guard while protruding boulders provide sculpture. A smaller courtyard garden sits silently against a stained glass window. A Shaker ice house complements this harmony as 'Sargent' cherry trees, a gift from Japan, commemorate peace among nations.

2015 |

➲ The Tilden Japanese Garden is at intersection of Routes 20 & 22. Through black gates of Tilden Mansion, garden is behind the Victorian-style house. Parking is across street at a white Shaker meetinghouse on South Meadow Road or look for signs on Routes 20/22.

SPENCERTOWN

 GARDEN OF LINDA B. HORN
5015 County Rt. 7, Spencertown

 DIGGING DEEPER

Artist Linda Horn began to create a one-acre native meadow/prairie when she and her husband moved to the area. The intent was to develop a biodiverse, beautiful substitute for the omnipresent American lawn, and allow her to create art based on actual experiences in nature. Increasingly fascinated with the process of landscape restoration, Ms. Horn applied this concept to other areas, including a woodland and wetland. The result is an ever-changing landscape that provides inspiration and a haven for beneficial insects, birds and wildlife, as well as people.

NEW

➲ From Hillsdale, take Route 22 north then turn right onto Route 7 about 3 miles to #5015 (driveway on left).If you pass it you'll immediately see Punsit Road on the right--you have to U-turn and go back to 5015 on right.

From Chatham take Route 203 about 5 minutes to Spencertown Country Store, stay right onto Route 7, 1 mile, first driveway on the right past Pratt Hill Road.

Parking on Punsit Road or side of driveway if not used.

🌀 DIGGING DEEPER

SUNDAY, JULY 17 | 2:30 PM

BRINGING BACK NATURAL LANDSCAPES

with Linda Horn, Barbara Hughey, and Heather Grimes

AT: Garden of Linda B. Horn,
    5015 County Rt. 7, Spencertown

Explore a one-acre meadow, a waterfall and surrounding wetland, and a sweeping woodland, all restored to native vibrance by owner and artist Linda Horn, land stewardship designer Barbara Hughey, and landscape designer Heather Grimes. This knowledgeable and passionate trio will introduce guests to this dynamic landscape, discuss the concepts and practices of landscape restoration, and provide participants at any level of expertise with inspiration and practical ideas for creating healthy, beautiful, and low maintenance native ecosystems on their own property.

Registration is required and space is limited. **Opendaysprogram.org or call 1(888) 842-2442**

Putnam County

Stonecrop Gardens Special Open Day featuring Tea in the Garden

SUNDAY, JULY 17

Garden is open 10 a.m. to 5 p.m.
$5 admission

☕ Visitors may purchase tea and cake from 12 p.m. to 4 p.m.

Other upcoming 2016 Open Days: August 14, September 18, and October 2. See Stonecrop Gardens' full listing on page 259.

Ulster County

Saturday, July 23

🕐 **Hours vary by garden**
(Starting at 10 a.m.)
$7 per garden

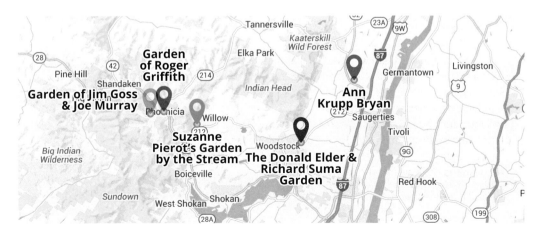

ULSTER COUNTY

PHOENICIA

 GARDEN OF JIM GOSS & JOE MURRAY
30 Circle Drive, Phoenicia

🕐 10 a.m. to 4 p.m.

Located in the heart of the Catskill Mountains, our modest house and grounds (just over one acre) serve as an example of what is attainable in deer country. What we may lack in time and other resources has been recouped with dedication. All design, installation, and maintenance is handled exclusively by us—the owners. This woodland property is unfenced and almost entirely open to deer and other herbivores. As a result, resistance to browsers has been a primary focus over the garden's twenty-year history. Research, trial and error, and the occasional spritz of Deer Defeat has resulted in a lush landscape that we are proud to share. The site features a bog, mixed borders, and a wild garden, and includes many out-of-the- ordinary deer-resistant plants arranged in striking combinations. Throughout the garden, the plantings are punctuated with stone accents, both natural and in the form of carved, South Asian objects. Jim, a painter and the primary designer of the garden, relishes the prospect of working and reworking this horticultural canvas.

2015 | 📷

➲ From the New York State Thruway, take Exit 19 to traffic circle just beyond the exit, and go west onto Route 28. Travel approximately 22 miles and turn left at sign for Woodland Valley Road (look for Simpler Times Cabins on left side of Route 28). After crossing a bridge, turn right to continue on Woodland Valley Road. Travel 0.6 mile but do not cross the next bridge you will see off to the right. When you come to a bridge that you must cross to continue, cross and take the far right fork onto Woodland Clove Road. Travel 0.3 mile and turn left onto Circle Drive; #30 is on the right. Please park on the road.

 GARDEN OF ROGER GRIFFITH
72 State Route 214, Phoenicia

🕐 10 a.m. to 4 p.m.

Set on one acre of flat fertile land and enclosed by towering conifers and 100-year-old sugar maples is Roger's garden. The garden consists of three parts: flanking the back door of the 1928 clapboard Bungalow is a three-season perennial garden; adjacent to this is a kitchen herb garden; and nested in the center of the backyard is a semi-formal flower and vegetable garden. Only the perennial garden existed when the house was bought in 2004. The flower and vegetable garden is loosely modeled on formal English and French vegetable gardens in Europe with espalier fruit trees and perennial borders. The property abounds with simple stonework including a rocky driveway path, a rectangular pea gravel terrace and a lawn between the house and the garden.

NEW | ♿ | 📷

➲ The garden is located at 72 Route 214 at the corner of Romer Street in the Hamlet of Phoenicia. Route 214 begins from Main Street in Phoenicia and Romer Street is 0.2 mile from Main Street. Entrance to the garden is on Romer Street.

SAUGERTIES

 ANN KRUPP BRYAN
24 East Church Road, Saugerties

🕐 10 a.m. to 5 p.m.

Beginning as a gravel parking lot and the grounds of a country church, the garden has developed over the past twenty five years. Today, the church is a lovely house surrounded by extensive sunny borders, large old trees underplanted with shade gardens, a steep hillside shade garden, and an organic vegetable garden. Ann designed, planted, and has maintained this land including building the stone retaining walls. During the last seven years, foliage plants have taken center stage in both sun and shade. For the past four years, Ann's newly completed sculptures have been added to the landscape each year, and a new fifty-foot shrub border is just starting to come into its own. For the past three years the garden has been open in mid September, the bloom in the July garden is quite different.

2015 | 📷

➲ From the New York State Thruway South, take Exit 20 and turn right onto Route 32 North. Go 2.3 miles and turn right onto Old Route 32. Go 0.8 mile to top of hill and turn right onto Church Road, a dead end. There is a stone grotto on road, with a grey church visible. Follow signs to parking.

   From the New York State Thruway North take Exit 20. Turn left and go 0.2 mile. Turn right onto Route 32 North and proceed as directed above.

📍 **THE DONALD ELDER & RICHARD SUMA GARDEN**
   31 Adams Road, Saugerties
🕐 10 a.m. to 4 p.m.

This is an artists garden influenced by the randomness of the English cottage garden, the formality of the clipped-bordered garden, and the subtlety of the studied views of the Japanese garden. An Asian- style screened pavilion provides a restful retreat and moun-tain views. Nestled In the woods, this garden incorporates the elements of water and stone. Gravel paths link the garden together to form a balanced and tranquil place. The garden was started in 1991 by Richard Suma and Donald Elder. Richard's passing in 2003 left behind his presence and spirit with every changing season.

2014 | 📷

➲ From the south, take the New York State Thruway/I-87 to Exit 19/Kingston. Stay right as you pay toll and follow signs to Route 28 west. Go 6 miles to Woodstock. Turn right onto Route 375/Woodstock and go 2 miles to Route 212. Turn right and go 2 miles to driveway on left. Look for Adams Road, turn left, and go up dirt driveway to end, #31. From the north, follow signs to Route 212 west/Woodstock. Go

6.5 miles to Adams Road on right. Turn right and go up dirt driveway to end, #31.

WILLOW

📍 **SUZANNE PIEROT'S GARDEN BY THE STREAM**
   33 Hickory Road, Willow
🕐 10 a.m. to 4 p.m.

My six-acre shade garden that rambles down the hill to a tumbling mountain stream is brought to life with great swatches of color — lavender, pink, red, white, and purple. All this color is from astilbe, the greatest plant any shade garden can have. There are thousands of astilbe, and when massed together, not only is the color magnificent, the fragrance is a sensual experience. The collection of over seventy-five varieties range in size from the native plant which is several feet tall, to a three-inch miniature. Those of you who have visited my garden before will notice many new beds as I keep working my way into the densely wooded area. I hope you will find ideas for your own garden. Don't miss seeing the *Magnolia tricuspidata* with leaves that are over three feet across. This magnolia actually likes growing in the shade. Hostas are also a main feature and there are about 20,000 of more than 100 different varieties used both as specimen plants as well as groundcover. New this year is a large area where only yellow... [Read the full description online]

NEW | ♿ | 📷

➲ From south, take I-87/New York State Thru-way to Exit 19/Kingston onto Route 28 west towards Pine Hill. Turn right at traffic light onto Route 375 and go to end (2.9 miles). Turn left onto Route 212 into village of Woodstock. Go through Woodstock to Bearsville. Turn right (stay on Route 212 for 7.3 miles). Turn right onto Grog Kill Road. Go 0.3 mile to first paved road (no sign) and turn left. Go 0.4 mile and turn left onto Four Wheel Drive. Go 0.2 mile and turn left onto Hickory Road. Go 0.1 mile to dead end. Gate has a sign that reads

"Pierot." Enter gate and turn right down hill to main house. Drop off passengers and return to area outside gate to park.

From north, take New York State Thruway/

I-87 to Exit 20/Saugerties/Woodstock. Turn left after toll. Turn right onto Route 212 into village of Woodstock. Proceed as directed above.

Westchester County

Sunday, July 24

🕐 **Hours vary by garden (Starting at 10 a.m.)**

$7 per garden

The Native Plant Center at Westchester Community College in Valhalla will also be open on this day.

WESTCHESTER COUNTY

BEDFORD HILLS

📍 **HEFFERNAN GARDEN**
120 West Patent Road, Bedford Hills
🕐 10 a.m. to 4 p.m.

The inspiration for this garden was fairly simple—looking at the sweep of the land coming down the hill to our stream, it looked to be the perfect setting for a meadow with an orchard in the background. As I read about meadows, the name Neil Diboll, of Prairie Nurseries in Wisconsin, kept coming up. I contacted him, Neil flew out, took soil samples, and presented us with a few ideas. His ideas, expertise, and vision ultimately provided the inspiration for

how the garden looks now. Today our property is graced with ten acres of wildflowers and over 100 fruit trees in the two orchards including apples, peaches, plums, apricots, pears, Japanese pears, nectarines, and mulberries.

**NEW | **

From I-684, both north and south of Bedford, take Exit 4 onto Route 172/Bedford Road and turn right onto West Patent Road. Cross Guard Hill Road. Go down the hill, the property is on right with the barn and stone silo.

From the Saw Mill Parkway south of Bedford, take Green Lane to the end (cross Route 117). At the end, turn left onto Mclean. Turn right onto West Patent Road. The property is the first property on the left after the school.

If you drive past the stone silo you have gone too far.

PHILLIS WARDEN
531 Bedford Center Road, Bedford Hills

🕐 10 a.m. to 4 p.m.

This garden of many facets includes perennial borders, three water gardens, a formal vegetable garden, wildflower garden, a fern garden, a marsh garden, a tree platform overlooking the marshlands, a woodland walk, a hidden garden, and a formal croquet court. The garden extends over seven acres, the back four acres of which are a study in what deer do not eat.

2015 | 📷

➲ From Bedford Village, take Route 22 towards Katonah to intersection at Bedford Cross. Garden is on left. Please park at Rippowam School and walk to #531.

CORTLANDT MANOR

VIVIAN & ED MERRIN
2547 Maple Avenue, Cortlandt Manor

🕐 10 a.m. to 2 p.m.

The "STUMPERIE" garden is now complete and is open (what a wonder out of the hurricane Sandy). The Merrin garden has been featured in several books and magazines. The most spectacular of which is *The New Garden Paradise: Great Private Gardens of the World*. On a pond with a "pond house" is a paradise of lotus, 500 of them. More than 300 mountain laurels surround the garden, in a planting that makes them part of the total landscape. Mixed borders flow in and out of the six- or seven-acre garden, containing indigenous plants as well as species and rare cultivars. The Merrins have four greenhouse structures in which are kept the rare tropical plants, all of which are on display during the summer months. There is a lotus pond which will be in bloom. It is a sight to behold. A dramatic lookout of glass and wood takes the viewer to oversee the property and lake that is part of the property. The garden has been done with the expertise of Patrick Chassé. We also have an expanded new vegetable garden for you to see. In July, visitors will see fifty to seventy-five lotus in bloom, fifty to seventy-five tropical plants and orchids, three gardenia trees of various size, many hibiscus, some unique, a cactus garden, the Stumperie, and the giant bamboo garden.

2015 | 📷

➲ From the Taconic State Parkway, take Route 202 exit. Turn left towards Peekskill. Go 2.5 miles, then turn left at traffic light onto Croton Avenue, just past Cortland Farm Market. Go 1.2 miles to blinking light/stop sign and turn right onto Furnace Dock Road. Go 0.8 mile to blinking light/stop sign and turn left onto Maple Avenue. Go 0.9 mile to private road on right. Go 0.2 mile to #2547 on left.

POUND RIDGE

SARA STEIN GARDEN
8 Fox Hill Road, Pound Ridge

🕐 10 a.m. to 4 p.m.

This ecological restoration by Sara Stein, the native plant pioneer, spans five-and-one-half-acres and includes upland and wetland meadows, woodlands, and thickets. Documenting her planting experiences in her books (Noah's Garden, Planting Noah's Garden, My Weeds), she included many native species important to wildlife but not often used in landscaping. Other features include a planted stone terrace with grasses and sedges, an herb garden within openings in a brick patio and a planted moss garden and path around the pond. There are numerous paths through the various habitats, all showing a viable, sustainable alternative to the conventional suburban landscape design. The meadows will be in full bloom. Ellen and James Best acquired the property in 2007 and have been maintaining it since then.

2015 | ♿ | 📷

➲ From I-684, take Exit 4/Route 172 east to the blinking light at the gas station. Turn left, merging onto Routes 172 & 22 through Bedford. Go 1 mile, bearing right at the Bedford Village Green, staying on Route 172. At light (Gulf gas station), turn right onto Long Ridge Road, south toward Stamford, CT. Continue 2.4 miles to Fox Hill Road. Turn right. Number 8 is the first driveway on the left. Please park on Fox Hill Road.

From the Merritt Parkway, take Exit 34/Long Ridge Road/Route 104. Go 6.5 miles north toward Bedford. Turn left onto Fox Hill Road. Number 8 is the first driveway on the left. Please park on Fox Hill Road.

SOUTH SALEM

 GARDEN OF BERNARD MARQUEZ & TIM FISH
74 Hemlock Road, South Salem

🕐 10 a.m. to 6 p.m.

The Garden is a hybrid of design discipline and fun! It consists of several garden rooms on different levels. Plantings consist of a variety of boxwoods, some uncommon in the northeast. There are also a variety of conifer cultivars and other broadleaf evergreens. Water elements, stone work and a view of the Pound Ridge Reservation are highlights. Annuals, perennials, artifacts and containers complete the experience.

2015 | ♿ | 📷

⮐ From the west take I-684 to Exit 6/Route 35. Go east to Route 123, south to Mill River Road to Lake Kitchawan Road to Hemlock Road. All are one directional turns.

PUBLIC GARDEN

VALHALLA

📍 **THE NATIVE PLANT CENTER AT WESTCHESTER COMMUNITY COLLEGE**
75 Grasslands Road, Valhalla
(914) 606-7870

Special Garden Conservancy Open Day guided tours, Sunday, July 24, 2016, 12 p.m. to 4 p.m.

💲 Free

See this garden's listing on page 261.

Dutchess County

Saturday, July 30

🕙 **10 a.m. to 4 p.m.**
$7 per garden

🏷️ Pop-up Nursery
Twin Brooks Gardens,
garden shop by Squirrel Hall

There are also gardens open on this day and Digging Deeper events in nearby Litchfield County, CT. See page 90.

 DIGGING DEEPER: Exploring Twin Maples—The Evolution of a Garden; Douglas Dockery Thomas & Deborah Munson; Salisbury, CT; 4:30 p.m. See page 93.

 DIGGING DEEPER: Garden Revolution —Exploring Natural Gardens with Larry Weaner; Lakeville, CT; 1:30 p.m. See page 93.

DUTCHESS COUNTY

MILLBROOK

📍 **SQUIRREL HALL**
83 Maple Avenue, Millbrook

🏷️ Twin Brooks Gardens &
garden shop by Squirrel Hall

Squirrel Hall is a surprisingly witty garden, formally designed on a tiny village lot of less than one acre. The central axis is defined by an allée of sixteen hornbeams with two secret niches. The garden is organized into a series rooms with features usually reserved for large estates. The front lawn is enclosed by shrubs and an asparagus bed, a boxwood walkway leads to the front door and through an antique gate to the sunken garden, across the gravel and up the steps to a pavilion terrace and dining courtyard. Up a few more steps to the allée. The apiary is to the east, the petite orchard to the west, and a border of peonies is enclosed by a collection of hydrangea and other shrubs to the north. Two English terracotta chimneys mark the entrance to a secret woodland stroll garden featuring hemlocks, shade loving perennials and shrubs, and a bungalow.

NEW |

⮫ From Taconic State Parkway take Route 44 exit, go east toward Millbrook. From west, follow directions on Route 44 from here. Go 1.8 miles from the Taconic State Parkway and turn left to stay on Route 44 East. In 2.7 miles, turn right onto Ciferri Drive. Take first left onto Hillside Drive and then first right onto Haight Avenue. Continue to first left onto Maple Avenue.

From the east, Take 44 West and turn right onto Franklin Avenue. (Twin Brooks Gardens is on left) Take first right onto Maple Avenue.

MILLERTON

HYLAND/WENTE GARDEN
95 Taylor Road, Millerton

The property consists of a modern barn-like structure located on rolling farmland overlooking Indian Mountain and Indian Lake. The house has eight doors leading to a series of distinct gardens, intentionally blurring house and gardens. Emphasizing grasses, textures, colors, and plant combinations, the gardens blend with surrounding wildflower meadows and are designed for interest in all seasons. There is a rill with bamboo, a secret garden, a pool garden, a garden of solar panels, and a wooded walk down to Indian Lake.

2015 |

⮫ From Route 22 in Amenia, drive north 4.1 miles to Coleman Station Road/Route 58, and turn right. Go 1.1 miles, crossing Harlem Valley Rail Trail. Turn left immediately onto Regan Road, which, after 0.8 mile, dead-ends into Taylor Road. Turn right and go 0.1 mile up hill, and driveway, #95, is on left.

From clock tower in Sharon, Connecticut, drive north on Route 41along Sharon Green. Turn left onto Route 361 West at stop sign 0.1 mile in middle of Sharon Green, then make an

immediate right, just after fire station, remaining on Route 361/Millerton Road. Follow for 2.1 miles and turn left onto Dakin Road (at a sign for Mole's Hill Farm Stables). Go up hill on Dakin Road, which becomes Taylor Road 0.4 mile from Route 361; #95 is on right.

PUBLIC GARDEN

MILLBROOK

INNISFREE GARDEN
362 Tyrell Road, Millbrook
(845) 677-5268,
www.innisfreegarden.org

See this garden's listing page 257.

Dutchess County

Saturday, August 6

🕐 **Hours vary by garden
(Starting at 10 a.m.)**
$7 per garden

📚 Book Signings
Amy Goldman Fowler, Rhinebeck
Bettina Mueller, Tivoli

DUTCHESS COUNTY

RHINEBECK

📍 **CEDAR HEIGHTS FARM**
Address and directions will be provided at nearby gardens

🕐 10 a.m. to 4 p.m.

Cedar Heights Farm is the quintessential Hudson Valley Romantic landscape. This 21st century house was built following plans for a Cottage-Villa in the Bracketed Mode, from Andrew Jackson Downing's influential 1842 book, *Cottage Residences*. While the landscape was "subconsciously influenced" by Downing, who inspired Frederick Law Olmsted and Calvert Vaux, it nonetheless bears his stamp. The house atop a hill looks over apple orchards at sweeping Catskill Mountain views. Lawns are dotted with shrub borders, horse barns, and specimen trees. The effect is bold, yet serene, exactly what Downing would have done in this decidedly American place.

NEW | ♿ | 📷

➲ Directions to this garden are available by calling the Garden Conservancy office at 888-842-2442 or at additional gardens open on this date.

📍 **CEDAR HEIGHTS ORCHARD
—ARVIA MORRIS**
8 Crosby Lane, Rhinebeck

🕐 10 a.m. to 4 p.m.

The gardens near the house, pool house and barn include informal plantings of a large variety of bulbs, perennials and shrubs designed for low maintenance and bloom from

March to November. Yew hedges, specimen trees and stone walls lend structure. Further on the large vegetable garden/cutting garden includes a new border planting to attract butterflies and pollinators. From there a long path through a meadow leads past several ponds (with duck house in the rustic style) toward a large woodland garden of native plants and a large stand of bamboo. There are various structures along the way for rest and focus. A one-acre new apple orchard of 240 trees including twenty-four heirloom and new varieties for cider making was planted two years ago. The hillside orchard faces west with a stunning view of the Catskill Mountains.

2014 | |

➲ From Taconic State Parkway, take Rhinebeck/Red Hook exit and follow Route 199 West to traffic light (about 4 miles). Take Route 308 straight for 2 miles to Cedar Heights Road. Turn right and take second right onto Crosby Lane. Follow to dead end and into Cedar Heights Orchard. Park in barnyard and in marked areas. Please call (845) 876-3231 for more information.

📍 **AMY GOLDMAN FOWLER**
164 Mountain View Road, Rhinebeck

🕐 10 a.m. to 2 p.m.

 Book Signing
Heirloom Harvest: Modern Daguerrotypes of Historic Garden Treasures, by Amy Goldman Fowler

On two hundred acres in the Hudson Valley, Amy Goldman grows heirloom fruits and vegetables—two orchards full of apples, pears, peaches; and three plots of squash, melons, tomatoes, peppers, and more. In her fourth book, *Heirloom Harvest: Modern Daguerreotypes of Historic Garden Treasures* (Bloomsbury 2015), illustrated by Jerry Spagnoli, Amy describes her long-term collaboration with the land on the historic 1788 Abraham Traver farmstead. The place she fell in love with at first sight across a marshy expanse is different today. The house has been restored and incorporated into a larger whole. Farm outbuildings have cropped up, as have livestock and poultry. What was once a field of golden-colored little bluestem is now a more fruited plain filled with gardens (perennial, herb, vegetable) and orchards, intricacies, and delights.

2008 |

➲ From the Taconic State Parkway, take the Bull's Head Road exit heading west towards Rhinebeck. Go 4.2 miles on Bull's Head (also known as Slate Quarry Road or County Route 19) until you see Mountain View Road on left. Turn left and go 1.5 miles until you see 1,000 feet of split-rail fence on your left and mailbox #164. Turn left into the driveway and go past the cottage and barn, 0.5 mile to the house.

TIVOLI

📍 **A TEA GARDEN IN TIVOLI**
14 North Road, Tivoli

🕐 10 a.m. to 4 p.m.

 Book Signing
A Tea Garden in Tivoli, by Bettina Mueller

Drawing from a three decades long study of the Japanese Tea tradition where great—even legendary—gardens are small by necessity, award-winning author and garden designer Bettina Mueller set out to turn her one-eighth

---

📖 BOOK SIGNING

SATURDAY, AUGUST 6| 10 AM – 2 PM

HEIRLOOM HARVEST: MODERN DAGUERROTYPES OF HISTORIC GARDEN TREASURES
BY AMY GOLDMAN FOWLER

AT: Amy Goldman Fowler's garden
        164 Mountain View Road, Rhinebeck

of an acre backyard in the small village of Tivoli, New York into a private world of beauty and tranquility. Bettina created a Japanese-inspired tea garden that won Gardenista's 2015 Best Garden Design Award. A bamboo fence and gate, stone paths, naturalistic planting, and an antique Chinese water basin reinforce the beauty of the natural surroundings. The garden leads to a tea house nestled in the back of the property where Bettina hosts Japanese tea ceremonies for her guests. One passes from the colorful flower gardens at the front of the 1860s farmhouse to the quiet back-yard Roji (tea garden). It is said that the way to the tea house should feel like a mountain path in the midst of a forest; with every step you leave the dust of the world behind. Her recent book about the garden *A Tea Garden in Tivoli— American Garden Design Inspired by the Japanese Way of Tea* can be seen on her website with views of the garden. www.TeaGardenBook.com.

NEW | ♿ | 📷

➲ From Route 9G, turn west onto Route 78 to Tivoli. Drive to the first stop sign in the middle of the village and turn right onto North Road. The mailbox has the #14 on it. The garden is at the first Victorian house on left.

 ## BOOK SIGNING

SATURDAY, AUGUST 6| 10 AM – 4 PM
A TEA GARDEN IN TIVOLI
BY BETTINA MUELLER
AT: A Tea Garden in Tivoli, 14 North Road, Tivoli

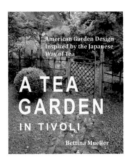

Schuyler & Tompkins County

SATURDAY, AUGUST 6

🕐 **10 a.m. to 4 p.m.**
$7 per garden

OUR PARTNER IN TOMPKINS COUNTY

THE TOMPKINS COUNTY COMMUNITY BEAUTIFICATION PROGRAM
was established in 2002 to improve the landscaping and appearance of places where tourists might go. In the City of Ithaca, this is accomplished through the efforts of a group of volunteers called the Beautification Brigade. This program also hosts a Rural Beautification Grant program through which matching funds are made available to rural Tompkins County Towns and Villages for beautification projects. Schuyler County

ALPINE

LIPARI GARDEN
3991 Route 228, Alpine

This ga'den, planted by Susanne Lipari, surrounds an 1840s farm house with borders, vegetable garden, and orchard. Over the years, most of the lawn has been replaced with borders, gravel paths, and thyme lawns. Most of the shrubs were grown from cuttings. The gardener loves the process of gardening as much as the result, and delights in the thought that many of the plants in the garden started as seeds or cuttings. She uses metal frames as plant supports and borrows from her years in the plant pathology labs at Cornell University with an abundance of old lab glassware perched on the metal frames. New last year are several installations of stone by Susanne's landscaper son, Daniel Lipari. A dry laid stone wall anchors a new garden on the hillside. It uses local stone and incorporates large boulders as a defining element. A small pond is also surrounded by laid stone. At this time of year, the garden displays many daylilies, lilies, and a wide selection of summer-blooming perennials.

2010 | ♿ |

➥ From Ithaca, take Route 79 west to Mecklenburg (about 10 miles). Turn left onto Route 228 South and go 2.4 miles. Please park on the road.

From Watkins Glen, take Route 79 east to Mecklenburg, turn right onto Route 228 South and go 2.4 miles. Please park on the road.

TOMPKINS COUNTY
FREEVILLE

MANZANO GARDEN
418 Caswell Road, Freeville

Spacious gardens surround the Ann and Carlton Manzano's 1800s farmhouse and are well-integrated with the sloping topography near the house and the surrounding woodlands beyond. Near the house, the pool area is softened with lush, tropical plantings, while the steep slopes behind the house are planted with a dense mix of perennials, shrubs, and groundcovers. Be sure to visit the barn that houses the art studio—Carlton is a *plein air* artist and dozens of his paintings are on display in the barn, which he built himself using a style that matches the era of their historic farmhouse. Carlton's whimsical sculptures made of natural wood pieces can be found along the woodland edge and paths.

2007 |

➥ From Route 13 in Ithaca, turn north onto Hanshaw Road. Go 2.7 miles and turn right onto West Dryden Road. Go 2.9 miles, and turn left onto Caswell Road. Go 0.5 mile to #418.

ITHACA

 ORCUTT GARDEN
130 Brook Way, Ithaca

Dianne and Jim Orcutt have developed their suburban lot into a series of garden rooms that make their property feel much larger than it is. Plantings in front of the house and adjacent to the driveway consist of trees, shrubs, groundcovers, ornamental grasses and perennials and are chosen for their low appeal to deer, as these areas are not fenced and deer pressure is high in this part of Tompkins County. Inside the fenced area lush, colorful perennials gardens completely surround the pool, and the deck is planted with large containers. A woodland garden next to the pool is planted with a textural mix of shade-tolerant perennials. This garden is a great example of how to transform a level, rectangular lot into an interesting, colorful, and varied series of gardens, some of which are deer-resistant.

NEW | 🚹 | 📷

➲ From Route 13 in Ithaca, turn north onto North Triphammer Road. Go 0.8 mile and turn right onto Brook Drive. Continue to left turn onto Brook Way.

TRUMANSBURG

 FILIOS GARDEN
9243 Route 89 North, Trumansburg

For decades. Candy and Achilles Filios have been creating their own Greek paradise overlooking Cayuga Lake. The gardens are anchored by beautiful stone walls and outbuildings, including a potting shed that will make you drool with envy, all built by Achilles in the style of his native Greece. The gardens include many flowers and ornamental plantings but also have a strong focus on food production. Candy's vegetable garden displays her passion for heirloom pumpkins and an heirloom tomato collection featuring more than thirty varieties. A unique feature of this garden are the "figgeries", based on a technique for growing fig trees that Candy and Achilles observed in an English garden. Ten-foot-deep recessed chambers are lined with stone walls to retain the heat, and the top is open during the frost free months. In winter the chambers are covered with layers of plastic and the fig trees have thrived despite two very extreme winters in the northeast. The Filios' also cultivate grapevines, an apple orchard and chestnut trees that provide them with abundant fruit and nuts each fall, and chickens in a special stone- lined run adjacent to one of the figgeries.

NEW | 🚹 | 📷

➲ From Ithaca, take Route 89 North/ Taughannock Road for 13.8 miles. The garden is on the right.

 HERON RIDGE
9531 Route 89, Trumansburg

Louie Larson and Peter O'Connell's gardens are incredibly exuberant, colorful and whimsical. A sculptural welcome garden greets visitors at the top of the driveway, made with large boulders, faux pier posts and large container plantings. Walk through the stone hedge and down the steps to the terraced gardens that lead down to the lakeside house. The gardens are carved out of a woodland and include stone features, container plantings, a tiny water garden, statuary, quaint outbuildings and hundreds of blooming annuals and perennials. A boulder-enclosed vegetable garden is sited in a sunny spot next to the driveway. The plantings continue around the house—be sure to enjoy the colorful planters on the back deck, Peter's hand built brick pizza oven and the beautiful view of Cayuga Lake.

NEW | 🚹 | 📷

➲ From Cass Park in Ithaca, take Route 89 11 miles north. Turn right at Old Orchard Beach Road. Follow signs to Heron Ridge. Follow signs for parking.

Putnam County

Stonecrop Gardens Special Open Day featuring Tea in the Garden

SUNDAY, AUGUST 14

Garden is open 10 a.m. to 5 p.m.
$5 admission

☕ Visitors may purchase tea and cake from 12 p.m. to 4 p.m.

Other upcoming 2016 Open Days:
September 18 and October 2.
See Stonecrop Gardens' full listing on page 259.

Columbia County

Saturday, August 20

🕐 **Hours vary by garden**
   (Starting at 10 a.m.)
$7 per garden

🏷 Pop-up Nursery
Broken Arrow Nursery

 DIGGING DEEPER: Planting in a Post-Wild World, with Thomas Rainer, Copake Falls

COLUMBIA COUNTY

COPAKE FALLS

📍 **MARGARET ROACH**
99 Valley View Road, Copake Falls

🕐 10 a.m. to 4 p.m.

🏷 Broken Arrow Nursery

The garden, about twenty-five years of age, reflects my obsession with plants, particularly those with good foliage or of interest to wildlife, and also my belief that even in Zone 5B, the view out the window can be compelling and satisfying all 365 days. Sixty kinds of birds have been my longtime companions, along with every native frog and toad species, and we are all happy together. Informal mixed borders, shrubberies, frog-filled water gardens and container groupings cover the steep two-and-one-third-acre hillside, a former orchard with a simple Victorian-era farmhouse and little outbuildings set in Taconic State Park lands on a rural farm road.

2015 | 📷

⮑ From Route 22 (5 miles south of Hillsdale, 13 miles north of Millerton) take Route 344 towards Taconic State Park signs. Bear right onto Valley View Road after park entrance and brown store, over metal bridge and past camp. After High Valley Road on left, stay right another 100 feet to green barn and house on left. Parking on High Valley or opposite house.

⭐ **CHURCH OF ST. JOHN**
IN THE WILDERNESS
261 State Route 344, Copake Falls

 DIGGING DEEPER VENUE ONLY

HUDSON

📍 **VERSAILLES ON HUDSON**
5 Rossman Avenue, Hudson

🕐 10 a.m. to 2 p.m.

We wanted to create a garden that looked as if it had been planted when the house was built in 1903. The entire land formation presented a real challenge—from the house to the bottom of the garden was a steep thirty-foot drop. We needed to create an elegant way to move through the garden—so we carefully designed multi- level stone patios and easy access stairways to guide you down to the fountain. We chose a most unexpected plan that would take advantage of the dramatic views of the river, hills, and sunsets. By turning the garden on its axis, we have created the illusion of a massive property—with grand sweeping lawns, long flowing hydrangea and hornbeam hedges, and architectural boxwood balls. Our fountain and the hornbeam curve are the highlights of this quiet garden—complete with fish, frogs and water plants. In the spring and early summer, the garden is predominately white but turns ever more pink as the summer progresses. In the winter, this garden makes an equally strong statement framed by the many evergreens. Versailles on Hudson... [Read the full description online]

NEW | 📷

⮑ Warren Street is the main street of Hudson. It runs gently uphill from the river for about 1.5 miles. Cross streets start at 1st Street near the river and go up in numbers from there. For our garden (5 Rossman Avenue), go to the top of Warren Street, turn left onto Prospect Avenue, and then right onto Rossman Avenue. (Columbia Memorial Hospital is on Prospect Avenue opposite Rossman Avenue.) Our house is a big pink Victorian on the right the third house from the corner. From the south, take the Sawmill Parkway North to the Taconic State Parkway. Take the Hudson exit onto Route 82 west. It becomes Routes 9 and 23. Continue straight until Route 9 turns right toward Hudson at a traffic light (Route 23 goes straight on to the Rip Van Winkle Bridge). WARNING: Do not turn right onto Route 9H at an earlier traffic light. Route 9 runs straight into Prospect Avenue with the top of Warren Street on left. Proceed as directed above.

From the New York State Thruway/I-87 North to Exit 21/Catskill. Exit toll plaza and turn left onto Route 23B, then left again onto

Route 23 East. Soon after crossing the Rip Van Winkle bridge turn left onto Route 9G and go north toward Hudson. You will enter Hudson on 3rd Street. The second traffic light is Warren Street. Turn right and proceed as directed above.

From Massachusetts and New England, take the Massachusetts Turnpike West to Exit B-2/Taconic Parkway South. Take the Parkway until the exit for Route 23 West, Hudson. This will turn into Route 23B take you directly into Hudson. Turn left onto Prospect Avenue. You will be at the non-Warren Street end of Prospect and so Rossman Avenue is the first on the left. Proceed as directed above. Please park anywhere on the right side of Rossman Avenue going uphill. Do not park in the driveway.

VALATIE

 KEVIN LEE JACOBS
3007 Main Street, Valatie

🕐 10 a.m. to 4 p.m.

Kevin Lee Jacobs wears three hats: cookbook author, serious gardener, and creator of the well-known website "A Garden for the House" (www.agardenforthehouse.com). His house is on the National Register of Historic Places. He has designed numerous gardens on his urban property: a Woodland Garden, a winding Serpentine Garden, two Kitchen Gardens, and a formal Boxwood Garden.

2014 | ♿ | 📷

➲ From Claverack and points south, take Route 9H north. Take the Valatie exit. Turn left onto Route 9 North. Continue 0.6 mile to Main Street. Turn left onto Lake Street (the first left) and then an immediate left into the driveway. The house is a big white Victorian with green shutters.

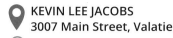 DIGGING DEEPER

SATURDAY, AUGUST 20

PLANTING IN A POST-WILD WORLD

AT: Church of St. John in the Wilderness
  261 State Route 344, Copake Falls

Join us for an afternoon lecture and workshop with landscape architect Thomas Rainer. He is co-author with Claudia West of a new book called *Planting in a Post-Wild World* that inspires us to design plantings that function like naturally occurring plant communities. It also instructs how to manage them, not doing painstaking and often impractical garden maintenance, plant by plant, as in traditional horticulture.

Registration is required and space is limited. **Opendaysprogram.org or call 1(888) 842-2442**

WaveHill

"One of the greatest living works of art"

A public garden and cultural center

West 249 Street and Independence Avenue
Bronx, NY 10471 • wavehill.org • 718.549.3200

New York City

Thursday, September 8

 DIGGING DEEPER

THURSDAY, SEPTEMBER 8 | 5:30 PM

INTO THE BLUE—PUSHING BOUNDARIES ON A ROOFTOP GARDEN

Fred Rich, Mark K. Morrison & Annie Novak

AT: Battery Park City, NYC
    (address sent to ticket holders only)

Thirty-five stories above the southern tip of Manhattan sits a grand experiment—the 2,000 square-foot Battery Rooftop Garden with panoramic skyline and water views. Owner Fred Rich set out to create a complex ecosystem with trees, shrubs, and plants to enhance environmental performance, provide edibles and horticultural interest year round, and attract wildlife. He turned to landscape architect Mark K. Morrison and urban farmer Annie Novak to push the boundaries, making this garden a living laboratory and agitprop for green roof technology and urban agriculture, and a garden of delight. Come talk to this trio about their extraordinary creation and linger a while yourself.

Registration is required and space is limited. **Opendaysprogram.org or call 1(888) 842-2442**

Nassau County

Saturday, September 17

 DIGGING DEEPER

SATURDAY, SEPTEMBER 17 | 10 AM | $15

TEA CEREMONY

AT: John P. Humes Japanese Stroll Garden
  Oyster Bay Road and Dogwood Lane, Mill Neck, NY

Tour of the very special John P. Humes Japanese Stroll Garden with its curator Stephen Morrell. Stephen will explain the design aspects of Japanese gardens and the art of the tea ceremony. A landscape architect specializing in Japanese-style gardens, Stephen has studied in Japan and is a practitioner of Zen Buddhism and the tea ceremony. He will explain the history of tea ceremony and present formal tea to one lucky guest recipient.

This program will be held again on October 1.

Registration is required and space is limited. **Opendaysprogram.org or call 1(888) 842-2442**

Westchester County

Sunday, September 18

🕐 **Hours vary by garden
  (Starting at 10 a.m.)**

$7 per garden

There are also gardens open on this day in Fairfield County, CT. See page 102.

 DIGGING DEEPER: Making Visual Sense of Your Outdoor Space, with Bernard Marquez & Tim Fish, South Salem, 2 p.m.& 4:30 p.m.

WESTCHESTER COUNTY

LEWISBORO

 **THE WHITE GARDEN
199 Elmwood Road, Lewisboro**

🕐 10 a.m. to 3 p.m.

The native oak-hickory forest provides a "sacred grove" setting for the modern Greek Revival-style house. The gardens were designed by Patrick Chassé, ASLA, and completed in 1999. Nearest the house the gardens are classically inspired, including a nymphaeum, pergola garden, labyrinth, and theater court, and additional hidden gardens

Dick Button—Ice Pond Farm, featured in *Outstanding American Gardens: A Celebration—25 Years of the Garden Conservancy*. Photo by Marion Brenner.

include a perennial ellipse and "annual" garden, a conservatory "jungle" garden, and an Asian-inspired moss garden. Several water features accent the landscape, and native plantings dominate in areas outside the central gardens. Many sculptures enrich this landscape and one can visit a Temple of Apollo on an island in the main pond. In spring, over 300,000 daffodils bloom in the woodland. Woodland walking paths weave over a meandering brook and through a shady dell. Several glasshouses can be seen, including a new state-of-the-art greenhouse that supports the gardens. Head gardener Eric Schmidt, who ably orchestrates the rich garden plantings throughout the property, is on hand for questions.

2015 | 📷🎟

➲ From Route 15/Merritt Parkway, take Exit 38 and follow Route 123 North through New Canaan into New York state. Town of Lewisboro and village of Vista are first signs encountered. Go past Vista Fire Department about 0.25 mile. Just after shingled Episcopal church on right, Route 123 bears left and Elmwood Road bears right. Go about another 0.25 mile

just over a hill. At beginning of a gray stockade fence on right is driveway at #199.

NORTH SALEM

DICK BUTTON—ICE POND FARM
115 June Road, North Salem
🕙 10 a.m. to 3 p.m.

Forget last year and my hopes to do a tribune to Stephen Sondheim's "Into The Woods"... will hopefully get in a few trees to start the woods...The real change is a border along the pool. I noticed last year no one looked at the border underneath the circle garden and in fact I didn't either...it had gotten too messy. So, being enamored with the materials used in a Japanese garden...water, gravel, rock, clipped box, Japanese maples, rhodies and Ilex, (but not with a full Japanese garden...too difficult to create with effective authority) I ripped out all but the lilacs Page Dickey suggested I plant years ago and started. Hope you will come and jeer or cheer!

2015

➲ Going south on I-68 Hardscrabble Road and go east about 5 miles to Old Route 124/ June Road. Turn right onto June Road and go

0.75 mile to #115. Going north on I-684, take Exit 7/Purdys. Take Route 116 east for about 3 miles to North Salem. Turn left onto June Road/Old Route 124. Go 0.5 mile to #115. Please park in the field as directed.

 GARDEN OF BERNARD MARQUEZ & TIM FISH
74 Hemlock Road, South Salem

 DIGGING DEEPER ONLY

 **DIGGING DEEPER**

SUNDAY, SEPTEMBER 18 | 2:30 PM & 4 PM

MAKING VISUAL SENSE OF YOUR OUTDOOR SPACE

AT: Garden of Bernard Marquez & Tim Fish
74 Hemlock Road, South Salem

Garden designers and long-time Open Days hosts, Bernard Marquez and Timothy Fish, will use their own spectacular garden, recently featured in Garden Design Magazine and always a favorite with Open Days visitors, as a way to explore design ideas they find essential in any project. They will open a conversation with participants on maximizing what any given space has to offer, making a space relevant to how you live, and creating a pleasing and functional composition.

A Native of California, Bernard is a horticulturalist inspired by the great outdoors and natural compositions, with a relaxed design discipline. Tim is a native of Nebraska, a gardener, painter, and sculptor. As a member of the International Design Police, he possesses an uncompromising design discipline.

Registration is required and space is limited. **Opendaysprogram.org or call 1(888) 842-2442**

Dutchess County

Saturday, September 24

🕐 **10 a.m. to 4 p.m.**
$7 per garden

 Pop-up Nursery
Atlock Farm / Broken Arrow Nursery /
Ellen Hoverkamp / Merritt Bookstore /
Orchard Jewelry

 Book Signing with Merritt Bookstore
Katie Ridder & Peter Pennoyer,
Millbrook, 2 p.m. to 3 p.m.

 DIGGING DEEPER: A House in the
Country—The Garden of Katie Ridder &
Peter Pennoyer, Millbrook, 4:30 p.m.

OUR PARTNER IN DUTCHESS COUNTY

INNISFREE GARDEN

INNISFREE GARDEN

We are proud to partner with Innisfree Garden to bring you the May 21, July 30, and September 24 Dutchess County Open Days. Innisfree Foundation preserves and shares Innisfree Garden and the legacy of landscape architect Lester Collins. His iconic mid-twentieth century design exalts the beauty of nature enhanced by subtle and sustainable human intervention. A small nonprofit, Innisfree has opened this sublime 185-acre landscape to the public since 1960, and is now expanding its educational offerings and working to preserve and protect this living landmark.

Innisfree is a post-war masterpiece — PERIOD.
Charles Birnbaum, President, TCLF

INNISFREE GARDEN
www.innisfreegarden.org
Millbrook, New York

DUTCHESS COUNTY

CLINTON CORNERS

JUNTO FARM
99-100 Dr. Harrington Road,
Clinton Corners

"Gardens (and children) are for me among our most sincere expressions of hope and optimism. Our gardens now have unfolded over nearly fifteen years of thought, planning, experimentation, and effort. Many of the trees and plants selected have a direct connection to a powerful memories from my past: lilacs, azaleas, tulip poplars, and magnolias from my early childhood in DC; elms and ivy remind me of my years in Shaker Heights Ohio; bamboo and Japanese maples from seven years living in Asia; London plane trees after five years of admiring them in Regent's Park from the windows of my nash terrace. The house and gardens reflect some contrasting ideas and impulses; stark modernism versus a need for romance and whimsy, rigid geometry versus organic sweeps of plants; formal organization and carefully planned beds and defined view corridors versus wild, instinctive and impro-visational elements. The gardens are full of scents to evoke emotion, bouquets for the picking, and everywhere food to harvest—..."
[Read the full description online]
NEW

➲ From the Taconic State Parkway and Route 44 E, head east toward Millbrook and turn left onto Route 82. In 3.4 miles, turn right onto the Shunpike. In 0.7 miles, turn right onto Dr. Harrington Road.

From Route 44 W/Sharon Turnpike, turn right onto Stanford Road. In 2.6 miles, turn left on Shunpike. In 1 mile, turn left onto Dr. Harrington Road.

MILLBROOK

CLOVE BROOK FARM—
CHRISTOPHER SPITZMILLER
857 North Clove Road, Millbrook

The garden at Clove Brook Farm was designed by P. Allen Smith in collaboration with potter Christopher Spitzmiller in 2014. It was design to complement the 1830's Greek Revival farm house, complete with a custom fence, inspired by the balustrade on the Louisiana Plantation "Felicity" in the movie 12 Years A Slave. The garden, planted in 2014, sprung from the earth with great gusto and was inspired by the many visits to the garden of close friend Bunny Williams. The horseshoe-shaped layout begins with two long, mixed perennial beds towards the front, filled with vibrant blooms, and the additional rectangular beds include a mix of mostly flowers and some vegeta-bles planted to bloom seasonally, so there is always something to enjoy. In the spring and early summer, the wattle fence supports sweet peas and snap peas. Then dahlias grow up in their place, resembling colorful fireworks in late summer. Allen chose topiaries, Japa-nese willows, and white 'Phantom' hydrangeas to accent the front perennial beds and...
[Read the full description online]
2015 | ♿ | 📷

➲ From the South and East, take the Taconic State Parkway to the Beekman Road/Hopewell Junction/Sylvan Lake exit. Turn right onto Beekman Road. Go 10 miles to the farm off the Taconic. Go through two stop signs and then straight through a roundabout. Beekman Road becomes Clove Road. Where Clove Road turns into Chestnut Ridge Road, turn left onto North Clove Road. Clove Brook is the first farm on your right.

From the North, take Route 44 south. Across from the Verbank Fire House turn left onto North Clove Road. Clove Brook, is the last house on the left. When you see the Union Vale Highway department, slow down and park. Parking available at 851 North Clove Road or street parking; white building with a purple door.

From the West, take Route 343 to Chestnut Ridge Road. Take Chestnut Ridge Road and bear right through the stop sign at Halls Corner Road. Chestnut Ridge Road ends, then turn right onto North Clove Road. The farm is the first house on the right.

 KATIE RIDDER & PETER PENNOYER
366 Ludlow Woods Road, Millbrook

 DIGGING DEEPER

 Book Signing: 2 to 3 p.m.
A House in the Country,
by Katie Ridder and Peter Pennoyer

Our hornbeam-enclosed flower garden with formal bluestone paths framing fourteen beds was inspired by the flower garden at Wave Hill. Our house, designed by my husband, Peter Pennoyer, faces directly onto the garden. Our landscape architect, Edmund Hollander, designed our property with simple hedgerows and trees reserving the flower garden area for me to unleash a less disciplined approach. With a minimalist pergola supporting New Dawn roses, white wisteria and clematis serving as our outdoor dining room at its center, the garden is quite architectural in its overall structure. But my design is loose— a celebration of large scale flowers and saturated colors. Though only two years old it has flourished to the point where it has required major editing. And even as I edit, I am careful not to remove the surprising proliferation of volunteers from my annuals grown from seed. I am inspired by local gardens that I visit frequently: Wave Hill, New York Botanical

Garden, Untermeyer Garden, Stonecrop, as well as Open Day gardens. I continue to learn… [Read the full description online]
2015 | &. | ◉

➲ Ten minutes from the Taconic Parkway or five minutes from Route 22 in Millbrook.

STANFORDVILLE

 BEAR CREEK FARM
6187 Route 82, Stanfordville

Ornamental trees, hostas, three season flower gardens, massive dahlia gardens plus an organic vegetable garden. All using local native plants and some Japanese bushes and trees. A restful walk around about nine acres of a thirty-eight-acre property.
NEW | &. | ◉

➲ From the New York Taconic State Parkway traveling north, take Exit for US Route 44 E to Millbrook (sign also says Poughkeepsie, though you will have passed prior exits for that) and turn right at end of ramp. Go 1.0 mile, and turn left onto Route 82 N, the turn is just after mini- mall on left and only gas station on the left side of the road. Go 7.7 miles to garden on left. (Note: just after 7 miles you will see a fork in the road with Stissing Bank in center of fork, continue to bear left on Route 82 North and slow down. On left, you will pass a house with a brown fence close to the road and our driveway is a bit hidden but marked by two small stone pillars just after the fenced house. Note: If you pass Carousel Antiques Center on right, you have gone too far.

 ELLEN & ERIC PETERSEN
378 Conklin Hill Road, Stanfordville

Our garden keeps getting bigger! We keep making small changes, refining, and renovating older plantings and beginning new areas. We try to have interest every month of the year. In September, both annual and perennial sunflowers come into their own, along with many other tall daisy type plants. The pokeweeds trained into standards by my helper will be looking spectacular. The heptacodium should be showing its decorative red sepals and possibly the *Franklinia* will be in bloom. Probably the most spectacular part of the garden at this time is the meadow of *Sporobolus heterolepsis* (prairie drop seed), which frames a sculpture by Vivian Beer. On a sunny day, its scent is delicious. While I would definitely not call this a low- maintenance garden, we rarely water anything after the second year and fertilize only container plants. Compost suppresses weeds and feeds the soil without making it too rich. Consequently, in spite of all the very tall perennials, we need very little staking. My collection of plants includes more natives... [Read the full description online]

2014 |

➲ From Route 82 north, pass firehouse in Stanfordville. Go 5 miles to Old Conklin Hill Road and turn right. You will come to a "T" very soon. Turn right again there. Now you are on Conklin Hill Road. Continue about 2 miles up hill. The garden is on right after a sharp uphill turn. Please pull into the field on left. The house and garden are on right.

✿ PUBLIC GARDEN

MILLBROOK

📍 **INNISFREE GARDEN**
362 Tyrell Road, Millbrook
(845) 677-5268,
www.innisfreegarden.org

🏷 Atlock Farm / Broken Arrow Nursery / Ellen Hoverkamp / Merritt Bookstore / Orchard Jewely

See this garden's listing on page 257.

🌱 DIGGING DEEPER

SATURDAY, SEPTEMBER 24 | 4:30 PM

A HOUSE IN THE COUNTRY—THE GARDEN OF KATIE RIDDER & PETER PENNOYER

AT: 366 Ludlow Woods Road, Millbrook

Join renowned architect Peter Pennoyer and sought-after interior designer Katie Ridder for a talk about the conception, design, decoration, and landscaping of their new country house in Millbrook, New York. The couple bought the property in 2009 as a family getaway and have spent the last seven years transforming the land and building an exuberant, one-of-a-kind Greek Revival-inspired house with lush woodland, flower and cutting gardens.

Eric Piasecki

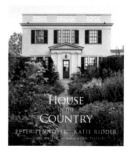

📗 Katie and Peter chronicle their entire process in the new book, *A House in the Country* (Vendome Press, 2016) which will be available.

Registration is required and space is limited. **Opendaysprogram.org or call 1(888) 842-2442**

The Hamptons: North Fork

Saturday, September 24

🕐 **12 p.m. to 4 p.m.**
$7 admission

SUFFOLK COUNTY

CUTCHOGUE

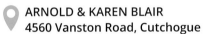
ARNOLD & KAREN BLAIR
4560 Vanston Road, Cutchogue

Our three-acre Peconic Bayfront property overlooks a seventeen-acre beach and wetland protected preserve deeded to The Nature Conservancy—a haven for migratory and nesting sea birds. The gardens flow from an eighty-foot elevation down to sea level via numerous winding paths with various landings and overlooks. A park- like one-and-one-half acre woodland garden features numerous spring flowering shrubs and trees under towering oaks. A wandering rustic path leads to a massive log gazebo fronting a wetland we lovingly rescued from invasive vines and replanted with indigenous bayberry, high tide bush, and native grasses which put on a late Fall delightful burst of color. Extensive stone walls surround a pool tucked into the hillside. Rolling lawns, numerous specimen evergreens, antique and salvaged garden ornaments, and 180-degree bay views with magnificent sunsets enhance a magical spot on the North Fork. Our garden is self-designed and features plenty of natives. It has evolved over twenty seven years of experimenting, transplanting, learning, and re-transplanting. Our garden is a living, breathing, perpetual work that will never finish.

2015 | 📷

➲ Take Route 25 East from Riverhead. At the second traffic light in Cutchogue, turn right onto Eugenes Road. Turn right onto Skunk Lane. Bear right and continue all the way to the Bay where road curves right over causeway. At end of causeway road forks. Take right fork which is Vanston Road. House is 0.9 mile on right on Vanston Road.

Nassau County

Saturday, October 1

 DIGGING DEEPER

SATURDAY, OCTOBER 1 | 10 AM | $15

TEA CEREMONY

AT: **John P. Humes Japanese Stroll Garden**
  Oyster Bay Road and Dogwood Lane, Mill Neck, NY

Tour of the very special John P. Humes Japanese Stroll Garden with its curator Stephen Morrell. Stephen will explain the design aspects of Japanese gardens and the art of the tea ceremony. A landscape architect specializing in Japanese-style gardens, Stephen has studied in Japan and is a practitioner of Zen Buddhism and the tea ceremony. He will explain the history of tea ceremony and present formal tea to one lucky guest recipient.

Registration is required and space is limited. **Opendaysprogram.org or call 1(888) 842-2442**

Putnam County

Stonecrop Gardens Special Open Day featuring Tea in the Garden

SUNDAY, OCTOBER 2
Last one of the season!

Garden is open 10 a.m. to 5 p.m.
$5 admission

☕ Visitors may purchase tea and cake from 12 p.m. to 4 p.m.

See Stonecrop Gardens' full listing on page 259.

Dutchess County

Saturday, October 15

🕐 **12 p.m. to 6 p.m.**
$7 admission

DUTCHESS COUNTY

PAWLING

📍 **THE BRINE GARDEN—
DUNCAN & JULIA BRINE
21 Bluebird Inn Road, Pawling**

🕐 12 p.m. to 6 p.m.

With an emphasis on native plants, this naturalistic, six-acre garden and arboretum connects ecologically and horticulturally diverse areas. The twenty-six-year-old garden has a maturing plant collection including an allée of *Taxodium d*. (with knees), groups of *Chionanthus v*. (with drupes), and more than twenty viburnum (native and non-native), some with showy berries. Several imposing hedges of *Miscanthus giganteus* structure the areas and relate to the *Phragmites* of this formerly agrarian landscape. You will receive a property map and a plant list which indicates U.S. and Dutchess County natives. Anne Raver of the New York Times profiled this landscape designer's garden. The Brine Garden is a chapter of *Private Gardens of the Hudson Valley* and *Gardens of the Hudson Valley* and is featured in *Designer Plant Combinations, 50 Beautiful Deer-Resistant Plants, Horticulture*, and *Hudson Valley Magazine*, among others. Duncan Brine speaks and writes about naturalistic landscape design and he's an instructor at the New York Botanical Garden. See images on www. gardenlarge.com.

2015 |

➲ From the South (Westchester County, New York City), take Route I-684 North all the way to the end where Route I-684 becomes Route 22. Continue north on Route 22 for about 25 minutes. From the intersection of Routes 55

and 22 in Pawling continue north on Route 22 about 3 miles (passing Trinity Pawling High School and gazebos on right.) Turn right onto Route 68/North Quaker Hill Road. Bear left at the first intersection onto Hurd's Corner Road. Go 0.5 mile. Park on right side of Hurd's Corner Road across from Bluebird Inn Road on left. Walk in on Bluebird Inn Road to the last house on left.

From the North (Northern Dutchess County, Columbia County), take Route 22 south. At the intersection with Route 55 in Wingdale continue south on Route 22 about 4 miles. Turn left onto Route 68/North Quaker Hill Road. Proceed as directed above. From Northwestern Connecticut, take Route 7 in Gaylordsville, CT, west on Route 55 into New York. At the "T" intersection turn left and continue to Route 22. Turn left (south) onto Route 22 and go 4 miles. Turn left onto Route 68/North Quaker Hill Road. Proceed as directed above.

❀ PUBLIC GARDENS

BRONX COUNTY

BRONX

WAVE HILL
West 249th Street & Independence Avenue, Bronx, (718) 549-3200, www.wavehill.org

Often called one of the most beautiful places in New York, this southern-most of the great estates along the east bank of the Hudson River features spectacular views of the river and the Palisades, a wide variety of specimen trees and a great range of imaginative plantings in an intimate setting. Wave Hill's mission is to celebrate the artistry and legacy of its gardens and landscapes, to preserve its magnificent views, and to explore human connections to the natural world through programs in horticulture, education and the arts. Amenities include The Shop, Café, restrooms and parking. Wave Hill House, the Perkins Visitor Center, Glyndor Gallery and the Great Lawn are wheelchair-accessible. The Ecology Building can only be reached by stairs. Most areas of the garden are accessible, and those that are not accessible are indicated on the seasonal Map & Guide.

🕐 March 15 through October 31: Tuesday through Sunday, 9 a.m. to 5:30 p.m. November 1 through March 14: Tuesday through Sunday, 9 a.m. to 4:30 p.m. Closed Mondays, except Memorial Day, Labor Day and Columbus Day. Closed New Year's Day, Thanksgiving, and Christmas.

$ Free Tuesday and Saturday until 12 p.m., otherwise, $8 adults, $4 seniors/students, $2 children 6+. Children under 6 free.

➲ From West Side and New Jersey, take Henry Hudson Parkway to Exit 21/246-250th Street. Continue north to 252nd Street. Turn left at overpass and left again. Turn right at 249th Street to Wave Hill gate.

From Westchester, take Henry Hudson Parkway south to Exit 22/254th Street. Turn left at stop sign and left again at traffic light. Turn right onto 249th Street to Wave Hill gate.

Wave Hill provides free shuttle service between the front gate and the Metro-North Riverdale, station as well as the #1 subway station at West 242nd Street. Shuttle schedules at wavehill.org. Purchase Metro-North Getaway Package from Grand Central Terminal or Harlem-125 Street, and receive discounts on round-trip rail fare and admission to Wave Hill.

COLUMBIA COUNTY

AUSTERLITZ

STEEPLETOP—POET EDNA ST. VINCENT MILLAY'S GARDEN
440 East Hill Road, Austerlitz (518) 392-3362, www.millay.org

Pulitzer-prize winning poet, Edna St. Vincent Millay's home Steepletop, named for the wildflower found in its high fields, served the poet in very unique ways. This secluded sanctuary provided Millay with space to create gardens that satisfied her earth-ecstatic nature and gave her endless inspiration for some of her most beloved work. Over the twenty five years that Millay lived at Steepletop she wrote volumes of poetry and created a series of garden rooms, a kitchen garden, and a spring-fed pool with an adjoining outdoor bar dubbed "The Ruins" where she could entertain her guests. Though some of these features are in various stages of restoration, they all can be toured and appreciated by today's visitors to Steepletop.

🕐 Special Garden Conservancy Open Day on Saturday, August 20; discounted house tours offered at 12 p.m. and 2 p.m. Space is limited so reservations are requested. Otherwise open Friday through Monday 10 a.m. to 4:30 p.m.

$ On August 20 Open Day, grounds $7; house tours $12. Otherwise, grounds and garden guided tours are $16. Please note Open Days admission tickets are not accepted here.

➲ East Hill Road is just off of Route 22 in Austerlitz, NY, just 4 miles south of I-90 and the Massachusetts Turnpike.

From the Taconic Parkway go east on Route 203 and follow the signs to Steepletop.

DUTCHESS COUNTY

AMENIA

WETHERSFIELD
214 Pugsley Hill Road, Amenia
(845) 373-8037,
www.wethersfieldgarden.org

Ten acres of formal classical style and outer gardens surround Chauncey D. Stillman's Georgian-style brick house. The original garden around the perimeter of the house was created in 1940 by Bryan J. Lynch. Starting in 1952, Evelyn N. Poehler designed and maintained the formal garden and wilderness garden over a twenty year period. The formal Garden, blending with the natural landscape, features trimmed hedges, sculpture, water features and spectacular panoramic views.

🕐 Special Garden Conservancy Open Days June 20, July 25 and August 15, 10 a.m. to 4 p.m. Special guided tours of the garden will be offered at 11 a.m. and 2:15 p.m. The Main House will be open from noon to 2 p.m. for viewing Stillman's art collection. Don't miss this special opportunity. Regular visiting hours for Garden are June through September, Wednesday, Friday and Saturday, noon to 5 p.m. Reservations required for tours of Carriage House and Main House.

➲ From the Taconic State Parkway, take Route 44 east for 10.8 miles, turn left onto Route 86 for 1.4 miles, and turn right onto Pugsley Hill Road. Follow signs for 1.3 miles to estate entrance on left.

HYDE PARK

BEATRIX FARRAND GARDEN
AT BELLEFIELD
4097 Albany Post Road (Route 9),
Hyde Park, (845) 229-9115,
www.beatrixfarrandgarden.org

The enclosed formal garden and surrounding wild garden were designed in 1912 by the acclaimed landscape gardener Beatrix Farrand. Thought to be her earliest surviving residential project, it has been restored and is maintained by a small, nonprofit organization, The Beatrix Farrand Garden Association, in partnership with the National Park Service. Adjacent to a magnificent eighteenth-century house that was remodeled by the architects McKim, Mead & White in 1911, the garden evidences Colonial American, Arts and Crafts, and formal European influences. Typical of Farrand's work, the subtle elegance of the plan and built elements is set off by lush borders in sophisticated color schemes. A self-guided audio tour, installed in 2012, helps visitors appreciate the garden and its extraordinary history.

🕐 Year round, daily, 7 a.m. to sunset. Closed Christmas Day, Thanksgiving, and New Year's Day

$ Free

➲ Bellefield is part of the Roosevelt-Vanderbilt National Historic Sites and located on a public campus along Route 9 that includes Franklin Delano Roosevelt Home and Presidential Library. Park at Wallace Visitor Center and follow signs to garden.

MILLBROOK

INNISFREE GARDEN
362 Tyrrel Road, Millbrook
(845) 677-5268, www.innisfreegarden.org

Recognized as one of the world's ten best gardens, Innisfree is a powerful icon of mid-twentieth century design. Over fifty years in the making, it is the work of landscape architect Lester Collins, FASLA (1914 – 1993), with important contributions by his clients, artist and teacher Walter Beck and gardener and heiress Marion Burt Beck. Innisfree merges the essence of Modernist ideas with traditional Chinese and Japanese garden design principles in a form that evolved through subtle handling of the landscape and slow manipulation of its ecology. The result is a distinctly American stroll garden—a sublime composition of rock, water, wood, and sky achieved with remarkable economy and grace.

🕐 Saturday, April 16, 23 & 30, 2016, 11 a.m. to 5 p.m. Regular hours May 7, 2016 through October 16, 2016: Wednesday through Friday, 10 a.m. to 4 p.m.; weekends and bank holidays, 11 a.m. to 5 p.m.; closed Mondays and Tuesdays except bank holidays. Guided curator's tours and wildflower walks offered monthly. Garden opens before sunrise three times each year. Please see website for calendar details.

$ $6 weekdays; $8 weekends and holidays; children 3 and under free.

➲ Tyrrel Road is on the south side of Route 44, 1.6 miles east of the Taconic State Parkway overpass and 1.9 miles west of the traffic light at the intersection of Routes 82, 343, and Franklin Avenue. Blue and white signs for Innisfree on Route 44 mark the turn. Innisfree is about 1.1 miles off Route 44, on the left side of Tyrrel. The street number is out of order so watch for the white Innisfree sign and a dirt driveway through stone pillars to the right of a stone gatehouse. The parking area is about .5 miles in along the drive. If coming from the Taconic, please do NOT take the Tyrrel Road exit (it is impassible in the middle). Instead take the Route 44 exit east toward Millbrook. If using GPS, the Innisfree driveway is now called Innisfree Lane. You can key in Tyrrel Road & Innisfree Lane, Millbrook, NY 12545.

NASSAU COUNTY
MILL NECK
JOHN P. HUMES JAPANESE STROLL GARDEN
Oyster Bay Road & Dogwood Lane, Mill Neck, (516) 676-4486

A seven-acre gem of landscape design, the garden provides a retreat for passive recreation and contemplation. The views, textures, and balance of elements in the garden follow Japanese aesthetic principles, encouraging a contemplative experience. The garden suggests a mountain setting beside a sea, where gravel paths represent streams forming pools and cascades, eventually flowing into the ocean, represented by a pond.

🕐 April 30 through October, Saturdays and Sundays, 11:30 a.m. to 4 p.m. Private tours and tea ceremony demonstrations by appointment. Call for reservations.

$ $10 adults

➲ The garden is located on the North Shore of Long Island about 26 miles from Manhattan and one mile from Planting Fields Arboretum, and the Long Island Railroad's Oyster Bay Line. Taxis are available.

By car from west, take I-495/Long Island Expressway to Exit 39/Glen Cove Road. Follow Glen Cove Road north to Route 25A/Northern Boulevard. Turn right and continue past LIU Post on the right, past Route 107 to the next traffic light at Wolver Hollow Road. The Old Brookville Police station is on the left. Turn left, and follow Wolver Hollow Road to the "T". Turn right onto Chicken Valley Road. Pass Planting Fields Arboretum on right and continue straight through yellow blinking light and continue one half mile to Dogwood Lane. Turn right. Parking is immediately on right.

From the east: Take I-495/Long Island Expressway to Exit 41N to Route 106N to Route 25A/Northern Boulevard. Turn left onto Route 25A and follow to the second traffic light. Turn right onto Wolver Hollow Road. Old Brookville Police State is on the right.

Proceed as directed above.

PUTNAM COUNTY

COLD SPRING

STONECROP GARDENS

81 Stonecrop Lane, Cold Spring
(845) 265-2000, www.stonecrop.org

Stonecrop Gardens, originally the home of Frank and Anne Cabot, became a public garden in 1992 under the direction of Caroline Burgess. Frank Cabot is also the founder of the Garden Conservancy. At its windswept elevation of 1,100 feet in the Hudson Highlands, Stonecrop enjoys a Zone 5 climate. The display gardens cover an area of about twelve acres and incorporate a diverse collection of gardens and plants including woodland and water gardens, a grass garden, raised alpine stone beds, a cliff rock garden, perennial beds, and an enclosed English-style flower garden. Additional features include a conservatory, display alpine house, a pit house with an extensive collection of choice dwarf bulbs, and systematic order beds representing over fifty plant families.

🕐 Special Garden Conservancy 2016 Open Days featuring Tea in the Garden, April 24, May 8, June 12, July 17, August 14, September 18, October 2; 10 a.m. to 5 p.m. Visitors may purchase tea and cake from 12 p.m. to 4 p.m. Also open, April through October, Monday through Saturday, 10 a.m. to 5 p.m.

💲 $5

➲ From Taconic State Parkway, take Route 301/Cold Spring exit. Travel 3.5 miles to Stonecrop's entrance on right. A sign reading "Stonecrop Gardens" marks the driveway.

From Route 9, take Route 301 east 2.7 miles and turn left at the entrance.

SUFFOLK COUNTY

BRIDGEHAMPTON

BRIDGE GARDENS

36 Mitchell Lane, Bridgehampton
www.PeconiclandTrust.org/
bridge_gardens.html

Bridge Gardens is a unique public garden, donated to the Peconic Land Trust, a non-profit conservation organization on Long Island, in 2008 by Harry Neyens and Jim Kilpatrick. Bridge Gardens serves as a multi-purpose, multi-disciplinary outdoor classroom, demonstration garden and community resource. Covering five acres, Bridge Gardens features an herb garden with 180 different culinary, medicinal, ornamental, textile and dyeing herb, vegetable garden, perennial beds and borders, a collection of antique and modern roses, animal topiaries, water garden, woodland paths, double hedgerow of privet, and specimen shrubs and trees. Bridge Gardens offers a variety of educational and recreational programs throughout the year, including programming on toxin-free lawn and landscape care.

🕐 April through October, Saturdays, 10 a.m. to 5 p.m. Sundays noon to 5 p.m. From Memorial Day to Labor Day, Bridge Gardens is also open Wednesdays and Thursdays from 10 a.m. to 5 p.m. and on Fridays from 10 a.m. to dusk.

💲 $10 or $20 up to a party of 4

➲ From the West: Take the Long Island Expressway to exit 70, onto CR 111 to Route 27/CR 39 and head East through Southampton and into the hamlet of Bridgehampton. Turn north (left) onto Butter Lane, and immediately after the railroad trestle turn left onto Mitchell Lane. Bridge Gardens is the first entrance on the left.

EAST HAMPTON

LONGHOUSE RESERVE
133 Hands Creek Road, East Hampton
(631) 329-3568, www.longhouse.org

By far, the sixteen acres of LongHouse Reserve are the most exciting gardens in The Hamptons. From the moment you enter through the impressive allée of statuesque cryptomeria, you know you are in for a rarified experience. The varied and fascinating landscape includes a gigantic lotus pond, numerous walks, a dune garden, and a grass amphitheater. Collections of bamboo, conifers, broadleaf evergreens, and grasses are a compendium of each genus and the springtime entices with more than 200 varieties of daffodils and 1,000 times as many blooms, at least. Aside from the fantastic gardens and arboretum, there is a museum-worthy collection of contemporary sculpture to intrigue you at every turn of every path. This is the one East End garden that is not to be missed. The large new house (not open to the public) was inspired by the seventh-century Shinto shrine at Ise, Japan.

🕐 April through Columbus Day weekend, Wednesday and Saturday, 2 p.m. to 5 p.m.; July and August, Wednesday through Saturday, 2 p.m. to 5 p.m. Winter hours are by appointment.

$ $10 adults, $8 seniors, members free

⮑ From East Hampton at the intersection at Main Street, go to Cooper Street, turn right, and go to end. Turn left onto Cedar Street and bear right at fork onto Hands Creek Road. Go 0.7 mile to #133, on left.

SAGAPONACK

MADOO CONSERVANCY
618 Main Street, Sagaponack
(631) 537-8200, www.madoo.org

The *New York Times* salutes it as "Robert Dash's ever-changing masterpiece" while The Garden Club of America asserts that Madoo is "one of America's most beautiful gardens." The renowned garden eminence, Rosemary Verey embraced it as "...my favorite American garden." This much published horticultural jewel began in 1967 on two acres of turn-around land that had never been farmed and opened to the public in 1994. It has leapt forward to constitute a cornucopia, an exuberant encyclopedia, of the garden's most exalted and admired classical themes. The visitor will come across an over-and-under Tudor knot garden in box, a 120-foot rope walk with subtended water rill representing the forced perspectives of the High Renaissance and a fifth-century Greek exedra complete with domed oculus. Four quincunx beds reinterpret a plan of Cyrus the Great, the earliest western European garden plan extant. There is a free-standing curve bower of six little-leafed beech, a child's maze, an intricate berried potager, a fifty-foot long laburnum arbor, hermitage, Giordan Segreto, woodland, sculpture by Henri Matisse, a maple-tree water fountain by Win Knowlton, ponds, mirrored walls, unique benches and seats. Bold mauves, chartreuses and blues give zest to fences, sheds and furnishings. Orientalisms abound, including a curved-roof Japanese bridge in black, scarlet and yellow and rare and native specimens, uniquely pruned. Walkways in stone, brick, pebbles, grass, and sliced telephone poles wind through this entirely organic, impeccably maintained, hallmark. On the National Register of Historical Places, this artist's garden is both refuge and immediately available learning experience.

🕐 May 15 through September 15, Friday and Saturday, 12 p.m. to 4 p.m. Private visits may be arranged in advance at other times of the year.

$ $10

⮑ From Long Island Expressway/I-495, take Exit 70 and follow signs to Montauk. Sagaponack is on Route 27, 1 mile east of Bridgehampton. Turn right at traffic light onto Sagg Main Street (first light east of Bridgehampton on Route 27). Madoo Conservancy is a little over 1 mile from highway and entrance is on Sagg Lake Lane, first road on right after post office.

WESTCHESTER COUNTY

OSSINING

THE WILDFLOWER ISLAND AT TEATOWN LAKE RESERVATION
1600 Spring Valley Road, Ossining
(914) 762-2912

Wildflower Island is a woodland garden of over 200 species of native plants, including rare Lady's-slipper orchids nestled among the abundant spring ephemerals. Experienced volunteers guide visitors on their tour of the island. This day also marks the annual Plant-Fest, celebrating its 25th year. Many unusual annuals, perennials, native plants, herbs and vegetables are for sale. Knowledgeable volunteers on habitat, bee and butterfly attractors, combinations for spectacular mixed containers, and nature friendly gardening offer expert advice. Other offerings include herbal vinegars, bee keeping and honey, tool sharpening.

🕐 Special Garden Conservancy Open Day, May 7. Tours at 10 a.m., 12:00 p.m. & 2 p.m. Reservations are required. $5pp. (914) 762-2912, ext.110 by May 5. Wildflower Island is open mid-April through mid-September by reservation.

⮕ From Route 134, turn right onto Spring Valley Rd. Drive for about 1 mile bearing left at the fork/Teatown sign. The Nature Center will be on your right over the crest of the hill. The main parking lot is on your right immediately after the Nature Center.

VALHALLA

THE NATIVE PLANT CENTER AT WESTCHESTER COMMUNITY COLLEGE
75 Grasslands Road, Valhalla
(914) 606-7870
www.nativeplantcenter.org

The Native Plant Center's demonstration gardens feature plants native to the northeastern United States. Lady Bird Johnson Demonstration Garden: Located near the College's East Grasslands entrance. Established in 1998 and dedicated in 1999 with a ceremony attended by Mrs. Johnson and her daughters, Lynda Johnson Robb and Luci Baines Johnson. Expanded and rededicated in 2012. Featured gardens: Native wildflower meadow planted in 1998 and now under restoration and berry-producing native shrubs and trees beneficial to birds, planted in 2012. Stone Cottage Garden: Behind the headquarters of The Native Plant Center. Installation began in 2002; dedicated in 2005. This garden is divided into four themes that display ways native plants can be utilized: to attract hummingbirds and butterflies; low groundcovers and lawn substitutes; foundation plantings; fall and winter interest. Rain Garden: Also located behind the headquarters of The Native Plant Center. Established 2008. The central element is a gravel/stone bed that carries stormwater runoff from the roof and downspouts of the cottage. The native plants in this garden can tolerate extreme fluctuations in moisture.

🕐 Special Garden Conservancy Open Day guided tours, Sunday, July 24, 2016, 12 p.m. to 4 p.m.; otherwise year round, daily, dawn to dusk.

$ Free

⮕ From northern Westchester, take Sprain Brook Parkway south to Eastview exit. Turn left onto Route 100. Enter Westchester Community College at East Grasslands Gate and bear right. Park in Lot #1. Greeting table at far edge of lot, near garden.

From southern Westchester, take Sprain Brook Parkway to Eastview exit. Turn right onto Route 100. Proceed as directed above.

From I-287, take Exit 4/Route 100A and go north 0.5 mile to entrance to Westchester Community College on right. At end of entrance road, turn right and follow to Parking Lot #1. Proceed as directed above.

NORTH CAROLINA

Raleigh Durham

Saturday, October 29

🕐 **10 a.m. to 3 p.m.**
$7 admission

 DIGGING DEEPER: Designing with Nature at Deer Chase Gardens, with Justin Waller, 3 p.m.

ORANGE COUNTY

DURHAM

 DEER CHASE GARDENS
221 Deer Chase Lane, Durham

 DIGGING DEEPER

Deer Chase Gardens is a magical Eden located in the heart of Duke Forest. For invited guests, it offers year-round appeal with a stunning display of perennials, 200-year-old oaks, mature cedars, and showy maples. The property offers an expansive vista from one of the highest points in Orange County, adjacent to some of the best- preserved forestland

in the North Carolina Piedmont. Guests will enjoy the experience of wandering through ingeniously cultivated outdoor rooms which highlight many creative combinations of plantings in different settings, including an Asian garden with an authentic hand-built Japanese tea house, an organic orchard, a native pocosin habitat, a poolside butterfly garden, and formal sun garden, connected by an alluring combination of cultivated allée, rustic handmade bridges, and arched passages. Sit and enjoy the garden's many water features (including streams, fountains, and a formal reflective pool), and marvel at the variety of avian and amphibian visitors to this wildlife paradise. Sculptures from local artists, elaborate stonework, and handsomely... [Read the full description online]
NEW

➲ From Raleigh, follow I-40 West, towards Chapel Hill, and exit onto Route 15/Route 501 marked "to Chapel Hill & Durham". Turn right (east, towards Durham) and get in the left lane. At the next intersection, Sage Road, turn left and go straight to "T" intersection with Old Erwin Road. Turn right (east) onto Erwin, and continue, pass Hollow Rock Racquet and Swim Club. Turn left onto Kerley Road (you will not have a stop sign). Follow Kerley Road across Mt. Sinai Road (first stop sign) to the second stop sign at Cornwallis. Turn left (west) onto West Cornwallis, then immediately take your first right onto Bay Meadows Lane (gravel road). Follow Bay Meadows Lane to the first marked driveway on left, Deer Chase Lane (semi-paved driveway), and follow Deer Chase Lane to parking directions.

From Durham, via Freeways, take Route 15/Route 501 South towards Chapel Hill, and exit Cornwallis Road. Turn right (west) onto Cornwallis and continue through light at Erwin Road. In about 1 mile, cross the Orange County line at Kerley Road. Immediately after Kerley, turn right onto a gravel road, Bay Meadows Lane. Continue to first marked left, semi-paved driveway, Deer Chase Lane. Follow Deer Chase Lane straight uphill, over the deer-grate; there will be signs for parking.

 # DIGGING DEEPER

SATURDAY, OCTOBER 29 | 3 TO 4:30 PM

DESIGNING WITH NATURE AT DEER CHASE GARDENS

with Justin Waller

At: Deer Chase Gardens, 221 Deer Chase Lane, Durham

Horticulturist Justin Waller will lead an in-depth tour of Deer Chase Gardens with ample opportunity for guests to comment and ask questions. Justin will discuss how he and the garden owners have used existing features and contours to create water features and moss gardens as well as site garden structures and rooms. He will also talk about using plants effectively, and the use of natural building materials. Justin notes, "Having gardened at Deer Chase for over 20 years, I have had the opportunity to see it transform from a thoughtfully laid out plan to a mature but ever changing space in which I envisage nature to dictate design."

Refreshments will be served following the tour.

Registration is required and space is limited. **Opendaysprogram.org or call 1(888) 842-2442**

❋ PUBLIC GARDEN

MECKLENBURG COUNTY

CHARLOTTE

WING HAVEN
248 Ridgewood Avenue, Charlotte
(704) 331-0664,
www.winghavengardens.com
Two Gardens. One experience. Wing Haven now includes the Elizabeth Lawrence House & Garden as well as Wing Haven Gardens & Bird Sanctuary. Since its creation in 1927 by Elizabeth and Edwin Clarkson, Wing Haven Gardens & Bird Sanctuary has been a special part of Charlotte. The gardens, encompassing approximately three acres in the heart of Charlotte, are enclosed on all sides by brick walls and include both formal and woodland areas. Throughout, the emphasis is on plantings for birds and other wildlife, providing food, cover, and nesting sites. Plaques and

statuary integrated into the garden wall and paths reflect the spirit and beauty of Wing Haven and its creators. Visitors marvel not only at the gardens but the frequent sightings of birds and the small wildlife scampering throughout the property. Elizabeth Lawrence was already a recognized garden designer and writer when, in 1948, she moved from Raleigh to Charlotte, and began building the house and making a garden. Lawrence, the first woman to graduate with a degree in landscape design at North Carolina State University, is regarded as a preeminent figure in the region's horticultural history. A graceful refuge that doubled as a living laboratory for her study and appreciation of plants and design, the garden was a frequent reference and inspiration for her writing for thirty-five years. The House and Garden on Ridgewood Avenue were entered in the National Register of Historic Places in September of 2006.

🕐 Fridays and Saturdays 10 a.m. to 2 p.m.

$ $10 for individuals ages 10 and up / Members free. Includes admission for both gardens. Children under 10 free. Educators bringing a group of youngsters to the garden must schedule a guided tour by calling (704) 331-0664 x103.

➲ From I-77, take Exit 6A/Woodlawn, follow about 3 miles, and turn left onto Selwyn Avenue. Follow 0.5 mile and turn left onto Ridgewood Avenue. Wing Haven is at #248.

ORANGE COUNTY

HILLSBOROUGH

MONTROSE
320 St. Mary's Road, Hillsborough
(919) 732-7787

Montrose is a sixty-one acre property listed in the National Register of Historic Places. The grounds, laid out in the nineteenth century, contain several nineteenth-century buildings, a rock garden, scree garden, woodland gardens, and sunny gardens with unique color and planting schemes. There are mass plantings of bulbs including rain lilies, cyclamen, galanthus, and crocus species. Unusual trees, shrubs, trellises, fences, and arbors provide structure in winter and large urns planted with spectacular color combinations brighten the summer gardens. The winter gardens are a special feature.

🕐 September through May guided tours by appointment only, Tuesday, Thursday and Saturday at 10 a.m. Tours for groups of 6 or more may be arranged at other times.

$ $11 adults, $5 children 6 to 12, children under 6 and Garden Conservancy members free.

➲ From I-85, take Exit 164 and go north into Hillsborough. Turn right onto East King Street. At stop sign, bear left and go up hill onto St. Marys Road (not a sharp left). Pass St Matthew's Church on right and Cameron Park Elementary School. Montrose is just past school on right. There are large red brick gateposts with a plaque on right that reads: Montrose 320. Parking available at Montrose for smaller tours.

From I-40 take Exit 261. Go north toward Hillsborough and pass under I-85. Proceed as directed above.

PENNSYLVANIA

Bucks County

Saturday, June 11

🕐 **Hours vary by garden
(Starting at 10 a.m.)**

$7 per garden

🏷 Pop-up Nursery
Tiffany Perennials
Paxson Hill Farm

 EXPERTS IN THE GARDEN: Spring
Crops, Plant Hybridizing & Burpee's
Top Plant Picks; George Ball & Henk
van der Veldt, at Fordhook Farm,
Doylestown

 DIGGING DEEPER: Listening to the
Land, Jack Staub & Renny Reynolds, at
Hortulus Farm, Wrightstown, 4 p.m.

BUCKS COUNTY

DOYLESTOWN

📍 **FORDHOOK FARM OF
W. ATLEE BURPEE CO.**
105 New Britain Road, Doylestown

🕐 10 a.m. to 4 p.m.

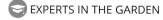 EXPERTS IN THE GARDEN

You will have the opportunity to take a
behind-the-scenes tour of the Burpee and
Heronswood's famed trials and testing

operations. In 1888, W. Atlee Burpee acquired
several hundred acres of farmland in bucolic
Bucks County. Today at Fordhook Farm, as
before, hundreds of new vegetables, annuals,
and perennials are grown, tested, and evaluated on a sixty-acre test farm and network of
gardens to guarantee Burpee's high standards
of quality. Once home to the Burpee family,
the eighteenth-century manor has been
designated a National Historic Site. The house
features the richly paneled study where W.
Atlee Burpee compiled and edited the first

Burpee catalogs. Burpee Hall, located in an adjoining stone barn, has been fully renovated as a conference center. It features a 360° hand-painted mural of Fordhook Farm during the late nineteenth century. Once the hub for seed processing at Fordhook, the one-of-a-kind Seed House is located across the drive from the manor. Be sure to visit the many trial gardens—birthplace of culinary favorites such as Golden Bantam, the first...
[Read the full description online]

2015 | ♿ |

⮎ From Philadelphia, take I-95 north to Route 332 west towards Newtown. Take Route 332 for 3.7 miles to Route 413 north. Take Route 413 for 10.4 miles to Route 202 south. Take Route 202 for 3.5 miles to State Street. Follow State Street south past the hospital and over Route 611, then go 0.25 mile and turn left onto New Britain Road (the first road on the left next to Delaware Valley College). The entrance to Fordhook Farm is 0.25 mile on the left through two stone pillars. From New York and points north, take I-287 south to Route 202 towards Flemington. Cross the Delaware River to Doylestown (about 45 miles from Somerville). Proceed as directed above.

From Baltimore/Washington, D.C., take I-95 north. At Chester, Pennsylvania, exit onto I-476, towards Plymouth Meeting. Stay on I- 476, then exit onto I-276 east. Take I-276 to Exit 343 (Willow Grove). Follow Route 611 north (follow bypass route not business route through Doylestown)11 miles to Route 202 south—Norristown exit. Bear right off of exit onto Route 202 south for 0.25 mile, turn left on New Britain Road (first road on left next to Delaware Valley College). Entrance to Fordhook is 0.25 mile on left through two stone pillars.

FURLONG

⬤ DARK HOLLOW FARM
937 Macclesfield Road, Furlong

🕐 10 a.m. to 4 p.m.

This garden is an eclectic mix of interesting plants on a beautifully manicured eight-acre property. A blend of mature trees, flowering shrubs, and an appealing selection of perennials all complement the meticulously appointed and cared for eighteenth-century house, barn, and cottage on this fantastic property. Enjoy the delightful perennial garden, the quaint barnyard vegetable garden, and the magical shade gardens. Throughout the season there is always a feast for the gardeners eye on Dark Hollow Farm.

2011 | ♿ |

⮎ From the corner of Route 263 and Edison Furlong Road, go southeast on Forest Grove Road (which becomes Swamp Road) 2.5 miles to Dark Hollow Road. Turn right and go to dead end at foot bridge. Turn left onto Macclesfield Road to #937 (third driveway on left).

NEW HOPE

⬤ PAXSON HILL FARM
3265 Comfort Road, New Hope

🕐 10 a.m. to 4 p.m.

 Paxson Hill Farm

Ten acres of landscape featuring a formal garden with a linear granite-edged parterre, reflecting pools with fountains, two 330-foot double perennial borders, weeping Tupelo tunnel, knot garden, yellow garden with bocce court, and a population of swans, geese, peacocks, emus, and guinea fowl (many are "rescues"). The garden is notable for several unusual and rare plants including seven mature *Heptacodium miconioides* (Seven Son Flower) bearing clouds of white flowers in late summer, followed by even more beautiful red calyces. An adjacent naturalistic garden with ponds and waterfalls, maze garden, and shady woodland garden are also open to visitors.

2015 |

⮕ From Lahaska, PA/Peddler's Village, at the intersection of Routes 202 and 263, take Route 263 north 3.2 miles then turn left onto Comfort Road. Go 1 mile and the farm is on left.

From New Hope, PA take Route 32 North and turn left onto Route 263 South. At the top of hill, turn right onto Comfort Road. Go 1 mile and farm is on left.

POINT PLEASANT

THE GARDENS AT MILL FLEURS
27 Cafferty Road, Point Pleasant

🚩 Guided Tours only: 10 a.m. / 1:30 p.m.

🏷 Tiffany Perennials

The Gardens at Mill Fleurs, a 1742 grist mill on the often-raging Tohickon Creek, are set into massive rock outcroppings and steep woodland slopes. We have drama and drainage—everything else is pure challenge. I am a hopeless collector of any plant family that thrives in shade; anything with a green or black flower, any plant we haven't seen before in Zone 6. Creating a landscape that will appeal to people who might be casual gardeners out of all these collections is a challenge I enjoy. Plants are organized by color families: all the plants in a given area will have either foliage or flowers of the same color. For more information and pictures please visit www.millfleurs.garden.

2013 |

⮕ Mill Fleurs is 100 yards off River Road/Route 32, 9 miles north of New Hope and 7 miles south of the bridge over the Delaware River at Frenchtown, NJ. The Point Pleasant Baptist Church is in the fork where Cafferty Road branches off Route 32. Please park in the church parking lot, entering it from River Road on the north side of the church. Walk around the split rail fence at the back of the church and cross Cafferty Road VERY CAREFULLY. The tour will gather behind the little white house that is signed: Cafferty One / Tiffany Perennials.

WRIGHTSTOWN

HORTULUS FARM
60 Thompson Mill Road, Wrightstown

🕐 10 a.m. to 4 p.m.

🛈 DIGGING DEEPER

🏷 Hortulus Farm Nursery

Our garden appears as an integral part of the Pennsylvania landscape, as befits an eighteenth-century farmstead with barns and a healthy population of animals. We are lucky enough to be nestled in our own little valley, quite far off the road and unusual for a house of this age. Our 100 acres try to respect the integrity of the farm's historical significance and the natural landscape, with the occasional whimsical or formal statement thrown in. There are lots of woods and pasture, lots of shrubs and naturalized perennial plantings in the stream and woodland gardens, yet also formal borders, follies, gazebos, and sizable herb and vegetable gardens. All are anchored by the formal simplicity of classic Bucks County architecture. In the past years, we have been fortunate enough to have had the gardens featured in *House & Garden*, *House Beautiful*, *Horticulture*, *Garden Design*, *Organic Gardening*, *Country Living*, *Quest*, and *Food & Wine* magazines, as well as on HGTV's "Secret Gardens of Philadelphia" and the Travel Channel.

2014 |

⮕ From New Hope, take Windy Bush Road/Route 232 South about 5 miles. At "Wrightstown Township" sign on right, turn immediately left onto Pineville Road. Go about 1 mile to right onto Thompson Mill Road. Go over bridge through series of steep, winding, up-hill turns and up into a clearing and straightaway. Go to #60 for parking. From Philadelphia, take I-95 North towards Trenton about 40 miles to Exit 31/New Hope. Turn left at end of exit ramp onto Taylorsville Road. Go north 3 miles to Wood Hill Road and turn left. Go about 2.7 miles to first stop sign. Turn right onto Eagle Road, go 0.3 mile, and make first left onto Pineville Road. Proceed as directed above.

DIGGING DEEPER

SATURDAY, JUNE 11 | 4 PM

LISTENING TO THE LAND
AT HORTULUS FARM

AT: Hortulus Farm, 60 Thompson Mill Road, Wrightstown

Renny Reynolds and Jack Staub, the owners and creators of the gardens at historic Hortulus Farm, will lead an educational tour through their thirty acres of gardens. Their journey began with allowing the property to, as they say, "speak for itself", the natural terrain and historic farm buildings describing to them what was appropriate in terms of planting. Over the last thirty-five years, they have transformed a rundown eighteenth-century farmstead with no gardens into the Garden Conservancy's newest affiliate garden and a garden described by *The Great Gardens Of The Philadelphia Region* thusly: "18th and 19th century buildings are surrounded by such horticultural opulence that the scene registers as both sublimely serene and surreal."

The hour and a half tour will conclude with a Q&A and light refreshments in the garden.

Registration is required and space is limited. **Opendaysprogram.org or call 1(888) 842-2442**

 # EXPERTS IN THE GARDEN

SATURDAY, JUNE 11 | THROUGHOUT THE DAY

SPRING CROPS, PLANT HYBRIDIZING &
BURPEE'S TOP PLANT PICKS

**AT: Fordhook Farm of W. Atlee Burpee Co.
    105 New Britain Road, Doylestown**

When Fordhook Farm is awash in late spring perennials and early summer edibles (leafy and podded vegetables), George Ball, Chairman and Chief Executive Officer of W. Atlee Burpee Company, will welcome visitors to this historic working farm. Joining him will be Henk van der Velde, Director of Research and Development, Burpee. Henk is based at Burpee NL and was flown in just for this Open Day. He has been responsible for many important introductions, both edibles and ornamentals. George and Henk will talk about the process of plant hybridization, as well as Burpee's best new varieties and long-time favorites. This is a very special opportunity so bring your gardening questions and quandaries!

Bucks County

Saturday, August 13

🕙 **10 a.m. to 4 p.m.**
$7 per garden

 EXPERTS IN THE GARDEN: Summer Crops, Plant Hybridizing & Burpee's Top Plant Picks; George Ball & Simon Crawford, at Fordhook Farm, Doylestown

 Pop-up Nursery
Paxson Hill Farm

BUCKS COUNTY

DOYLESTOWN

📍 **FORDHOOK FARM OF W. ATLEE BURPEE CO.**
105 New Britain Road, Doylestown

 EXPERTS IN THE GARDEN

You will have the opportunity to take a behind-the-scenes tour of the Burpee and Heronswood's famed trials and testing operations. In 1888, W. Atlee Burpee acquired several hundred acres of farmland in bucolic Bucks County. Today at Fordhook Farm, as before, hundreds of new vegetables, annuals, and perennials are grown, tested, and evaluated on a sixty-acre test farm and network of gardens to guarantee Burpee's high standards of quality. Once home to the Burpee family, the eighteenth-century manor has been designated a National Historic Site. The house features the richly paneled study where W. Atlee Burpee compiled and edited the first Burpee catalogs. Burpee Hall, located in an adjoining stone barn, has been fully renovated as a conference center. It features a 360° hand-painted mural of Fordhook Farm during the late nineteenth century. Once the hub for seed processing at Fordhook, the one-of-a-kind Seed House is located across the drive from the manor. Be sure to visit the many trial gardens—birthplace of culinary favorites such as Golden Bantam, the first...
[Read the full description online]
2015 | ♿ | 📷

➲ From Philadelphia, take I-95 north to Route 332 west towards Newtown. Take Route 332 for 3.7 miles to Route 413 north. Take Route 413 for 10.4 miles to Route 202 south. Take Route 202 for 3.5 miles to State Street. Follow

State Street south past the hospital and over Route 611, then go 0.25 mile and turn left onto New Britain Road (the first road on the left next to Delaware Valley College). The entrance to Fordhook Farm is 0.25 mile on the left through two stone pillars.

From New York and points north, take I-287 south to Route 202 towards Flemington. Cross the Delaware River to Doylestown (about 45 miles from Somerville). Proceed as directed above.

From Baltimore/Washington, D.C., take I-95 north. At Chester, Pennsylvania, exit onto I-476, towards Plymouth Meeting. Stay on I-476, then exit onto I-276 east. Take I-276 to Exit 343 (Willow Grove). Follow Route 611 north (follow bypass route not business route through Doylestown)11 miles to Route 202 south—Norristown exit. Bear right off of exit onto Route 202 south for 0.25 mile, turn left on New Britain Road (first road on left next to Delaware Valley College). Entrance to Fordhook is 0.25 mile on left through two stone pillars.

NEW HOPE

 PAXSON HILL FARM
3265 Comfort Road, New Hope

 Paxson Hill Farm

Ten acres of landscape featuring a formal garden with a linear granite-edged parterre, reflecting pools with fountains, two 330-foot double perennial borders, weeping Tupelo tunnel, knot garden, yellow garden with bocce court, and a population of swans, geese, peacocks, emus, and guinea fowl (many are "rescues"). The garden is notable for several unusual and rare plants including seven mature *Heptacodium miconioides* (Seven Son Flower) bearing clouds of white flowers in late summer, followed by even more beautiful red calyces. An adjacent naturalistic garden with ponds and waterfalls, maze garden, and shady woodland garden are also open to visitors.
NEW | 📷

⮩ From Lahaska, PA/Peddler's Village, at the intersection of Routes 202 and 263, take Route 263 north 3.2 miles then turn left onto Comfort Road. Go 1 mile and the farm is on left.

From New Hope, PA take Route 32 North and turn left onto Route 263 South. At the top of hill, turn right onto Comfort Road. Go 1 mile and farm is on left.

EXPERTS IN THE GARDEN

SATURDAY, AUGUST 13 | THROUGHOUT THE DAY

SUMMER CROPS, PLANT HYBRIDIZING & BURPEE'S TOP PLANT PICKS

**AT: Fordhook Farm of W. Atlee Burpee Co.
    105 New Britain Road, Doylestown**

When Fordhook Farm offers a rich bounty of peak summer annuals, perennials and edibles (fruited crops like tomatoes, peppers and eggplants), George Ball, Chairman and Chief Executive Officer of W. Atlee Burpee Company, will welcome visitors to this historic working farm. Joining him will be Simon Crawford, Managing Director Burpee Europe. Simon is based in the Cotswolds and was flown in just for this Open Day. A noted plant hybridizer, Simon serves on the prestigious RHS Herbaceous Plant Committee, the RHS Trials Advisory Committee, and judges at major RHS shows, including the Chelsea Flower Show. He is now re-establishing the Burpee range of vegetable and flower seed varieties across Europe. George and Simon will talk about the process of plant hybridization, as well as Burpee's best new varieties and long-time favorites. This is a very special opportunity so bring you gardening questions and quandaries!

Bucks County

Saturday, October 8

🕐 **10 a.m. to 4 p.m.**
$7 per garden

🏷 Pop-up Nursery
Paxson Hill Farm

There is also a garden open on this date in nearby Hunterdon County, NJ. See page 170.

There is also a garden open on this date in nearby Hunterdon County, NJ. See page 170.

 DIGGING DEEPER: Seeing the Garden for the Trees—Designing with Trees, Bruce Gangawer, at Paxson Hill Farm, New Hope, 4 p.m.

BUCKS COUNTY

NEW HOPE

📍 **JERICHO MOUNTAIN ORCHARDS**
136 Buckmanville Road, New Hope

🏷 Atlock Farm

This is a delightful terraced country garden surrounding a seventeenth-century stone-and-timber farmhouse on extensive acreage. Many varieties of old garden roses and climbers ramble over eighteenth-century walls, barns, trellises, and tuteurs, leading to lovely perennial borders and formally parterred beds. There are also charming shade pond and stream gardens, as well as a sizable nineteenth-century apple orchard.

2014 | ♿ | 📷

➲ From New Hope, take Route 232 to right. Go 3+ miles (pass Betts Equipment on right) to Street Road. Turn left and then first right onto Buckmanville. Number 136 is 0.5 mile on left.

From Doylestown, take Route 202 north to Route 413. Turn right, go through a traffic light at the intersection of Route 263. Continue 4 to 5 miles. After traffic light by Pineville Tavern on left, take first road on left, Pine Lane. Go 1 mile to stop sign at Route 232. Cross over Route 232 and take first left onto Buckmanville Road. Go 1 mile to #136 right.

From Philadelphia, take I-95 north to New Hope exit. At bottom of ramp, turn left onto

Taylorsville Road. Continue 3+ miles through traffic light at Route 532. Continue to "T" intersection at Route 32. Turn left and continue towards New Hope. Go 1+ mile and turn left onto Lurgan Road (Bowmans Tavern Restaurant on right). Continue 2+ miles to stop sign and "T" intersection at Street Road. Turn left onto Street and immediate right onto Buckmanville Road. Number 136 Buckmanville is 0.5 mile on left.

PAXSON HILL FARM
3265 Comfort Road, New Hope

DIGGING DEEPER

Paxson Hill Farm

Ten acres of landscape featuring a formal garden with a linear granite-edged parterre, reflecting pools with fountains, two 330-foot double perennial borders, weeping Tupelo tunnel, knot garden, yellow garden with bocce court, and a population of swans, geese, peacocks, emus, and guinea fowl (many are "rescues"). The garden is notable for several unusual and rare plants including seven mature *Heptacodium miconioides* (Seven Son Flower) bearing clouds of white flowers in late summer, followed by even more beautiful red calyces. An adjacent naturalistic garden with ponds and waterfalls, maze garden, and shady woodland garden are also open to visitors.
NEW | 📷

⮑ From Lahaska, PA/Peddler's Village, at the intersection of Routes 202 and 263, take Route 263 north 3.2 miles then turn left onto Comfort Road. Go 1 mile and the farm is on left.

From New Hope, PA take Route 32 North and turn left onto Route 263 South. At the top of hill, turn right onto Comfort Road. Go 1 mile and farm is on left.

🛈 DIGGING DEEPER

SATURDAY, OCTOBER 8 | 4 PM

SEEING THE GARDEN FOR THE TREES —DESIGNING WITH TREES AT PAXSON HILL FARM

with Bruce Gangawer

AT: Paxson Hill Farm, 3265 Comfort Road, New Hope

Paxson Hill Farm is a private pleasure garden—an expansive and varied landscape meant to delight. Here, owner, professional designer, and nurseryman, Bruce Gangawer has combined his inventive and astute eye with an extraordinary collection of rare and unusual plants, and more than a hint of whimsy. During this relaxed afternoon garden walk, Bruce will focus on how he uses trees to shape and punctuate garden rooms—both formal and naturalistic. He will also introduce visitors to some of his choice trees, including a weeping Tupelo walk (a la Barnsley House), a cluster of radiant yellow *Zelkova serrata* 'Ogon,' and a stunning grouping of mature *Heptacodium miconoides*, seven-son flower.

Refreshments will be served.

Registration is required and space is limited. **Opendaysprogram.org or call 1(888) 842-2442**

✱ PUBLIC GARDENS

CHESTER COUNTY

KENNETT SQUARE

LONGWOOD GARDENS
Route 1, Kennett Square
(610) 388-1000
www.longwoodgardens.org
One of the world's premier horticultural displays, Longwood offers 1,077 acres of gardens, woodlands, and meadows; twenty outdoor gardens; twenty indoor gardens within four acres of greenhouses; 11,000 types of plants; spectacular fountains; extensive educational programs; and 800 events each year.

🕐 Year round, daily, 9 a.m. to 6 p.m. Frequently open late for seasonal display.

$ Non-peak days, $20 adults, $17 seniors 62 and older, $10 students 5-18 or with student ID, children under 4 free. See website for additional pricing.

➲ Located on Route 1, 3 miles northeast of Kennett Square, Pennsylvania, and 12 miles north of Wilmington, Delaware.

DELAWARE COUNTY

WAYNE

CHANTICLEER
786 Church Road, Wayne
(610) 687-4163,
www.chanticleergarden.org
This thirty-five-acre pleasure garden was formerly the home of the Rosengarten family. Emphasis is on ornamental plants, particularly herbaceous perennials. The garden is a dynamic mix of formal and naturalistic areas, collections of flowering trees and shrubs, ponds, meadows, wildflower gardens, a ruin garden, and a garden of shade-loving Asian herbaceous plants.

🕐 April through October, Wednesday through Sunday, 10 a.m. to 5 p.m.; May through August, open until 8 p.m. on Friday

$ Adults (13 years and over) - $10.00
Pre-teen children (12 years and under) - Free
Members of Pennsylvania Horticultural Society and local arboreta - $8.00
Radnor Library Cardholders - $5.00
Garden professionals - Free

➲ Take I-76 West to I-476 South, Take Exit 13 toward Villanova. Turn right at the intersection of Routes 30 and 320 South. Turn right at the next traffic light onto Conestoga Road. Turn left on to Church Road. Go 0.5 mile to Chanticleer.

RHODE ISLAND

Little Compton

Saturday & Sunday, May 21 & 22

🕘 **9:30 a.m. to 6 p.m.**
$20 admission

Admission supports Sakonnet Garden, local wild meadow restoration, and the Garden Conservancy.

🏷️ Pop-up Nursery
Opus Nursery / Broken Arrow Nursery / Rare Finds Nursery / Peckham's Greenhouse

NEWPORT COUNTY

LITTLE COMPTON

📍 **SAKONNET**
510 West Main Road, Little Compton

🏷️ Opus Nursery / Broken Arrow Nursery / Rare Finds Nursery / Peckham's Greenhouse

Sakonnet Garden will open during the peak of bloom in late May (hard to predict exactly). These are the only Open Days in 2016. Several of the Northeast's best specialty nurseries will have connoisseur plants available for purchase. The Rhododendron Punchbowl, a confection of pinks and whites, and the Azalea Hedge should be in full bloom (see www.sakonnetgarden.com). Flowers on the dove tree and Asian species rhododendrons, plus soft orange and yellow rhodies should be at peak. Hundreds of woodland wildflowers are expected to still be in flower—from blue *Meconopsis* poppies to late trilliums. Sakonnet is an exotic cottage garden imbedded within a native coastal fields landscape, a long-term project of John Gwynne and Mikel Folcarelli. The main garden is slightly larger than an acre and is subdivided into a series of spaces separated by high tapestry hedges and stone walls. One space, planted with soft yellows seems to catch the sunlight on a gray, coastal Rhode Island day; a newly replanted zone is silver, punctuated with spires of weeping spruce ; another evokes the subtropics—its centerpiece a red "Mughal Pavilion" imported from India. A Gothic Woodpile is one of multiple tall wind barriers installed to create microclimates for experimental growing of rarely-seen Zone 7 plants. The beginnings of a half-acre, entirely new Pollinator Plus garden will be evident, designed as a biodiversity maze for high production of butterfly caterpillars and pollinating insects.

2015 | ♿ | 📷

➲ From north, go about 5.6 miles south of traffic light at Tiverton Four Corners (Gray's Ice Cream stand), on left 0.07 mile after sign "to Commons" and just after Taylor's Lane. Small sign on tree reads "510". Park along street.

Providence

Saturday, June 11

🕐 **10 a.m. to 4 p.m.**
$7 admission

There are also gardens open on this day in nearby Bristol County, MA. See page 128.

PROVIDENCE COUNTY

PROVIDENCE

📍 **COLLEGE HILL URBAN OASIS**
26 Diman Place, Providence

Designed by Andrew Grossman, this urban garden in the heart of College Hill near Brown University is a miniature paradise. Located at the intersection of two quiet streets in the Stimson Street historic district, it is enclosed by a tall board fence with lattice insets. The garden features a boisterous arrangement of white hydrangeas, hydrangea trees, and white roses accented by a contemporary fountain amidst pots of tall grasses and flowers.

NEW | ♿ | 📷

⮌ Street parking available on Diman Place and Stimson Avenue.

TEXAS

OUR PARTNERS IN HOUSTON

PECKERWOOD GARDEN CONSERVATION FOUNDATION

We are proud to partner with the Peckerwood Garden Conservation Foundation to bring you this Open Day. The foundation was established to preserve existing collections at Peckerwood, support continued plant explorations and trials, and develop, maintain, and preserve the land and facilities of Peckerwood Garden in Hempstead, Texas. In 1998, Peckerwood Garden was designated a preservation garden of the Garden Conservancy.

The garden has regular opportunities to visit and welcomes group tours. We hope you will make Peckerwood part of your garden-visiting plans this year.

Peckerwood Garden, featured in *Outstanding American Gardens: A Celebration—25 Years of the Garden Conservancy.* Photo by Marion Brenner.

Houston

Saturday, April 30

🕙 **10 a.m. to 4 p.m.**
$40 for all gardens or $7 per garden

🏷️ Pop-up Nursery
Plants from Peckerwood Garden will
be available at 1236 Studewood Street,
Houston

HARRIS COUNTY

BELLAIRE

📍 **BELLAIRE MEADOW**
505 South Third Street, Bellaire

This Texas native garden is located in the
suburban city of Bellaire. The owner's love of
the Texas Hill Country is the inspiration of this
garden. An exemplary use of Houston hardy
native plants in the context of a suburban
setting, this garden keeps the integrity of the
design while still in keeping with the neighborhood. An existing pool dictated the shape of
the planting bed in the delightful rear garden.
An inspired contemporary water feature was
added updating the feel of the space. Mature
olives in mammoth white pots anchor the
expertly designed planting of the backyard.
NEW | ♿ | 📷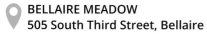

➲ Take I-610 south to Bissonnet Street and
turn right. Turn left onto South Rice Avenue.
Turn left onto Jessamine Street. Take the first
right onto South Third Road. The garden is on
the left. Parking is on one side of the street
only.

HOUSTON

📍 **ALBA GARDEN**
744 West 43rd Street, Houston

This garden is situated on an acre and a half
in the Garden Oaks neighborhood. Stepping
through the garden gate into this urban Eden, it
is evident that a true gardener lives here. Mostly hidden from street view, this garden features
a 15,000 gallon garden koi pond approximately
thirty feet long, bisected by a wooden bridge.
Though the pond is the highlight of the garden,
there are also flagstone pathways curving

around beautifully tended beds planted to provide a habitat for birds, butterflies, and bees. The garden features unusual collections of native and Houston-hardy plants.

NEW | ♿ | 📷

➲ From 610 North Loop, take the Durham/Shepherd Exit and go north on 43rd Street. Continue to #744 West. Park along West 43rd Street and surrounding streets.

📍 THE ART COMPOUND
1901 West 14th Street, Houston

The property of a prominent artist, Dixie Friend Gay, this garden is an ongoing project by the owner and her son. The garden, house, and art studios are located on an acre of land off a tributary of White Oak Bayou in the Clark Pines neighborhood, built by the artist in 1992. The garden is a collection of native and tropical plants intermixed with beautifully placed art and found objects. Features of the garden include a beautiful mixed-media gate by the artist, artfully designed meandering plant beds, and a goldfish pond.

NEW | 📷

➲ Garden is on 14th Street, 3 blocks west of intersection of Durham and 14th street. If you reach Beall Street, you have gone too far west. Please park on the street.

📍 BALDRIDGE RESIDENCE
2111 Bolsover Street, Houston

This neo-traditional garden is located in the city of West University Place. It is the home of prominent garden designer Cedar Baldridge. The main space of the backyard is situated around a pool and water feature, flanked by containers of citrus. Architectural features include a Chippendale trellis for the owners beloved sweet peas, beautifully detailed gates, flagstone terrace, and a collection of 1940s Saltorini outdoor furniture. The planting design includes espaliered magnolias and citrus trees, a topiary holly colonnade, olive trees, and cutting flowers.

NEW | ♿ | 📷

➲ Take Route 59 N toward downtown. Exit at Greenbriar and turn right onto Greenbriar Drive. Then turn left onto Bolsover Street. Garden is on right.

📍 CAMBERG GARDEN
3250 Reba Drive, Houston

This new garden, designed by Cedar Baldridge, surrounds a recently built Bobby McAlpine house in River Oaks. The traditional front yard and drive with lawn and foundation planting accentuates the dramatic neo-traditional vernacular architecture and beautifully detailed fence and gates. The more contemporary rear courtyard is centered around a small pool. The space includes a boxwood and seasonal flower parterre, a crape myrtle screen set in gravel, a small lawn, and a container garden. The plant palette includes boxwood, camellias, and multi-trunk Natchez crape myrtles.

NEW | ♿ | 📷

➲ Take I-610 South to Westheimer Road and turn left. Then turn left onto Bellmeade Street. Take second left onto Reba Drive. The garden is on the right.

📍 HABITAT GARDENS
802 Woodland Street, Houston

A garden planned to provide a habitat highway for birds and pollinators that celebrates the spring with wildflowers. This is a smaller Woodland Heights garden. Once the spring extravaganza is over, the perennials are the focus of this compact but impressive cottage garden.

NEW | ♿ | 📷

➲ Take the I-10 east to Exit at Taylor/Sawyer/Watson. Travel a few blocks north on Watson to Woodland street. This is an old neighborhood with small lots. Please be considerate of the neighbors when parking.

KYLE-LASSETER GARDEN
5 West 11th Place, Houston

The recently built home of architect Dillon Kyle and Sam Lasseter is located in the gated neighborhood, West 11th Place, near the Museum District. The garden is inspired by vernacular southern gardens. The backyard garden is centered on a circular pool with brick coping set in a manicured lawn edged surrounded by repurposed brick paths and planted beds. Small raised water gardens are placed asymmetrically within the lawn area. The owners' casual lifestyle and love of gardening is evident in planning of the outdoor spaces. An eclectic container garden is set off by a brick serpentine wall and informal seating areas with vintage furniture, a mix of recycled pavers are set in loosely planted mixed beds.
NEW | ♿ | 📷

➲ Take Route 59 North toward downtown. Take the Main Street exit and turn right. Turn right onto Bissonnet Street. Take the third left onto West 11th Place. The garden is on the left. Park on Bayard Lane or Yoakum Boulevard and walk to #5 West 11th Place.

SOUTHSIDE PLACE

SOUTHSIDE GLADE
6510 Auden Street, Southside Place

Part of the success of the garden in the city of Southside Place is the juxtaposition of the owners' contemporary art collection and the unique plant selection of the garden's landscape architect, Mark McKinnon. Bold texture and colors are evident in the foundation planting at the front of the house. The garden has a contemporary feel. The garden was designed around a large sculpture/water feature that is set in the large swimming pool. A shade garden with unusual plant specimens runs the length of the pool garden behind a modern shade structure. A substantial potager garden with raised vegetable beds is located on the property.
NEW | ♿

➲ Take I-69 North toward downtown. Turn right onto Wesleyan Street and then left onto University Boulevard. Take the second right onto Auden Street. The garden is on right.

✳ PUBLIC GARDEN

WALLER COUNTY

HEMPSTEAD

PECKERWOOD GARDEN
20571 FM 359, (979) 826-3232, www.peckerwoodgarden.org

🏷 Selling plants at pop-up nursery for the April 30 Houston Open Day at **1236 Studewood Street, Houston, 10 a.m. to 4 p.m.**

Peckerwood Garden is an artist's garden uniquely combining aesthetic experience and scientific exploration. It holds an unrivaled collection of plants from around the world with emphasis on plants collected in Mexico by its founder, John G. Fairey. Recently enlarged to thirty-nine acres, the cultivated garden occupies about ten acres and includes a woodland garden along the banks of a creek, a higher dry garden, and a meadow garden that is being developed into an arboretum. More than 3,000 species and cultivars can be found here.

🕐 March 12 & 26, April 9 & 23, May 8, May 21 (Friends of Peckerwood Day). Plant sales, weekends, 12 p.m. to 5 p.m. Garden tours at 1 p.m. and 3 p.m. See our website for more dates.

🚩 $10 for garden tour. Call for private tour rates. Available year round.

➲ From Houston, take Highway 290 west past Prairie View. Before reaching Hempstead, take Exit FM359 towards Brookshire. Proceed through traffic light at intersection with Business 290. Garden is located 1 mile past this intersection on right. Enter at sign for parking, nursery, and garden entry.

EL PASO COUNTY

EL PASO

CHIHUAHUAN DESERT GARDENS
University of Texas at the Centennial Museum, 500 West University Avenue, El Paso (915) 747-5335, www.museum.utep.edu

The garden hosts a collection of Chihuahuan Desert plants designed in a landscape setting amid natural rock boulders and landscape features such as pergolas, benches, fountains and a pond.

🕐 Year round, daily, dawn to dusk.

🚩 Free

⮑ Take I-10 to Schuster/Sun Bowl Exit, turn north onto Sun Bowl Drive. Turn right at stop sign, stop at guard house. Continue east on University Avenue about 200 feet. Turn south at driveway entrance to back parking lot of the Centennial Museum on the campus of UTEP. The gardens surround the Centennial Museum.

VERMONT

Manchester Area

Saturday, July 9

🕐 **Hours vary by garden
(Starting at 10 a.m.)**

$7 per garden

⭐ Start your day Hildene, The Lincoln Family Home, 1005 Hildene Road, Manchester. Tickets and maps will be available there.

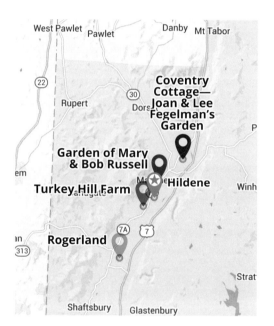

BENNINGTON COUNTY

EAST ARLINGTON

📍 **ROGERLAND
1308 & 1268 East Arlington Road**

🕐 10 a.m. to 4 p.m.

When, in 1989, we purchased the two houses and twenty acres, the gardens were simple and overgrown with weeds. What is today the focal section was a hay field. The challenge was to merge my desire for a symmetrical, structured, formal English garden around the

1830 farmhouse, fulfilling my enjoyment of golf, chess, and lawn bowls, while concurrently integrating my late wife's preference for a minimalist, locally traditional garden around the more modern ranch. A dry river bed divides the two styles, and there are many water features, iron fenced kitchen gardens, topiaries, and patios round out the property. Key to the garden is the merging of the structured hardscape—stone walks and dry-laid walls, many sitting areas, extensive custom iron work—with the softscape—thousands of perennials, annuals, trees and shrubs. Different areas include the golf putting green, lawn bowls, "Alice-in-Wonderland", alpine, a granite raised-bed vegetable gardens, vineyard walk, hops production, and seven different water features. Several new features have been added since the last Open Day in 2011. I recommend you plan to spend one and a half to two hours to enjoy the gardens. A brochure and map with suggested route will be provided at the entrance.

2013 | ♿ | 📷

➲ From Bennington, go north on Route 7 towards Manchester. Take Exit 3 off Route 7/Route 313 West/Arlington. At the bottom of the ramp, turn left under the bridge onto Route 313 West. Take the first right (after the southbound exit ramp) onto South Road. Continue to end at "T" intersection and turn left onto Old Mill Road. Stay on Old Mill Road, staying right at all "Y" junctions through the Village of East Arlington. At the end of Old Mill Road, turn right onto East Arlington Road/ Maple Street. The two houses are 8 and 9 houses on right from corner and just past the Arlington Antique Center. The mailboxes are numbered 1268 and 1308 respectively, but look for Garden Conservancy signs.

From Bennington or Manchester take Route 7A and in the center of the Town of Arlington turn east onto East Arlington Road. Follow about 1 mile past the schools, library and Antique Center, to the garden. Parking will be marked and is available in the empty lot opposite the 1268 house.

From Manchester go south on Route 7 towards Bennington. Take Exit 3/Route 313 West/Arlington. At the bottom of the ramp, turn right and stay right on Route 313 West. Proceed as directed above. The distance from Bennington or Manchester is about 12 miles.

MANCHESTER

GARDEN OF MARY & BOB RUSSELL
275 High Fields Lane

🕐 10 a.m. to 4 p.m.

This grand summer home with views across Manchester Valley to the Green Mountains was built by Mary & Bobby Russell in 1999. It is based on the Georgian Revival tradition of Robert Todd Lincoln's 1902 Hildene. The landscape design emanates from the lines, proportions, style and viewlines of this elegant home. Gordon Hayward, nationally recognized garden designer, worked closely with Mary Russell to create gardens that reflect the Colonial Revivalist style of the house with its clean, elegant lines. The entry garden on the west side of the house is punctuated by finely built stone walls that form the backdrop for ferns and birch gardens at the woodland edges while a refined boxwood partitioned garden near the front door introduces a more

formal and colorful note. Off the south end of the house is a grove of Stewartia pseudo-camellia trees with a backdrop of ferns and woodland. The walk through this grove leads to the east-facing 90' long open porch which establishes an intimate relationship between house and the east gardens. A fine stone re-taining wall creates a level lawn acting like an extension of the grand porch. A gray garden sits atop the wall while a far more colorful high summer border stretches out below it. A boxwood-edged four-quadrant garden sits within an ell of the house punctuated by a... [Read the full description online]

NEW | &. | 📷

➲ From Manchester Center: head south on Route 7A. Just after Stewart's, turn right onto Way's Lane. At the end, turn right onto West Road, then take first road on left towards Southern Vermont Arts Center. Before the Arts Center, turn left onto Highland Avenue. Con-tinue on the driveway to the very end, passing through white gate. Parking at the top.

📍 **TURKEY HILL FARM**
317 Silver Springs Lane
🕐 10 a.m. to 4 p.m.

The gardens around the main house were designed during the 1930s and have been cared for since by four generations of commit-ted gardeners. The layout remains the same as the original; the plantings have changed over the years. In 2004, we began a project to convert five acres of pasture into gardens. Like most projects, this one took on a life of its own and is now a sculpture garden with a winding arroyo, a pergola, and mowed walking paths. Across the road near the barn are the vegeta-ble gardens; a small orchard of apple, cherry, and pear trees; a pond; a screen house; and a greenhouse. A converted corncrib is a one-room guest cottage. Turkey Hill Farm gets its name from the wild turkeys that graze in the apple orchard. Last year a new path was added through the woods featuring a mean-dering boardwalk through an azalea garden, a

vine-covered arbor and gazebo. Many exotic woodland plants are also featured. Last year we completed a new traditional Japanese Garden, designed by landscape architect Ray Smith, featuring a Viewing Pavilion, Japanese bridge, lanterns, and varied plantings.

2013 | &. | 📷

➲ Follow Route 7A South from Manchester. Turn right onto Silver Spring Lane (3 miles south of the Equinox Hotel). Turn right at "T" intersection and follow road as it winds up hill to left. Turkey Hill Farm is first property up hill.

MANCHESTER CENTER

📍 **COVENTRY COTTAGE—**
JOAN & LEE FEGELMAN'S GARDEN
42 Coventry Lane
🕐 12 p.m. to 4 p.m.

In the spring of 1991, our gardens began as three large perennial beds on a former horse pasture. Today our gardens encom-pass over an acre. As you meander through the perennial garden room on wide grass pathways, you will witness a riot of color that is in various stages of bloom from spring until frost. Leaving the perennial garden through an arbor, you wander along a peony/daylily walkway, the vista opens, and, to the right, you see a pergola garden room featuring rocks, a sundial, and interesting shrubs. From there, meander on a thyme-scented stone path through the herb garden, which then flows into the grass. The rose garden features roses that are at home in Vermont. Unusual hostas enhance the beauty of the pool area.

2009 | &. | 📷

➲ From Manchester Center, take Route 7A north to Barnumville Road. Go 0.7 mile to second left, Canterbury Road. Go 0.6 mile to second right, Coventry Lane. House is first driveway on right.

PUBLIC GARDEN

MANCHESTER

 HILDENE, THE LINCOLN FAMILY HOME
1005 Hildene Road, Manchester

🕘 9:30 a.m. to 4:30 p.m.

⭐ Start your day here on July 9 for the Manchester Area Open Day. Tickets and maps will be available.

Discounted admission for Garden Conservancy Open Days: participants may present their garden tour tickets at Hildene's Welcome Center on either July 9 or July 10, 2016 to receive $10 off the admission price to Hildene.

See this garden's listing on page 288.

Windham County

Sunday, August 21

🕘 **10 a.m. to 4 p.m.**

$7 admission

There are also gardens open on this day in the nearby Monadnock Area, NH. See page 151.

 Pop-up Nursery
Broken Arrow Nursery / Opus Plants

 DIGGING DEEPER: Walking Design Workshop, at Gordon & Mary Hayward's Garden, Westminster West, 4 PM

WESTMINSTER WEST

 GORDON & MARY HAYWARD'S GARDEN
508 McKinnon Road, Westminster West

 Broken Arrow Nursery / Opus Plants

 DIGGING DEEPER

Gordon and Mary Hayward's one-and-one-half acre garden surrounds their 220-year-old farmhouse in southeastern Vermont. Over the past thirty-two years they have developed a hybrid of Old England and New England gardens to reflect Gordon's past growing up

on an orchard in northwestern Connecticut and Mary's past growing up on a farm outside Chipping Campden in the North Cotswold Hills of England. The garden, the subject of their book *The Intimate Garden* (WW Norton, 2005) is comprised of fourteen garden rooms. One area includes a pair of ninety-foot-long perennial borders that terminates in a post-and-

beam gazebo framing views of surrounding twenty acres of meadows. Over forty planted terra cotta pots and many garden ornaments, several from England, figure into the mood of this garden. Go to their website, www.haywardgardens.com for photos.
2014 |

➲ From I-91 north or south, take Exit 4/ Putney. When off the ramp, take Route 5 North 0.5 mile into Putney Village center. Turn left onto Westminster Road and go 4 miles, making no turns, to the second entrance to McKinnon Road. That is, McKinnon is a "U"-shaped road that enters Westminster Road at two points. Pass the first and then take the second entrance to McKinnon and then immediately turn right into the field to park. (Please use zip code 05346 for GPS or mapping software).

🌷 DIGGING DEEPER

Richard Brown

AUGUST 21, SUNDAY | 4 PM
WALKING DESIGN WORKSHOP
with Gordon and Mary Hayward
AT: Gordon & Mary Hayward's Garden,
      508 McKinnon Road, Westminster West

Gordon and Mary Hayward have been developing their Vermont garden, and their design skills, for thirty-five years. Gordon has written eleven books on how to design a garden and he lectures nationwide on the subject.

In this one to one-and-one-half- hour walking design workshop, Gordon and Mary will follow the itinerary of their garden and highlight essential design elements they put into play to create their one-and-one-half- acre garden. They will illustrate how they put universal elements of composition to work as they designed their garden: the role of paths to initiate a garden design which integrates house and garden, theme and variation, elements of coherence, positive and negative space, contrasting textures and forms, the many roles of itinerary, variations in mood, color contrast, scale and proportion... The Haywards will use their garden to illustrate universal design principles you can take home to put to work in your new or existing garden. At the very least, this workshop will enable you to see your garden and those of others in a new way."

Registration is required and space is limited. **Opendaysprogram.org or call 1(888) 842-2442**

✽ PUBLIC GARDEN

BENNINGTON COUNTY

MANCHESTER

HILDENE, THE LINCOLN FAMILY HOME
1005 Hildene Road, Manchester
(802) 362-1788, www.hildene.org

President Lincoln's granddaughter, Jessie, designed the formal garden on the south lawn of her parents' Manchester home, Hildene, in 1907. A gift to her mother, Mary Harlan Lincoln, it is an American version of the European parterre, with closely cropped privet hedges laid out to resemble a stained glass window when seen from her mother's second floor sitting room. The formal garden has been restored and replanted with like-colors using updated hybrids of turn-of-the-century flowers. In addition, a pergola inspired by the original one that framed the garden was constructed and the hedges pruned back to their original height. The garden contains 1,000s of peony blooms, many of them from the original 1907 plants.

Year round, daily, 9:30 a.m. to 4:30 p.m. Closed Easter, Thanksgiving, and Dec. 24, 25, and 26.

$ $20/adults; $5 youth ages 6-14; Youth under 6 and Hildene members are free. Discounted admission for Garden Conservancy Open Days: participants may present their garden tour tickets at Hildene's Welcome Center on either July 9 or July 10, 2016 to receive $10 off the admission price to Hildene.

➲ Located just 2 miles south of junction of Routes 7A, 11 & 30.

WASHINGTON

South Sound

Saturday, June 4

🕐 **10 a.m. to 3 p.m.**
$7 per garden

🏷️ Pop-up Nursery
Old Goat Farm

OUR PARTNER IN THE SOUTH SOUND

CHASE GARDEN

We are proud to partner with Chase Garden to bring you this Open Day. All of the gardens open on this day support the maintenance and development of public programs at Chase Garden. Read more about our preservation work at this special garden and throughout the Pacific Northwest later in this chapter.

PIERCE COUNTY

GRAHAM

📍 **OLD GOAT FARM**
20021 Orting Kapowsin Highway East, Graham

🏷️ Pop-up Garden Shop

Old Goat Farm is a small nursery located in the foothills below Mt. Rainier. The property includes a very small farm with a 100-year-old farm house and a large garden featuring both sun and shade beds. A substantial part of the garden is used for growing vegetables. The nursery specializes in unusual plants, many of which also flourish in the garden. Another highlight of the farm are the animals: two old goats, nine peacocks, ten ducks, and about sixty chickens.

2015 | ♿ | 📷

➲ From Seattle, take I-5 south to Highway 405 North towards Renton. Follow to Highway 167 South towards Kent-Auburn and then

take Highway 410/Sumner-Yakima exit onto Highway 162 to Orting. Turn right at traffic light and go 7 miles to Orting. Turn right at light onto Calistoga. Follow up winding hill; road flattens out. Pass first major cross street, 200th Street, which veers to right. Go to third driveway on left.

From Olympia, take I-5 North to Highway 512 East towards Puyallup. Then take Exit 161 (second Puyallup exit) and turn right onto Meridian (past South Hill Mall), go 6 miles. Turn left onto 200th Street (left turn lane) and go about 2 miles to stop sign. Turn right onto Orting-Kapowsin Highway. Go to third driveway on left.

ORTING

 VANCOR GARDENS
23517 Orville Road East, Orting

Nestled against a steep ridge of mixed deciduous/coniferous forest, VanCor Gardens wide sweep of manicured lawns encircle beautiful mature Douglas fir and Western red cedar trees and seemingly endless meandering flowerbeds are filled with rhododendrons, azaleas, and perennials. The center core of the garden has been left in its natural state providing birds (more than forty species recorded), chipmunks and squirrels living space. The cutting garden provides constant color throughout the growing season and the rose garden is filled with lovely blooms if not too recently visited by the deer. Numerous garden "creatures" greet you as you wander about and a cabana and outdoor barbecue provide for summer entertainment. Strategically placed rustic benches give resting spots to allow full appreciation of the area. At feeding time, the small pond's very tame koi readily take food from your fingers. A small orchard assures a bountiful crop of apples and pears.

2015 | ♿ | 📷

⮕ From I-405, take Exit 2A. Go 18 miles on Route 167 and 2 miles on Route 410 to Route 162. Continue through Orting 1.5 miles, turn-

ing right on Orville Road. "Homeranch" is on left about 2 miles.

PUYALLUP

 ERNIE & JULIA GRAHAM GARDEN
13715 Military Road East, Puyallup

Situated on a sloped acre looking out to Mt. Rainier, this peaceful, award-winning garden focuses on foliage color, texture, and contrast. Paths lead visitors through several distinct areas, including: a tranquil Japanese maple woodland featuring plantings native to the Pacific Northwest and Asia; a colorful poolside container garden; a purple & black courtyard; Ernie's vegetable garden; and eclectic spaces in between. The garden is a wildlife sanctuary organically maintained solely by its owners. It is a mature garden although always undergoing redesign here and there. Especially now that we have a year old standard poodle who delights in "playing" amongst the special plants.

2015 | 📷

⮕ From I-405, take the Auburn exit heading south on Route 167/Valley Freeway. Go south past Auburn. Exit right at the Sumner/Yakima Exit onto Route 410. Go about a mile to the Orting/Valley Avenue exit. Turn right and go south toward Orting for about 3 miles. Turn right onto Military Road East and head up the hill. Part way up the hill, turn right again at the Military Road East sign and proceed uphill to 13715. Please use parking strip outside of fence.

From I-5 south of Tacoma, go east on Route 512 for about 10 miles. Take the Eatonville Exit, veering right onto Meridian. Turn left onto 37th Avenue East (which becomes 39th). Go about 1 mile to end of road, then turn right onto Shaw Road. Proceed about 0.75 miles to stoplight (gas station on corner), then turn left onto 122nd Street East. Go about 0.25 miles, then turn left onto Military Road East to 13715.

 ED HUME'S EDUCATIONAL GARDEN
11504 58th Avenue East, Puyallup

Twelve-plus small gardens are designed to be

interactive with each having points of interest that challenge both young and older minds. The goal is that one goes away with a better understanding of the wonders of nature. It is a place where adults and children can learn the basics of gardening, but have fun at the same time. Gardens include a small Japanese Garden, Puzzle Garden, Insectivorous Garden, Butterfly & Hummingbird Garden, Tunnel (vines) Garden, Herb Garden, Maze, Crazy garden and others. Tours are conducted through the garden, by Ed Hume and staff.

2010 | ♿ | 📷

➲ Located in Summit area of Puyallup, just off Highway 512. From I-5, take Exit 127 east onto Highway 512. Go about 6 miles to Canyon Road/Summit exit. Turn right at exit, and get in left lane. Go about 2 blocks and turn left at second traffic light onto 112th Street East. Stay on 112th Street for 1 long block, and turn right onto 58th Avenue East. The garden is about 3 blocks on right at end of 58th Avenue.

✤ PUBLIC GARDENS

KING COUNTY

AUBURN

📍 **SOOS CREEK BOTANICAL GARDEN & HERITAGE CENTER**
29308 132nd Avenue SE, Auburn
(253) 639-0949,
www.sooscreekbotanicalgarden.org
🕐 10 a.m. to 3 p.m.

The twenty-three-acre garden was created over five decades by Maurice Skagen and his partner James Daly. Maurice transformed the acreage into eleven beautiful garden rooms. Frequent trips to England and Japan in the 1980s inspired his design of the parallel long borders beyond the Schaffer Pond. It is a garden of many colors and textures, with native and exotic collections. Paths lead from one garden room to the next with song birds, but-terflies and other wildlife enjoying the quiet relaxing atmosphere of nature.

🕐 Wednesday through Saturday, Mid-March to Mid-November from 10 a.m. to 3 p.m. Docent tours are available by appointment.

$ Free, donations accepted

➲ From I-5, take Auburn-North Bend exit Highway 18 and go east. Take the SE 304th Street exit toward SE 312th Street. Turn right onto SE 304th, turn right onto 132nd Avenue SE. Follow 132nd Avenue SE about 0.5 mile. The Garden entrance gate is on right, follow the driveway to the graveled parking lot.

PIERCE COUNTY

ORTING

📍 **CHASE GARDEN**
16015 264th Street East, Orting
(360) 893-6739, www.chasegarden.org
🕐 10 a.m. to 3 p.m.

A naturalistic, four-and-one-half-acre garden was created and lovingly tended by Ione and Emmott Chase. This modernist, Japanese-in-spired garden includes a reflecting pool, gravel paths, and moss-covered boulders, designed by landscape architect A. Rex Zumwalt with Ione Chase. Other areas including a wildflow-er carpeted forest of native trees, perennial shade borders, a rock garden, and a ground-cover meadow inspired by the alpine mead-ows of nearby Mount Rainier. This garden has an inspiring sense of place with its majestic view of Mount Rainier across the Puyallup River Valley.

🕐 Open Wednesday through Sunday, March through October from 10 a.m. to 3 p.m. Guided tours for individuals are available at 1:30 p.m. on the fourth Saturday of each month throughout the season, March through October.

$ $8 per person, Members: Free, Children 12 and under: Free, Military rate with valid active or retired ID: Buy one, get one free

➲ From Tacoma/I-5 North or South, take

The Chase Garden, Orting, Washington

This quintessential modernist garden of the Pacific Northwest represents the lifework of Emmott and Ione Chase, who spent more than forty years creating and refining it. In the late 1950s, they hired a young architect, K. Walter Johnson, to design their modest house, and they engaged a newly graduated landscape architect, Rex Zumwalt, to plan a Japanese-style garden around it. Using mostly native plants in a naturalistic arrangement, they created a garden of serene beauty in a dramatic setting atop a bluff with a majestic view of Mount Rainier.

...The plan included a concrete terrace and a covered lanai, narrow stepping-stones and bridges, and pebbled reflecting pools. Though a novelty to the Pacific Northwest at the time, it later defined the region's prevailing garden style.

—Excerpted from *Outstanding American Gardens: A Celebration—25 Years of the Garden Conservancy*. Photo by Marion Brenner.

Highway 512 East toward Puyallup. From Highway 512, take the Canyon Road exit (fourth exit) and turn right onto Canyon Road. Go about 4.1 miles to 176th Street East. At this major intersection, turn left and continue about 3 miles to Meridian Avenue East. Stay in the right lane and turn right onto Meridian Avenue East/Highway 161. Continue south for 5.6 miles, going through Graham and over a steep hill to 264th Street East. Turn left onto 264th Street East and continue about 3.5 miles. The driveway is on left. Take the drive on the right down to the visitor's center.

Vancouver Area

Saturday, June 11

🕐 **10 a.m. to 4 p.m.**
$7 per garden

OUR PARTNER IN THE NORTHWEST

HARDY PLANT SOCIETY OF OREGON

For more than ten years, we have been proud to partner with the Hardy Plant Society of Oregon to share private gardens throughout the Pacific Northwest. Widely known as HPSO, this is a non-profit volunteer organization for all gardeners: beginning or experienced, amateur or professional. Founded in 1984 and dedicated to the promotion of hardy herbaceous perennials, HPSO now has more than 2,400 members in the Pacific Northwest and beyond. This year, the Open Day explores the glorious gardens in and around Vancouver, Washington on Saturday June 11.

CLARK COUNTY

BATTLE GROUND

📍 THE BAILEY HAVEN
9601 NE 177th Street, Battle Ground

In April 1999, I found myself staring at an empty, slick, wet, flat acre of clay with two stark buildings and an ugly blacktop drive for inspiration. But, with handy ruler, graph paper, and ignorant bliss I laid out a design and husband Al built all I asked for. This garden has three distinct areas: the public garden, a relaxing-entertaining space with ponds and gazebo, and the working garden. This last area contains arbors, nine pergola beds, a rock garden, a loop garden, a Lady walk, a vegetable garden, paths, benches, trees, a conifer collection, a potting area, and topiary.

NEW | ♿ | 📷

➲ From the south, take I-5 north to Exit 9/ Fairgrounds/179th Street. Turn right, going east to 96th Avenue and turn right. Go 2 blocks to 177th Street.

From Battle Ground or Orchards on Highway 503, go to 189th Street. Turn west and follow 189th as it gradually turns into 179th Street. Turn south onto 96th Avenue and go to 177th Street.

📍 RITCHIE GARDEN
7619 NE 192nd Way, Battle Ground

In 2001, the five acres that was to become our garden sported one scrubby tree near a wetland. Gradually the area has evolved into a gracious setting characterized by weeping, contorted, and variegated perennials and trees looking out onto earthen ponds. We are always adding native plants that we hope will thicket and make berries to feed and protect local wildlife. We draw hummingbirds by growing plants with trumpet-shaped flowers—especially hardy fuchsias. The constantly changing fragrances and vistas are delightful!

NEW | ♿ | 📷

➲ Travel north on I-5 to 179th Street/Fair-grounds Exit. Go right (east) on 179th Street 3 miles to 72nd Avenue (at the traffic signal at John Deere and Manor Church) Turn left (north) and go about 0.5 mile to 192nd Way. Look for the Tiger Lily sign; 192nd Way on the right.

Coming north on the I-205 take Exit 32/ Padden Parkway W. Turn right off the exit to Andresen, then turn right and head north. Andresen joins St. Johns Boulevard and becomes 72nd Avenue. Continue north to 192nd Way (about 5 miles from Andresen.) Look for the Tiger Lily sign; 192nd Way on the right.

Coming from Battle Ground or northeast, go west on 219th Street to 72nd Avenue. Turn south onto 72nd and go to 192nd Way. The Tiger Lily monument doesn't face in your direction, but look for the first street on left after the light at 199th Street.

Look for the address on a rock out at the street. The garden is on the right in a yellow house with lots of plants and trees. PLEASE park on our side of the street, in front of or beyond our house. All 4 tires must be on the pavement (not in the bioswale).

VANCOUVER

📍 DRAGONFLY HOLLOW
12517 NE 20th Avenue, Vancouver

During our garden's twenty-five years, we've removed many old trees, eliminated our lawn, added a crop circle, outdoor living areas, and have responded to increasing shade. We continue to edit, removing and adding many new plants each year so there is a mix of mature and new. With one of us being a landscape designer/garden author, there always seems to be 'opportunity'. Our garden is in an ever-evolutionary state but its colorful flowers, swaying grasses, clipped hedges, award-winning garden art, and dramatic plants never cease to delight us.

2005 | ♿

➲ Drive north on either I-5 or I-205. If on I-5 turn right at the off-ramp, go to the first signal, turn right, go to the next signal, turn right onto Highway 99 South. If on I-205, turn left at the ramp signal, go to the next signal and turn left onto Highway 99 South. Continue through the 129th Street signal and about half-way down the hill turn left onto NE 20th Avenue. Turn left immediately at the dead-end sign and drive to the first mailbox on right. (It is red with a dark brown base with our house numbers in silver.) Park on the road and walk up the driveway to the garage area where there will be hosts to check you into the garden. For those who are physically-challenged, you can move the barrier at the bottom of the driveway and drive up to turn around at the top of the parking area and drop off someone.

THE GARDEN OF ROGER & JUDY MCELHANEY'S MATSU KAZE (WIND IN THE PINES)
12506 North 109th Avenue, Vancouver

I designed and developed our Asian-inspired garden fourteen years ago when this two-and-one-half acre property was a horse pasture. It is now filled with rare and unusual plants including many varieties of conifers, ginkgos, Japanese maples and dogwoods, as well as lilies, peonies, daphnes, clematis, rhododendrons and other perennials. Meandering pathways lead to various seating areas, a pond with a waterfall, a covered bridge over a dry creek bed, a fire pit, an outdoor kitchen, and a guest house. We created this garden to give us something to do in our retirement. It has given us that and so much more.

NEW | ♿ | 📷

⮑ From I-205 North, take Exit 32/Padden Parkway and go east. At the second light, turn left onto 117th Avenue/Highway 503. Continue north through 4 or 5 lights, past a Shell station on right and a WinCo on left. About 0.25 mile more, turn left onto 131st Street, just before you get to a white farm house on right. If you get to Chapman's Nursery on left, you've gone too far. Once on 131st Street, go a country block and turn left onto 110th Avenue. 110th jogs to the right and then jogs to the left onto

109th Avenue. Ours is the last house on right where the road dead ends.

From I-5 North, take the 78th Street exit east. After a few lights beyond Highway 99, 78th Street continues to right and the left fork becomes Padden Parkway. Stay to left on Padden and go over the I-205 overpass. Proceed as directed above. Please park on the side of the road in the grassy area.

SEYMOUR-LUECK
218 NW 88th Street, Vancouver

Our garden is influenced by Japanese landscaping and showcases water features, sculptures, and glass art. Ornamental grasses and moss play a prominent role in establishing the garden as part of the greenway behind it. Designed by Vanessa Nagel, stone pathways lead past a koi pond to several secluded sitting areas which are particularly nice for contemplation.

NEW | ♿ | 📷

⮑ From I-5, take Exit 4 for NE 78th Street. Travel west on 78th Street and turn right onto NE Hazel Dell Avenue, then left onto 83rd. Turn right onto NW Greenbriar Drive. Follow the curve and turn right onto NW 87th Street. Turn right again onto NW 4th Street, then right onto NW 88th Street. There is plenty of street parking. House is on a large cul-de-sac.

Bainbridge Island

Sunday, June 26

🕐 **Hours vary by garden**
 (Starting at 10 a.m.)

$7 per garden

KITSAP COUNTY

BAINBRIDGE ISLAND

📍 **CHAPMAN'S GARDEN**
 10666 Manitou Park Boulevard N.W.,
 Bainbridge Island

🕐 10 a.m. to 4 p.m.

The garden is in an old High Bank neighborhood that once housed vacation cabins or lumber worker's homes. In those days the mosquito fleet operated around this coast. In planning our garden, we took into account the old trees on and around the surrounding properties. It is not a "shade garden", but it is shaded. It provides color and interest year round with blooms beginning in February and finishing with a Forest Pansy leaf turn in October. It is loose and rambling. As you walk down past the cyprus hedge there are rhododendrons, varieties of hydrangea, lemon fuchsia, azalea, hosta, hellebores and heather. Succulents and herbs grow over the low rock walls. Trial and error ground covers show up here and there. It is a charming northwest garden. Around to the front of the house is a spectacular view from the high bank toward Seattle. Large pots on the main deck are filled with tropicals. Here, the side yard plantings are simple: ornamental grasses, flax, yarrow, purple thistle, and a small lawn. A magnificent old fir is right in the middle—its twisted branches providing shade through the long summer days.

NEW | 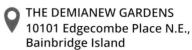

⮕ From Seattle take the Bainbridge Island Ferry from Coleman Dock. On the Island, follow 305 to the fourth traffic light; turn right onto

Manitou Beach Drive. Within 100 yards is a fork, follow left onto North Madison. At Valley Road (4-way stop) turn right and follow the road past Bay Hay, continuing down around a curve where the name changes to Manitou Beach Road. Continue about 0.25 mile and turn left onto Manitou Park Boulevard. Number 10666 is the eighth driveway on the right. Park on the sides and walk down.

📍 **THE DEMIANEW GARDENS**
 10101 Edgecombe Place N.E.,
 Bainbridge Island

🕐 10 a.m. to 5 p.m.

We are situated on a hill overlooking beautiful Puget Sound. Our property includes both shady woodland and full sun areas, so we are able to have a diverse collection of plants. Our goal is to always have something in bloom from early spring through fall. We also love fragrance, so we have used many different types of plants. In spring we have a profusion of bulbs and early blooming perennials such as epimediums and terrestrial orchids. As spring gives way to summer, we have blue Himalayan poppies, peonies, delphiniums, and finally roses. Mid summer is full of day lilies, Asian and Oriental lilies, and many other perennials. Late summer gives us perennial lobelia, sedum, and many fuchsias. We have fruits and vegetables mixed into our sunny beds, so we enjoy our own organic produce throughout the season.

2010 | 📷

➲ From the Bainbridge Ferry Terminal, take Highway 305 north to the fourth traffic light and turn right onto Manitou Beach. Keep right and go about 100 yards to Edgecombe Place and turn right. We are the first house on the right. Park on the street and walk up the driveway. Distance is just under 3 miles from the ferry. From Kitsap Peninsula, take Highway 305 to Bainbridge Island. Once on Bainbridge, go about 3 miles to Manitou Beach/Sportsman Club Road intersection. Turn left onto Manitou Beach and proceed as directed above. We live on a private road, please park on the street and walk up the driveway. The driveway is steep, but it is worth the effort!

📍 **PEYTON GULLY GARDEN**
3948 El Cimo Lane N.E.,
Bainbridge Island

🕐 10 a.m. to 4 p.m.

My garden started in 2000, after our house was built, and it was quite an experience for me, as I had never grown a garden in the ground, only in garden pots. It was empty soil, and it was almost two acres with a gully down each side of the property. There was about an acre left to plant. I started with trees, mainly Japanese maples, but also redbud 'Forest Pansy', Persian parrotia, mountain hemlocks, birch, and conifers. I added shrubs and finally

a few perennials. As my garden aged so did I, so I have simplified my planting, mostly to these trees and shrubs, with rhododendrons, pieris, grasses, berberis, leucothoe, and nandina. I have developed my garden down into the gully. It is surrounded by a creek bed and features paths and bridges. I describe my garden as "serenity with an Asian flair!"

NEW | ♿ | 📷

➲ From Lynwood Center Drive, turn west onto Baker Hill Road. Go up hill and as it curves and starts downhill and levels out, Palomino will come in from the left. Turn left onto Palomino and drive to dead end. Turn left onto Buckskin Road. Go down short hill to El Cimo Lane and turn right. Continue to dead end and turn left. Continue to 3948 El Cimo, with the stone circle fence.

📍 **OLAF RIBEIRO/NANCY ALLISON**
10744 Manitou Beach Drive N.E.,
Bainbridge Island

🕐 10 a.m. to 4 p.m.

The Olaf Ribeiro/Nancy Allison garden is a small one-third-acre garden surrounding a 1920s-era English-style cottage. It was originally established as a "Last Chance" garden. Ailing plants that were sent to Olaf (a plant pathologist) for diagnosis were brought back to health and placed in the garden. This has resulted in an eclectic garden with a wide diversity of plants, each with its own story of survival. Spring is welcomed by primulas, rhododendrons, aquilegias, and a variety of bulbs. The Japanese laceleaf maples provide a splendid fall palette. The owners now strive to maintain a tranquil garden that has flowering plants throughout the year balanced with evergreens. The backyard has a signature forty-plus-year-old *Styrax japonica*, a *Magnolia grandifolia*, and a towering western red cedar (*Thuja plicata*). The sixty-foot-long privet hedge has been shaped into a dragon and other creatively shaped shrubs are scattered through the front yard. A row of exceptional pink roses, bred over forty years by a rose aficionado line, the south wall. All walkways and the fountain were constructed by the owners. The garden is shared with a wide variety of birds, squirrels, and visiting deer. **NEW** | ♿ | 📷

⮑ Take the Seattle ferry to Bainbridge Island (a 30 minute ride). Once on the Island, go past the first and second stoplights (second stop light has a gas station on the left and a McDonald's on the right). Go past a yellow caution light and down the hill to another stop light. Turn right at this stoplight onto Sportsman Club/Manitou Beach. Take the right fork (0.1 mile) and continue along the waterfront to stop sign (0.5 mile). Turn left onto Falk Road and go to the top of the hill to "T" intersection (0.5 mile). At the T-junction, turn left and follow road down the hill past Messenger house. We are the third house on left past the Messenger house soon after the white picket fence (0.5 mile).

📍 THE SKYLER GARDEN
9734 Manitou Place, Bainbridge Island
🕐 10 a.m. to 5 p.m.

Gracefully surrounded by waves of cedar pickets, this private third-of- an-acre site sits at the end of a quiet cul-de-sac. Nestled among tall firs, vine maples, rhododendrons, azaleas, viburnum, and magnolias, these gardens have been a work in progress for more than thirty years. Stroll the pathways through serene surroundings, each leading to a different garden room, and you will discover seemingly endless groupings of hosta, hellebores, hebes, barberries, spirea, farfugium, euphorbias, and more than 100 varieties of ferns—the gardeners passion. These gardens have interest throughout the year with hardscape, garden rocks, and water features. Enjoy the serenity of these gardens.

2015 | ♿ | 📷

⮑ From Seattle take the Bainbridge Island Ferry from Coleman Dock on the waterfront (a 30-minute crossing). On Bainbridge Island, take Highway 305 to fourth traffic light and turn right onto Manitou Beach Drive. Imme-

diately turn left at fork onto North Madison. Turn right onto Beach Crest Drive. Turn left onto Manitou Place. Please park in cul-de-sac and walk through the steel gates.

KINGSTON

📍 LEAF WORKS
28212 Hansville Road N.E., Kingston
🕐 10 a.m. to 4 p.m.

A garden to keep you warm. Leaf Works includes a tropical valley through the palms and bananas, a sunny patio with a stream, yuccas, eucalyptus, and other drought-tolerant plants. A courtyard gives the affect of a terrarium. Our house is tucked into the extensive gardens with every window a framed view into the garden. **NEW** | 📷

⮑ From the Edmonds-Kingston Ferry Terminal Path go northwest on Kingston Ferry Slip toward Edmonds-Kingston Ferry Terminal Path. Merge onto Route 104 West/N.E. 1st Street/N.E. Highway 104. Continue 2.6 miles. Turn right onto Hansville Road N.E. Go 0.6 mile and turn right. Garden will be on left in 0.3 mile.

The Garden Conservancy in the Pacific Northwest

Photo by Marion Brenner

The Chase Garden: Taking a Private Gem Public in Orting, WA

This striking modernist garden was the life-work of Emmott and Ione Chase, who spent more than fifty years creating this special place. In the late 1950s, they built their house in a dramatic setting atop a bluff with a majestic view of Mount Rainier. Inspired by Japanese design and using mostly native plants, they created a landscape of serene beauty. Though a novelty to the Pacific Northwest at the time, it later typified the region's prevailing garden style. Today the garden's outstanding features are its native, naturalistic woodlands, alpine meadows, and stylized rock gardens.

We began working with Emmott and Ione Chase in 1995 establishing the Friends of the Chase Garden to build local support and to operate the garden. After Emmott's and Ione's deaths, we inherited the garden and hold a conservation easement on the site, protecting the scenic value of the garden for future generations.

We continue to raise funds to maintain the garden, open it to the public, and plan for its future. Learn more about events and developments at the Chase Garden at **www.chasegarden.org**.

Gaiety Hollow:
Preserving a Cultural Legacy
in Salem, OR

Gaiety Hollow was the home garden and office of Elizabeth Lord and Edith Schryver, the first all-female landscape architecture firm in the Pacific Northwest. From 1929 to 1969, Lord & Schryver designed more than 250 landscapes throughout the Northwest and their firm was a major force in shaping the city of Salem.

The Lord & Schryver Conservancy was formed to "preserve and interpret the legacy of Lord and Schryver to promote a greater understanding of their contribution to Northwest landscape architecture." They have listed the garden on the National Register of Historic Places and raised the funds to purchase the site in 2015.

We partnered with Lord & Schryver Conservancy in 2014 and have been advising them on the restoration and preservation of Gaiety Hollow, as well as marketing and staffing plans. For more information about Gaiety Hollow, visit www.lord-schryverconservancy.org.

The Garden Conservancy
Northwest Network:
Facilitating Collective Action

Our Northwest Network is a collective of public gardens, city parks, plant societies, and botanic gardens that have come together to share resources offering professional education for members throughout Washington, Oregon, and British Columbia.

Gardens and horticultural organizations can enjoy an exchange of ideas among garden preservation advocates across the Pacific Northwest. Here are our members.

- **The Bellevue Botanical Garden**, Bellvue, WA
- **Bloedel Reserve**, Bainbridge Island, WA
- **Chase Garden**, Orting, WA
- **E.B. Dunn Historic Garden Trust**, Seattle, WA
- **Gaiety Hollow**, Salem, OR
- **Hardy Plant Society,** Portland, OR
- **Kruckeberg Botanic Garden**, Shoreline, WA
- **Lakewold Gardens**, Lakewood, WA
- **Lan Su Chinese Garden**, Portland, OR
- **Meerkerk Gardens**, Greenbank, WA
- **The Elisabeth Carey Miller Botanical Garden**, Seattle, WA
- **Milner Gardens & Woodland** Qualicum Beach, BC
- **The Moore-Turner Heritage Gardens**, Spokane, WA
- **Ohme Gardens**, Wenatchee, WA
- **PowellsWood, A Northwest Garden**, Federal Way, WA
- **Rhododendron Species Botanical Garden**, Federal Way, WA
- **The Rogerson Clematis Collection Botanical Garden**, West Linn, OR
- **Seattle Chinese Garden**, Seattle, WA
- **South Seattle Community College Arboretum**, Seatte. WA
- **Soos Creek Botanical Garden & Heritage Center**, Auburn, WA
- **Streissguth Gardens**, Seattle, WA
- **Yakima Area Arboretum**, Yakima, WA

All Northwest Network members are listed in the Public Gardens Index at the back of the *Directory*. Learn more at **www.gardenconservancy.org** or **www.northwestgardens.org**.

WISCONSIN

OUR PARTNERS IN THE MILWAUKEE AREA

FRIENDS OF VILLA TERRACE

We are proud to partner with the Friends of Villa Terrace to bring you the July 16 Milwaukee Area Open Day. Since 1997, the Friends of Villa Terrace have been working to restore the Renaissance Garden at Villa Terrace. The Renaissance Garden is maintained entirely through private donations. Please stop in and explore the gardens during this Open Day or their regular hours. A portion of the proceeds from this Open Day will support this important garden.

See their garden listing on page 310.

BOERNER BOTANICAL GARDENS

We are proud to partner with Boerner Botanical Gardens to bring you the August 6 and 13 Milwaukee Area Open Days. To celebrate this public garden's 77th year, the Friends of Boerner Botanical Gardens are hosting a variety of classes (including many for children) and events year-round. There are regular opportunities to visit and group tours are welcome. We hope you will make Boerner Botanical Gardens part of your garden-visiting plans during this Open Day and through the year. See their complete listing at the end of this chapter. A portion of the proceeds from these Open Days will support this important garden.

See their garden listing on page 310.

Milwaukee Area

Saturday, July 16

🕐 **Hours vary by garden**
(Starting at 10 a.m.)

$7 per garden

MILWAUKEE COUNTY

RIVER HILLS

📍 **THE CHIMNEYS**
1105 West Dean Road, River Hills
🕐 10 a.m. to 5 p.m.

The gardens feature a formal rose garden, perennial and vegetable gardens, water and woodland gardens, and an extensive arboretum. Located on fifteen acres of land with beautiful vistas, the gardens were created by the current owners after clearing the land of invasives, but preserving standout specimen native trees. The arboretum includes collections of native, European, and Asian trees and shrubs to frame the vistas and water gardens.

NEW

➲ Take Highway 43 to Exit 82/Brown Deer Road west. Turn left onto North Spruce Road and continue to West Heather Lane. Turn left and West Heather Lane which becomes North Pheasant Lane. Turn right onto West Dean Road. Park on West Dean Road and walk south down private road to end and bear left at sign labeled Knox 1105 West Dean Road through gatehouse. Park on West Dean Road only.

📍 **HILL TOP HOUSE**
2280 West Dean Road, River Hills
🕐 10 a.m. to 5 p.m.

This fifteen-acre estate is composed of interconnecting pathways circumnavigating the property; manmade ponds and a recirculating stream; parterre, fountain and sculpture gardens; and woodland gardens colonized by ferns, lilies, wild geranium, ginger, sweet woodruff and spring ephemerals. The 1929 English Georgian-style residence sits hilltop, overlooking five acres of manicured lawn irrigated with water from one of the two ponds. Formally clipped evergreen hedges define the foundation gardens and terraces, as well as the pea gravel pathways and circular drive. The numerous tree, shrub and perennial species throughout the property make for enchanting surprises every step of the way.

1999 | ♿ | 📷

⮑ Take I-43 to Good Hope Road. Proceed west for 0.5 mile to the second road on the right, River Road. Go north on River Road to Dean Road (at a stop sign). Turn left and go west for 0.5 mile to #2280 on the north side of the road. Please park along the road.

OZAUKEE COUNTY

GRAFTON

📍 **TWO OAKS**
1776 Lake Shore Road, Grafton
🕐 10 a.m. to 5 p.m.

Two Oaks is a marriage of buildings and gardens harmonizing with strong architectural lines and landscape vistas on thirteen acres. Two Oaks—in the making for more than thirty years—is the vision of owners Bryan Gore his sons. Multiple building structures designed in an eighteenth-century American Tidewater Plantation Tradition are embraced by authentic landscape features with an overlook which descends to a two-axis English garden and park replete with many water features, statuary, and garden ornaments, temple mount, and obelisk graveyard. The formal gardens are bordered by a pond, overflow stream, swamp, planted collections such as a beech wood, a woodland, and a pasture with grazing sheep. The grounds of Two Oaks are graced with a myriad of butterflies, bluebirds, hummingbirds, thrashers, and more. Adjacent to the nature preserve park "Lion's Den Gorge" on the shores of Lake Michigan in Ozaukee County, Two Oaks is a private threshold with its unique setting and is the perfect invitation to explore the magic to be discovered while exploring the gorge.

NEW | ♿ | 📷

⮑ The garden is 25 minutes north of downtown Milwaukee. From I-43, take Exit 92/Grafton. Turn right (east) from off ramp onto County Highway "C." Turn left, (north) and go 1.5 miles to 1776 County C (also known as Lake Shore Road). Two Brick Pillars denote the entrance to the property and garden.

MEQUON

📍 **DRAGONFLY FARM**
3200 West Bonniwell Road, Mequon
🕐 10 a.m. to 5 p.m.

Dragonfly Farm is fifteen and one-half acres in Mequon, Wisconsin, about thirty minutes north of Milwaukee. We have been gardening on the property since 1998. During that time we have restored a one-and-one-half-acre wetland, built a barn for our poultry, and created about two miles of walking trails to "destinations" on our property. Approximately thirteen and one-half acres of our land is held in a conservation easement by the Ozaukee-Washington Land Trust in perpetuity. The "homestead footprint" and its gardens take up the other two acres. Still a fairly young garden by many standards, the "bones" of our garden are in place and maturing nicely. You will find a berry and soft fruit garden, a cutting garden, a veggie garden, and a small orchard near the barn. Our hens are free range and kept for egg production. Other destinations are an oak grove, a grape arbor, an allée of chestnut crabapples, and two ponds where we treat/direct our sump water. We focus heavily on native selections and use them in both traditional design and in our meadows and wetland.

NEW | 📷

⮑ Take I-43 to Exit 89/Highway C/Pioneer Road. Go west 1.5 miles to Riverland Road. Continue south on Riverland Road to Bonniwell Road 1.1 miles. Go east on Bonniwell Road to #3200. Look for the sign that reads "Dragonfly Farm" Proceed down to the end of the road and use the turn around at the dead end to park on the NORTH SIDE of Bonniwell

Road. OR the lower gravel road off the turn-around. DO NOT PARK ON the south side of Bonniwell Road or on Riverland Road. Do not block our neighbors driveways. Pull off onto shoulders only. Take care, ditches are DEEP.

 PUBLIC GARDEN

MILWAUKEE COUNTY

MILWAUKEE

RENAISSANCE GARDEN AT VILLA TERRACE
2220 North Terrace Avenue, Milwaukee

🕐 10 a.m. to 4 p.m.

See this garden's listing on page 310.

Milwaukee Area

Saturday, July 23

🕐 **10 a.m. to 4 p.m.**
$7 admission

The Christopher Farm & Gardens

SHEBOYGAN COUNTY

SHEBOYGAN

 THE CHRISTOPHER FARM & GARDENS
W 580 Garton Road, Sheboygan

The Christopher Farm & Gardens has transformed from a horse farm to a fifty-plus-acre groomed garden drained by a complex swale system that creates an ideal environment for plants, trees, and shrubs to flourish. With every twist and turn in the paths there is something new to see. Thousands of plants, shrubs, and tree species sprawl the grounds—some specifically selected for the many specialized gardens nestled throughout the property, including: a Specialty Conifer Garden, Peony Garden, Children's Educational Farm, Asian Water Garden, Fruit Orchards and Vegetable Gardens, Natural Prairie, and Greenhouses featuring a cacti and orchid displays, living walls, tropical plants, a koi pond and many other interesting and unusual plants.

NEW | ♿ | 📷

➲ Take I-94 North into Milwaukee. In Milwaukee take I-43 North to the last Sheboygan exit 128/Route 42/Sheboygan/Howards Grove Exit. Turn right onto Route 42 and immediately get into the left lane and turn left onto 40th Street/Dairyland Road (just after the Hardees Restaurant). Turn left onto 40th Street. Proceed north for 2 miles to Garton Road. Turn right (east) onto Garton Road and go about 2 miles to the end of the road. Drive through the white fence to W580 Garton Road. Follow parking signs into the designated field area.

Milwaukee Area

Saturday, August 6

🕐 **Hours vary by garden (Starting at 10 a.m.)**

$7 per garden

🏷 Pop-up Garden Shop
Monches Farm

 DIGGING DEEPER: Preserving Beauty at Ramhorn Farm, Newburg Village Hall, 10:30 AM, 2 p.m. & 4:30 p.m.

MILWAUKEE COUNTY

RIVER HILLS

📍 **GREEN FIRE WOODS**
Park at St. Christopher's Church, 7845 North River Road, River Hills. A shuttle will be provided to the garden.

🕐 10 a.m. to 4 p.m.

My goal has always been two fold, first to provide healthy food for my family and secondly to proved a safe haven for native plants in the forest and field areas. The vegetable garden has always been organic and now I am working on converting to bio-dynamic. The natural areas are managed to preserve the woodland ephemerals and prairie natives. Our fence provides a sanctuary from the deer.

1998 | ♿ | 📷

➲ The garden is 1 mile north of the intersection of River Road and Good Hope Road. Visitors must park at St. Christopher's Church,

7845 North River Road. A shuttle will be provided to Green Fire Woods.

 KUBLY GARDEN
8245 North Range Line Road, River Hills
🕐 10 a.m. to 4 p.m.

The garden is a vivid array of purple, pink, red, blue, yellow, and white flowers bordering three sides of a large square of lawn featuring arborvitae at the four corners and a fountain in the center circled by boxwood. There is a family area with swimming pool beyond the garden.

NEW | 📷

➲ Range Line Road between Brown Deer Road and Green Bay Road.

From Milwaukee, take I-43 North and travel approximately 9 miles to Exit 80/Good Hope Road. Follow Good Hope Road approximately 2.5 miles to North Range Line Road and turn right. Number 8245 is on the left, opposite the Milwaukee Country Club.

OZAUKEE COUNTY

NEWBURG

 RAMHORN FARM
**Park at Newburg Village Hall,
614 Main Street, Newburg.
A shuttle will be provided to
the garden.**
🕐 10 a.m. to 4 p.m.

 Monches Farm

 DIGGING DEEPER

Ramhorn Farm, home to the owners of Monches Farm, consists of 130 acres in Ozaukee County, Wisconsin with natural woodlands, wetlands, creeks, ponds and thirty-five acres of tillable land, of which we took fifteen acres to recreate a native prairie. We preserve our farm through the Washington/Ozaukee County Land Trust. Over the last ten years we have moved and restored eight historic structures of half timber and log construction

on our property to create this historic European looking farmstead. Our house is of half-timber construction and consists of three different historic Wisconsin structures that where originally build by German immigrants in the 1840s. We have moved and restored them to create what is now Ramhorn Farm. Many of the interior historic components were brought from Europe such as 1700s doors, floors, windows, fireplaces and furnishings. Our gardens include a fenced in garden with edible plants, herbs, vegetables, and flowering plants as well as a young orchard, areas for fruits, berries and naturalistic gardens with native and non-native perennials and grasses. Our gardens are cultivated in an organic and biodynamic way.

NEW | ♿ | 📷

➲ A shuttle will be provided to the garden from the Newburg Village Hall, 614 Main Street, Newburg, WI 53060. The Village Hall has a parking lot and there is plenty of on-street parking nearby.

✹ PUBLIC GARDEN

MILWAUKEE COUNTY

HALES CORNERS

 BOERNER BOTANICAL GARDENS
9400 Boerner Drive, Hales Corners
★ Start your day here for the August 6 Milwaukee Area Open Day
🕐 8 a.m. to 6 p.m.

See this garden's listing on page 310.

Green Fire Woods, featured in
*Outstanding American Gardens: A
Celebration—25 Years of the Garden
Conservancy*. Photo by Marion Brenner.

DIGGING DEEPER

SATURDAY, AUGUST 6 | 10:30 AM, 2 PM & 4:30 PM

PRESERVING BEAUTY AT RAMHORN FARM

AT: Newburg Village Hall, 614 Main Street, Newburg
A shuttle will be provided to the garden from the Village Hall.

Owners of the renowned Monches Farm, Matt Kastell & Scott Sieckman, have combined backgrounds in archeology, horticulture, landscape architecture, anthropology, art, and ornamental horticulture. They will lead a tour of their own garden, the 130-acre Ramhorn Farm—the land, the prairie, the gardens, and historic buildings. They will show first-hand how architecture can influence the natural landscape, and how gardens and outdoor spaces with fences, hedges, and water features harmonize with the natural setting. The pair will also talk about keeping bees, chickens, and making tea from your own plants.

Refreshments will be served in the barn and a pop-up garden shop will be available.

Registration is required and space is limited. **Opendaysprogram.org or call 1(888) 842-2442.**

Milwaukee Area

Saturday, August 13

🕐 **Hours vary by garden (Starting at 10 a.m.)**

$7 per garden

 DIGGING DEEPER: Going Green— Communing with Moss, The Sievert Garden, Waukesha, 4 p.m.

MILWAUKEE COUNTY

GREENFIELD

RADLER'S ROSARIUM
10020 West Meadow Drive, Greenfield

🕐 10 a.m. to 4 p.m.

Will is the developer of the popular Knock Out® series of roses. His two-acre garden is extensively landscaped with all types of interesting plants, even a reconstructed prairie. This is a gardener's garden. It includes ponds filled with tame goldfish, gazebos, arbors, and sculpture. The sloping garden uses stone to create seating, terraces, raised garden beds, a fire pit, an outdoor fireplace, waterfalls, and a meandering stream linking it all together. There is even an outdoor shower.

NEW | ♿ | 📷

➲ From I-43 going south (west), take the Highway 45 South/108th Street Exit. Continue south on Highway 100 and quickly get into the left lane to turn left at the first stop light onto Edgerton Avenue. Continue to 102nd Street, turning left (you can't turn right). At the first intersection on 102nd Street the street name changes to Meadow Drive. Meadow Drive is only two blocks long and my garden is at the bottom of the hill on the left (the tan and green English Tudor with too many plants). Meadow Drive is a narrow street. Park only on one side, or in the Rose Innovation's Playground's parking lot or on Root River Parkway.

WAUKESHA COUNTY

DOUSMAN

LARK'S GARDEN
S28 W36123 Scuppernong Circle, Dousman

🕐 10 a.m. to 4 p.m.

I view my garden as a painter views their canvas—an ever-changing piece of art. My goal was to have color, texture, form, and movement throughout the year in my Zone 5 landscape. Creating garden art is another passion of mine. Vermicomposting and vegetable, herb, perennial, and bog gardens keep me busy. A couple of years ago I started making my own herbal, medicinal oil infusions—drying enough herbs to supply me with plenty of herbal teas for the long Wisconsin winter.

NEW

➲ From Milwaukee or Waukesha, take I-94 South to Highway 67/ Oconomowoc/Dousman exit. Turn left (south) onto Highway 67 for 5 miles to Beverly Lane. Turn right (west) onto Beverly Lane. Go to stop sign at Scuppernong Drive and turn left. Stay on Scuppernong DRIVE to Scuppernong Circle. Garden is on the south side of the street. There is a flag pole with a brick planter. Please park on street.

WAUKESHA

THE SIEVERT GARDEN
W231 S5977 Molla Drive, Waukesha

🕐 10 a.m. to 4 p.m.

🌀 DIGGING DEEPER

The one-acre property is surrounded by shade gardens with perennials selected for their foliage, including 700 hostas. Many moss gardens appear, including containers and mossy rocks. There are three water systems in the water garden. There is a Japanese-style garden, a cactus and succulent garden, a sunken garden, a hillside garden, and a Williamsburg-inspired formal garden. Five thousand antique bricks and 2,000 antique cobblestones were used for walks and planters. Begonias and impatiens appear in a single-color-plus-white pattern. All trees are deciduous to blend with nearby wooded areas.

NEW | 📷

➲ From the east, take National Avenue/Highway 164 and turn onto Glengarry Road. Go west 2.1 miles to Molla Drive. Turn left (south), and the garden is at the second last house on Molla Drive on the right.

From the west, take National Avenue/ Highway 164 (north of the Highway 164 Exit on I-43), take Highway 164 north to Townline Road. Turn right (east) and go 0.6 mile to Big

Bend Road, then continue a 0.5 mile east to Charles Drive. Turn left (north) onto Charles, then turn right onto Fern Drive, then turn left onto Molla Drive. The garden is at the second house on the left. Please park on the east side of Molla Drive, if possible.

❋ PUBLIC GARDENS

MILWAUKEE COUNTY
HALES CORNERS

BOERNER BOTANICAL GARDENS
9400 Boerner Drive, Hales Corners

Known for its unusual topography, historic forty-acre gardens within 500 acre Whitnall Park. Collections: Perennial & Shrub Malls, Herb, Rose, Annual, Peony, Rock Gardens, Wetlands, Trial Gardens, NEW Rotary ADA path. Seasonal displays: wildflowers, tulips, crab apples, peonies, iris, roses, day lilies. Café & Gift Shop available.

🕐 April 29 through October 4, daily, 8 a.m. to 6 p.m.

$ Adults $5.50; Seniors & Students $4.50; Children 6 to 17 $3

➲ Located in the southwest suburbs of Milwaukee. I-894 to Exit 5A (Forest Home). Forest Home SW to 92nd Street; travel south approximately 1 mile to College Avenue. Or enter Boerner from 5879 South 92nd street.

MILWAUKEE

RENAISSANCE GARDEN AT VILLA TERRACE
2220 North Terrace Avenue, Milwaukee

The Renaissance Garden at Villa Terrace surrounds the Villa Terrace Decorative Arts Museum in Milwaukee, Wisconsin. The house was designed by architect David Adler for Milwaukee industrialist Lloyd R. Smith and his family, and was built on the bluff above Lake Michigan in the style of an Italian Villa. The family called it Sopra Mare—"Above the Sea"—because its beautiful setting reminded

---

 DIGGING DEEPER

SATURDAY, AUGUST 13 | 4 PM

GOING GREEN: COMMUNING WITH MOSS IN DALE SIEVERT'S GARDEN

AT: W231 S5977 Molla Drive, Waukesha

A passionate moss gardener, Dale Sievert's garden has been featured in a wide array of books and magazines, and he has written articles on moss for several national magazines.

In this special afternoon tour and discussion, Dale will highlight some of the many moss varieties he grows, as well as the culture of moss, showing how he uses them on the ground, on rocks, and in containers. Dale started to garden when he was seven, and ran a tree and shrub nursery for many years. He embraced shade gardening in the late 1980s when the trees in his own yard got bigger. Dale began his Japanese-style garden in 2000 and became interested in moss gardening after visiting gardens in Japan a few years later.

them of the Mediterranean Sea. The garden was originally designed by Bostonian Rose Standish Nichols in the formal Italianate style, with a central axis running from the wrought iron entry gates by Austrian blacksmith Cyril Colnik, to the Hermes fountain in the elegant courtyard, through the Great Hall, across the terrace, down the water stairs, across the meadow and finally to the grand Neptune Gate. Statuary and garden features are arranged symmetrically along the sides of the central axis. The garden was renovated in 2002 according to the design of Dennis Buettner, FASLA. The lakeside portion of the garden is approximately three acres and is inspired by the classical themes of order and beauty. It is initially viewed from the museum's Terrace d'Luna atop the bluff, allowing a broad and inspiring view of the garden and the waters of Lake Michigan. The second terrace, called Parnassus, features small putti statues, representing the four seasons and the fine arts. Descending the bluff is the Bride's Orchard of flowering crabapple trees, divided by the Scaletta d'Aqua (a water stairs), and at the bottom of the pedestrian stairway is a statue of Ceres, the goddess of agriculture. The center of the lower portion of the garden is a large meadow, with a fish pond, ("Vasca") at one end, and a wrought iron Neptune Gate at the other. Just beyond the Vasca is a small building resembling a Roman temple, providing space for public restrooms. Rows of Armstrong maples stand at each side of the meadow and an obelisk with surrounding flowering annuals marks its center. Rows of hydrangeas lie beneath the trees, and at their far end are two ironwood arbors, providing welcome shade for visitors. Nearby are semicircular benches, placed conveniently for conversation and rest, and just beyond these are two roundels, with statues of Hercules and Diana, goddess of the Hunt. All of the features echo those of the traditional Renaissance Garden and are designed to delight, amuse and inspire.

🕐 Special Garden Conservancy Open Day, July 16, 2016; 10 a.m. to 4 p.m. Otherwise, Wednesday–Sunday, 1 p.m. to 5 p.m., closed Thanksgiving day, Christmas eve, Christmas day, New Year's Eve, and New Years day.

$ $7 Adults, $5 Seniors (62+), Military and students. Free for Members and children 12 and under.

⮕ From Interstate 43 heading north from downtown Milwaukee, take Locust Avenue east until it ends at Lakd Drive. Turn right (south) and follow Lake Drive about 10-12 blocks, past the traffic light at North Avenue. The second block after the traffic light is East Ivanhoe Place. Turn left (east), and in one block the Villa Terrace Museum will be straight ahead. The garden reaches to Lincoln Memorial Drive at the lake front, but there is no access there.

Public Gardens

There are so many great public gardens around the country, we wanted to list them all. This listing include our partners in preservation, our Northwest Network, and Open Days, as well as members of the American Public Garden Association, and some of the museum properties managed by the National Society of the Colonial Dames of America.

ⓖ **The Garden Conservancy** preservation partners

ⓞ **Open Days** partners

ⓝ **Garden Conservancy Northwest Network** members

ⓐ **American Public Gardens Association (AGPA)** members

ⓒ **The National Society of the Colonial Dames of America** properties

ALABAMA

ANNISTON
Longleaf Botanical Gardens
P.O. Box 1587, Anniston, 36202
annistonmuseum.org

AUBURN
Donald E. Davis Arboretum
College St and Garden Dr,
Auburn, 36849
auburn.edu/arboretum

BIRMINGHAM
Aldridge Gardens
3530 Lorna Rd,
Birmingham, 35216
aldridgegardens.com
ⓐ

Birmingham Botanical Gardens
2612 Lane Park Rd,
Birmingham, 35223
bbgardens.org
ⓐ

DOTHAN
Dothan Area Botanical Gardens
5130 Headland Ave,
Dothan, 36303
dabg.com

HUNTSVILLE
Huntsville Botanical Garden
4747 Bob Wallace Ave,
Huntsville, 35805
hsvbg.org

MOBILE
Conde-Charlotte Museum House & Garden
104 Theatre St, Mobile, 36602
ⓒ

Mobile Botanical Gardens
5151 Museum Dr,
Mobile, 36689
mobilebotanicalgardens.org

THEODORE
Bellingrath Gardens & Home
12401 Bellingrath Gardens Rd,
Theodore, 36582
bellingrath.org

ALASKA

ANCHORAGE
Alaska Botanical Garden
4601 Campbell Airstrip Rd,
Anchorage, 99507
alaskabg.org

JUNEAU
Jensen-Olson Arboretum
23035 Glacier Highway,
Juneau, 99801
juneau.org/parkrec

ARIZONA

CAREFREE
Carefree Desert Gardens
101 Easy St, Carefree, 85377
carefree.org

FLAGSTAFF
Arboretum at Flagstaff
4001 South Woody Mountain
Rd, Flagstaff, 86001
thearb.org
ⓐ

GLENDALE
Glendale Xeriscape Demonstration Garden
5959 W. Brown St,
Glendale, 85302
glendaleaz.com/waterconservation

MESA
Rose Garden at Mesa Community College
1833 W. Southern Ave,
Mesa, 85202
mesacc.edu/rosegarden

PHOENIX
Desert Botanical Garden
1201 N. Galvin Pkwy,
Phoenix, 85008
dbg.org

SUPERIOR
Boyce Thompson Arboretum
37615 E US Highway 60,
Superior, 85173
arboretum.ag.arizona.edu

TUCSON
Arizona-Sonora Desert Museum
2021 N. Kinney Rd,
Tucson, 85743
desertmuseum.org

Tohono Chul Park
7366 N. Paseo del Norte,
Tucson, 85704
tohonochulpark.org

Tucson Botanical Gardens
2150 N. Alvernon Way,
Tucson, 85712
tucsonbotanical.org

**University of Arizona
Campus Arboretum**
101 Herring Hall, Tucson, 85721
arboretum.arizona.edu

ARKANSAS

BENTONVILLE
Compton Gardens
312 N. Main St,
Bentonville, 72712
peelcompton.org

**Crystal Bridges Museum
of American Art**
600 Museum Way,
Bentonville, 72712
crystalbridges.org

HOT SPRINGS
Garvan Woodland Gardens
550 Arkridge Rd,
Hot Springs, 71903
garvangardens.org

LITTLE ROCK
Wildwood Park for the Arts
20919 Denny Rd,
Little Rock, 72223
wildwoodpark.org

SPRINGDALE
Botanical Garden of the Ozarks
4703 N Crossover Rd
Springdale, 72764
bgozarks.org

CALIFORNIA

ARCADIA
**Los Angeles County
Arboretum Foundation**
301 N. Baldwin Ave,
Arcadia, 91007
arboretum.org

BERKELEY
**University of California
Botanical Garden**
200 Centennial Dr, #5045,
Berkeley, 94720
botanicalgarden.berkeley.edu

CLAREMONT
**Rancho Santa Ana
Botanic Garden**
1500 North College Ave,
Claremont, 91711
rsabg.org

CLOVIS
Clovis Botanical Garden
945 N Clovis Ave, Clovis, 93611
clovisbotanicalgarden.org

CORONA DEL MAR
Sherman Library & Gardens
2647 East Coast Highway,
Corona del Mar, 92625
slgardens.org

DAVIS
**UC Davis Arboretum
& Public Garden**
One Shields Ave, Valley Oak
Cottage, Davis, 95616
arboretum.ucdavis.edu

**UC Davis Haagen-Dazs
Honey Bee Haven**
1 Shields Ave, Davis, 95616
hhbhgarden.ucdavis.edu/welcome

DUNSMUIR
Dunsmuir Botanical Gardens
4841 Dunsmuir Ave,
Dunsmuir, 96025
dunsmuirbotanicalgardens.org

EL CAJON
Water Conservation Garden
12122 Cuyamaca College Dr
West, El Cajon, 92019
thegarden.org

ENCINITAS
Leichtag Foundation
441 Saxony Rd,
Encinitas, 92126
leichtag.org

San Diego Botanic Garden
230 Quail Gardens Dr,
Encinitas, 92023
qbgardens.org

ESCONDIDO
San Diego Zoo Safari Park
15500 San Pasqual Valley Rd,
Escondido, 92027
sandiegozoo.org

EUREKA
Humboldt Botanical Garden
7707 Tompkins Hill Rd,
Eureka, 95503
hbgf.org

FRESNO
Jordan College of Agricultural Sciences
California State University, Fresno, 93740

FT. BRAGG
Mendocino Coast Botanical Gardens
18220 N. Highway 1,
Ft. Bragg, 95437
gardenbythesea.org

FULLERTON
Fullerton Arboretum
1900 Associated Rd,
Fullerton, 92831
fullertonarboretum.org

GLEN ELLEN
Quarryhill Botanical Garden
12841 CA-12,
Glen Ellen, 95442
quarryhillbg.org

LA CANADA FLINTRIDGE
Descanso Gardens
1418 Descanso Dr,
La Canada Flintridge, 91011
descansogardens.org

LONG BEACH
Earl Burns Miller Japanese Garden
1250 Bellflower Blvd,
Long Beach, 90840
csulb.edu/~jgarden

LOS ANGELES
J. Paul Getty Museum
1200 Getty Center Dr,
Los Angeles, 90049
getty.edu

Mildred E Mathias Botanical Gardens
777 Tiverton Dr,
Los Angeles, 90095
botgard.ucla.edu

OAKLAND
Children's Fairyland
699 Bellevue Ave,
Los Angeles, 94610
fairyland.org

Regional Parks Botanic Garden
C/o East Bay Regional Park District, Los Angeles, 94605
nativeplants.org

PALM DESERT
The Living Desert
47-900 Portola Ave,
Palm Desert, 92260
livingdesert.org

PALO ALTO
Gamble Garden
1431 Waverley St,
Palo Alto, 94301
gamblegarden.org

PALOS VERDES PENINSULA
South Coast Botanic Garden Foundation
26300 Crenshaw Blvd,
Palos Verdes Peninsula, 90274
southcoastbotanicgarden.org

PASADENA
La Casita del Arroyo Garden
177 South Arroyo Blvd, 91105
lacasitadelarroyo.org

RIVERSIDE
LaSierra University
4500 Riverwalk Pkwy,
Riverside, 92515
lasierra.edu

ROSS
Marin Art & Garden Center
30 Sir Francis Drake Blvd,
Ross, 94957
magc.org

SAN DIEGO
San Diego Zoo
2920 Zoo Dr, San Diego, 92101
sandiegozoo.org

SAN FRANCISCO
Gardens of Alcatraz
Alcatraz Island, San Francisco
alcatrazgardens.org

Octagon House
2645 Gough St,
San Francisco, 94123
nscda-ca.org

San Francisco Botanical Garden
Golden Gate Park, San Francisco
sfbotanicalgarden.org

San Francisco Conservatory of Flowers
Golden Gate Park, San Francisco
conservatoryofflowers.org

SAN JOSE
Guadalupe River Park Conservancy
438 Coleman Ave,
San Jose, 95110
grpg.org

SAN LUIS OBISPO
Cal Poly Arboretum & Gardens
1 Grand Ave,
San Luis Obispo, 93407

San Luis Obispo Botanical Garden
3450 Dairy Creek Rd,
San Luis Obispo, 93403
slobg.org

SAN MARINO
Huntington Library, Art Collections, & Botanical Gardens
1151 Oxford Rd,
San Marino 91108,
huntington.org

SANTA ANA
Fairhaven Memorial Park
1702 E. Fairhaven Ave,
Santa Ana, 92705
fairhavenmemorial.com

SANTA BARBARA
Casa del Herrero
1387 East Valley Rd,
Santa Barbara, 93108
casadelherrero.com

Ganna Walska Lotusland
695 Ashley Rd,
Santa Barbara, 93108
lotusland.org

Santa Barbara Botanic Garden
1212 Mission Canyon Rd,
Santa Barbara, 93105
sbbg.org

SANTA CRUZ
Santa Cruz Arboretum
1156 High St, MS Arboretum,
Santa Cruz, 95064
arboretum.ucsc.edu

SANTA ROSA
Luther Burbank Home & Gardens
100 Santa Rose Ave,
Santa Rosa, 95404
lutherburbank.org

SUN VALLEY
Theodore Payne Foundation for Wild Flowers and Native Plants
10459 Tuxford St,
Sun Valley, 91352
theodorepayne.org

TEMECULA
Rose Haven Heritage Garden
30592 Jedediah Smith Rd,
Temecula, 92592
temeculavalleyrosesociety.org

VENTURA
Ventura Botanical Gardens
398 Ferro Dr, 93001
venturabotanicalgardens.com

VISTA
Alta Vista Botanical Gardens
200 Civic Center Dr,
Vista, 92084
altavistagardens.org

WALNUT CREEK
Gardens at Heather Farms
1540 Marchbanks Dr,
Walnut Creek, 94598
gardenshf.org

Ruth Bancroft Garden
1552 Bancroft Rd,
Walnut Creek, 94598
ruthbancroftgarden.org

WOODSIDE
Filoli
86 Canada Rd,
Woodside, 94062
filoli.org

COLORADO

BOULDER
Colorado Shakespeare Gardens
P.O. Box 20355, Boulder, 80308
coloradoshakespearegardens.org

COLORADO SPRINGS
Colorado Springs Utilities
2855 Mesa Rd,
Colorado Springs, 80918
csu.org

DENVER
Denver Botanic Gardens
909 York St, Denver, 80206
denverbotanicgardens.org

Regis University, Physical Facilities F-16
3333 Regis Blvd, Denver, 80221

DURANGO
Durango Botanic Gardens
1400 Main Ave, Denver, 81301

FORT COLLINS
Gardens on Spring Creek
2145 Centre Ave,
Fort Collins, 80526
fcgov.com/horticulture

GRAND JUNCTION
Western Colorado Botanical Gardens
655 Struthers Ave,
Grand Junction, 81501
wcbotanic.org

JULESBURG
Colorado State University Extension, Golden Plains Area Extension—Sedgwick
315 Cedar St, Suite 100,
Julesburg, 80737

LITTLETON
Hudson Gardens & Event Center
6115 S. Santa Fe Dr,
Littleton, 80120
hudsongardens.org

STEAMBOAT SPRINGS
Yampa River Botanic Park
1000 Pamela Ln,
Steamboat Springs, 80487
yampariverbotanicpark.org

TRINIDAD
Trinidad History Museum
312 East Main St,
Trinidad, 81082
historycolorado.org

VAIL
Betty Ford Alpine Gardens
530 South Frontage Rd East,
Vail, 81657
bettyfordalpinegardens.org

CONNECTICUT

BRIDGEPORT
Colorblends House and Spring Garden
893 Clinton Ave,
Bridgeport, 06604
colorblendsspringgarden.com

NEW HAVEN
Marsh Botanical Garden,
Yale University
227 Mansfield St,
New Haven, 06511
marshbotanicalgarden.yale.edu

NEW LONDON
Connecticut College Arboretum
270 Mohegan Ave, Campus Box
5201, New London, 06320
arboretum.conncoll.edu

REDDING
Highstead
127 Lonetown Rd,
Redding, 06896
highstead.net

STAMFORD
Bartlett Arboretum & Gardens
151 Brookdale Rd,
Stamford, 06903
bartlettarboretum.org

STORRS
University of Connecticut,
Ecology & Evolutionary Biology
Plant Growth Facilities
floraeeb.uconn.edu

WATERFORD
Harkness Memorial State Park
275 Great Neck Rd,
Waterford, 06385
ct.gov/deep/harkness

WASHINGTON
Hollister House Garden
300 Nettleton Hollow Rd,
Washington, 06793
hollisterhousegarden.org

WETHERSFIELD
Webb House Colonial
Revival Garden at the Webb-
Deane-Stevens Museum
211 Main St,
Wethersfield, 06109
webb-deane-stevens.org

DELAWARE

BETHANY BEACH
Delaware Botanic Gardens
at Pepper Creek
Buckhill Ln, Dagsboro, 19939
delawaregardens.org

HOCKESSIN
Mt. Cuba Center
3120 Barley Mill Rd,
Hockessin, 19707
mtcubacenter.org

LEWES
Mill Pond Garden Inc.
31401 Melloy Court,
Lewes, 19958
millpondgarden.com

NEWARK
Longwood Graduate Program
University of Delaware,
Newark, 19716
udel.edu/LongwoodGrad

University of Delaware
Botanic Gardens
University of Delaware,
Newark, 19716
ag.udel.edu/udbg

WILMINGTON
Delaware Center for Horticulture
1810 N. DuPont St,
Wilmington, 19806
thedch.org

Nemours Mansion & Gardens
1600 Rockland Rd,
Wilmington, 19803
nemoursmansion.org

Stonegates
4031 Kennett Pike,
Wilmington, 19807
stonegates.com

WINTERTHUR
Winterthur
Route 52, Winterthur, 19735
winterthur.org

DISTRICT OF COLUMBIA

WASHINGTON
American University
4400 Massachusetts Ave, NW,
Washington, 20016
american.edu/arboretum

Dumbarton House & Gardens
2715 Q St, NW
Washington, 20007
dumbartonhouse.org

Dumbarton Oaks
1703 32nd St, NW,
Washington, 20007
doaks.org

Hillwood Estate,
Museum & Gardens
4155 Linnean Ave, NW,
Washington, 20008
hillwoodmuseum.org

Smithsonian Gardens
600 Maryland Ave. SW,
Washington, 20013
gardens.si.edu

Tudor Place Historic
House & Garden
1644 31st St, NW,
Washington, 20007
tudorplace.org

U.S. National Arboretum
3501 New York Ave, NE,
Washington, 20002
usna.usda.gov

U.S. Botanic Garden
245 First St, SW,
Washington, 20024
usbg.gov

Washington National Cathedral
3101 Wisconsin Ave. NW,
Washington, 20016
cathedral.org

FLORIDA

CORAL GABLES
**University of Miami—
Gifford Arboretum**
1301 Memorial Dr,
Coral Gables, 33146
bio.miami.edu/arboretum

Fairchild Tropical Botanic Garden
10901 Old Cutler Rd,
Coral Gables, 33156
fairchildgarden.org

FORT MYERS
Berne Davis Botanical Garden
9329 Garden Pointe Court,
Fort Myers, 33908
fmlcgardencouncil.com

Lakes Park Botanic Garden
7330 Gladiolus Dr,
Fort Myers, 33908
lakesparkenrichmentfoundation.
org

FORT PIERCE
Heathcote Botanical Gardens
210 Savannah Rd,
Fort Pierce, 34982
heathcotebotanicalgardens.org

GOTHA
Nehrling Gardens
2267 Hempel Ave,
Gotha, 34734
nehrlinggardens.org

HOMESTEAD
Fruit and Spice Park
24801 SW 187 Ave,
Homestead, 33031
fruitandspicepark.org

Redland Tropical Gardens
24050 SW 162 Ave,
Homestead, 33031
redlandtropicalgardens.org

JACKSONVILLE
**Cummer Museum of
Art & Gardens**
829 Riverside Ave,
Jacksonville, 32204
cummer.org

Evergreen Cemetery Association
4535 Main St,
Jacksonville, 32206
evergreenjax.com

KEY LARGO
**The Botanic Gardens
at Kona Kai Resort**
97802 Overseas Highway,
Key Largo, 33037
kkgb.org

KEY WEST
**Key West Botanical
Garden Society**
5210 College Rd,
Key West, 33040
keywestbotanicalgarden.org

LAKE WALES
Bok Tower Gardens
1151 Tower Blvd,
Lake Wales, 33853
boktower.org

LOXAHATCHEE
White Fences Equestrian Center
3978 Hanover Circle,
Loxahatchee, 33470
WhiteFencesFlorida.com

MIAMI
Block Botanical Gardens
7299 SW 79 Court,
Miami, 33143

**Florida International University
College of Arts & Sciences**
11200 SW 8th St,
Miami, 33199

**Miami-Dade Zoological
Park & Gardens**
12400 SW 152 St,
Miami, 33177
zoomiami.org
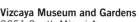

Montgomery Botanical Center
11901 Old Cutler Rd,
Miami, 33156
montgomerybotanical.org

Vizcaya Museum and Gardens
3251 South Miami Ave,
Miami, 33129
vizcayamuseum.org

Miami Beach Botanical Garden
2000 Convention Center Dr,
Miami, 33139
mbgarden.org

NAPLES
Naples Botanical Garden
4820 Bayshore Dr,
Naples, 34112
naplesgarden.org

Naples Zoo at Caribbean Gardens
1590 Goodlette-Frank Rd,
Naples, 34102
napleszoo.com

OCALA
**Horticultural Arts &
Park Institute, Inc.**
8435 SW 80th St, Suite 2,
Ocala, 34481
sholompark.com/main.html

ORLANDO
Exploration Gardens
6021 S. Conway Rd,
Orlando, 32812
orange.ifas.ufl.edu

Harry P. Leu Gardens
1920 N. Forest Ave,
Orlando, 32803
leugardens.org

**University of Central
Florida Arboretum**
12443 Research Pkwy,
Orlando, 32816
arboretum.ucf.edu

PINECREST
Pinecrest Gardens
11000 SW 57th Ave,
Pinecrest, 33156
pinecrestgardens.com

PUNTA GORDA
**Peace River Botanical &
Sculpture Gardens**
5950 Riverside Dr,
Punta Gorda, 33982
PeaceRiverGardens.org

QUINCY
**Gardens of the Big Bend
at University of Florida**
155 Research Rd,
Quincy, 32351
nfrec.ifas.ufl.edu/gardens.shtml

SANIBEL
**Botanical Gardens at
Sanibel Moorings Resort**
845 East Gulf Dr,
Sanibel, 33957
sanibelmoorings.com

SARASOTA
Marie Selby Botanical Gardens
811 S. Palm Ave,
Sarasota, 34236
selby.org

TALLAHASSEE
**Alfred B. Maclay
Gardens State Park**
3540 Thomasville Rd,
Tallahassee, 32309
floridastateparks.org

TAMPA
**University of South Florida
Botanical Gardens**
4202 E. Fowler Ave, NES107,
Tampa, 33620
gardens.usf.edu

VERO BEACH
McKee Botanical Garden
350 U.S. Hwy. 1,
Vero Beach, 32962
mckeegarden.org

WEST PALM BEACH
Mounts Botanical Garden
559 N. Military Trail,
West Palm Beach, 33415
mounts.org

**Unbelievable Acres
Botanic Gardens, Inc.**
470 63rd Trail North,
West Palm Beach, 33413

WINTER PARK
Mead Botanical Garden
1500 S Denning Dr,
Winter Park, 32789
meadgarden.org

GEORGIA

ADAIRSVILLE
Barnsley Resort
597 Barnsley Gardens Rd,
Adairsville, 30103
barnsleyresort.com

ATHENS
**State Botanical Garden of
Georgia, University of Georgia**
2450 S. Milledge Ave,
Athens, 30605
uga.edu/botgarden

ATLANTA
Atlanta Botanical Garden
1345 Piedmont Ave NE,
Atlanta, 30309
atlantabotanicalgarden.org

**Atlanta History Center,
Goizueta Gardens**
130 W. Paces Ferry Rd, NW,
Atlanta, 30305
AtlantaHistoryCenter.com

Historic Oakland Foundation
248 Oakland Ave, SE,
Atlanta, 30312
oaklandcemetery.com

Trees Atlanta
225 Chester Ave, SE,
Atlanta, 30316
TreesAtlanta.org

CARROLTON
University of West Georgia
1601 Maple St,
Carrolton, 30118

COLUMBUS
Columbus Botanical Garden
3603 Weems Rd,
Columbus, 31909
columbusbotanicalgarden.org

DECATUR
Woodlands Garden of Decatur
932 Scott Blvd, Decatur, 30030
woodlandsgarden.org

KENNESAW
Smith-Gilbert Gardens
2382 Pine Mountain Rd,
Kennesaw, 30152
smithgilbertgardens.com

MACON
**Waddell Barnes
Botanical Gardens**
100 College Station Dr,
Macon, 31206
mga.edu/botanical/default.aspx

MILLEDGEVILLE
Lockerly Arboretum
1534 Irwinton Rd,
Milledgeville, 31061
lockerly.org

MT. BERRY
Oak Hill & The Martha Berry Museum, Berry College
2277 Martha Berry Hwy NW,
Mt. Berry, 30149
berry.edu/oakhill

PINE MOUNTAIN
Callaway Gardens
17800 US Hwy 27
Pine Mountain, GA 31822
callawaygardens.com

SAVANNAH
Coastal Georgia Botanical Gardens
2 Canebrake Rd,
Savannah, 31419
coastalgeorgiabg.org

Andrew Low House & Garden
329 Abercorn St,
Savannah, 31401
andrewlowhouse.com

HAWAII

CAPTAIN COOK
Amy B. H. Greenwell Ethnobotanical Garden
82-6160 Hawaii Belt Rd,
Captain Cook, 96704
bishopmuseum.org/greenwell

HALEIWA
Waimea Valley
59-864 Kamehameha Hwy,
Haleiwa, 96712
waimeavalley.net

HONOLULU
Honolulu Botanical Gardens
50 N. Vineyard Blvd,
Honolulu, 96817
co.honolulu.hi.us/parks/hbg
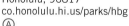

Honolulu Zoo Society
151 Kapahulu Ave,
Honolulu, 96815
honzoosoc.org

Lyon Arboretum, University of Hawaii
3860 Manoa Rd,
Honolulu, 96822
manoa.hawaii.edu\lyonarboretum

KALAHEO
National Tropical Botanical Garden
3530 Papalina Rd,
Kalaheo, 96741
ntbg.org

PAPAIKOU
Hawaii Tropical Botanical Garden
27-717 Old Mamalahoa Hwy,
Papaikou, 96781
hawaiigarden.com

PEARL CITY
University of Hawaii Urban Garden Center
955 Kamehameha Highway,
Pearl City, 96782
ctahr.hawaii.edu/ougc

IDAHO

BOISE
Idaho Botanical Garden
2355 Old Penitentiary Rd,
Boise, 83712
idahobotanicalgarden.org

COEUR D ALENE
Great Gardens In North Idaho
4221 Moccasin Rd,
Coeur D Alene, 83815
ggini.org

MOSCOW
University of Idaho Arboretum & Botanical Garden
1200 West Palouse River Dr
Moscow, 83844
uidaho.edu/arboretum/

SUN VALLEY
Sawtooth Botanical Garden
11 Gimlet Rd, Ketchum, 83340
sbgarden.org

ILLINOIS

BLOOMINGTON
Illinois Wesleyan University
1312 Park St,
Bloomington 61701

CHICAGO
Chicago Women's Park & Gardens at Clarke House Museum
1827 S Indiana Ave,
Chicago, 60616
clarkehousemuseum.org

Garfield Park Conservatory
300 North Central Park Ave,
Chicago, 60624
garfieldconservatory.org

Lincoln Park Zoo
2001 N. Clark St,
Chicago, 60614
lpzoo.org

Lurie Garden
201 East Randolph St,
Chicago, 60601
luriegarden.org

University of Chicago
5555 S. Ellis Ave, Room 300,
Chicago, 60637
uchicago.edu/docs/gardbroNS

EAST PEORIA
Illinois Central College Arboretum
One College Dr,
East Peoria, 61635
icc.edu/ait/horticulture/arboretum.asp

ELMHURST
Elmhurst College
190 S. Prospect Ave,
Elmhurst, 60126
public.elmhurst.edu/collections/arboretum

EVANSTON
The Shakespeare Garden
Northwestern University
Evanston, 60208
thegardenclubofevanston.org/
html/gardens.php

GLENCOE
Chicago Botanic Garden
1000 Lake Cook Rd,
Glencoe, 60022
chicagobotanic.org

GODFREY
**Lewis and Clark
Community College**
5800 Godfrey Rd,
Godfrey, 62035

LAKE FOREST
The Garden at Elawa Farm
1401 Middlefork Dr,
Lake Forest, 60045

LISLE
Morton Arboretum
4100 Illinois Route 53,
Lisle, 60532
mortonarb.org

MAHOMET
Mabery Gelvin Botanical Gardens
650 N. Lombard,
Mahomet, 61853

NORMAL
**Fell Arboretum at
Illinois State University**
Normal, 61790
ilstu.edu/depts/arboretum

OAK PARK
Oak Park Conservatory
615 Garfield St,
Oak Park, 60304
pdop.org

PEORIA
Luthy Botanical Garden
2520 N. Prospect Rd,
Peoria, 61603
peoriaparks.org/luthy/
luthymain.html

PETERSBURG
**Starhill Forest Arboretum
of Illinois College**
12000 Boy Scout Trail,
Petersburg, 62675
StarhillForest.com

ROCK ISLAND
Quad City Botanical Center
2525 4th Ave,
Rock Island, 61201
qcgardens.com

ROCKFORD
**Klehm Arboretum &
Botanic Garden**
2715 South Main St,
Rockford, 61102
klehm.org

Rockford Park District
401 S. Main St,
Rockford, 61101
rockfordparkdistrict.org

SPRINGFIELD
**Washington Park
Botanical Garden**
1740 West Fayette Ave,
Springfield, 62704
springfieldparks.org/facilities/
botanical

URBANA
University of Illinois Arboretum
1201 South Dorner Dr,
Urbana, 61801

WHEATON
Cantigny Foundation
1 S. 151 Winfield Rd,
Wheaton, 60189
cantignypark.com

INDIANA

ELKHART
Wellfield Botanic Gardens
1101 North Main St,
Elkhart, 46514
wellfieldgardens.org

INDIANAPOLIS
Indianapolis Museum of Art
4000 Michigan Rd,
Indianapolis, 46208
imamuseum.org

MADISON
**Lanier Mansion State
Historic Site & Gardens**
601 West First St,
Madison, 47250
indianamuseum.org

MARION
Gardens at Matter Park
1899 N. Matter Park Dr,
Marion, 46952
aneveninginthegardens.com

MUNCIE
Minnetrista
1200 N. Minnetrista Pkwy,
Muncie, 47304
minnetrista.net

NEW HARMONY
David Lenz House & Garden
324 North St,
New Harmony, 47631
newharmony.org

VALPARAISO
Taltree Arboretum & Gardens
71 North 500 West,
Valparaiso, 46385
taltree.org

WEST LAFAYETTE
**Purdue University,
Dept. of Horticulture &
Landscape Architecture**
695 Agriculture Mall Dr,
West Lafayette, 47907
hort.purdue.edu

IOWA

AMES
**Reiman Gardens,
Iowa State University**
1407 University Blvd,
Ames, 50011
reimangardens.iastate.edu

DALLAS CENTER
Brenton Arboretum
25141 260th St,
Dallas Center, 50063
thebrentonarboretum.org

DAVENPORT
Vander Veer Botanical Gardens
214 W. Central Park Ave,
Davenport, 52803
Ⓐ

DES MOINES
**Better Homes & Gardens
Test Garden**
1716 Locust St,
Des Moines, 50309
Ⓐ

**Greater Des Moines
Botanical Garden**
909 Robert D. Ray Dr,
Des Moines, 50309
dmbotanicalgarden.com
Ⓐ

DUBUQUE
**Dubuque Arboretum &
Botanical Gardens**
3800 Arboretum Dr,
Dubuque, 52001
dubuquearboretum.com
Ⓐ

MADRID
Iowa Arboretum
1875 Peach Ave,
Madrid, 50156
iowaarboretum.org

WATERLOO
**Cedar Valley Arboretum
& Botanic Gardens**
1927 E. Orange Rd,
Waterloo, 50701
cedarvalleyarboretum.org
Ⓐ

KANSAS

HESSTON
Dyck Arboretum of the Plains
177 W. Hickory St,
Hesston, 67062
dyckarboretum.org
Ⓐ

KANSAS CITY
**University of Kansas
Medical Center**
3901 Rainbow Blvd,
Kansas City, 66160
kumc.edu

MANHATTAN
Kansas State University Gardens
2021 Throckmorton Hall,
Manhattan, 66506
ksu.edu/gardens

OVERLAND PARK
**Overland Park Arboretum
& Botanical Gardens**
8909 West 179th St,
Overland Park, 66085
opkansas.org/_vis/arboretum
Ⓐ

WICHITA
Botanica, The Wichita Gardens
701 North Amidon,
Wichita, 67203
botanica.org

KENTUCKY

BOWLING GREEN
Baker Arboretum
4801 Morgantown Rd,
Bowling Green, 42101
wku.edu/bakerarboretum/

CRESTWOOD
Yew Dell Gardens
6220 Old LaGrange Rd,
Crestwood, 40014
yewdellgardens.org
Ⓖ

FRANKFORT
Liberty Hall Historic Site
202 Wilkinson St,
Frankfort, 40601
libertyhall.org
Ⓒ

CLERMONT
**Bernheim Arboretum
& Research Forest**
2499 Clermont Rd,
Clermont, 40110
bernheim.org

LEXINGTON
Gainesway Farm
3750 Paris Pike,
Lexington, 40511

**The Arboretum, State Botanical
Garden of Kentucky**
500 Alumni Dr,
Lexington, 40503
ca.uky.edu/arboretum

LOUISVILLE
Cave Hill Cemetery
701 Baxter Ave,
Louisville, 40204
cavehillcemetery.com

OWENSBORO
**Western Kentucky
Botanical Garden**
25 Carter Rd,
Owensboro, 42301
wkbg.org

UNION
Boone County Arboretum
9190 Camp Ernst Rd,
Union, 41091
bcarboretum.org

VERSAILLES
Gainsborough Farm
7200 Steele Rd,
Versailles, 40383
darleyamerica.com

LOUISIANA

AVERY ISLAND
Jungle Gardens
LA-329, Avery Island, 70513
junglegardens.org

BATON ROUGE
Friends of Hilltop Arboretum
11855 Highland Rd
Baton Rouge, 70810
lsu.edu/hilltop

**LSU AgCenter Botanic
Gardens at Burden**
4560 Essen Lane,
Baton Rouge, 70809
lsuagcenter.com

NEW ORLEANS
Longue Vue House & Gardens
7 Bamboo Rd,
New Orleans, 70124
longuevue.com/

New Orleans Botanical Garden
1 Palm Dr,
New Orleans, 70124
neworleanscitypark.com

SHREVEPORT
**Gardens of The American
Rose Center**
8877 Jefferson Paige Rd,
Shreveport, 71119
ars.org

MAINE

BOOTHBAY
**Coastal Maine
Botanical Gardens**
132 Botanical Gardens Dr,
Boothbay, 04537
mainegardens.org

PORTLAND
Tate House Museum & Garden
1270 Westbrook St,
Portland, 04102
tatehouse.org

SEAL HARBOR
**Mount Desert Land &
Garden Preserve**
92 Cooksey Dr,
Seal Harbor, 04675
gardenpreserve.org

SOUTH PARIS
**McLaughlin Garden
& Homestead**
97 Main St,
South Paris, 04281
mclaughlingarden.org

MARYLAND

BALTIMORE
**Baltimore Conservatory
Association, Inc.**
3100 Swann Dr,
Baltimore, 21217

CHEVY CHASE
Chevy Chase Club
6100 Connecticut Ave,
Chevy Chase, 20815
chevychaseclub.org

COLLEGE PARK
**University of Maryland
Arboretum & Botanical Garden**
1600 Service Bldg,
College Park, 20742
arboretum.umd.edu

DOWELL
**Annmarie Sculpture
Garden & Arts Center**
13480 Dowell Rd,
Dowell, 20629
annmariegarden.org

EDGEWATER
**Historic London Town
and Gardens**
839 London Town Rd,
Edgewater, 21037
historiclondontown.org

FREDERICK
High Glen Gardens
6450 Christopher's Crossing,
Frederick, 21702
facebook.com/HighGlenGardens

MIDDLETOWN
Surreybrooke
8537 Hollow Rd,
Middletown, 21769
surreybrooke.com

MONKTON
Ladew Topiary Gardens
3535 Jarrettsville Pike,
Monkton 21111
ladewgardens.com

POTOMAC
Glenstone Museum
12002 Glen Rd,
Potomac, 20854
glenstone.org

RIDGELY
Adkins Arboretum
12610 Eveland Rd,
Ridgely, 21660
adkinsarboretum.org

ROCKVILLE
Linden Botanic Garden
13304 Ardennes Ave,
Rockville, 20851
lindenbg.org

SALISBURY
Salisbury University Arboretum
1101 Camden Ave,
Salisbury, 21801
salisbury.edu/arboretum

WHEATON
Brookside Gardens
1800 Glenallan Ave,
Wheaton, 20902
brooksidegardens.org

MASSACHUSETTS

BEVERLY
The Trustees, Long Hill
572 Essex St,
Beverly, 01915
thetrustees.org

BOYLSTON
Tower Hill Botanic Garden
11 French Dr,
Boylston, 01505
towerhillbg.org

CAMBRIDGE
Mount Auburn Cemetery
580 Mount Auburn St,
Cambridge, 02138
mountauburn.org

FALMOUTH
Highfield Hall & Gardens
56 Highfield Dr,
Falmouth, 02541
highfield.org

FRAMINGHAM
**New England Wild Flower
Society, Garden In The Woods**
180 Hemenway Rd,
Framingham, 01701
newenglandWILD.org

MILTON
Mary M. B. Wakefield Estate
1465 Brush Hill Rd,
Milton 02186
wakefieldtrust.org

NEWTON
Newton Cemetery
791 Walnut St,
Newton, 02459
newcemcorp.org

NORTHAMPTON
**Botanic Garden of Smith
College, Lyman Conservatory**
16 College Lane,
Northampton, 01063
smith.edu/garden

QUINCY
**The Gardens at Quincy
Homestead**
24 Butler Rd, Quincy 02169
nscda.org/museums2/
ma-quincyhomestead.html

ROSLINDALE
**Arnold Arboretum of
Harvard University**
1300 Centre St,
Roslindale, 02131
arboretum.harvard.edu

SANDWICH
Heritage Museums & Gardens
67 Grove St,
Sandwich, 02563
heritagemuseums.org

STOCKBRIDGE
Berkshire Botanical Garden
5 W Stockbridge Rd,
Stockbridge, 01262
berkshirebotanical.org

WELLESLEY
**Massachusetts
Horticultural Society**
900 Washington St,
Wellesley, 02482
masshort.org

WELLESLEY
Wellesley College Botanic Gardens
106 Central St,
Wellesley, 02481
wellesley.edu/wcbg

WEST TISBURY
Polly Hill Arboretum
809 State Rd,
West Tisbury, 02575
pollyhillarboretum.org

MICHIGAN

ANN ARBOR
**Matthaei Botanical Gardens
& Nichols Arboretum**
1800 North Dixboro Rd,
Ann Arbor, 48105
mbgna.umich.edu

BERRIEN SPRINGS
Andrews University Arboretum
8475 E. Campus Circle Dr,
Berrien Springs, 47104

EAST LANSING
**W.J. Beal Botanical Garden,
Michigan State University**
408 West Circle Dr, Rm 412,
East Lansing, 48824
cpp.msu.edu/beal

FLINT
**Applewood—The C.S.
Mott Estate**
1400 East Kearsley St,
Flint, 48503
applewood.org

GRAND RAPIDS
**Frederik Meijer Gardens
& Sculpture Park**
1000 East Beltline NE,
Grand Rapids, 49525
meijergardens.org

GROSSE POINTE SHORES
Historic Ford Estates
1100 Lake Shore Rd,
Grosse Pointe Shores, 48236
fordhouse.org

HILLSDALE

**Slayton Arboretum of
Hillsdale College**
Dept. of Biology, 33 E. College
St, Hillsdale, 49242
hillsdale.edu/arboretum

HOLLAND

Windmill Island Gardens
1 Lincoln Ave,
Holland, 49423
windmillisland.org

MIDLAND

Dow Gardens
1018 W. Main St,
Midland, 48640
dowgardens.org

NILES

Fernwood Botanical Garden
13988 Range Line Rd,
Niles, 49120
fernwoodbotanical.org

TAYLOR

Taylor Conservatory Foundation
Box 1903, Taylor, 48180
taylorconservatory@sbcglobal.
net

TIPTON

Hidden Lake Gardens,
Michigan State University,
Tipton, 49287
hiddenlakegardens.msu.edu

TRAVERSE CITY

**Botanic Garden at
Historic Barns Park**
1490 Red Dr,
Traverse City, 49684
northwestmichigangarden.org

MINNESOTA

CHASKA

Minnesota Landscape Arboretum
3675 Arboretum Dr,
Chaska, 55318
arboretum.umn.edu

MINNEAPOLIS

Project Sweetie Pie
1418 Oliver Ave. N,
Minneapolis, 55411
projectsweetiepie.org

ST. PAUL

Como Park Zoo & Conservatory
1225 Estabrook Dr,
St. Paul, 55103
comozooconservatory.org

ST. PETER

**Linnaeus Arboretum,
Gustavus Adolphus College**
800 West College Ave,
St. Peter, 56082
gustavus.edu/arboretum

MISSISSIPPI

JACKSON

The Oaks House Museum
823 North Jefferson St,
Jackson, 39202
theoakshousemuseum.org

PICAYUNE

Crosby Arboretum
370 Ridge Rd, Picayune, 39466
crosbyarboretum.msstate.edu

UNIVERSITY

**Maynard W Quimby
Medicinal Plant Garden**
301 Insight Park Ave,
University, 38677

MISSOURI

COLUMBIA

Mizzou Botanic Garden
181 General Services Building,
Columbia, 65211
gardens.missouri.edu

KINGSVILLE

Powell Gardens
1609 NW U.S. Hwy. 50,
Kingsville, 64061
powellgardens.org

NEW BLOOMFIELD

Prairie Garden Trust
3914 Foxdale Rd,
New Bloomfield, 65063
prairiegardentrust.org

STE. GENEVIEVE

Bolduc House Museum
125 South Main St,
Ste. Genevieve, 63670
bolduchouse.org
ⓒ

ST. LOUIS

Bellefontaine Cemetery
4947 W. Florissant Ave,
St. Louis, 63115
bellefontainecemetery.org
Ⓐ

Missouri Botanical Garden
4344 Shaw Blvd,
St. Louis, 63110
mobot.org
Ⓐ

Tower Grove Park
4256 Magnolia Ave,
St. Louis, 63110
Ⓐ

SPRINGFIELD

**Springfield-Greene County
Botanical Center**
2400 S. Scenic,
Springfield, 65807
botanicalcenter.org
Ⓐ

STRAFFORD
Lovett Pinetum
2706 Pearson Valley Dr,
Strafford, 65757
lovettpinetum.org

NEBRASKA

LINCOLN
Nebraska Statewide Arboretum
University of Nebraska-Lincoln,
Lincoln, 68583
arboretum.unl.edu

**University of Nebraska Lincoln
Botanical Garden & Arboretum**
1309 N. 17th, Lincoln, 68588
unl.edu/landscape/bga/

OMAHA
Lauritzen Gardens
100 Bancroft St,
Omaha, 68108
omahabotanicalgardens.org

NEVADA

LAS VEGAS
Springs Preserve
333 S Valley View Blvd,
Las Vegas, 89107
springspreserve.org

RENO
**Wilbur D. May Arboretum
& Botanical Garden**
1595 North Sierra St,
Reno, 89503
maycenter.com

NEW HAMPSHIRE

LEE
Bedrock Gardens
45 High Rd, Lee, 03861
bedrockgardens.org

NEWBURY
The Fells
456 NH-103A, Newbury, 03255
TheFells.org

PORTSMOUTH
**Moffatt-Ladd House &
Garden Museum**
154 Market St,
Portsmouth, 03801
moffattladd.org

NEW JERSEY

HAMILTON
Grounds For Sculpture
80 Sculptor Way,
Hamilton, 08619
groundsforsculpture.org

HIGHTSTOWN
**Meadow Lakes—The Robert
A. Winters Arboretum**
300 Etra Rd,
Hightstown, 08520
phsnet.org/meadow.asp

LAKEWOOD
**Sister Mary Grace Burns
Arboretum, Georgian
Court University**
900 Lakewood Ave,
Lakewood, 08701
georgian.edu/arboretum

MEDFORD
**Barton Arboretum & Nature
Preserve of Medford Leas**
One Medford Leas Way,
Medford, 08055
medfordleas.org

MONTCLAIR
Van Vleck House & Gardens
21 Van Vleck St,
Montclair, 07042
vanvleck.org

MORRISTOWN
Morris County Park Commission
300 Mendham Rd
Morris Township, 07960
morrisparks.net

**North American Butterfly
Association**
4 Delaware Rd,
Morristown, 07960
naba.org

NEW BRUNSWICK
**Rutgers Gardens, Cook
College/Rutgers University**
112 Ryders Lane,
New Brunswick, 08901
rutgersgardens.rutgers.edu

RINGWOOD
**Skylands Association, New
Jersey State Botanical Garden**
2 Morris Rd, Ringwood, 07456
njbg.org

SHORT HILLS
Greenwood Gardens
274 Old Short Hills Rd,
Short Hills, 07078
greenwoodgardens.org

SUMMIT
Reeves-Reed Arboretum
165 Hobart Ave,
Summit, 07901
reeves-reedarboretum.org

VERNON
Meadowburn Farm
41 Meadowburn Rd,
Vernon, 07462
meadowburnfarm.com

WAYNE
Friends of Laurelwood Arboretum
725 Pines Lake Dr W,
Wayne, 07470
laurelwoodarboretum.org

WESTFIELD
Fairview Cemetery
1100 E BRd St,
Westfield, 07090
westfieldnj.com/fairview/

NEW MEXICO

ALBUQUERQUE
ABQ BioPark Botanic Garden
2601 Central Ave, NW,
Albuquerque, 87104
cabq.gov/biopark/garden/index.
html

SANTA FE
Santa Fe Botanical Garden
715 Camino Lejo,
Santa Fe, 87505
santafebotanicalgarden.org

NEW YORK

AMENIA
Wethersfield
214 Pugsley Hill Rd,
Amenia, 12501
wethersfieldgarden.org

ANNANDALE ON HUDSON
Bard College Arboretum
30 Campus Rd,
Annandale on Hudson, 12504
inside.bard.edu/horticulture

Blithewood Garden
Bard College, Blithewood Rd,
Annandale on Hudson, 12504
inside.bard.edu/horticulture

AUSTERLITZ
**Steepletop—Poet Edna St.
Vincent Millay's Garden**
436 East Hill Rd,
Austerlitz, 12017
millay.org

BRIDGEHAMPTON
**Peconic Land Trust—
Bridge Gardens**
36 Mitchells Ln,
Bridgehampton, 11932
peconiclandtrust.org

BRONX
**American Society of
Botanical Artists**
The New York Botanical Garden,
2900 Southern Blvd,
Bronx, 10458
asba-art.org

**Bartow-Pell Mansion
Museum and Gardens**
895 Shore Rd, Bronx, 10464
bpmm.org

New York Botanical Garden
2900 Southern Blvd,
Bronx, 10458
nybg.org

Van Cortlandt House Museum
6035 BRdway, Bronx, 10471
vchm.org

Wave Hill
675 W. 252nd St,
Bronx, 10471
wavehill.org

BROOKLYN
Brooklyn Botanic Garden
1000 Washington Ave,
Brooklyn, 11225
bbg.org

Brooklyn Bridge Park
334 Furman St,
Brooklyn, 11201
brooklynbridgeparknyc.org

Green-Wood Cemetery
500 25th St,
Brooklyn, 11232
greenwoodcemetery.org

BUFFALO
**Buffalo & Erie County
Botanical Garden**
2655 S. Park Ave,
Buffalo, 14218
buffalogardens.com

**Forest Lawn Cemetery
& Arboretum**
1411 Delaware Ave,
Buffalo, 14209
forest-lawn.com

CANANDAIGUA
Sonnenberg Gardens & Mansion
151 Charlotte St,
Canandaigua, 14424
sonnenberg.org

COBLESKILL
**Cobleskill College, SUNYPlant
Science Dept.State**
Route 7, Cobleskill, 12043
cobleskill.edu

COLD SPRING
Garden Conservancy
20 Nazareth Way,
Cold Spring, 10524
gardenconservancy.org

Stonecrop Gardens
81 Stonecrop Lane,
Cold Spring, 10516
stonecrop.org

EAST HAMPTON
LongHouse Reserve
133 Hands Creek Rd,
East Hampton, 11937
longhouse.org

ESPERANCE
Landis Arboretum
Lape Rd, Esperance, 12066
landisarboretum.org

FLUSHING
Queens Botanical Garden
43-50 Main St,
Flushing, 11355
queensbotanical.org

GARDEN CITY
Arboretum at Adelphi University
150 South Ave,
Garden City, 11530
adelphi.edu

GENEVA

Cornell University NY State Agricultural Experiment Station
630 W. North St,
Geneva, 14456

GREAT RIVER

Bayard Cutting Arboretum
440 Montauk Hwy,
Great River, 11739
bayardcuttingarboretum.com

HOLBROOK

Sachem Public Library
150 Holbrook Rd,
Holbrook, 11741
sachemlibrary.org

HYDE PARK

Roosevelt Vanderbilt National Historic Site
4097 Albany Post Rd,
Hyde Park, 12538
nps.gov/hofr/roosevelt-vanderbilt-national-historic-sites.htm

ITHACA

Cornell Plantations
One Plantations Rd,
Ithaca, 14850
cornellplantations.org

KATONAH

Lasdon Park And Arboretum
Route 35, Katonah, 10536

LOCUST VALLEY

Bailey Arboretum
194 Bayview Rd,
Locust Valley, 11560
baileyarboretum.org

MILLBROOK

Innisfree
362 Tyrell Rd,
Millbrook, 12545
innisfreegarden.org

MILL NECK

The John P. Humes Japanese Stroll Garden
Dogwood Ln, Mill Neck, 11765

NEW YORK

Battery Park City Parks Conservancy
75 Battery Place,
New York, 10280
bpcparks.org

Friends of the High Line
thehighline.org

NSCDA Museum House & Garden
215 East 71st St,
New York, 10021
nscdny.org

OLD WESTBURY

Old Westbury Gardens
71 Old Westbury Rd,
Old Westbury, 11568
oldwestburygardens.org

OYSTER BAY

Planting Fields Arboretum
1395 Planting Fields Rd,
Oyster Bay, 11771
plantingfields.org

POCANTICO HILLS

Historic Hudson Valley
639 Bedford Rd,
Pocantico Hills, 10951
hudsonvalley.org

POUGHKEEPSIE

Locust Grove
2683 South Rd,
Poughkeepsie, 12601
lgny.org

ROCHESTER

George Eastman Museum
900 East Ave,
Rochester, 14607
eastmanhouse.org

SLINGERLANDS

Pine Hollow Arboretum
34 Pine Hollow Rd,
Slingerlands, 12159
pinehollowarboretum.org

TANNERSVILLE

Mountain Top Arboretum
County Rd 23C & Maude Adams Rd, Tannersville, 12485
mtarboretum.org

VALHALLA

The Native Plant Center at WCC
75 Grasslands Rd, 10595
nativeplantcenter.org

NORTH CAROLINA

ASHEVILLE

Botanical Gardens at Asheville
151 W.T. Weaver Blvd,
Asheville, 28804
ashevillebotanicalgardens.org

North Carolina Arboretum
100 Frederick Law Olmsted Way,
Asheville, 28806
ncarboretum.org

BELMONT

Daniel Stowe Botanical Garden
6500 S. New Hope Rd,
Belmont, 28012
dsbg.org

CHAPEL HILL

North Carolina Botanical Garden
UNC at Chapel Hill,
Chapel Hill, 27517
ncbg.unc.edu

CHARLOTTE

Bartlett Tree Research Laboratories & Arboretum
13768 Hamilton Rd,
Charlotte, 28278
bartlett.com

UNC Charlotte Botanical Gardens
9201 University City Blvd,
Charlotte, 28223
gardens.uncc.edu

Wing Haven
248 Ridgewood Ave,
Charlotte, 28209
winghavengardens.org

DURHAM
Sarah P. Duke Gardens
Duke University, 420 Anderson
St, Durham, 27708
gardens.duke.edu

ELON COLLEGE
Elon University
Campus Box 2000,
Elon College, 27244
elon.edu

FAYETTEVILLE
Cape Fear Botanical Garden
536 N Eastern Blvd,
Fayetteville, 28301
capefearbg.org

HIGH POINT
**Mariana H. Qubein Arboretum
& Botanical Gardens at
High Point University**
833 Montlieu Ave, Drawer 53,
High Point, 27262
highpoint.edu

HILLSBOROUGH
Montrose
320 St. Mary's Rd, Hillsborough,
27278

KERNERSVILLE
Paul J. Ciener Botanical Garden
215 S. Main St,
Kernersville, 27284
cienerbotanicalgarden.org

LAKE LURE
Lake Lure Flowering Bridge, Inc.
Town Center Walkway,
Lake Lure, 28746
lakelurefloweringbridge.com

LAKE TOXAWAY
Southern Highlands Reserve
558 Summit Ridge Rd, 2
Lake Toxaway, 8747
southernhighlandsreserve.org

PINEHURST
Sandhills Horticultural Gardens
3395 Airport Rd,
Pinehurst, 28374
sandhillshorticulturalgardens.com

RALEIGH
Haywood Hall
211 New Bern Place,
Raleigh, 27601
haywoodhall.org

JC Raulston Arboretum
4415 Beryl Rd, Raleigh
ncsu.edu/jcraulstonarboretum

**Joel Lane Museum
House & Garden**
160 Main St, Raleigh
joellane.org

Juniper Level Botanic Garden
9241 Sauls Rd,
Raleigh, 27603
juniperlevelbotanicgarden.org

WILMINGTON
Airlie Gardens
300 Airlie Rd,
Wilmington, 28403
airliegardens.org

Burgwin-Wright House & Gardens
224 Market St,
Wilmington, 28401

**New Hanover Extension
Arboretum**
6206 Oleander Dr,
Wilmington, 28403
gardeningnhc.org

WINSTON-SALEM
Old Salem Museums & Gardens
900 Old Salem Rd,
Winston-Salem, 27101
oldsalem.org

**Reynolda Gardens of
Wake Forest University**
100 Reynolda Village,
Winston-Salem, 27106
reynoldagardens.org

OHIO

AKRON
Akron Zoological Park
500 Edgewood Ave,
Akron, 44307
akronzoo.org

ALLIANCE
**Beech Creek Botanical
Garden & Nature Preserve**
11929 Beech St NE,
Alliance, 44601
beechcreekgardens.org

AVON
Miller Nature Preserve
2739 Center Rd, Avon, 44011

BOWLING GREEN
Simpson Garden Park
1291 Conneaut Ave,
Bowling Green, 43402

CINCINNATI
The Betts House
416 Clark St,
Cincinnati, 45203
thebettshouse.org

Cincinnati Zoo & Botanical Garden
3400 Vine St,
Cincinnati, 45220
cincinnatizoo.org

Spring Grove Cemetery & Arboretum
4521 Spring Grove Ave,
Cincinnati, 45232
springgrove.org

CLEVELAND
Cleveland Botanical Garden
11030 East Blvd,
Cleveland, 44106
cbgarden.org

Lake View Cemetery
12316 Euclid Ave,
Cleveland, 44106
lakeviewcemetery.com

COLUMBUS
Franklin Park Conservatory & Botanical Gardens
1777 E. BRd St,
Columbus, 43203
fpconservatory.org

Friends of the Topiary Park
480 E Town St,
Columbus, 43215
topiarygarden.org

Chadwick Arboretum & Learning Gardens
Ohio State University, 2001
Fyffe Court, Columbus, 43210
chadwickarboretum.osu.edu

COSHOCTON
Clary Gardens
588 W. Chestnut St,
Coshocton, 43812
clarygardens.org

DAYTON
American Veterans Heritage Center
Building 120, 4100 W. Third
St,Dayton, 45428
americanveteransheritage.org

GROVE CITY
Gardens at Gantz Farm
4035 BRdway,
Grove City, 43123
grovecityohio.gov/gantz

INDIAN HILL
Stanley M. Rowe Arboretum
4600 Muchmore Rd,
Indian Hil,l 45243

KIRTLAND
Holden Arboretum
9500 Sperry Rd,
Kirtland, 44094
holdenarb.org

The Herb Society of America
9019 Kirtland Chardon Rd,
Kirtland, 44094
herbsociety.org

MANSFIELD
Kingwood Center Gardens
50 North Trimble Rd,
Mansfield, 44906
kingwoodcenter.org

NEWARK
Dawes Arboretum
7770 Jacksontown Rd, SE,
Newark, 43056
dawesarb.org

SHARONVILLE
Kemper Log House Museum— Historic Kitchen & Herb Garden
11450 Lebanon Rd,
Sharonville, 45241
heritagevillagecincinnati.org
Ⓒ

TOLEDO
Toledo Botanical Garden
5403 Elmer Dr, Toledo, 43615
toledogarden.org

WAKEMAN
Schoepfle Garden
11106 Market St,
Wakeman, 44889
metroparks.cc

WARREN
Draime Estate Gardens of Kent State University
8473 Hunters Trail SE,
Warren, 44484
kent.edu/horticulture

WESTERVILLE
Inniswood Metro Gardens
940 S. Hempstead Rd,
Westerville, 43081
inniswood.org

WOOSTER
Secrest Arboretum
1680 Madison Ave,
Wooster, 44691
secrest.osu.edu

YOUNGSTOWN
Fellows Riverside Gardens
123 McKinley Ave,
Youngstown 44509,
millcreekmetroparks.org

ZANESVILLE
Mission Oaks Gardens
1901 Norwood Blvd,
Zanesville, 43701

OKLAHOMA

OKLAHOMA CITY
Myriad Gardens Foundation
301 West Reno,
Oklahoma City, 73102
myriadgardens.com

Oklahoma City Zoo & Botanical Garden
2101 NE 50th St,
Oklahoma City, 73111
okczoo.com

STILLWATER
Botanic Garden at Oklahoma State University
360 Agriculture Hall,
Stillwater, 74078
hortla.okstate.edu

TULSA
Philbrook Museum of Art
2727 S Rockford Rd,
Tulsa, 74114
philbrook.org

Tulsa Botanic Garden
3900 Tulsa Botanic Dr,
Tulsa, 74127
tulsabotanic.org

Tulsa Garden Center
2435 S. Peoria Ave,
Tulsa, 74114
tulsagardencenter.com

OREGON

ELKTON
Elkton Community Education Center
15850 Hwy 38 W,
Elkton, 97436
elktonbutterflies.com

LAKE OSWEGO
Friends of the Rogerson Clematis Collection
PO Box 734,
Lake Oswego, 97034
rogersonclematiscollection.org

NEWBERG
Hoover-Minthorn House
115 South River St,
Newberg, 97132
thehoover-minthorn
housemuseum.org

PORTLAND
Hoyt Arboretum And Herbarium
4000 SW Fairview Blvd,
Portland, 97221
HoytArboretum.org

Lan Su Chinese Garden
239 NW Everett St,
Porland, 97209
lansugarden.org

Leach Botanical Garden
6704 SE 122nd Ave,
Portland, 97236
leachgarden.org

Oregon Zoo/Horticulture
4001 SW Canyon Rd,
Portland, 97221
oregonzoo.org

SALEM
Gaiety Hollow
545 Mission St,
Salem, 97308
lord-schryverconservancy.org

SILVERTON
Oregon Garden Foundation
879 W. Main St,
Silverton, 97381
oregongarden.org

PENNSYLVANIA

ALLENTOWN
Cedar Crest College
100 College Dr,
Allentown, 18104
cedarcrest.edu

AMBLER
Temple University
580 Meetinghouse Rd,
Ambler, 19002
temple.edu/Ambler

BATH
Graver Arboretum of Muhlenberg College
1597 Bushkill Center Rd,
Bath 18014
muhlenberg.edu/cultural/graver

BRYN MAWR
Bryn Mawr College
101 N. Merion Ave,
Bryn Mawr, 19010

CALIFORNIA
California University of Pennsylvania
Box 31, 250 University Ave,
California, 15419
calu.edu

CHADDS FORD
Brandywine Conservancy & Museum of Art
1 Hoffman's Mill Rd/Route 1,
Chadds Ford, 19317
brandywinemuseum.org

DEVON
Jenkins Arboretum & Gardens
631 Berwyn Baptist Rd,
Devon, 19333
jenkinsarboretum.org

DOYLESTOWN
Henry Schmieder Arboretum
Delaware Valley College,
700 E. Butler Ave,
Doylestown, 18901
delval.edu/arboretum

EDINBORO
Goodell Gardens & Homestead
221 Waterford St,
Edinboro, 16412
goodellgardens.org

ERIE
Arboretum at Penn State Erie, Behrend College
4701 College Dr, Erie, 16563
psbehrend.psu.edu

Erie Zoological Society
423 W. 38th St, Erie, 16508
eriezoo.org/discover_gardens.htm

GERMANTOWN
Stenton House Museum & Gardens
4601 N. 18th St,
Germantown, 19140
stenton.org

GLADWYNE
Henry Foundation for Botanical Research
801 Stony Lane,
Gladwyne, 19035
gladwyne.com/henry_foundation.htm

HARRISBURG
HACC, Central Pennsylvania's Community College
1 HACC Dr,
Harrisburg, 17110
hacc.edu

HAVERFORD
Haverford College Arboretum
370 Lancaster Ave,
Haverford, 19041
haverford.edu/arboretum

INDIANA
Allegheny Arboretum at Indiana University of Pennsylvania
650 South 13th St,
Indiana, 15705
iup.edu/arboretum

KENNETT SQUARE
Longwood Gardens, Inc.
Route 1, Kennett Square, 19348
longwoodgardens.org

KUTZTOWN
Kutztown University
427 Baldy St,
Kutztown, 19530
kutztown.edu

MEADOWBROOK
PHS Meadowbrook Farm
1633 Washington Lane,
Meadowbrook, 19046
meadowbrookfarm.org

MEADVILLE
Allegheny College
520 North Main St Box 28,
Meadville, 16335

MEDIA
Tyler Arboretum
515 Painter Rd, Media, 19063
TylerArboretum.org

MERION
Arboretum of the Barnes Foundation
300 N. Latch'S Lane,
Merion, 19066
barnesfoundation.org

NEW HOPE
Bowman's Hill Wildflower Preserve
1635 River Rd,
New Hope, 18938
bhwp.org

PHILADELPHIA
Awbury Arboretum
One Awbury Rd,
Philadelphia, 19138
awbury.org

Bartram's Garden
54th St & Lindbergh Blvd,
Philadelphia, 19143
bartramsgarden.org

Cathedral Village
600 East Cathedral Rd,
Philadelphia, 19128
cathedralvillage.com

Morris Arboretum of the University of Pennsylvania
100 East Northwestern Ave,
Philadelphia, 19118
morrisarboretum.org

Shofuso Japanese House & Garden
5070 Parkside Ave. #2104,
Philadelphia, 19131
japanesehouse.org

PITTSBURGH
Phipps Conservatory & Botanical Gardens
One Schenley Park,
Pittsburgh, 15213
phipps.conservatory.org

Pittsburgh Botanic Garden
850 Poplar St,
Pittsburgh, 15220
pittsburghbotanicgarden.org

Pittsburgh Parks Conservancy
2000 Technology Dr, Suite 200,
Pittsburgh, 15206

POINT PLEASANT
Gardens at Mill Fleurs
27 Cafferty Rd,
Point Pleasant, 18950
thegardensatmillfleurs.com

POTTSTOWN
Welkinweir
1368 Prizer Rd,
Pottstown, 19465
welkinweir.org

SCRANTON
Marywood University Arboretum
2300 Adams Ave,
Scranton, 18509
marywood.edu/arboretum

SWARTHMORE
Scott Arboretum of Swarthmore College
500 College Ave,
Swarthmore, 19081
scottarboretum.org

UNIVERSITY PARK
Arboretum at Penn State
320 Forest Resources Building,
University Park, 16802
arboretum.psu.edu

Penn State University
Office of Physical Plant
159 A Office of Physical Plant,
University Park, 16802
opp.psu.edu

WAYNE
Chanticleer Foundation
786 Church Rd, Wayne19087
chanticleergarden.org

WRIGHTSTOWN
Hortulus Farm Gardens
60 Thompson Mill Rd,
Wrightstown, 18940
hortulusfarm.com

RHODE ISLAND

BRISTOL
Blithewold Mansion,
Gardens & Arboretum
101 Ferry Rd, Bristol, 02809
blithewold.org

NEWPORT
Newport Tree Society
P.O. Box 863, Newport, 02840
newportarboretum.org

MIDDLETOWN
Whitehall Museum House
311 Berkeley Ave,
Middletown, 02842
whitehallmuseum.org

PROVIDENCE
The Stephen Hopkins
House & Garden
15 Hopkins St,
Providence, 02903
nscdarhodeisland.org

Swan Point Cemetery
585 Blackstone Blvd,
Providence, 02906
swanpointcemetery.com

SOUTH CAROLINA

CHARLESTON
Magnolia Plantations & Gardens
3550 Ashley River Rd,
Charleston, 29414
magnoliaplantation.com

CLEMSON
South Carolina Botanical Garden
Clemson University,
Clemson, 29634
virtual.clemson.edu/groups/scbg

COLUMBIA
Historic Columbia Foundation
1601 Richland St,
Columbia, 29201

Riverbanks Zoo &
Botanical Garden
500 Wildlife Pkwy,
Columbia, 29210
riverbanks.org

HARTSVILLE
Kalmia Gardens of Coker College
1624 W. Carolina Ave,
Hartsville, 29550
coker.edu/kalmia

LAKE CITY
Moore Farms Botanical Garden
100 New Zion Rd,
Lake City, 29560
moorefarmsbg.org

PAWLEYS ISLAND
Brookgreen Gardens
1931 Brookgreen Garden Dr,
Murrells Inlet, 29576
brookgreen.org

SPARTANBURG
Spartanburg Community College
107 Community College Dr,
Spartanburg, 29303
sccsc.edu

SOUTH DAKOTA

BROOKINGS
McCrory Gardens
South Dakota State University,
Brookings, 57007
mccrorygardens.com

CHARLESTON
The Powder Magazine Museum
& Colonial Revival Garden
79 Cumberland St,
Charleston, 29401
powdermag.org

HERMOSA
Great Plains Native Plant Society
P.O. Box 321, Hermosa, 57744
gpnps.org

TENNESSEE

CHATTANOOGA
Reflection Riding Arboretum
& Nature Center
400 Garden Rd,
Chattanooga, 37419
reflectionriding.org

KNOXVILLE
Knoxville Botanical
Garden and Arboretum
2743 Wimpole Ave,
Knoxville, 37914
knoxgarden.org

Lakeshore Park
6410 S Northshore Dr,
Knoxville, 37919
cityofknoxville.org/parks/
lakeshore.asp

University of Tennessee Gardens
2431 Joe Johnson Dr,
Knoxville, 37996
utgardens.tennessee.edu

University of Tennessee-
Facilities Services,
2233 Volunteer Blvd,
Knoxville, 37996
pp.utk.edu

MEMPHIS
Dixon Gallery & Gardens
4339 Park Ave,
Memphis, 38117
dixon.org

NASHVILLE
Cheekwood Botanical
Garden & Museum of Art
1200 Forrest Park Dr,
Nashville, 37205
cheekwood.org

Historic Travellers
Rest Plantation
636 Farrell Pkwy,
Nashville, 37220
travellersrestplantation.org

Vanderbilt University
122 Bryan Bldg,
Nashville, 37240

UNION CITY
Discovery Park of America
830 Everett Blvd,
Union City, 38261
discoveryparkofamerica.com

WHITE BLUFF
Arboretum at Interstate
Packaging
2285 Hwy. 47 North
White Bluff, 37187
interstatepkg.com/AboutIP.htm

TEXAS

AUSTIN
Lady Bird Johnson
Wildflower Center
La Crosse Ave, Austin, 78739
wildflower.org

CORPUS CHRISTI
South Texas Botanical
Gardens & Nature Center
8545 S. Staples St,
Corpus Christi, 78413
stxbot.org

DALLAS
Dallas Arboretum &
Botanical Society
8617 Garland Rd,
Dallas, 75218
dallasarboretum.org

Dallas Baptist University
3000 Mt. Creek Pkwy,
Dallas, 75211

Texas Discovery Gardens
3601 Martin Luther King
Jr Blvd, Dallas, 75210
texasdiscoverygardens.org

EL PASO
Chihuahuan Desert Gardens
University of Texas at El Paso
500 W. University Ave,
El Paso, 79968
utep.edu/museum

FORT DAVIS
Chihuahuan Desert
Research Institute
43869 TX-118,
Fort Davis, 79734
cdri.org

FORT WORTH
Fort Worth Botanic Garden
3220 Botanic Garden Blvd,
Fort Worth, 76107
fwbg.org

HEMPSTEAD
Peckerwood Garden
20559 FM 359 Rd,
Hempstead, 77445
PeckerwoodGarden.org

HOUSTON
Houston Botanic Garden
3701 Kirby Dr, Houston, 77027
houstonbotanicgarden.org

HUMBLE
Mercer Botanic Gardens
22306 Aldine Westfield Rd,
Humble, 77338
hcp4.net/mercer

MINERAL WELLS
Clark Gardens Botanical Park
567 Maddux Rd,
Weatherford, 76088
clarkgardens.com

ORANGE
Shangri La Botanical
Gardens & Nature Center
2111 W Park Ave,
Orange, 77630
shangrilagardens.org

SAN ANTONIO
San Antonio Botanical Garden
555 Funston Place,
San Antonio, 78209
sabot.org

San Antonio Zoo
3903 N. St. Mary's St,
San Antonio, 78212

TEMPLE
Bend of the River Botanic Garden
2 N. Main St, Ste. 201,
Temple, 76501
templeparks.com

WOODWAY
Carleen Bright Arboretum
1 Pavilion Way, Woodway, 76712
woodway-texas.com/lev1.cfm/9

UTAH

KAYSVILLE
Utah State University
Botanical Center
920 S 50 W, Kaysville, 84037
utahbotanicalcenter.org

LEHI
Thanksgiving Point Garden
3003 N. Thanksgiving Way,
Lehi, 84043
thanksgivingpoint.org

OGDEN
Ogden Botanical Garden
1750 Monroe Blvd,
Ogden, 84401
ogdenbotanicalgardens.org

SALT LAKE CITY
Red Butte Garden & Arboretum
300 Wakara Way,
Salt Lake City, 84108
redbuttegarden.org

Tracy Aviary
589 East 1300 South,
Salt Lake City, 84105
tracyaviary.org

WASHINGTON
Boiling Springs Ecoseum
& Desert Preserve
4234 S. Washington Fields Rd.
#2, Washington, 84780
theboilingsprings.org

WEST JORDAN
Conservation Garden Park
8215 S.1300 W,
West Jordan, 84088
conservationgardenpark.org

VERMONT

MANCHESTER
Hildene, The Lincoln
Family Home
1005 Hildene Rd,
Manchester, 05254
hildene.org

VIRGINIA

ALEXANDRIA
American Horticultural Society
7931 E. Blvd Dr,
Alexandria, 22308
ahs.org

Green Spring Gardens
4603 Green Spring Rd,
Alexandria, 22312
greenspring.org

BLACKSBURG
Hahn Horticulture Garden
at Virginia Tech
200 Garden Lane,
Blacksburg, 24061
hort.vt.edu/hhg

BOYCE
Orland E. White Arboretum
400 Blandy Farm Lane,
Boyce, 22620
blandy.virginia.edu

CHANTILLY
National Botanic Garden
26175 Ticonderoga Rd,
Chantilly, 20152
nationalbotanicgarden.org

CHARLOTTESVILLE
Monticello
931 Thomas Jefferson Pkwy,
Charlottesville, 22902
monticello.org

HARRISONBURG
Edith J. Carrier Arboretum at
James Madison University
MSC 3705, 780 University
Blvd, Harrisonburg, 22807
jmu.edu/arboretum

LEXINGTON
Boxerwood Nature Center
& Woodland Garden
963 Ross Rd,
Lexington, 24450
boxerwood.org

LYNCHBURG
Old City Cemetery
Museums & Arboretum
401 Taylor St,
Lynchburg, 24501
gravegarden.org

MASON NECK
Gunston Hall & Garden
10709 Gunston Rd,
Mason Neck, 22079
www.gunstonhall.org

MONTPELIER STATION
Montpelier Foundation
13384 Laundry Rd,
Montpelier Sta, 22957
montpelier.org

NORFOLK
Hermitage Museum & Gardens
7637 North Shore Rd,
Norfolk, 23505
thehermitagemuseum.org

Norfolk Botanical Garden
6700 Azalea Garden Rd,
Norfolk, 23518
norfolkbotanicalgarden.org

RICHMOND
Lewis Ginter Botanical Garden
1800 Lakeside Ave,
Richmond, 23228
lewisginter.org

Maymont Foundation
1700 Hampton St,
Richmond, 23220

STRATFORD
Stratford Hall
483 Great House Rd,
Stratford, 22558
stratfordhall.org

VIENNA
Meadowlark Botanical Gardens
9750 Meadowlark Gardens Ct,
Vienna, 22182
nvrpa.org

WHITE HALL
McIntire Botanical Garden
P.O. Box 350, White Hall, 22987
mcintirebotanicalgarden.org

WILLIAMSBURG
College of William & Mary
200 Stadium Dr,
Williamsburg, 23185
wm.edu

Colonial Williamsburg
313 1st St,
Williamsburg, 23185
history.org/history/cwland/index.
cfm

WINCHESTER
Museum of the
Shenandoah Valley
901 Amherst St,
Winchester, 22601
themsv.org

WASHINGTON

AUBURN
Creek Botanical Garden
& Heritage Center
29308 132nd Ave SW, Auburn
sooscreekbotanicalgarden.org

BAINBRIDGE ISLAND
Bloedel Reserve
7571 NE Dolphin Dr,
Bainbridge Island, 98110
bloedelreserve.org

BELLEVUE
Bellevue Botanical Garden
12001 Main St,
Bellevue, 98005
bellevuebotanical.org

FEDERAL WAY
Powellswood Garden
29607 8th Ave. S,
Federal Way, 98003
powellswood.org

Rhododendron Species
Botanical Garden
PO Box 379, Federal Way, 98063
rhodygarden.org

GREENBANK
Meerkerk Rhododendron Gardens
PO Box 154, Greenbank, 98253

KINGSTON
Heronswood Garden
7530 288th St NE,
Kingston, 98346
heronswoodgarden.org

LAKEWOOD
Lakewold Gardens
12317 Gravelly Lake Dr SW,
Lakewood, 98499
lakewoldgardens.org

ORTING
Chase Garden
16015 264th St East,
Orting, 98166
chasegarden.org

SEATTLE
E.B. Dunn Historic Trust
13533 Northshire Rd NW,
Seattle, 98177
dunngardens.org

Elisabeth Carey Miller
Botanical Garden
P.O. Box 77377, Seattle, 98177
millergarden.org

Highline Sea Tac
Botanical Garden
13735 24th Ave S, SeaTac,
98168highlinegarden.org

Seattle Chinese Garden
6000 16th Ave SW, Seattle
seattlechinesegarden.org

Streissguth Gardens
900 East Blaine St,
Seattle, 98102
streissguthgardens.com

University of Washington
Botanic Gardens
3501 NE 41st St,
Seattle, 98195
uwbotanicgardens.org

SHORELINE
Kruckeberg Botanic Garden
20312 15th Ave NW,
Shoreline, 98177
kruckeberg.org

SPOKANE
The Moore-Turner
Heritage Gardens
507 West 7th Ave,
Spokane 99204
heritagegardens.org

TACOMA
W.W. Seymour Botanical
Conservatory
4702 S. 19th St,
Tacoma, 98405
metroparkstacoma.org

Point Defiance Zoo & Aquarium
5400 N. Pearl St,
Tacoma, 98405
poza.org

WENATCHEE
Ohme Gardens
3327 Ohme Rd,
Wenatchee, 98801
ohmegardens.com

YAKIMA
Yakima Area Arboretum
1401 Arboretum Dr,
Yakima 98901
ahtrees.org

WOODINVILLE
Cottage Lake Gardens
17301 191st Ave NE,
Woodinville, 98072

WEST VIRGINIA

CHARLESTON
**Craik-Patton House &
Parterre Garden**
2809 Kanawha Blvd, 25311
www.craik-patton.org

CHEYENNE
Cheyenne Botanic Gardens
710 S. Lions Park Dr,
Cheyenne, 82001
botanic.org

HUNTINGTON
Huntington Museum of Art
2033 McCoy Rd,
Huntington, 25701
hmoa.org

JACKSON
Teton Botanical Garden
P.O. Box 13281, Jackson, 83002
tetonbotanicalgarden.org

MORGANTOWN
Core Arboretum
Monongahela Blvd,
Morgantown, 26505
arboretum.wvu.edu/

West Virginia Botanic Garden
PMB # 121, 714 Venture Dr,
Morgantown, 26508
wvbg.org

WISCONSIN

CLINTONVILLE
Arbor View Gardens
E 10540 County Rd C,
Clintonville, 54929
arborviewgardens.org

DELAVAN
Congdon Gardens
Box 185, Delavan, 53115
congdongardens.org

GREEN BAY
Green Bay Botanical Garden
2600 Larsen Rd,
Green Bay, 54303
gbbg.org

HALES CORNERS
Boerner Botanical Gardens
9400 Boerner Dr,
Hales Corners, 53130
countyparks.com

JANESVILLE
Rotary Botanical Gardens
1455 Palmer Dr,
Janesville, 53545
rotarybotanicalgardens.org

KENOSHA
Carthage College
2001 Alford Park Dr,
Kenosha, 53140
carthage.edu

KOHLER
Gardens of Kohler
1115 W. Riverside Dr,
Kohler, 53044
destinationkohler.com

MADISON
Allen Centennial Gardens
University of Wisconsin-Madison,
Madison, 53706
allencentennialgardens.org

Olbrich Botanical Gardens
3330 Atwood Ave,
Madison, 53704
olbrich.org

University of Wisconsin Arboretum
1207 Seminole Hwy,
Madison, 53711
uwarboretum.org

MILWAUKEE
**Mitchell Park Horticultural
Conservatory**
524 South Layton Blvd,
Milwaukee, 53215
countyparks.com

**Renaissance Gardens
at Villa Terrace**
2220 North Terrace Ave,
Milwaukee, 53202
villaterracemuseum.org/
renaissance_garden.html

PORTAGE
Historic Indian Agency House
1490 Agency House Rd,
Portage, 53901
agencyhouse.org

SHEBOYGAN
Bookworm Gardens
1416 Campus Dr,
Sheboygan, 53081
bookwormgardens.org

Christopher Farm & Gardens
W736 Orchard Beach Dr,
Sheboygan, 53083
christopherfarmandgarden.org

WALWORTH
Al's Autobody & Arboretum
W6866 North Walworth Rd,
Walworth, 53184
alsautobodyandarboretum.com

WAUSAU
Monk Botanical Gardens
518 South 7th Ave,
Wausau, 54401

BRITISH COLUMBIA

QUALICUM BEACH
Milner Gardens & Woodland
2179 West Island Highway,
Qualicum Beach,
milnergardens.org